Reckoning with

Winslow Homer:

His Late Paintings

and Their Influence

The Cleveland Museum of Art, Cleveland
September 19-November 18, 1990

Columbus Museum of Art, Columbus
December 16, 1990-February 10, 1991

The Corcoran Gallery of Art, Washington
March 16-May 12, 1991

The exhibition is made possible by
Squire, Sanders & Dempsey, an
international law firm, marking its
centennial with this tribute to
three cities in which it has offices.

Reckoning with

Winslow Homer:

His Late Paintings

and Their Influence

BRUCE ROBERTSON

Published by The Cleveland Museum of Art
in cooperation with Indiana University Press

The following publishers have generously given
permission to use quotations from copyrighted works:
From *The Poetry of Robert Frost* edited by Edward
Connery Lathem. Copyright 1923, 1928 © 1969 by Holt,
Rinehart and Winston. Copyright 1951, © 1956 by
Robert Frost. Reprinted by permission of Henry Holt
and Company, Inc. Excerpts from "The Dry Salvages"
in *Four Quartets,* copyright 1943 by T. S. Eliot and
renewed 1971 by Esme Valerie Eliot, reprinted by
permission of Harcourt Brace Jovanovich, Inc.

Distributed by Indiana University Press, Bloomington

Publication Staff: Thomas Barnard, Emily S. Rosen,
and Jo Zuppan

Printed in Great Britain by Balding + Mansell
International.

Jacket/Cover: Winslow Homer. *Early Morning after a
Storm at Sea,* 1902. Oil on canvas, 30-1/2 x 50 inches.
The Cleveland Museum of Art, Gift of J. H. Wade,
24.195.

Library of Congress Cataloging-in-Publication Data

Robertson, Bruce, 1955-

Reckoning with Winslow Homer: his late paintings and
their influence / Bruce Robertson
   p. cm.
   Includes bibliographical references.
   ISBN 0-940717-02-6. —ISBN 0-940717-03-4 (pbk.)
   1. Homer, Winslow, 1836-1910—Exhibitions. 2.
Homer, Winslow, 1836-1910—Influence—Exhibitions. I.
Cleveland Museum of Art. II. Title.

ND237.H7A4 1990

759.13—dc20   90-31989   CIP

Contents

List of Lenders

Addison Gallery of American Art, Phillips Academy, Andover, Massachusetts

The Art Institute of Chicago, Chicago

Berry-Hill Galleries, Inc., New York

Bowdoin College Museum of Art, Brunswick, Maine

The Brooklyn Museum, Brooklyn, New York

The Cleveland Museum of Art

Colby College Museum of Art, Waterville, Maine

Collection of Mr. and Mrs. Arthur G. Altschul

Collection of Joseph M. Erdelac, Cleveland

Collection of Robert Dance, New York

Collection, Glen Echo Farm, Virginia

Collection of Elie Hirschfeld, New York

Collection of Chris Huntington

Collection of Robert A. Mann

Collection of Remak Ramsey

Columbus Museum of Art, Columbus, Ohio

The Corcoran Gallery of Art, Washington

Hirshhorn Museum and Sculpture Garden, Smithsonian Institution, Washington

Kraushaar Galleries, New York

Los Angeles County Museum of Art, Los Angeles

Maier Museum of Art, Randolph-Macon Woman's College, Lynchburg, Virginia

Memphis Brooks Museum of Art, Memphis, Tennessee

The Metropolitan Museum of Art, New York

Milwaukee Art Museum

The Montclair Art Museum, Montclair, New Jersey

Munson-Williams-Proctor Institute Museum of Art, Utica, New York

The Museum of Modern Art, New York

National Academy of Design, New York

National Gallery of Art, Washington

National Museum of American Art, Smithsonian Institution, Washington

The New Britain Museum of American Art, New Britain, Connecticut

The Norton Gallery of Art, West Palm Beach

Philadelphia Museum of Art, Philadelphia

The Phillips Collection, Washington

Private collection

The Regis Collection, Minneapolis

Sterling and Francine Clark Art Institute, Williamstown, Massachusetts

Wadsworth Atheneum, Hartford

Whitney Museum of American Art, New York

William A. Farnsworth Library and Art Museum, Rockland, Maine

Yale University Art Gallery, New Haven

Foreword

Winslow Homer is a far more complex person than a casual consideration of his instantly pleasing works would suggest. Remarkably responsive to the various undercurrents of his times, Homer was wide-ranging in his choice of subjects to a degree matched by few of his contemporaries. Whether it be genre scenes, war subjects, or landscapes; related subjects such as American attitudes toward relaxation, coming to terms with the wilderness, or man's eternal battle with the elements—or stylistic issues such as the various European influences upon American artists—Winslow Homer's achievement must be considered in any pursuit of a greater understanding of nineteenth-century America and its art. Such complexity in his point of view is what one might expect of an artist who, at the end of his life, was generally considered the most important artist that the United States had yet produced.

In his many different subjects, the ocean was a recurring leitmotif. His manner of portraying it, however, constantly shifted throughout his career, reflecting his own growth. Initially, the beach with gently breaking waves was a suitable setting for scenes of leisure and flirtation—rarely is a sinister note even suggested; these pictures epitomized the new spirit of freedom and prosperity that characterized the North in the years immediately following the Civil War. His memorable paintings done in 1880, representing the children of Cape Ann at play—clamming, berrying, communing companionably—remain even today the perfect expression of the American dream of carefree childhood. Yet within a year or so, the character of his seaside subjects changed radically. Living in the small English village of Cullercoats on the North Sea, he observed the constant seaside drama of lifesaving crews and women keeping watch, anxiously scanning the wild seas. Few artists have grasped so grandly the stark loneliness and anxiety of waiting.

Shortly after he returned to America, in 1882, he pursued further the subjects that had absorbed him in England by going to Atlantic City to study and then paint American lifesavers at work. Afterward he reversed his role as observer of those left behind and instead sought to experience firsthand the drama of those who had gone to sea. In 1884 he joined the New England herring fleets on a trip to the Grand Banks. That trip triggered a series of pictures that are truly epic in their consideration of man's frightening battle with the sea. (Rudyard Kipling was to treat the same subject, albeit somewhat more romantically, in *Captains Courageous,* published thirteen years later).

That year, 1884, became pivotal in Homer's career because he joined his brother's family in Maine at their newly built house in what was still a small fishing settlement, Prout's Neck, near Portland. He soon constructed his own studio nearby. From then on Prout's Neck increasingly dominated his life and became the primary subject of his pictures or, at least, of his oil paintings. One must remember always that even as he synthesized his feelings and refined his perceptions about the northern seas in these works, each winter he usually traveled to southern climes and painted extraordinarily luminous watercolors that capture the bright light and colors of the tropical waters. The grand formality of the northern paintings and the charged intimacy of the southern subjects display a dichotomy of attitudes that stress the complexity of this withdrawn man's thoughts.

Curiously, the late marine oil paintings of the Maine coast are the most underestimated aspect of Homer's work. They are admired certainly, even revered, but they have not been considered with the method they deserve. That is hardly surprising, however, because the earlier drama of figures watching the sea, so convenient for critical analysis, was eliminated from these canvases. Instead, the subject became simply the dynamics of waves crashing against massive rocks, incoming tides battling receding undertows, and shifting cloud masses. Such a vivid understanding of the relationship between these various elements could only be achieved after years of studying the seasonal changes at Prout's Neck, constantly analyzing the facts and gradually achieving a most remarkable empathy with the changing conditions. Such absolute identification with the forces of nature is hard to realize, but it is even more difficult for others to appreciate when done. It requires extended contemplation of the painting, but proper appreciation seems only more exacting now because, with the notable exception of sailors, most of us have little sense of the shifting elements of nature and their effects on the landscape. Morning talk shows convey a consuming concern about the weather, yet most are oblivious of its visual implications, especially in a world too much dominated by pollution.

Bruce Robertson's suggestion that he undertake a study of Homer's late marine subjects was a complex enterprise, but there could be no doubt that such an analysis was much needed. As he observed, in discussing the idea for the exhibition, in these late marines Homer played a pivotal role for American art not unlike the one that Cézanne fulfilled at the same time in France. Thus, in creating this exhibition, Robertson considered a factor in Homer's life that is too little dealt with: the artist's impact upon the younger generation. Increasingly a loner, depending upon nature, his father, and his brothers for companionship, Homer certainly had no students and is generally seen as having little or no influence upon younger artists. This exhibition, however, disproves such an assumption. Instead of being dealt with as the end of nineteenth-century traditions, Homer's great marine subjects are seen here as the beginning of significant new ones—and appropriately so.

Yet, in terms of most exhibitions, this is an unusual one.

Normally in considering the pictures of an earlier period one is some distance removed from the experience motivating the work. Here, however, the very sites on the Maine coast that so deeply moved Homer and the younger artists who followed his example still nurture similarly moving encounters for those seeking them. Perhaps, therefore, such immediacy becomes a contributing factor in explaining the sensitivity and understanding of Robertson's perceptive essay.

The Cleveland Museum of Art and the museums sharing this exhibition, The Columbus Museum of Art and The Corcoran Gallery of Art, owe a great debt to many. As is indicated elsewhere, many scholars, collectors, and dealers have contributed in a variety of ways to our understanding of the subject and to the realization of this exhibition and its catalogue. The institutions and collectors who have lent works have done so with a splendid spirit of support, which has been highly valued. As chance would have it, the Memorial Art Gallery of the University of Rochester has simultaneously created the exhibition *Winslow Homer in the 1890s: Prout's Neck Observed.* Happily the two will be shown simultaneously in Washington, beginning in March 1991, so this extraordinary moment in the history of American art can briefly be better discerned in all its complexity.

In Cleveland *Reckoning with Winslow Homer: His Late Paintings and Their Influence* is viewed as a significant beginning for our extended celebrations of the Museum's 75th anniversary. This seems only appropriate since Winslow Homer's *Early Morning after a Storm at Sea* is one of the greatest of the Museum's early acquisitions (see Figure 20). This masterpiece epitomizes the time and care Homer was prepared to invest in a work. After initially sketching out the idea in a quick watercolor of 1883 (see Figure 10), he waited for seventeen years before undertaking the subject in oil and then, waiting patiently for the right conditions, he painted it in four successive two-hour sessions, which were, however, spread over two years. An astonishing feat!

That the Cleveland law firm of Squire, Sanders & Dempsey should have decided in celebration of its 100th anniversary to show its gratitude to three of the communities in which it has offices by generously underwriting the costs of the exhibition in Cleveland, Columbus, and Washington, as well as the publication of this catalogue, has been greatly appreciated. Their decision has an added felicity: Judge William B. Sanders, Harold T. Clark, James H. Dempsey, and Alton W. Whitehouse—four of this Museum's nine Presidents—have served with that firm.

Evan H. Turner, Director

Acknowledgments

My first thanks go to the owners, both public and private, of all the paintings I looked at during the last year: Arthur G. Altschul; Joseph Erdelac; Myron Kunin; Colles and John Larkin; Mrs. Janet Le Clair; Robert Mann; Stephen Naifeh; Remak Ramsey; and Gregory Vincent Smith. Also, Susan Faxon, Nicki Thiras, and Jock Reynolds, Addison Gallery of American Art, Andover; Carol Troyen, Peter Sutton, and Eleanor Jones, Museum of Fine Arts, Boston; Henrietta Tye and Donald Rosenthal, Bowdoin College Museum of Art; Linda Ferber and Barbara Gallati, Brooklyn Museum of Art; Milo Naeve, Art Institute of Chicago; Kristin Spangenberg, Cincinnati Art Museum; Steven Kern and David Brooks, Sterling and Francine Clark Art Institute; Hugh J. Gourley III and Lynn Marsden-Atlass, Colby College Museum of Art; Nanette Macyjunes and John Owens, Columbus Museum of Art; Franklin Kelly, The Corcoran Gallery of Art; Nancy Rivard Shaw, Detroit Institute of Art; Edith Murphy, William A. Farnsworth Library and Art Museum; Linda Merrill, Freer Gallery of Art; Judith Zilczer, Hirshhorn Museum and Sculpture Garden; Michael Quick, Los Angeles County Museum of Art; Ellen Schall and Barbara Jastrebsky, Maier Museum, Randolph-Macon Women's College; J. Richard Gruber, Memphis Brooks Museum; John Howat and Ida Balboul, Metropolitan Museum of Art; David Derringer and Barbara Krulik, National Academy of Design; Elizabeth Broun and Virginia Mecklenburg, National Museum of American Art; Susan Danly, Pennsylvania Academy of the Fine Arts; Joe Rishel, Larry Nichols, and Innis Shoemaker, Philadelphia Museum of Art; Joe Halbach and Eliza Rathbone, The Phillips Collection; Martha Severens and Michele Butterfield, Portland Museum of Art; Dan Rosenfeld, Museum of Art, Rhode Island School of Design; Betsy Kornhauser, Wadsworth Atheneum; Denis Evans, Whitney Museum of American Art; Mildred Staib, The Woodmere Art Museum; Sally Freitag and Susan

Stickler, Worcester Art Museum; Helen Cooper and Paula Freedman, Yale University Art Gallery. And Jay Cantor, Christie's; Bruce Chambers, Berry-Hill Galleries; John Driscoll, Babcock Galleries; Jill Frankel and Sandra Leff, Graham Galleries; Kenneth Lux, Kenneth Lux Gallery; Glenn Peck and Franklin Riehlman, H. V. Allison Galleries; Carole Pesner, Kraushaar Galleries; Roger Ramsay, Roger Ramsay Galleries; Peter Rathbone, Sotheby's; and Vose Galleries.

I would also like to thank the librarians, archivists, and owners of documents for making my research so pleasant and for permision to quote from papers in their possession: Jean Bellows Booth; Annie Rutledge, Amherst College Library; Margaret Kinzer Meyers, Archives of American Art, Washington, and the staff of the Archives of American Art, New York; Iris Snyder, Delaware Museum of Art; Bowdoin College Museum of Art; Beinecke Library, Yale University; and Knoedler's, New York.

A number of colleagues and friends were also helpful, for putting me up and listening to my ideas, or for just answering questions: Jeff Cunard, David Curry, Robert Dance, Linda Docherty, Marianne Doezema, Bill Homer, Patty Junker, Clayton Koppes, Thomas Kren, Gail Levin, Margaretta Lovell, David and Libby Lubin, Steven Moore, Becky Morter, George Shackelford, Nissa Simon, Marc Simpson, Marc Stern, Daniel Walth, Richard West, Roberta Wollons, and Rebecca Zurier. I owe special thanks to the people who guided me around two magical landscapes: Philip Beam and Doris Homer, who showed me Prout's Neck, and the residents of Monhegan who showed me the island and Rockwell Kent's homes and studio—Bill Boynton, Ed Deci, and Edgar and Anne Hubert.

This book and exhibition had its genesis, ultimately, in a seminar led by Jules Prown, whose inestimable teaching has inspired nearly all his students to write on Winslow Homer. But the conclusion of my work has lain here in Cleveland, both in the Museum and Case Western Reserve University, and it is to my students, colleagues, and friends in both institutions that I owe my greatest thanks and debts, especially: Lynn Cameron, Anne A. Edwards, Karen Ferguson, Jane Glaubinger, Del Gutridge, Linda Lumbert, Jenifer Neils, Carolyn Roman, Adele Z. Silver, William S. Talbot, and Georgina Gy. Toth. The group who midwifed my work should be singled out: my students and research assistants Sabine Kretzschmar, Stephen Wicks, and especially Mark Cole, without whom none of the real work would have been done; Jo Zuppan, Thomas Barnard, Emily S. Rosen, and Laurence Channing, who miraculously wrought order out of the chaos of my text; and last and certainly not least, Evan Turner, whose support and guidance were both challenging and inspiring. Without their aid there would have been no book and no show.

B.R.

Juley. *Winslow Homer at Prout's Neck,* 1908.

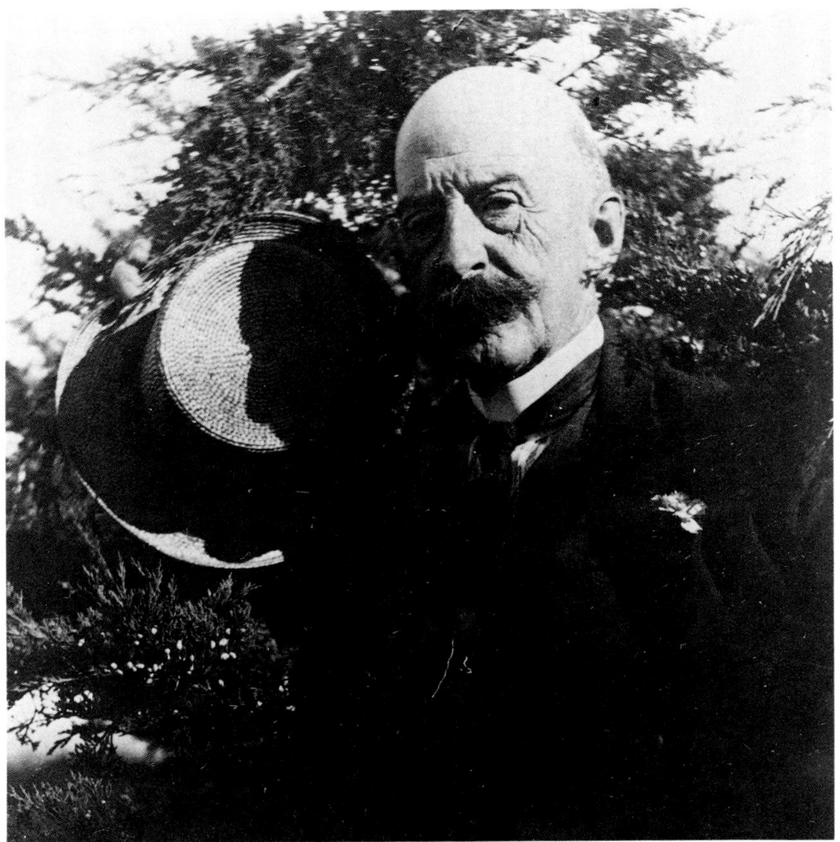

Introduction: Creating an American Tradition

Winslow Homer is as much an artist to reckon with today as he was one hundred years ago. His most famous paintings are recognizable to most Americans, and reproductions of them hang in classrooms, homes, and offices throughout the country. Despite this crush of popularity he does not grow stale: exhibitions of his art proliferate and books and articles weigh down shelves. Yet in a strange way, while we take him almost for granted, he evades our understanding. There is a curious opacity at the heart of his work that deflects our probing. Still we return to Homer again and again, seeking to understand the nature of his achievement. The subject is a vast one and for that reason has not been discussed with much vigor or clarity. This book and the exhibition which it accompanies attempt the task afresh by looking at what other artists made of him.

Because the possibilities are so enormous, several limits have been placed on the endeavor, with an eye to historical coherence. First, only the paintings he did between 1890 and his death in 1910 and their effect on the generation of artists succeeding him are considered. For the last twenty-seven years of his career, Homer lived in Maine and painted its coast. With only two exceptions, the other artists in this exhibition also painted the Maine coast. Furthermore, all began to paint while Homer was still alive, although in some cases their careers extended into the 1960s. These artists were also bound together by the particular need of their generation, in the first years of this century, to acknowledge modern European art and yet maintain an American identity. Winslow Homer was their guide.

Even though Winslow Homer was a great watercolor painter and his achievement in that medium has frequently been analyzed, only oil paintings are discussed at length here and are included in the exhibition. Homer often used his watercolors as studies for his canvases, and they outnumber his oils. Watercolor came to be the medium that satisfied him most; toward the end of his life, painting in oil became increasingly toilsome and problematic. Because of the easy assurance and beauty of his watercolors, they have always been appreciated. As a result, almost any later American artist who also used the medium has come under their influence.[1] Nonetheless, it was for oil painting that Homer reserved his deepest thoughts and dilemmas, and it was his oil paintings that were most frequently displayed and reproduced during his lifetime.[2] They, not the watercolors, were the Homers that younger artists most excitedly measured themselves against.

Finally, there is the question of procedure and method. Because this book and exhibition are not so much about Homer's influence as they are about the act of looking at Homer's paintings, I have thought it worthwhile to explore several different types of responses. The exhibition is centered on Homer's paintings and arranged thematically around the motifs that inspired the next generation of artists. The book is organized somewhat differently and includes many more observers. Proceeding more or less chronologically, the first two chapters recount the last twenty years of Homer's career; Chapters 3 and 4 the reactions of his immediate contemporaries, both critics and artists. Chapters 5 and 6 are concerned with the response of the next generation of artists during the first two decades of this century, while the last chapter covers the period between World Wars I and II. Inevitably, my own views and readings of Homer's paintings have intruded into the discussion, which is quite intentional. This gathering of paintings and observations, inspired by Homer's paintings, should reveal both the differences and the validity of all of them, and encourage the viewer's individual response. No single reading of Winslow Homer's painting can capture all its meanings and resonances. His art is as steady and yet as changeable as the rocks and waves he painted.

Writing just before World War II, the painter John Sloan exclaimed: "There is so much talk today about the American Scene. As though it had been discovered in the last decade!... But we really didn't start it. What about Homer, [Thomas] Eakins, and lesser men?"[3] Despite such acknowledgments, Homer has generally been seen as a self-contained figure, not only free of influence but essentially having none. For the most part, we have preferred to see him as an isolated, cantankerous American original.

This myth has a certain truth to it. After 1883 Homer appeared to have abandoned his colleagues and the city for Prout's Neck, a small spit of land on the Atlantic coast just south of Portland, Maine. He guarded his privacy fiercely; another painter, Marsden Hartley, was delighted to relate how Homer scared off visitors with a gun. Alone, with just painting tools and the rocks and waves of the North Atlantic coast for inspiration, Homer produced the forbiddingly austere and mysterious masterpieces with which he ended his career. In reality, however, he was seldom alone for more than a few weeks at a time. His family lived nearby for much of the year, and Prout's Neck was a busy summer resort. Homer visited Boston and New York frequently. The urbanity of appearance and manner, which marked his New York years, was not put aside. He kept abreast of the latest developments in the art world and the work of other artists.

But the mythic Homer has a greater presence than the real one. His contemporaries saw his art and life as synonymous, and what they saw reveals the nature of the myth. Cast as a distinctively American painter, Homer was the only major artist among his fellows without European training or taint, "the most truly national of all our painters."[4] But while critics praised his strength, they felt ambivalent about his pictorial sophistication. Today Homer's debts to James McNeill Whistler seem obvious, as does his study of tonalism, the school of late nineteenth-century American painting devoted to softly painted, subdued colors and other similarly quiet aesthetic concerns; Homer's technical mastery of the brush and the sensuousness of his color are unquestionable. To his audience in 1905, however, to quote one writer: "His drawing is not always sure, his colouring rather neutral, his handling is never brilliant, but a strong personality marks everything he does, and figure or landscape is seen with a true artist's vision."[5] Homer's paintings were described as big, strong, crude, and powerful. They were also American, virile, and real. For these critics and many more, Homer was the quintessential American and this was incompatible with ideas of beauty; by definition his work could not be seen as decorative or suave.

The great dilemma facing American artists at the end of the

nineteenth century was how to assimilate modern European art without losing their own voice. The debate was one of style and technique as much as subject matter. After 1880 the introduction of many European painterly fashions into America produced both exhilaration and great anxiety for painters and their audiences. For the first time, American painters began to explore systematically the expressive qualities of texture, brushstroke, and color. Simultaneously, many felt that artists were losing their identities as Americans and were merely reproducing the styles of Munich, Paris, and The Hague. Many critics were contemptuous of the younger, European-trained artists, sensing an effeminacy of style and a loss of manly vigor through their too-long exposure to Europe. At the same time, the older artists appeared heavy and crude in comparison.

In the midst of this debate Homer stood alone.[6] His late landscapes, the first dating from 1890, proposed a solution. Drenched in the rigorously selected facts of Prout's Neck, his landscapes also tackled the painterly issues faced by his contemporaries. Homer planted his feet firmly on the hard rocks of the Maine coast and faced out across the Atlantic toward Europe, a landscape and situation that enabled him to condense his vision of the world into its elemental qualities: a margin of land, a distant scrim of air, and the boiling sea between. The distillation of motifs threw into sharp focus his artistic means—brushstroke, palette, and composition. This two-fold analysis of subject and style, so ruthlessly carried out, made Homer unique among American painters of his generation, brought his art almost to the point of abstraction, and made his voice a strong and compelling one for artists just after the turn of the century. Homer was almost the only artist of his generation to negotiate successfully the hurdles of European art and American character.

At the heart of his success lay his realism. *Realism, realistic,* and *real* are terms whose meanings vary widely, depending on the period and country of the object denoted, and on the ideology and sophistication of the speaker. Today, "realistic" might mean "looking just like a photograph," "representing the proletariat authentically," or "belonging to the school of painting engendered by Gustave Courbet in mid-nineteenth century France." In Homer's day most viewers took his paintings as realistic because they believed that the works expressed something true about American life in a direct and uncomplicated way. For us, his realism consists not so much of his style and subjects but his emphasis on the tangible physicality of experience in this world, something that is felt most strongly not in our contact with other people but in the physical sensations, even pain, that the world inflicts on us. But however we interpret it, Homer's version of the real is fundamental to American painting of this century.[7]

Homer's success spawned a host of imitators and a school of American marine painting. But one group of artists did more than just mimic him. The students and followers of Robert Henri were, like Homer, committed to a pragmatic study of the real world, the world in which they lived every day. They wished to be as American as Homer and, on the whole, rejected both the gentility of American impressionism and tonalism, and the alienation from direct, whole experience which characterized much European modernism. Many of these artists (George Wesley Bellows, Henri himself, George Luks, and John Sloan) were members of the Ashcan school, the group that painted the New York scene with a clarity that shocked turn-of-the-century audiences. But others, like Van Dearing Perrine, Leon Kroll, Rockwell Kent, and Edward Hopper, have not normally been associated with Ashcan realism. While all had opportunities to see Homer's work in New York City and elsewhere, nearly all engaged it most intensely on Homer's own turf, Maine. Led by Henri, for several summers just before and after Homer's death they visited Maine to study nature with Homer's eyes. To be sure, Homer was not the only influence; nor was every great wave or rocky coast Homeric. For example, in the summers after the Armory Show of 1913—that exhibition of avant-garde European art which is the watershed event of modern art in this country—Vincent van Gogh's paintings transformed the landscapes that Bellows and Sloan painted. But both Bellows and Sloan found their subject matter and compositions, the release to work, and the foundation on which to paint, in Homer's pictures.

Because of the Armory Show, we tend to divide American painters at the turn of the century into two separate, hostile camps: realists whom the Armory Show had humiliated and modernists who embraced the new art. But it is difficult to imagine Bellows ever feeling more than a moment's self-doubt, and it is wise to remember that they all knew each other, even visited the same resorts, like Ogunquit and Gloucester. Significantly, John Marin and Marsden Hartley, two artists older than Bellows and Kent, and belonging to the other camp, likewise felt Homer's influence. During the 1930s, looking back to the beginning of their careers as they each attempted to refashion their art, Homer's coastal landscapes became powerful models.

Some of these artists—such as Bellows and Henri—in the process of discovering Homer's work, explored the central, elemental scene in a profusion of works, producing scores of studies of waves beating on the shore. Others, like Luks, were satisfied with a handful of sketches. For some of the artists, the influence is obvious and pivotal; for others, it was an important but passing phase. For still others, in particular Hopper, the links are subterranean or spiritual: we know they are there, but they are almost impossible to discern. Nonetheless, for a significant group of America's most important painters during the first half of this century, the experience of Homer's late works was crucial.

Understanding that experience is a complicated task. It is apparent, reading the reviews, the correspondence of Homer and his peers, and other contemporary evidence, that the paintings Homer's audience saw in 1890 differ from those seen by his audience twenty years later, and are different again from the paintings that we see. The canvases themselves have, of course, changed only marginally physically, but their audience has changed significantly. To a certain degree, we may recover those earlier structures of thought that they took for granted; to a degree, even, we may objectively observe our own. The questions of identity and inequality concerning so many of us today, for instance, frequently have to do with gender, a change from only just a few years ago when race and class, or even epistemology, might have weighed more heavily. At the turn of the century issues of nationalism and modernity predominated, as American society seemed to many spectators to be besieged by immigration and new technology, while Homer's own generation was still consumed by the aftermath of the Civil War. The character of each generation of artists and audiences reflects these changes. Thus, many artists in the decade just before World War I displayed a remarkably confident energy, very different from Homer's pessimism and our own alienation.

Whatever the nature of the observer, Homer's paintings present themselves as a blank screen on which his audience can project its own meanings: the figures turn away, the landscape is bare, the seas are almost empty, the light is dim. Full of the import of meaning and change—crashing waves, lowering skies, strong winds—they are actually empty of it. We become conscious of this when reviewing the many interpretations of his paintings that either repeat endlessly what has always been said or contradict each other completely. The same painting may apparently project a positive or negative view of man's relationship to nature, depending perhaps on the disposition of the viewer. But Homer's paintings balance on just this cusp of ambiguity. They offer no simple dichotomy between life and death, being and nothingness.

Whatever the cultural resonances of Homer's early work, which continue to the very end, his last works seem to express more personal and more fundamental concerns. In Homer's hands the impact of wave on rock, nature, and man, expressed an elemental polarity that may be variously interpreted. Soon after Homer's death, one observer mused: "It is impossible to avoid the reflection that the Maine Coast had a sort of personal fascination for Homer."[8] More recently, Clement Greenberg has noted: "Perhaps there was some unconscious connection for [Homer] (as for Poe) between the sea and sex."[9] The land is an obvious symbol of certainty and security, while the sea may embody a primeval connection with sexuality: on the empty spaces of the open waters we have always projected our erotic preoccupations. Under the tuition of Sigmund Freud and many others over the last one hundred years, the discourse of sexuality has moved to center stage in western culture. The formation of sexual identity, while it may not determine our lives, lies at the core of our human experience. In our present condition—seemingly unable to connect with the world in any but the most oblique fashion—sexual aphasia excites our attention. One of Homer's great attractions for us is the sexual repression (its nature at this date impossible to guess) that we sense generating the energy and alienation of his work.[10] It is no coincidence that the two artists discussed below whom we regard as the most influential—Marsden Hartley and

Edward Hopper—are the two who most profoundly explored Homer's note of alienation and who had the most difficulty expressing their sexuality. Hartley's homosexuality bore the brunt of social and legal prohibitions. Hopper, for whatever reason, constrained the men and women in his pictures within the shackles of houses and offices, where they neither touch nor look at one another but gaze longingly at the great world beyond.

Interpreting Winslow Homer is a difficult feat, but we are in good company when we attempt it. There is a community of observers, and a continuum of interpretation, that began the moment Homer laid down his brush and continues to the present. Joining them, we recognize that we cannot, and should not, hope to offer a definitive view. As Homer himself demonstrated in a score of paintings of the same small stretch of the Maine shore, a slight shift in our standpoint offers new vistas and new meanings. Returning to the same spot, the same painting, we see new things every day. Nothing makes this clearer than the work of the artists in this exhibition.

Winslow Homer

As a young man of twenty-five, Winslow Homer first tasted public recognition in covering the Civil War for *Harper's Magazine.* Older, soberer, and alone, he spent the last twenty years of his life memorializing the rocks and surf of Prout's Neck, Maine. In the years between he painted as broad a range of subjects as any American artist: children and old men, languid society ladies at resorts and robust fisherwomen on the beach, cows being milked and boats being swamped, the Adirondacks and the Bahamas. By the time he died Homer had the reputation of a hermit, known to the rest of the world only through his oil paintings, which appeared, one or two at a time, annually in exhibitions in New York, Philadelphia, Boston, and Chicago. He had no students, no apprentices, and few artist friends. His flinty character and equally taciturn, granite-like canvases—elemental, even crude dramas of the ocean and shore—seemed an absolute to his contemporaries. At the time of his death, his reputation was fixed in the public's mind: a lonely figure who spurned society, he was a great marine artist and our greatest native painter.

How did he get to this place? His early career was solid and successful, but no more so than that of many of his contemporaries. Fortunate to be reviewed generously from the start, he had made the obligatory trip to Europe in 1867, as soon as he could, but apparently to little effect. There was no discernible change in his style or subjects after the excursion, although it was a handy thing to have been well reviewed in Europe and he had almost won a medal, a nice feather in his cap.

Homer lived in New York City for the next twenty years. For the first decade his studio was in the University Building on Washington Square, then in the Tenth Street Studios along with most of the other leading artists in the city. He joined the appropriate organizations, even a few clubs, but was never a leader. During the summer months, he sensibly left the city seeking

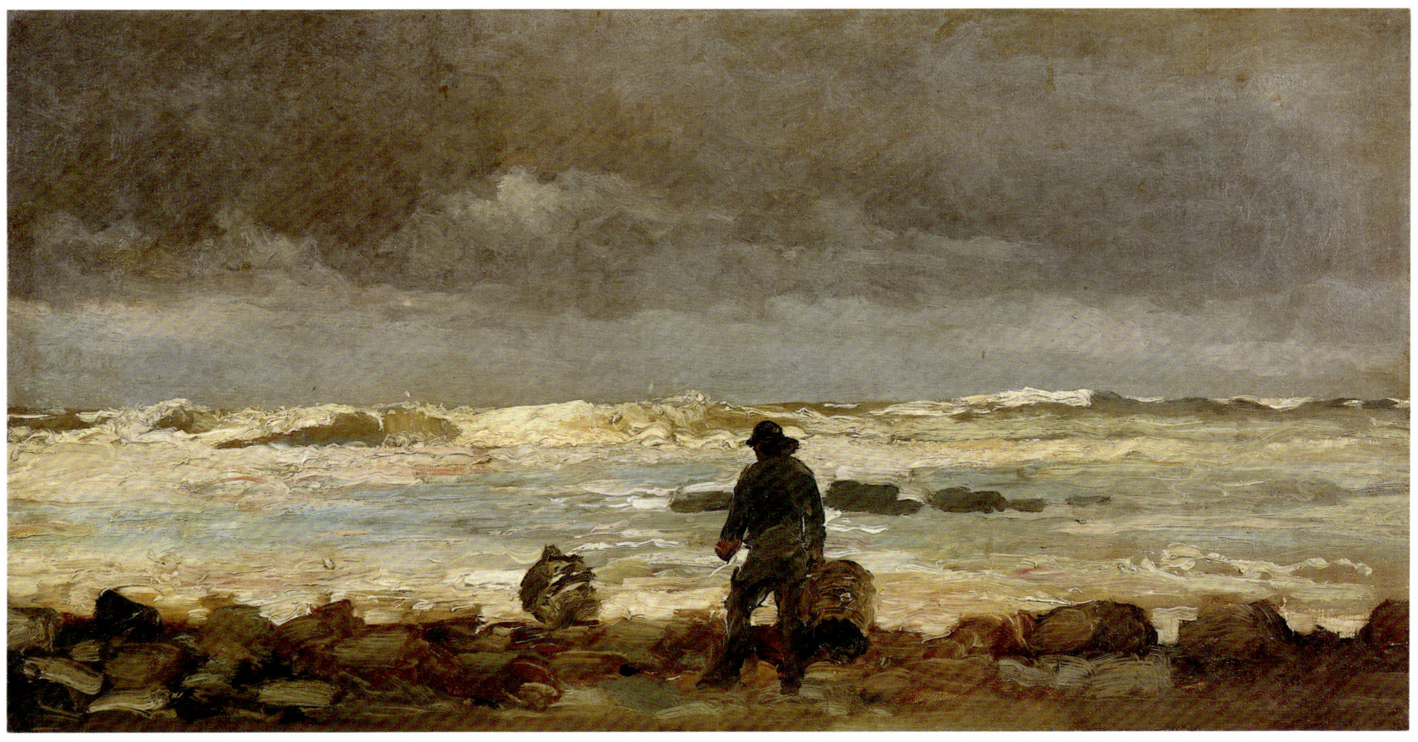

1. Homer. *Rocky Coast,* ca. 1883-1900.

material to paint, as did most of his artistic brethren. Looking back on his time in New York, his contemporaries struggled to find clues that would explain his later isolation. Under his convivial exterior they claimed to find a certain reserve, but that smacks of hindsight. Other accounts describe him as a dapper, presentable bachelor—qualities he retained to the end.

During this period he was grouped with other genre painters, always abreast of and generally helping to form the changing fashions in subject matter during the 1860s and 1870s. He supported himself by supplying drawings to such magazines as *Harper's* as well as by selling his paintings. By the end of the 1870s, he was able to cease commercial illustration and concentrate entirely on painting. His particular specialties—and everyone had to have one or two—were the New England farmer and the rural Southern black. In the New York art world of his day, he had a substantial but not a significant presence. As many of his contemporaries later remarked, if he had died before the age of forty-five, he would have been remembered for a few interesting pictures and not much else.

In 1881 Homer's life changed; he returned to Europe, not to

Paris but to London. Now a mature artist, even if he did not quite know what he wanted, he recognized what he did not want to do. He did not want to stay in his usual rut of places and subjects. He did not want to try the Continent again. He did not even want to explore London. In a sense, whatever London could have offered him in its urbanity, he could more comfortably have found in New York. And as for the Continent, he knew what was going on there; it was happening in New York City, right before his eyes.

A few years before, in 1877, there had been an uproar at the National Academy of Design, New York's only center for the display and promotion of contemporary art. The young turks who had gone away to train in Munich, Paris, and The Hague had come back and shaken everything up. They knew what art was all about and threatened to teach their elders, rebelliously founding the Society of American Painters. None of this dreary business of pretty and perfect, painting so much like a photograph that no one cared about the difference. They wanted paint and real painting. However diluted a version of the gospel of Whistler or the impressionists, their work was aesthetically minded and technically proficient.

Faced with the need to renew his art and life, Homer headed in the opposite direction, off to the little English fishing village of Cullercoats near Tynemouth, and began painting the hardy fishermen. Not the first artist to do so, he followed a trend made popular by Jules Breton (1827-1906) in France and, in England, Charles Napier Hemy (1841-1917) and Colin Hunter (1841-1904). The north of England, including Cullercoats, where the fishermen toiled on the rough North Sea, was already a favorite painting ground for many artists.

Returning to America at the end of 1882, Homer began to paint heroic scenes of action—or at least stressful inaction, scenes without leisure. Where before he had treated boys and girls in placid waters, now he saw men and women laboring against mighty turbulence (Figure 1). His models, and Homer, seem to have grown up and to have set aside childish delights. The next year he moved to Prout's Neck, abandoning New York.

The progress of Homer's career seems to have been one of renunciation: from the most horrific and widest fields of human action, the battlefields of the Civil War, to monotonously pound-

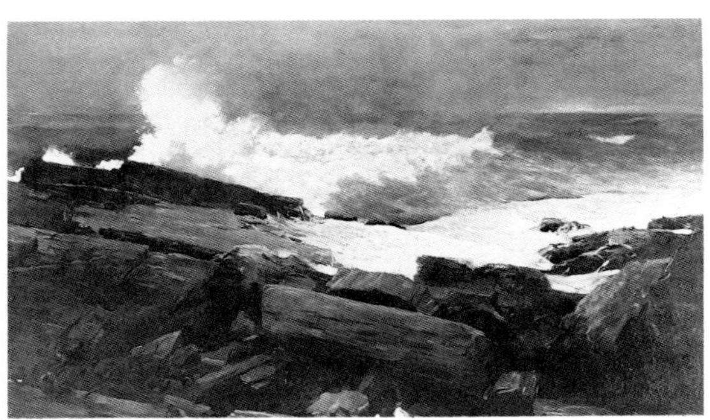

2. Homer. *Weatherbeaten, 1894.*

ing surf on a barren rock (Figure 2). He left behind the society and bustle of the city, the world of art, and the hope of love, for a life stripped down to its essentials.[1] He became as monolithic as his subjects. Yet few successfully abandon the accumulated memories and associations of a life. Although he may have turned his back on New York City, he occasionally looked over his shoulder; ties with his former life were not entirely severed.

But what is the balance of past and future in him? Interpreting Homer and his art—the significance of the move and its consequence for his paintings—is a difficult enterprise. Homer, the most reticent of artists, gives us little help. As he wrote to an early biographer: "It may seem ungrateful to you ... I should not agree with you in regard to that proposed sketch of my life. But I think it would probably kill me to have such [a] thing appear, and, as the most interesting part of my life is of no concern to the public, I must decline to give you any particulars in regard to it."[2] But we may, out of the skein of possibilities, weave a plausible picture of his emotions and motivations.

At the heart of this activity lies Homer himself. What he might have thought he was doing determined what he painted. But did his intentions determine the meaning of his works? We may imagine him in front of his easel: several sets of events comingling as he puts paint to canvas. First, the immediate experience of the rocks and water, the things the painting is most directly about. Second, a lifetime of looking at and making art: this is the knowledge he brings to bear on the task at hand, consciously and unconsciously fitting his direct experience into the patterns he found most satisfying after a lifetime. Third, the practical sensations of his body and situation. We might imagine his father blustering around the garden, intemperately ordering the servants about. Perhaps Winslow has a stomachache or new shoes that pinch his toes. After a lifetime of habit, most such realities could be shut out. Then, there are his emotions and his psychology, the life lived and felt outside the drama of the studio and his aesthetic perceptions. Today, his father grates on his nerves; perhaps he will give the deer a touch of his father's eyebrows. But we can seldom recover such private meanings and can only imagine that in ways he could not or would not bring to the surface, he felt alone, and the absolute and unyielding battle of rock and water was anesthetizing and oddly comforting. Finally, there was the fact of America: Homer was embedded in the culture of his day, both representing and interpreting it —consciously or not—in his depictions of the American landscape. Whatever Homer may have said about the overt meanings of his canvases, the forces that brought him to his final subject, Prout's Neck, were not always under his control.

The incidental causes for his move to Maine should not be underestimated. His brother Arthur had honeymooned at Prout's Neck in 1875 and returned each summer thereafter. The family business instincts scented a good opportunity for investment, and the Homers bought land there in 1883. Like any good unmarried child of his day, Winslow was the one responsible for looking after his parents, which presumably entailed living with them. But whatever his plans may have been, they were overturned by the death of his mother in 1884. What was to have been a summer place for the entire family became a year-round residence for Winslow. He lived in his own cottage, which was also his studio, a few feet from the main house where his family stayed. During the winter, his father lived in a hotel in Boston while Homer remained at Prout's Neck: distant, but not too far away.

Homer's existence at Prout's Neck during the summer was hardly reclusive. The place, if it did not crawl with people, certainly ambled. Several hotels were within a few hundred yards of his studio. However strenuously he tried to avoid their clientele, he could not evade them entirely. Although remaining aloof (after all, he was at work), he seems to have gotten on well with most of his summer neighbors at Prout's Neck, some of whom were professionals in other fields.[3] Artists who might be resident at the Neck during the summer occasionally entered his private circle. Only in the depths of winter did he live entirely alone and, even then, seldom for more than a few weeks. Nearly every January, he headed for New York City and then south to the Caribbean. Several times each year he went fishing with his older brother, Charles, to the Adirondacks or Quebec during the summer or fall, and to Florida in the winter.

Despite his busy life, we may guess that he longed for love and companionship beyond that of family and friends. Most viewers have read that loneliness in his work, but we can never be certain that we are not imposing the interpretation. Certainly Homer would never have admitted to it. Professionally, there was no particular need for the stimulation of New York City. For most culture (especially music, an abiding interest), he had Boston, which he visited frequently to see his father. Given the changed nature of his subject matter, Prout's Neck was the best place to be, and in his peculiarly literal fashion, he no doubt asked himself: "Why do anything else?" His stance was always deliberately inartistic: fishing, he would claim, was his major interest, and he would never have dreamed of introducing himself as an artist. Instead, he paid elaborate attention to the views of the local butcher, whom "he would let ... tear his pictures all to pieces."[4] His letters have the tone of a crafty Yankee trader, on the lookout for every dollar. He badgered his dealers constantly. Sounding like any tailor or small shopkeeper, to one of them he wrote: "I will paint for money at any time. Any subject, any size."[5] The society he created, of fishermen and local handymen, embraced people as remote from his career and professional interests as can be imagined. He stoutly denied any sense of deprivation (except in a few weak moments), just as he rejected the claims of the New York art world, threatening continually not to paint. "At present and for some time past I see no reason why I should paint any pictures," he exclaimed in 1893. In 1907 he informed one critic: "Perhaps you think that I am still painting and interested in art. That is a mistake. I care nothing for art. I no longer paint. I do not wish to see my name in print again."[6] Of course, he did continue to paint.

In trying to peer beneath his stony surface, to recover Homer's meanings in what he painted, we might begin with his family. His mother, Henrietta, was the artistic one and received full credit from Winslow for his interest in painting. He treasured her watercolors all his life, showing them proudly. As a second son he may always have been marked as hers; one intriguing argument that he was named after her pastor serves to underscore the point.[7] Homer regarded himself as her successor in other ways. Prophetically, the day before his birthday in 1895, he wrote to his older brother, Charles: "I suppose I may have 14 more [birthdays] (that was mother's age 73 years)"; he lived only one year longer, to the age of seventy-four.[8] Prout's Neck must have been tinged

with nostalgia and irony for him; after her death, he refused to
live in the main house with his father.

Charles Savage Homer, Sr., his father, was something of a
pompous windbag, full of the delusion of his own success, when in
fact he had repeatedly failed and abandoned his family. In a
sense, he represented all that Winslow rejected: commerce,
society, and the accumulation of things. Homer's early biogra-
phers often commented on the dissimilarities between the two: the
florid, imposing Charles, Sr., whose house was filled to overflow-
ing with everything consumable, and the trim, small Winslow,
whose studio was spartan. Visiting his father's house, across the
lawn from his studio, Homer would remove fruit from the over-
flowing bowls on the sideboard; his father would furiously put it
back. But Homer half-jokingly wrote at one point: "I find that
living with Father for three days, I grow to be so much like him
that I am frightened."[9] In sum, Homer's attitude seems to have
been one of jocular, waspish toleration and devotion; in other
words, it was contradictory, but the contradictions were balanced
by love.

Less is known about his brothers. Charles, Jr., two years older
than Winslow, was everything Homer, Sr., was supposed to be.
An industrial chemist of some repute, he became wealthy, married well and happily, but had no children. Winslow cared for
Charles' wife, Mattie, deeply. Not merely fishing partners, Charles and Winslow shared an interest in the same line of work.
Charles specialized in paints and varnishes, too—as a chemist.
His other brother, Arthur, was five years younger than Winslow,
and the two were never particularly close. Arthur's business
ventures, like their father's, were sometimes less than successful.
He and Winslow had heated discussions about who owned what
property on Prout's Neck. On the other hand, Arthur had two
sons, of whom Winslow was certainly fond and occasionally
helped. Both of his brothers represent the spheres that Homer
avoided: business and domesticity. And yet Homer remained in
the arms of his family all his life.

Homer might be said to have had the same relation to the
world beyond his family, the America of his day. Praised glibly all
too often as the most American of painters, he should perhaps be
taken to task for what he refused to paint: none of the drama of

city life found its way into his work, none of the business and urban bustle that was transforming America into an industrialized world power even as he painted. His paintings spurn the city and everything it represents, just as he himself did. Characteristically, as late as 1903, not understanding how "that thing" the telephone worked—although there were 2,371,000 of them in the country by 1902, one for every thirty-five Americans—he was unable to use one.[10]

In Homer's day urban growth threatened most observers of American life. The country felt filled in, completed; the American frontier was declared closed in 1893. Under the onslaught of mechanization, immigration, and incorporation, the normal relations of life threatened to dissolve or warp. The rationalization imposed on the economy and labor by the growth of national corporations provided seemingly limitless new comforts for consumers and increasing hardships for workers. Immigration brought to these shores large numbers of non-English speaking people to form new underclasses. Machines and innovative technology—such as the Corliss steam engine introduced at the Centennial Exposition, which stood 39 feet tall and weighed 650 tons—seemed to reduce human beings to the level of drones. Ostensibly Homer refused to deal with this. Standing with his face to the ocean, America behind him, he nonetheless felt the pressure of those forces at his back. His landscapes may be taken as his answer. As Ralph Waldo Emerson reminds us, "The land is the appointed remedy for whatever is false and fantastic in our culture."[11]

Proceeding along this path of analysis, however, will take us only so far. Homer deliberately left few clues behind, other than his paintings, and these, unlike verbal texts (which are ambiguous enough), evade all but the most obvious interpretations. In the end we must be content with our informed intuitions. We might compare with envy what we can responsibly say about Homer with what we know and can report about Henry Adams (1838-1918), only two years younger and a fellow-Bostonian. Adams, a self-revelatory writer, most conscious of being the direct descendant of presidents, displayed deliberately his motivations and reactions to contemporary culture and society. While we may differ in interpreting what Adams had to say, the nature and the depths of his dissatisfaction with the crass capitalism of American life are clear, his sense that in seeking material success in this world Americans were blunting themselves to authentic experience, that they were sacrificing the heart of life for the transitory satisfactions of power. Adams' critique of the materialist goals of American culture, as exemplified by, as one historian says, "modern man—urban, rootless, rational, immersed in the 'inauthentic' realm of commercial exchange," is one of the most articulate and extensive at the turn of the century.[12] This conflict between the outer life and the inner life is dramatized in many ways in Victorian experience and the gulf between the quiet self and the noisy world was one that many tried to bridge. Transcendentalism, belonging to the generation before Adams, is but one attempt.

Adams expressed his dilemma in several ways, but his basic terms for the two poles of experience were decidedly sexualized. The life of progress and action was identified with a Protestant male autonomy, as exemplified by his father, the diplomat Charles Francis Adams, while the life of reflection and true sensation was identified with a Catholic female dependence, as exemplified by his relations with women, including his beloved wife, Marian Hooper Adams. Or, as Adams called these sets of associations, the Virgin and the Dynamo.

For Adams, the Virgin embodied the connection we have lost between the here and now and the infinite, what Sigmund Freud called "oceanic feeling." She had been replaced by the Dynamo, mindlessly progressive, undirected energy, nominally in the charge of men but in reality controlling them. Adams addressed his ambivalence about being *in* the world but not *of* it in a poem, *Buddha and Brahmin,* in words that apply to Homer's characteristic situation:

> *But we, who cannot fly the world, must seek*
> *To live two separate lives; one, in the world*
> *Which we must ever seem to treat as real;*
> *The other in ourselves, behind a veil*
> *Not to be raised without disturbing both.*

As we will see, Homer, a realist to the core of his being, turned repeatedly from the reality of life to the world behind the veil.

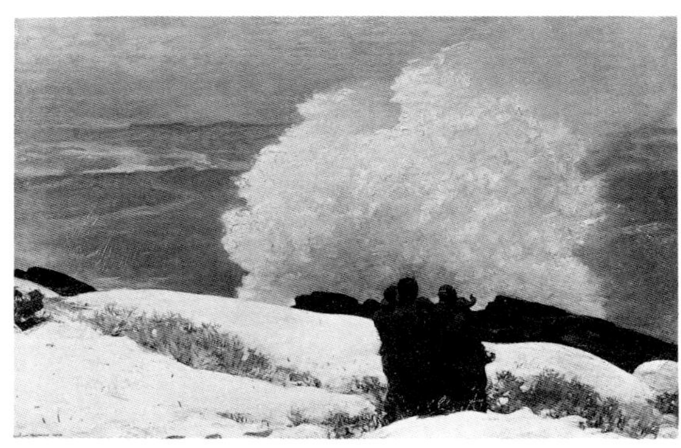

3. Homer. *Watching the Breakers: A High Sea,* 1896.

What Adams expressed in his poem, by telling the story of the Brahmin, Homer's paintings show us as unmetaphorically, as metonymically as they can. In matter-of-fact settings, the horizon is always muffled in fog and the figures, huddled together, gaze toward a curtain of mist, seeing nothing substantial (Figure 3). This is just the point: the horizon is a "veil not to be raised." Homer himself said: "a horizon is horrible—that straight line!"[13] Although we cannot be certain what his figures look at or what Homer felt and tried to say, as Henry Adams would tell us, the significant fact is that they rest in the balance between inner and outer worlds. Homer's art achieves a reciprocity between the simple, hard certainties of rock and ocean, loneliness and death, and everything else he and we might wish for.

Homer at Prout's Neck

If 1881 marked a major change in Homer's career, then 1890 marked another, the year of his first Prout's Neck marines, the paintings that represented for his contemporaries the pinnacle of his achievement. He had come back from England painting heroic men and women, pitting themselves against the sea, whether on the beach or in their boats. Now he began to paint just the shore and the water. He had been preparing for this moment since his arrival at Prout's Neck, recording the area in watercolors, but it had taken seven years for him to master the subject to the point where he could paint it in oil.

The five canvases completed in 1890 marked his first return to oil painting in nearly four years.[1] The exhibition of four of the paintings (*Cloud Shadows* was omitted) by his dealer Gustave Reichard in January 1891 prompted a storm of enthusiasm.[2] Among the newspaper clippings kept by his sister-in-law Mattie are over twenty reviews of the show. The exhibition confirmed what had been suspected since his return from England seven years before. The majority of the reviewers were highly favorable, despite a few of the same old criticisms. Homer was now unequivocally one of America's greatest painters, perhaps the truest delineator of her native character, a significant artist who had found his real voice. From this point on, his artistic presence was inescapable, even if his physical presence seemed to have vanished from the scene.

Yet, as his reputation grew, Homer seems to have embarked on oil painting more and more deliberately. Although he continued to paint watercolors prolifically, there are little more than thirty canvases to represent the last twenty years of his life. He became reluctant perhaps to expend the effort uselessly, either because he felt unappreciated by his audience (the years in which he painted nothing in oil often followed the hostile reception of a particular work or the failure to sell it) or because the subject did

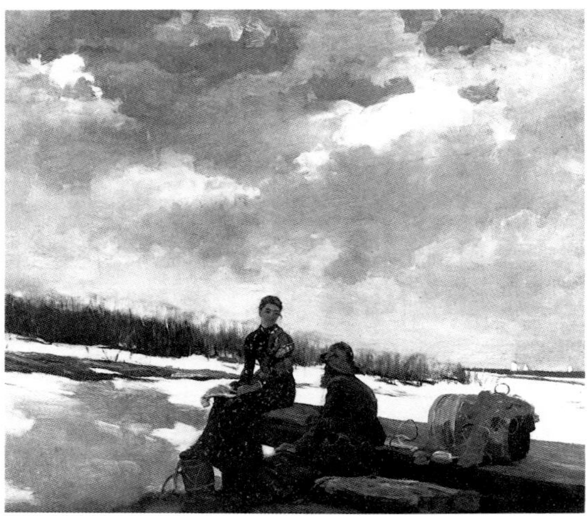

4. Homer. *Cloud Shadows,* 1890.

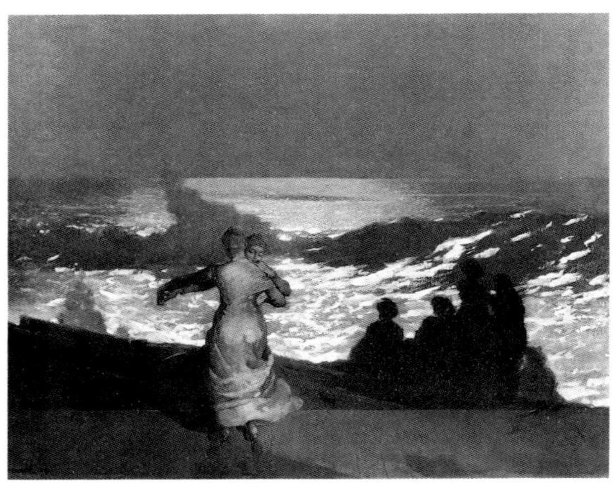

5. Homer. *A Summer Night,* 1890.

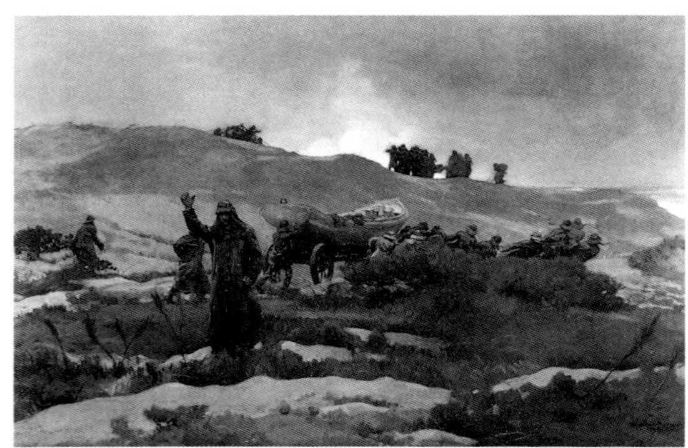

6. Homer. *The Wreck,* 1896.

not truly speak to him. We may take as axiomatic that every late canvas was important to him—all were self-consciously pondered, chosen carefully from the profusion of possibilities presented in his watercolors.

Although Winslow Homer never kept records of his works and claimed that once they were finished he was unconcerned with them, in fact in the last years of his life he constantly recalled canvases to paint on them a little more; many of the oil paintings in this exhibition were retouched at some later point by the artist.[3] In other words, out of sight was not out of mind. Finished or not, one way or another all his work remained alive to him. Given the tenacity and capacity of his visual memory, we may suggest that all his work moved toward the same themes, whatever the subject matter. Moreover, just as he could hold a watercolor motif in his memory for nearly twenty years before reworking it into an oil painting, so too could he hold the thread of a story and pick it up years later. It is therefore possible to see his last twenty years as a whole, each work commenting on, augmenting, and rereading the work that preceded it.[4]

What these later paintings reveal distinctly is the persistence of three interests: the paramount, almost obsessive attention to the formal qualities of the work; an abiding concern with narration; and the constant repetition of a few themes and motifs.

The five paintings completed in 1890 announced these concerns explicitly. *Cloud Shadows* and *A Summer Night* (Figures 4, 5) re-engaged the subject of women at their leisure, which Homer had been painting at least since 1865 but for the first time transplanted to Prout's Neck.[5] The first is quite conventional: a young lady seated on a piece of driftwood talking to an amusing old salt. The "cloud shadows" is a delicate allusion to the passage of time that stands between them but that will someday unite them. *A Summer Night,* the nighttime companion to the first piece, is altogether different. It looks forward in its ambiguous atmosphere to the light effects and psychological obscurity of the figures in his later works. The third painting, *A Signal of Distress* is another of the seafaring pictures so popular with the public. His print publisher issued a large photogravure of the work as a companion to *Hark! The Lark,* 1887, the one depicting men in danger, the other representing the women waiting for them. Homer did

7. Homer. *Winter Coast,* 1890.

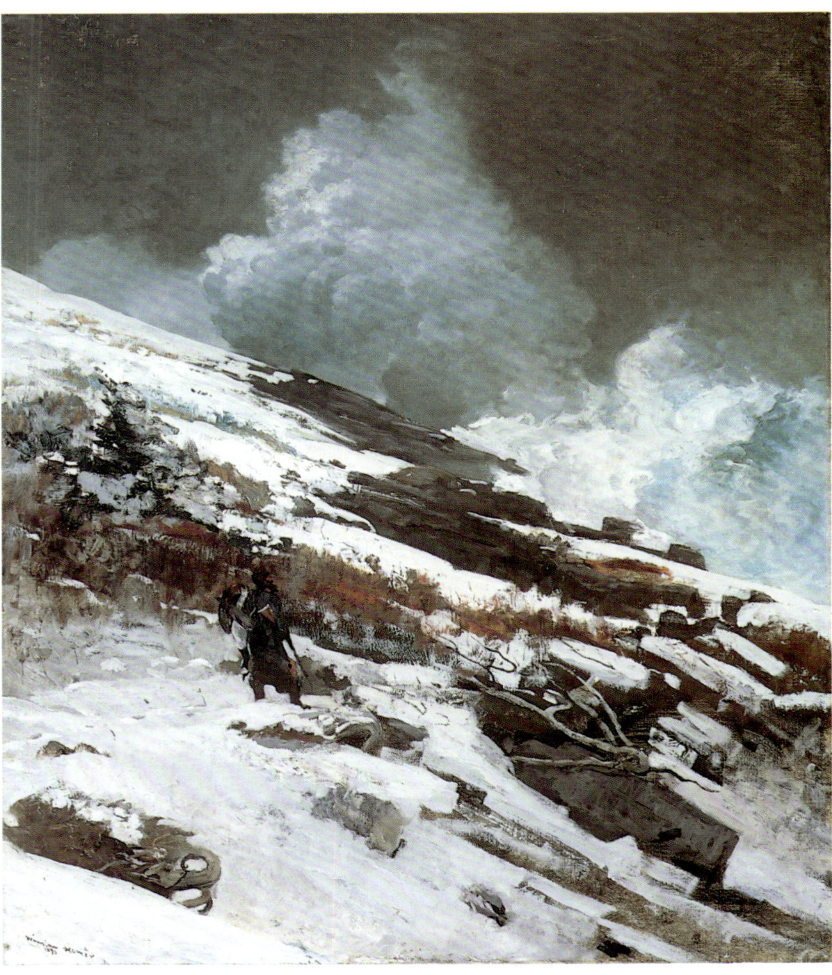

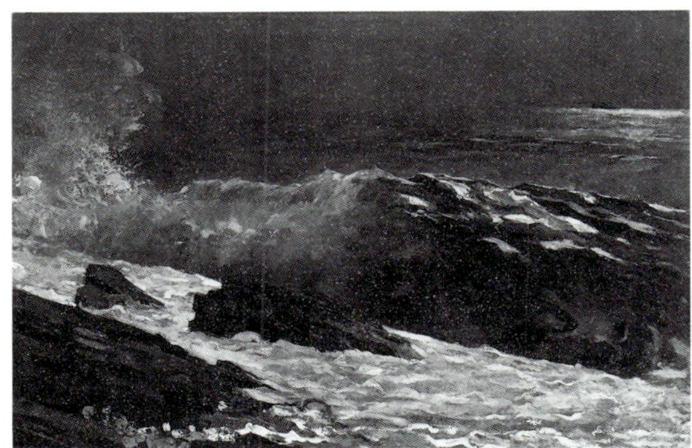

8. Homer. *Sunlight on the Coast,* 1890.

several more such paintings: *The Wreck* (Figure 6) and *The Lookout,* both in 1896, as well as *Gulf Stream,* 1899 (see Figure 24). The world of men in action also appears in several hunting paintings, such as *Huntsman and Dogs* (see Figure 60), 1891, and *Hound and Hunter,* 1892.[6]

The last two paintings of 1890 introduced the most important subjects of his last years: landscapes of winter and death, often containing figures watching the surf, and pure marines. *Winter Coast* (Figure 7) depicts a frozen coast on which stands a hunter staring at the surf, a dead goose hanging over his shoulder. *Sunlight on the Coast* (Figure 8) shows simply a wave, some rocks, and a distant steamer. Homer had been painting watercolors of the coast of Prout's Neck since first arriving there in 1883. That first summer seems to have been taken up with sketching

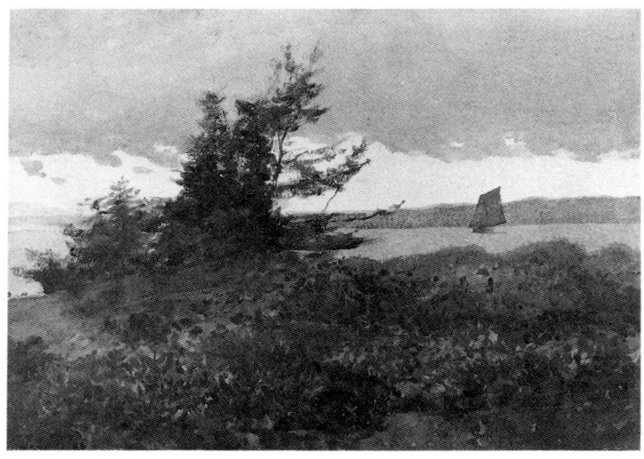

9. Homer. *Prout's Neck Surf, Looking Toward Old Orchard,* 1883.

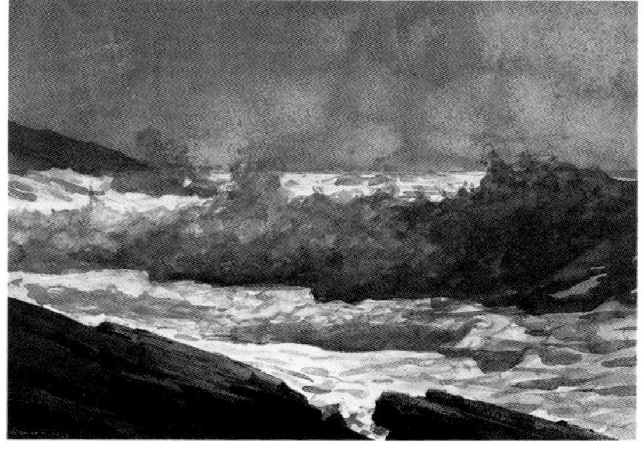

10. Homer. *Prout's Neck, Breakers,* 1883.

local views from every vantage point, as though he were mapping the place visually (Figures 9, 10). But the watercolors sat on a shelf until 1890, until he could finish distilling the essence of the place and decide which views were worth developing further. Homer narrowed the scores of viewpoints he painted down to one situation: a close-up of a small segment of the rocky shore, with strong waves pounding in. The setting of *Winter Coast* and *Sunlight on the Coast* was the sounding stage of his last dramas, a landscape he painted repeatedly for the next twenty years.

The limited number of motifs in Homer's late works, hammered at again and again, produces an effect close to serial imagery. Claude Monet's (1840-1926) series of haystacks and cathedral facades, begun at the same time, may instructively be compared with them (Figures 11, 12). Monet's are not only more analytically reductive but also more extended in their analysis: the compositions and viewpoints are more tightly controlled, and the study of light differentiates time more precisely and thoroughly. Monet's series are true sequences, however, while Homer's are repeated attempts to get the thing right or to see something new in the subject. Each time it was as if Homer progressed along the same road a little farther, telling what he had to say slightly more clearly.

Homer's condensation of his motifs, his stripping away of inessentials, can be seen at every level in his work, but it is most evident in the repetition of compositions. Perhaps the most

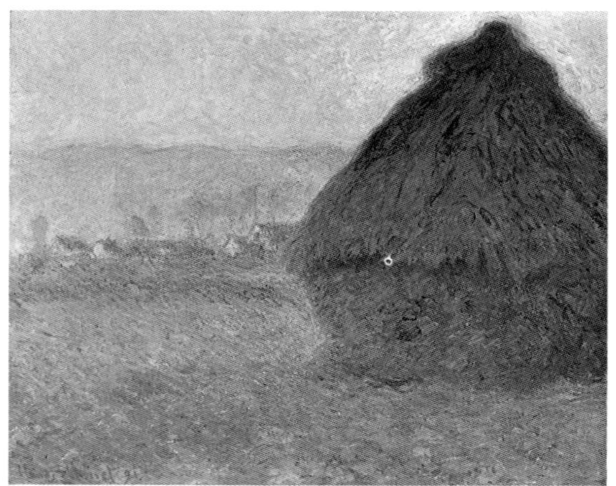

11. Monet. *Grainstack at Sunset near Giverney,* 1891.

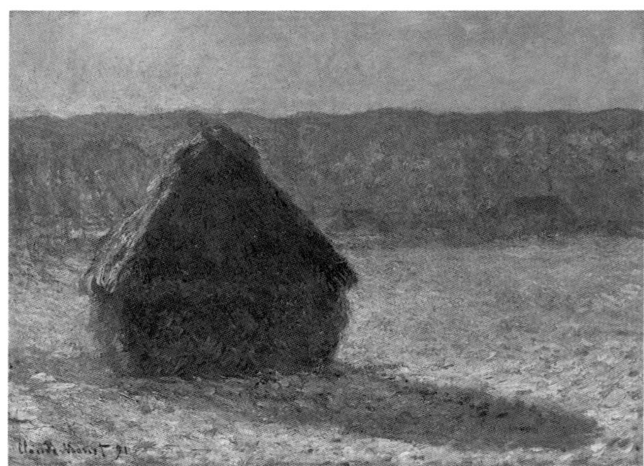

12. Monet. *Grainstack in Winter,* 1891.

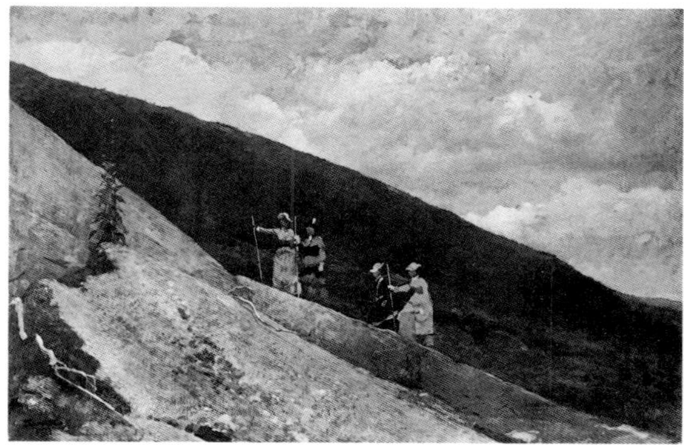

13. Homer. *In the Mountains,* 1877.

14. Homer. *Coast of Maine,* 1893.

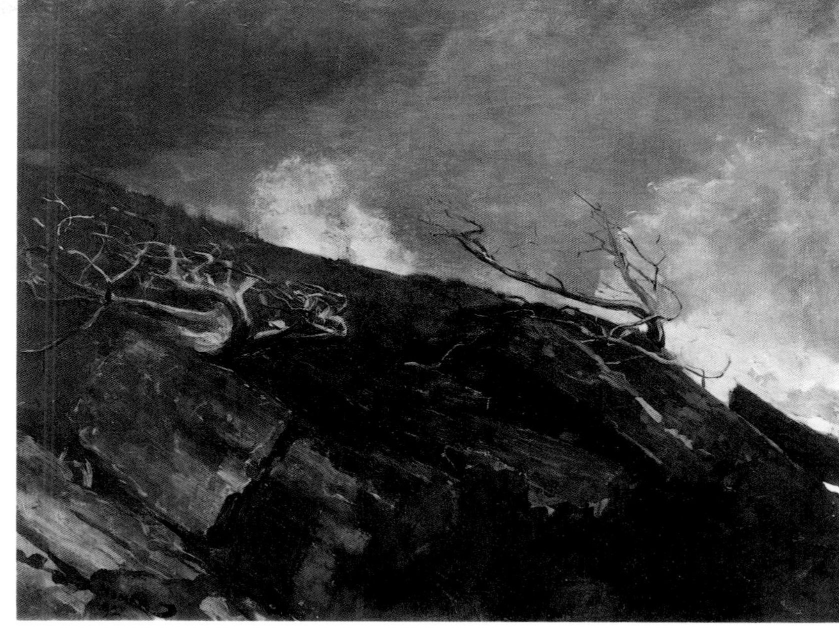

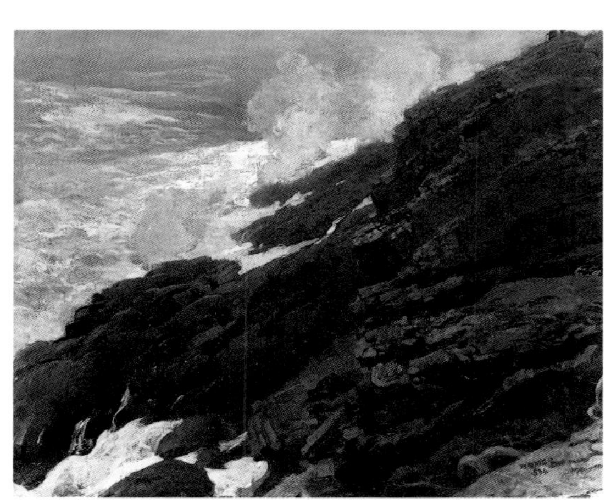

15. Homer. *High Cliffs, Coast of Maine,* 1894.

common device throughout his career was the composition ordered by a diagonal wedge, often of rock. *In the Mountains,* 1877 (Figure 13), for example, is dominated by the great decline of rock sloping from the summit to the left.[7] Compositionally, a later work such as *Coast of Maine,* 1893 (Figure 14), simplifies the earlier painting by eliminating the figures. In *High Cliffs, Coast of Maine,* 1894 (Figure 15), Homer depicted what at first glance seems to be the same scene as *Coast of Maine,* though reversed; but then we observe that instead of the shelf of rock coming toward us, the cliff wall recedes. The difference in scale and direction—which leads to this play of volumes—is sealed with the small figures at the top of the cliff to the right. Homer's manipulation of picture surface and depth here is typical of his work.

Homer's two most reductive compositions are *Northeaster* and *Cannon Rock* (Figures 16, 17), both marines painted in 1895. In *Northeaster* we have moved closer to the rock than ever before. The first impression is of four broad elements, decoratively arranged to form a flat composition: brown rock, green water, white spray, and gray sky. Then we realize that these flat areas of color are energetically articulated. The spray shoots up; the water advances. The broad rock contains smaller rocks that lift and

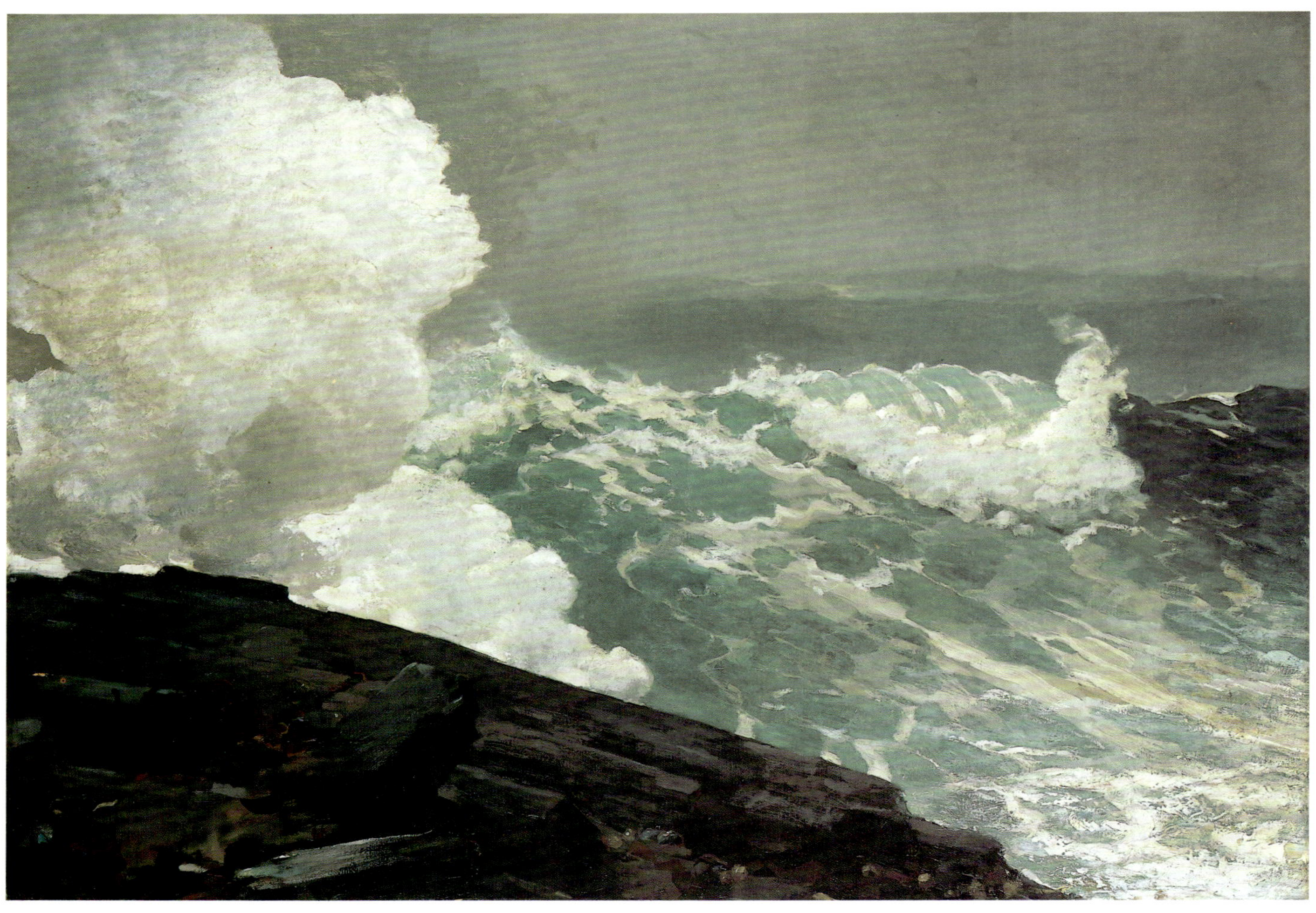

16. Homer. *Northeaster,* 1895.

point the eye across the scene, dramatizing earth's resistance to ocean. Even the gray sky conceals more waves beyond. The volume of the rocks to the left in the foreground is balanced by the yawning void of the water to the right, where the wave begins to recede before its next lunge at the land. The foreground to the left also is the area where Homer permits the purest, most saturated colors—the red seaweed and an odd speck of blue; to the far right, which is mostly white, the paint is thickly textured. Reading vertically, the left side offsets the broad white spray against the dark rock, the area of greatest value contrast; to the right, the most roughly brushed area steadies the most decorative, the little spray that dances on the crest of the wave.[8] The balancing act that binds the painting together is dynamic, not static.

Less decorative and somewhat ungainly, but just as striking, is

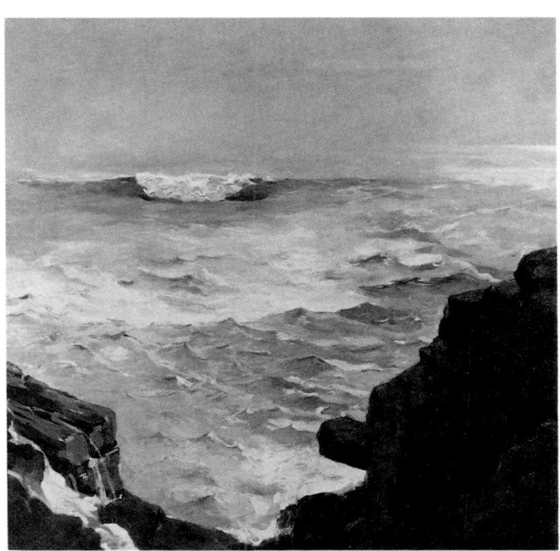

17. Homer. *Cannon Rock,* 1895.

Cannon Rock, a painting of the ocean on a calmer day. Its most important attribute is its square shape, which neutralizes any sense of lateral movement.[9] The two wedges of rock balance to left and right, an almost cubistic patterning of mass and void; the placement of the cresting wave a little to the left offsets the slightly greater mass of rock to the right. But the only strong line of the painting, Cannon Rock itself, points nowhere. There is a curious blankness to the work, as though it has no point other than its own existence, a disturbingly modern note.

These two paintings most vividly demonstrate the way Homer balanced on the knife-edge between realism and abstraction. Reducing the natural world to its fundamental elements, as he did his technique, he pushed his painting to an abstract arrangement of forms. But the inherent materiality of his subjects and their dynamism prevented him, willingly, from going further. Homer built a balcony on his studio where he could observe the sea and weather; from this vantage point he commanded an unbroken vista stretching to the horizon. Yet he chose to paint this panorama only in a few watercolors. For his canvases, he always stood on the shore, as though he could only paint with his feet planted on the rock. His low vantage point is consistent in every subject, not just the pure landscapes, and not only low but often looking down, concentrating on the near-at-hand, the material, and the immediate.[10]

Color and texture contribute strongly to the sense of abstraction and materiality in Homer's paintings. His color, despite his insistence on its absolute naturalism (asked if he ever modified the colors of nature, he replied "Never! Never!"),[11] was based on a theoretical understanding of its workings. From the very beginning of his career, he studied the most advanced ideas on color theory, having owned from 1867 a translation of Michel Eugene Chevreul's *The Laws of Contrast of Colours.* Chevreul, a French chemist and influential color theorist, both analyzed and advocated a scientific system of color oppositions and broken color. To achieve the greatest effects of vibrancy and also the greatest truth to experience, he maintained that the artist should place complementary colors side by side rather than blending them, or even glazing them. Homer practiced Chevreul's advice consistently, from his earliest works.[12]

Homer often enlivened his monochromatic color schemes with a dash of red: a touch of seaweed, a glimpse of stocking, or a scarf. Frequently, in the foreground he would juxtapose, in a few dabs of paint, the two dominant hues of the painting in either their purest form or else a hue complementary to the pervading color scheme. In the 1890s these color harmonies tended to be monochromatically sedate, but by 1900 they became much more varied, as in the lavender that pervades *Early Morning after a Storm at Sea* (see Figure 20). Homer also observed perceptual changes in color acutely. In *Winter Coast* (Figure 7), for instance, he transmuted the hunter's blue coat into brown as it drapes over the man's thigh into shadow.

By the 1890s Homer had an absolute command of his brush, varying the handling depending on the effect and the object at hand. He tended to reserve his most varied and dramatic brushwork for water, where the drama in most of his compositions resides. Thus, in *Early Morning after a Storm at Sea* the cotton-candy quality of the ocean spray is suggested with soft dabs of a fairly liquid paint on a lightly loaded brush, while in the foreground, where the water swirls on the rocks, a rich, creamy paint is used in long strokes. The rocks, in contrast, are directly painted without flourishes, suitable for their supporting role. One may contrast in many works, such as *Northeaster* (Figure 16) or *Maine Coast* (see Figure 23), the relatively thin handling of paint in the rocks with the richly varied treatment of the water.

Homer's working methods contributed to the freedom of his palette and texture. Much of his preliminary thinking was done in watercolor (although several oil sketches survive), which amplified his color sense. The ease of placing pure pigments on radiantly white paper spurred him on to experiment easily and prolifically with color in that medium, and then transfer the results to his oils. The gestation of his oils was sometimes long, based as they were on watercolors done years before; for example, *Early Morning after a Storm at Sea* (Figure 20), begun in 1900, is based on a watercolor of 1883, *Prout's Neck Breakers* (Figure 10).[13] Usually he would try to refresh his memory against the real thing before embarking on a canvas (although this was not always possible). But the actual execution was often swift. His marine paintings had the most direct relationship to the landscape and

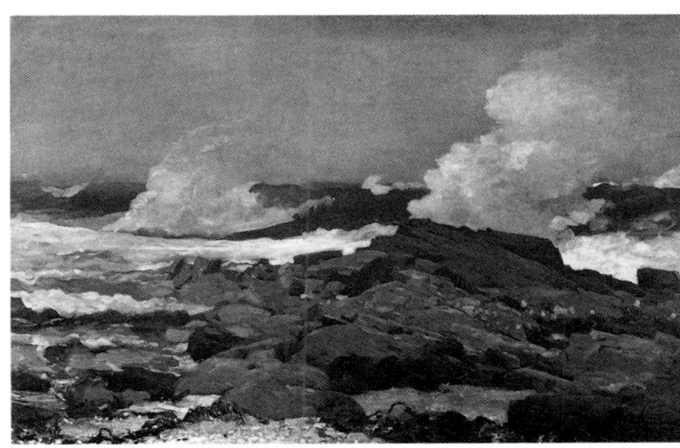

18. Homer. *Eastern Point,* 1900.

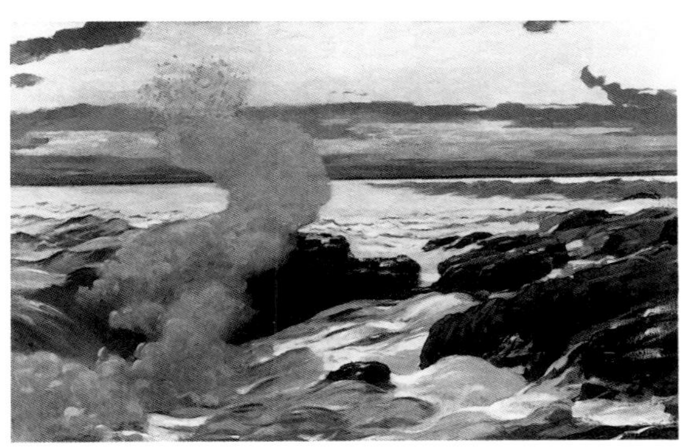

19. Homer. *West Point, Prout's Neck,* 1900.

event they depicted. These in a sense combined both the sketch and the finished painting, a technical fact that Homer exploited in the vigor of his paint handling. He commented once to a student: "Now those are nice little sketches [see Figure 91] ... but, you know, if you'd used larger brushes and a canvas, with exactly the same effort you would have had a picture instead of a sketch."[14]

For Homer, however, it was the subject that produced the technical effects, not the other way around. Three paintings, all begun in 1900, illustrate the point neatly: *Eastern Point; West Point, Prout's Neck;* and *Early Morning* (Figures 18-20), although Homer took two years to finish *Early Morning.* Each portrays, in a panoramic format, the rocks of the Neck, using the same basic elements. But it is the contrasts that are important. Taken in order of completion, *Eastern Point* depicts midday, under an overcast sky that seems to emphasize the straightforward palette: browns for the rocks, seacolors for the sea. Nothing is very strong or startling. *West Point* is an almost lurid demonstration of a sunset on the ocean, where the water seems a sheet of pearly ice because of the angles of reflection of the sunlight. *Early Morning* records a specific weather condition and has a very specific palette, a dark violet and golden cream. Along with each setting comes a different group of associations: the sober reality of midday; the ecstatic union of water, light, and sky at sunset; and the promise of serenity that comes with dawn.

"Meaning" in Homer's paintings normally resolves itself into a story, whether it is one contained within the painting or one seen in comparison with other works. Not surprisingly, Homer never entirely abandoned his roots as a journalist committed to recording events. Even within the simplest landscapes, there is always some action, something going on that implies a before and after. Although each work certainly exists on its own, we understand them better when we view them together, as Homer himself did. The juxtaposition of his paintings reshapes them into explicit sequences or into repetitions and adaptions of the same motif. Quite often, we have the sense that Homer has simply changed the position of his easel a few feet and that with that small change, everything else is modified. It is as though the only way for him to rethink a subject or to see it clearly is to stand and look. To achieve a different viewpoint, he had to change where he

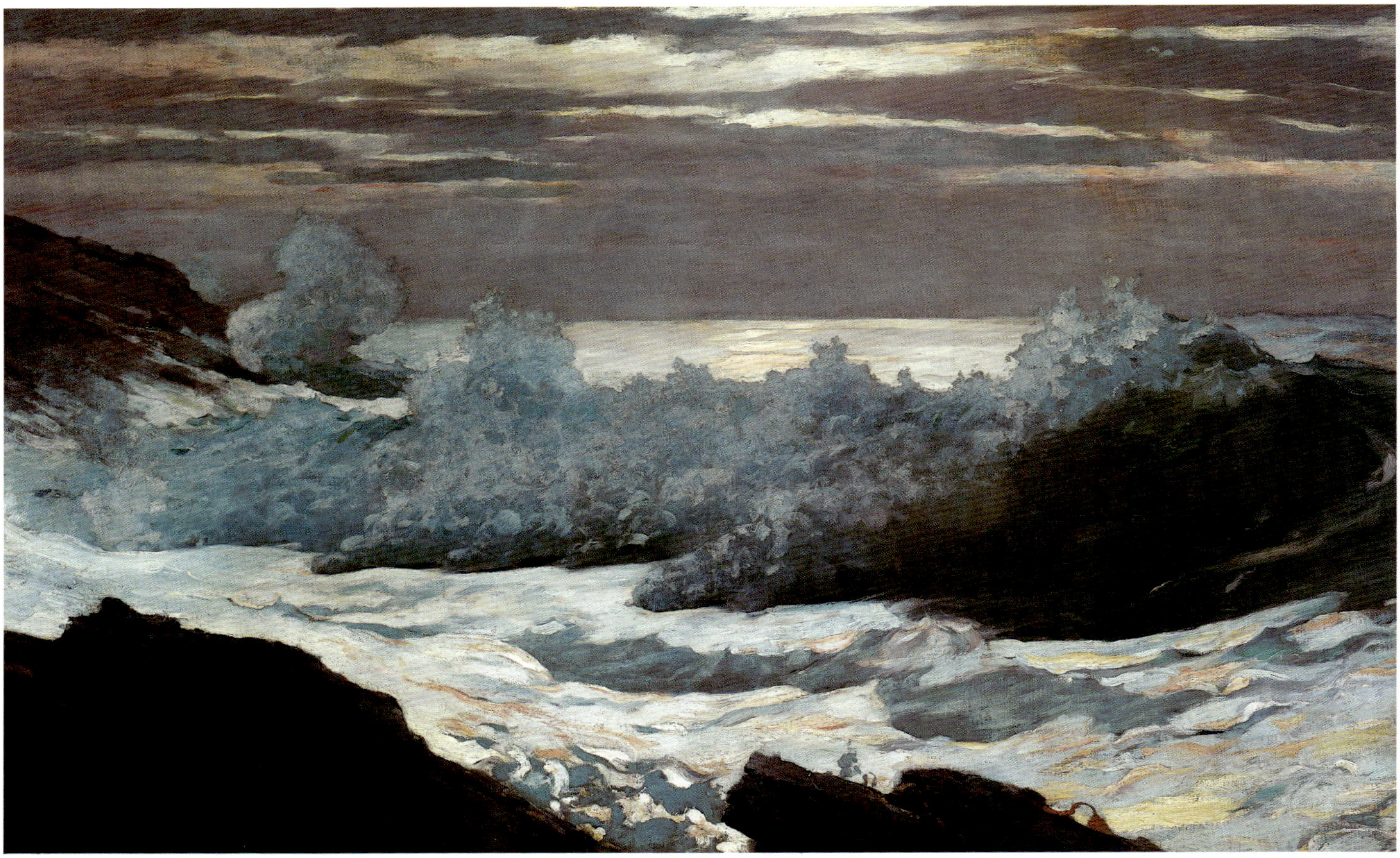

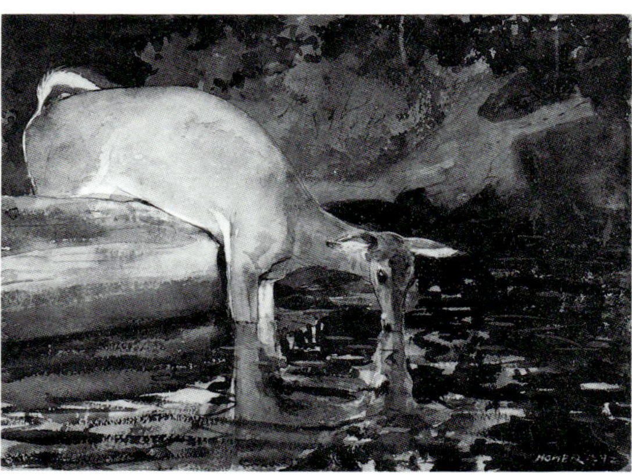

20. Homer. *Early Morning after a Storm at Sea,* 1902.

21. Homer. *Deer Drinking,* 1892.

stood. Homer had a weighty sense of the particularities of a scene, which he would not let go of until each angle had been described.

The watercolors depicting deer hunting, done in 1892, form the most concentrated and extended narrative sequence in his career. In them Homer recorded the hunt and death of a deer in several stages, where much of the significance of each scene is conveyed through the different vantage points. In *Deer Drinking* (Figure 21) we are stationed on the opposite bank of the stream from the deer, situated so that the log is angled diagonally from the left side of the drawing up and back into the picture space. In *The Fallen Deer* (Figure 22) our viewpoint has been shifted to the right so that the log parallels the picture plane, like a horizon line, while the deer is smaller in relation to the scene and placed closer to the center of the picture. The color changes as well, to

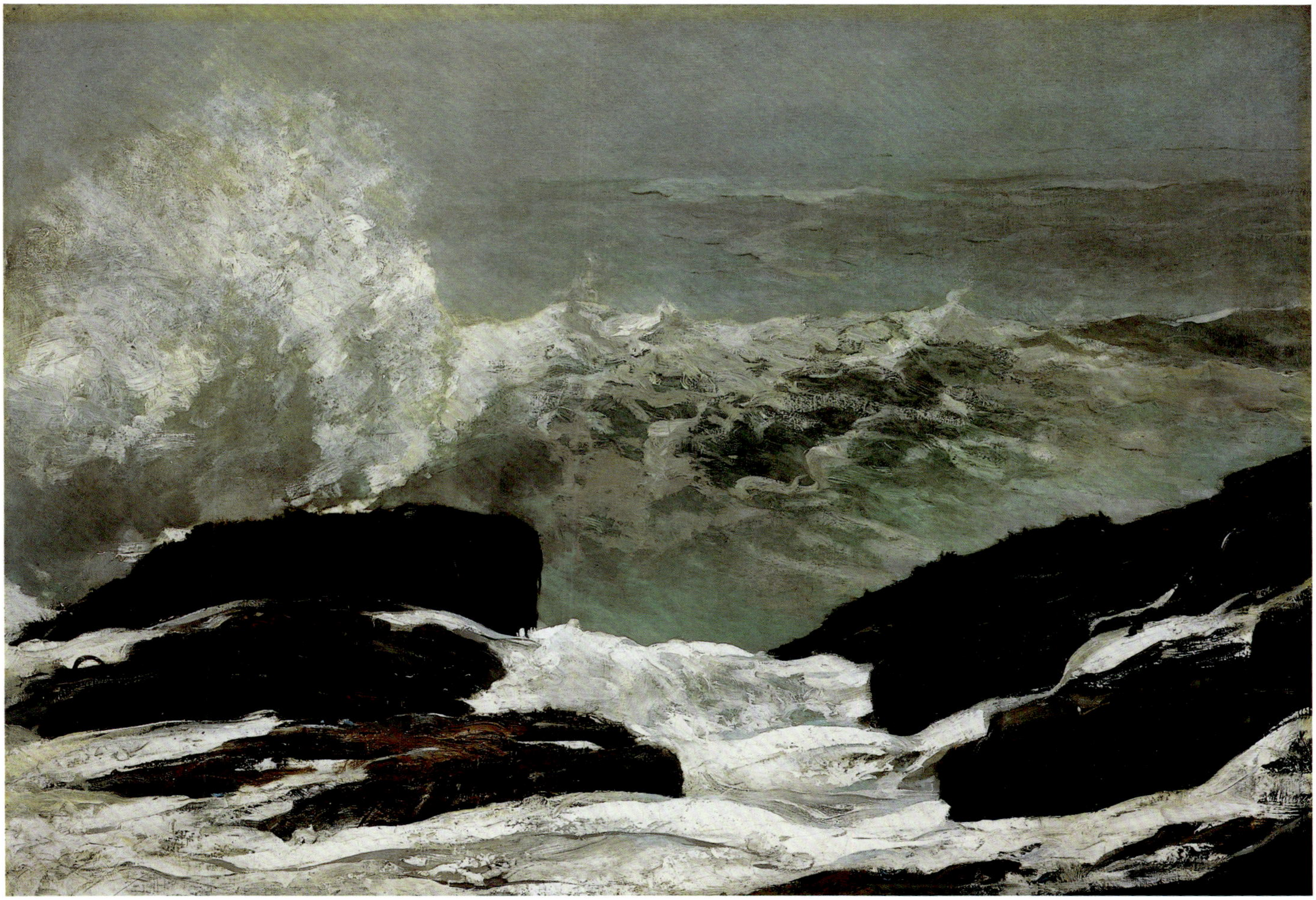

23. Homer. *Maine Coast,* 1896.

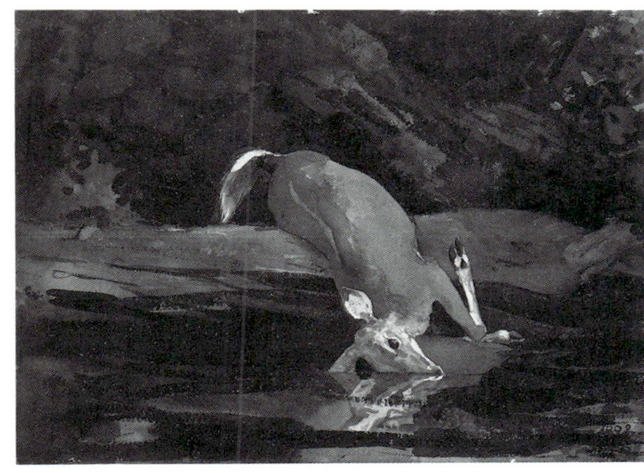

22. Homer. *The Fallen Deer,* 1892.

fewer and darker hues. The adjustments dramatize the loss of life and vitality; in the second work, we are distanced from the body in several subtle ways.

Homer also tried out different versions of the story simultaneously. The various scenes of deer hunting often include an old guide or a young man, or both. In several instances, the same moment in the hunt is repeated with different figures: Homer's paintings tell us how it happened with just the young man, then how it could have happened with both men.[15] As a good storyteller will, he continually thought up new wrinkles for old stories. And he embodied them in formally different treatments. The most appropriate analogy is with film making, also a sequence of images that tell a story. Homer approached his subjects as though reshooting them.

Thinking always in terms of the relationship between works, as well as the individual work, Homer invites us to consider groupings that may be separated by date of execution or size. Everything in his working method, slow and deliberate as it was, urges this course of interpretation. For example, the groups of marine paintings seem to form narratives, or at least implied narratives. *Sunlight on the Coast* (Figure 8) and *Early Morning after a Storm at Sea* (Figure 20), compositionally very alike, are versions of the same story. The slight changes in color and composition adjust the drama only slightly. In contrast, *Northeaster* (Figure 16) and *Maine Coast* (Figure 23) seem to be thesis and antithesis, the first constructing and the second deconstructing the elements of earth and water. In *Northeaster* the two are juxtaposed and unified, the picture is flat and decorative; in *Maine Coast* (as in *Cannon Rock,* Figure 17) the rocks have been split into teeth and chew the water violently, hollowing the space in on itself.

But the simple fact of action within a single work may also be construed as a narrative. In *Coast of Maine* (Figure 14), it is late afternoon toward the end of the year. It looks as though a storm were on the way, as well as night and snow: things will only get worse. Reading from center left to bottom right, we see a whole, although twisted and bent, tree and the burst of foam appearing mysteriously above it; then the merger of water and tree—in paint and placement on the canvas the two are intertwined—until we reach the threshing waves, the only water we actually see. The tree branches on the left are the most delicate and complex form in the painting. They are the only signs of life—a little tuft of leaves can be seen on the top left branch. As we proceed to the right, the simpler and more elemental become the shapes and things, and the more material: the action is greatest where the paint is thickest. The passage from left to right is also a movement from overall darkness to strong contrast of light and dark. The tendency to read the drama as one of progressive destruction—if one looks at the objects depicted—is contrasted with a movement toward energy and light—if one reads the painting in its formal elements.

The story Homer tended to tell in his marines is a simple one. The plot of stormy water and obdurate rock may not on the

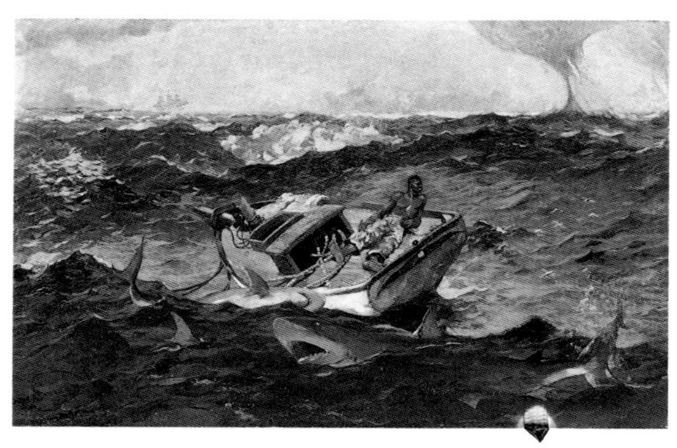

24. Homer. *The Gulf Stream,* 1899.

25. Homer. *To the Rescue,* 1886-1907.

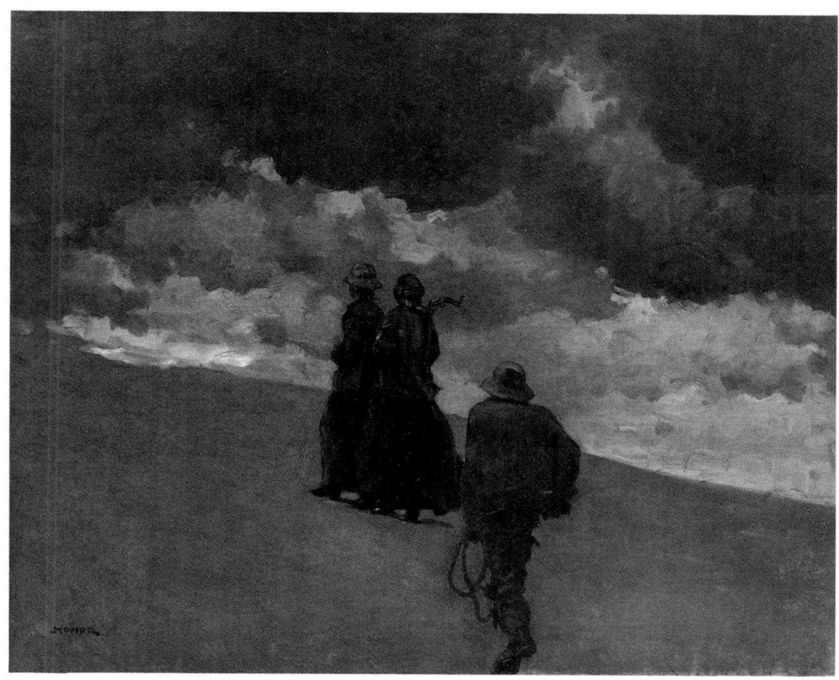

surface be as interesting as a novel, but it does have the same eternal truth as the basic boy-meets-girl. Nature's drama of aggression and resistance is usually held in balance in his work, but sometimes the balance tips one way or the other, toward the hardness of the rock or the violence of the water.[16] It is a bleak tale; Homer tells us of loneliness, danger, even death. His stories take place in a barren environment. Warmth is not part of this world; what is not snow might as well be. *Maine Coast,* for example, has a kind of piercing coldness to it; the raging water corresponds to a snowstorm. Even an oil Homer made from his Caribbean experiences—what he chose to distill from all his watercolors of those sun-drenched, welcoming islands—was about death. *The Gulf Stream* (Figure 24) depicts the same adversity as his northern scenes, although the predators are now sharks.

The human presence, despite this concentration on the powers of Nature, is never far away in Homer's work. During the 1880s he had reduced it to an elemental level (much as he would reduce his landscapes in the next period): men on the sea, women on the shore. Beginning in the 1890s, though fisher folk return on occasion, men appear more often as hunters—a more brutal engagement with nature than fishing—and women appear more

26. Homer. *Moonlight on the Water.*

remotely, even more passively. Or sometimes the figures shown watching the waves appear so swathed in clothes as to be almost lacking gender.

Always, however, the human is counterposed against the natural in a balance that hovers on the point of complete merger but never quite attains it. *To the Rescue* (Figure 25), which Homer worked on intermittently from 1886 to 1907, dramatizes this idea at several levels. In the painting, two women (followed by an old sailor) race toward a wall of foam and spray. Their faces are unreadable, since their backs are to us, but the haste of their gait expresses great urgency. Their goal, however, is entirely unclear: the rest of the picture is empty except for the ground beneath their feet and the boiling surf. Homer crops the scene to an ambiguous detail of some larger action, rendering the narrative of rescue almost pointless. At the same time the figures stand out distinctly against the grays and browns of their surroundings. The stormy maelstrom, rather than threatening to engulf them, reads as soft dabs of paint, and the delicate nuances of tone cushion the threat of the situation. The wind will never tear these solid figures off the rocks.

The most astonishing of all his scenes of people is the canvas with the least unusual subject, a picture of women at their leisure at a resort, *A Summer Night* (Figure 5), a subject Homer had painted since his earliest days.[17] In *Summer Night* two women "dance by the light of the moon" while a group of spectators sit off to one side in shadow against the water.[18] The women twirl in the foreground on a veranda in the light; the spectators seem to sit on the edge of the shore, and the smooth sea glitters with light. The music is quick-paced; the women, arm in arm, spin like tops. Behind them beats another rhythm, the soft susurration of the sea. The listeners seem to have turned to black stone, so quietly do they sit, unmoving for so long. On one side they hear the piano, on the other, the waves; on one side they see lamplight, on the other, the moon. To one side is humanity; to the other, the vastness of nature.

The many surviving related sketches in oil and watercolor testify to the unusual effort the painting cost. One study, *Moonlight on the Water* (Figure 26), is related to *A Summer Night* in an oblique manner. Given the almost violent freedom of the brushstrokes, it is difficult to consider the work more than a sketch, but comparably large and isolated strokes, in similarly abbreviated compositions, can be found in several exhibited paintings, such as *Maine Coast* and *Cape Trinity* (see Figures 23, 37), as well, of course, as many watercolors. Certainly, in size *Moonlight on the Water* is no smaller than many finished oils. But here the brushstroke has an unusually vivid life, almost becoming its own subject: the great slashes of white to the left leave the quiet dark figures to the right in shadow in every way. Little of this extraordinary attack can be found in the final work. Nonetheless, it is useful to realize that, in a sense, beneath the silent surface of *A Summer Night* heaves this energy.

In the finished painting the dancing women are circumscribed by the light and the platform in the foreground. They are young, or they would not dance so briskly; but they are old enough to be attractive, and for that reason they dance together: to dance with young men might be too exciting. They hold each other, not in a sexual embrace (except insofar as the touch of any person may be sexual) but in one that makes plain the power of music to bring people together against the loneliness of the night. This is the last time that people touch in Homer's art, and it is magical. Everything in the painting hangs in the balance, without resolution.

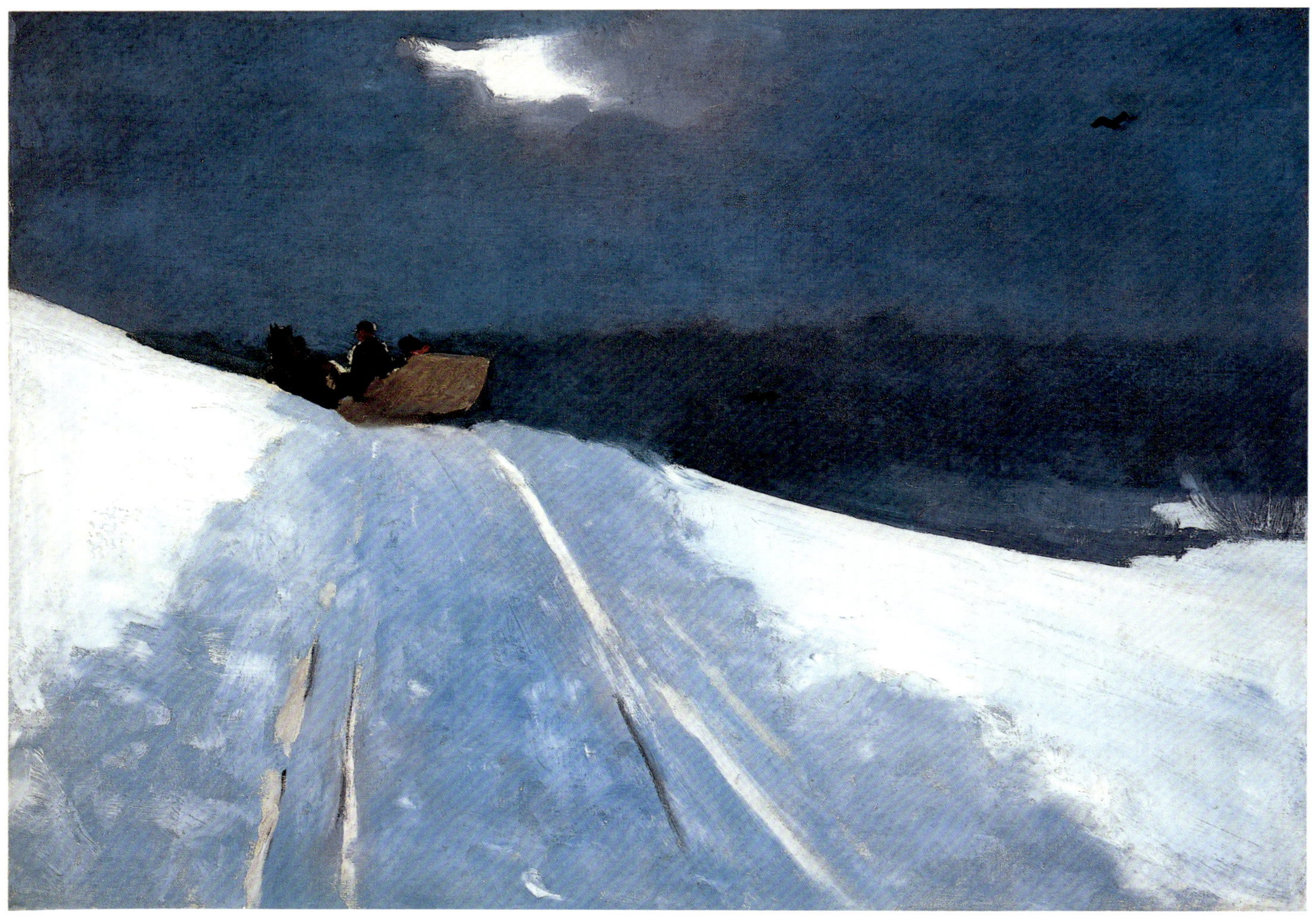

27. Homer. *Sleigh Ride,* ca. 1893.

For the next twenty years Homer pared down this softness and complexity until the last woman he painted, in *A Light on the Sea* (see Figure 39), is hard and heroic, and the last couple, a pair of ducks in *Right and Left* (see Figure 32), caught in the dance of flight, are severed by the hand of a hunter.

The quietness of mood in *A Summer Night,* perhaps a gentle irony at the ambiguities of love or a sweet sense of the slow withdrawal of the human presence into the picture's depths, are ideas not often associated with Homer, but they may be found in several late works. In *Sleigh Ride,* ca. 1893 (Figure 27), the design of the picture is its most striking feature. At its crux, where the two wedges of light and shadow balance, may be seen a sleigh. About to vanish from our sight, the sleigh carries a couple, a man and a woman. Their incipient vanishing does not provoke anxiety; rather it seems calmly inevitable, in the way ripples disappear into the surface of a pond. Above them, in a patch of sky showing through dark clouds, shines the last light of the day; two crows fly in the same direction as the sleigh travels. At the end of day, as night closes in, it is fitting that each returns home.

Another small painting begun that same fall and completed early the next year is equally quiet. *Below Zero,* finished December 1893 (Figure 28), is one of the key works that establishes the mood of many of the late paintings, one of the last to embed people in the landscape, in an indifferent nature which renders them mute. Bundled in fur, two presumably male figures pause in the snow to look at the mist on the sea.

The painting's mood and message have been variously interpreted: as expressing man's union with nature or as a statement of Nature as Other. In truth, the men depicted can see very little. The veil of gray paint acts like a curtain in front of their eyes as well as the viewer's. One contemporary found the mist rising from the sea to resemble "the busy spectacle of hundreds of factories."[19] A modern scholar sees it as a manifestation of the "Other: that against which the self is defined."[20] But the point is that their eyes are directed at a void, a blank screen; they can project whatever they wish onto it. The local reality of their standing there is one of the warmth of their bodies protected under the furs while the cold bites at their hands and noses. Having toiled through the crusty snow for some time, they now pause, balanced on the cusp of a moment. In seconds they will feel the cold, the hostility of the world, but for now, this moment, all they sense is its beauty. Their eyes, their aesthetic sense, momentarily take them out of their bodies. Homer's perceptions continually balance here, the willed optimism of an innate pessimist, knowing that in fact we can never know any "other" of any kind but content to avoid the matter for now. Loneliness is not the right label; perhaps indomitability in the face of isolation.

But, of course, from such stoic regard of the real face of nature, it is only a small step toward contemplating mortality. Death is perhaps the dominant subject of Homer's later paintings. He most directly dramatized Death in the form in which he personally experienced it: in hunting scenes. Surprisingly, since Homer was a fisherman, the majority of his sporting paintings

28. Homer. *Below Zero,* 1894.

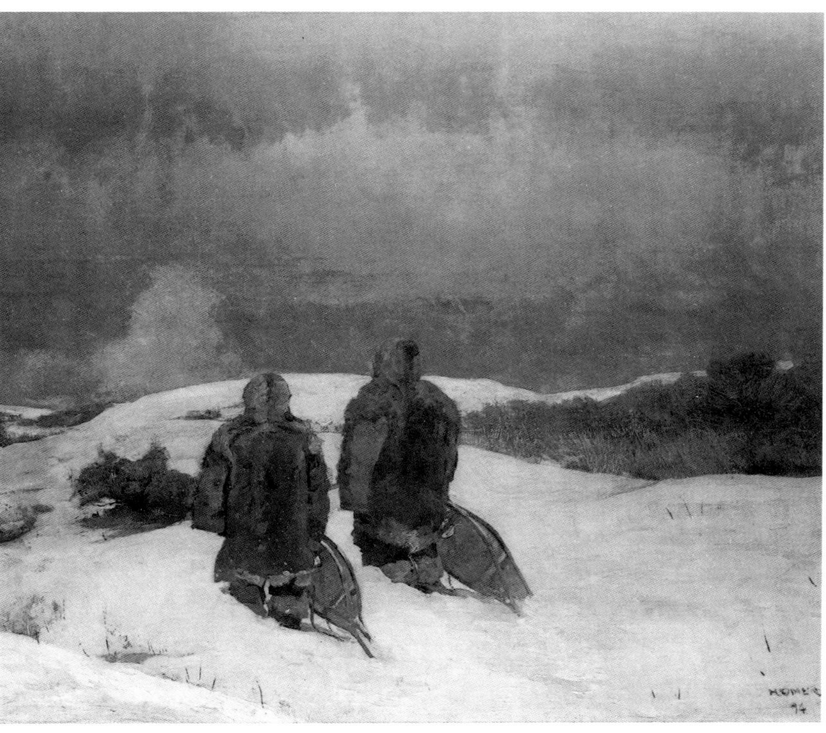

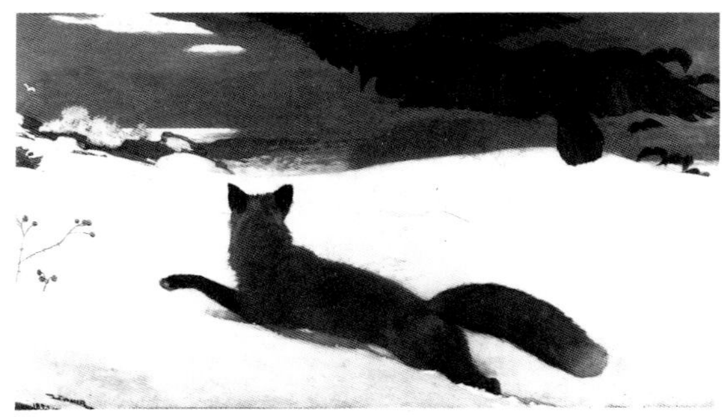

29. Homer. *Fox Hunt,* 1893.

depict different prey: mainly deer but also one fox.

Perhaps the most obvious feature of the hunting pictures is their matter-of-fact brutality, both in the manner of the death and in the nature of the hunter. The most extreme in this group is *Fox Hunt* (Figure 29), completed in first few months of 1893. Normally people hunt foxes, but here crows attack one. This startling reversal of aggression and resistance is matched at every point in the painting. The crows, smaller and less powerful than the fox, have the upperhand literally: with their wings spread they dwarf the fox. The sense of reversal rests on the formal level as well. Everyone has commented on the beauty of this painting, especially its color. Here, Homer's almost *japoniste* perfection of design is at its greatest dissonance with the harshness of the subject. He takes full advantage of the decorative possibilities of red fur and crisp outlines against white snow. The fox is splayed out across the canvas, slowed by snow and hunger as the crows spiral out from the copse on the right. Ahead of the fox lies only water and a small burst of white spray; there is no escape from fate. Coloristically the painted fur combines everything in the scene except the snow and the wave: the red of the berries, the green of the water, the blue of the shadow, the black of the crows. That is, the fox's coat includes everything except the ultimate cause of the animal's plight and its destination: snow and ice. But the white is as manifold as the fox: the white of the paralyzing snow is also the white of the sea-spray and the seagull. If we may read meaning into the colors, then the red and black of fox and crows—life and death—are balanced against the white which can be either.

It has often been felt that Homer identified with the fox, and the point is obvious: the painting is so exceptional.[21] *Fox Hunt* is Homer's most amazing tour-de-force, and his largest picture. But what is the nature of the identification? Homer avoids any obvious drama, as always understating the threat and the reaction. In Courbet's *Fox in the Snow* (Figure 30), 1860, a possible source for the subject, the fox is the successful predator, devouring a rodent.[22] In Homer's painting, not only are the crows not yet attacking the fox, but the fox may not have even noticed them. The animal turns not toward the crows but apparently looks steadily to the sea. Only the stretch of its body betrays haste and distress. The seagull and the burst of spray in the distance seem to belong to another world, where the blood-curdling drama of the foreground has been washed in white: the crows transformed into the gull and the life-and-death struggle turned into the impassive action of water against land. Again, a sense of equilibrium has been preserved, or rather a self-deprecating sense of cosmic order, in which the foreground is only a minor prelude to the expanse of the universe. The artist's identification with the fox is only the first of a series of identifications in which the sense of destabilized order is gradually returned to balance. But nothing erases the sense of isolation and death we perceive in this unforgiving world.

One final pair of hunting pictures returns to the human presence and its balance with nature. The paintings, *Kissing the Moon* (Figure 31), 1904, and *Right and Left* (Figure 32), 1909, are not a perfect pair, being slightly different in size: *Right and Left* is opened laterally to hold the flight and fall of the birds. But the juxtaposition illuminates each painting. In *Kissing the Moon* (also called *Sunset and Moonrise*) the hunter faces the sailors, who avoid his gaze, one looking at the moon. Instead of rowing, they scan the water for ducks. In *Right and Left,* the ducks have been

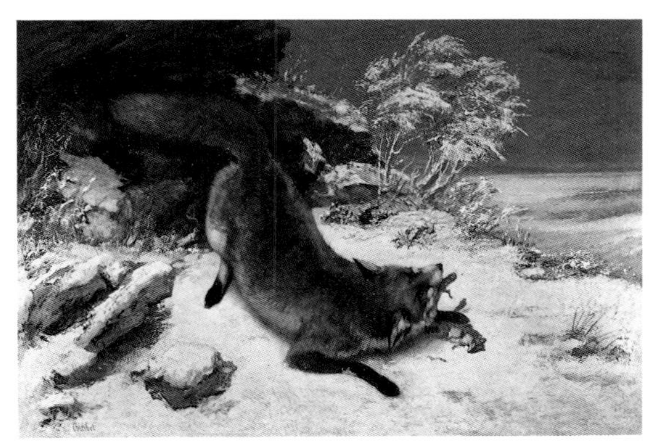

30. Courbet. *Fox in the Snow,* 1860.

31. Homer. *Kissing the Moon,* 1904.

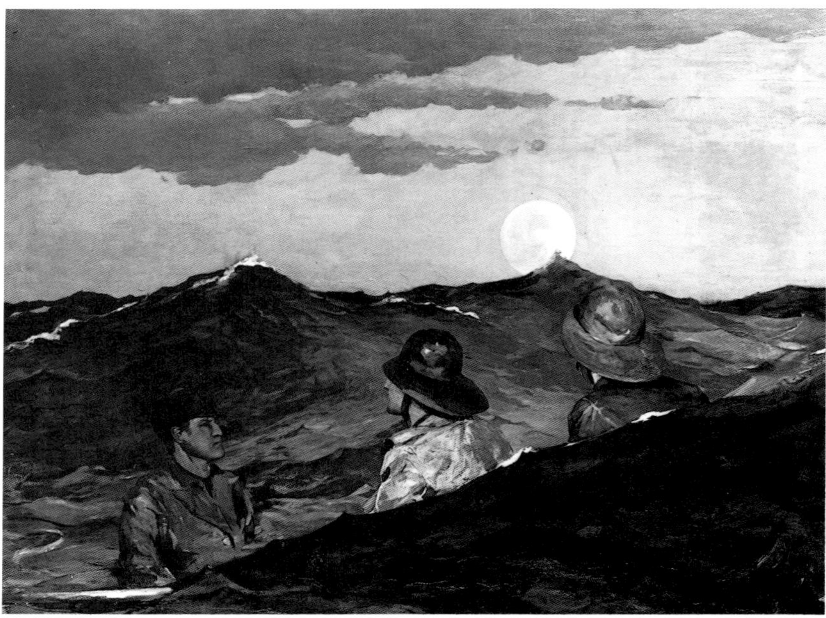

fired on, the hunter in the boat having risen and turned to do so. There are many oppositions at work here: patient waiting and swift action, human and animal, life and death. One basic reversal is surely male and female, despite the absence of any obvious female presence.[23] The titles hint at it. *Kissing the Moon* refers overtly to the viewpoint of the men: seen so low, the waves seem to kiss the moon. But the evocative sexuality of the title suggests that the men are about to kiss the globe of the moon, flushed warmly gold by the setting sun. In contrast, the prosaic title *Right and Left* grates, as it negates the lushness of the bird's bodies, their white breasts pressed toward us, and the misfortune of their fate.[24] Homer consistently shrouds gender in ambiguity. Whether overtly male or not, his victims often seem soft and feminine, in contrast to their hunters. Homer's "poignant identification with the hunted" achieves a final, richly ironic expression in *Right and Left.*[25] All that will remain of the ducks will be a feather or two floating on the waves.

The largest and most consistent group among Homer's late works are his paintings of the sea, where all these stories end. Here the themes of balance and struggle acted out by men and animals in the other works are recapitulated by nature herself, a much more stoic actor: rocks show no emotion.[26] The human presence is made marginal in these landscapes: footsteps in the snow or boats on the horizon. Homer's presence may be felt

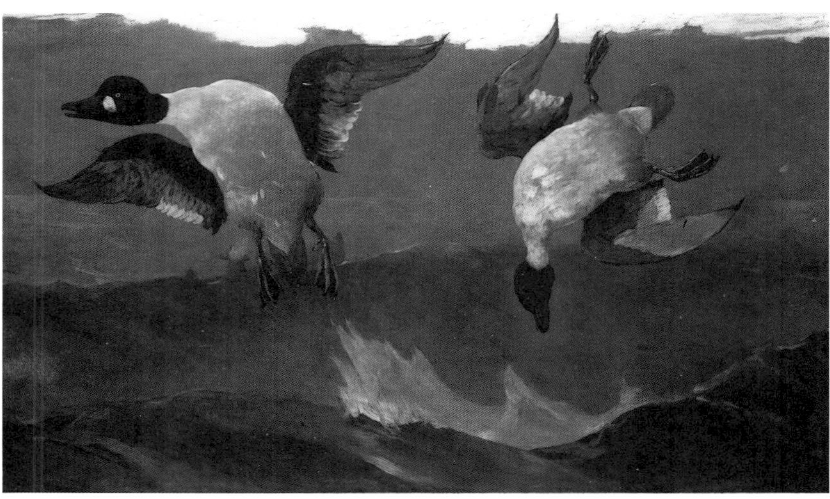

32. Homer. *Right and Left,* 1909.

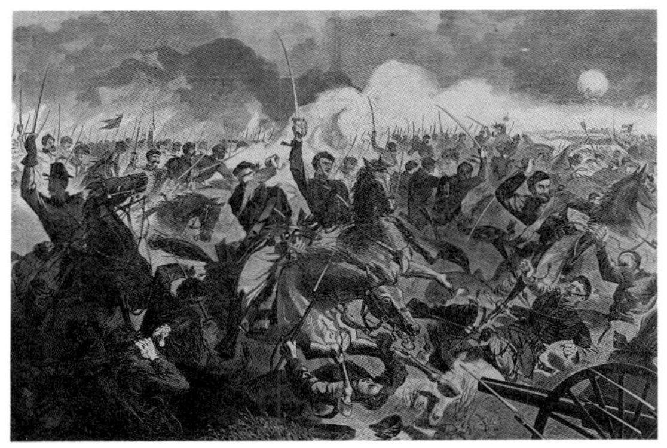

33. Homer. *The War for the Union, 1862—
A Cavalry Charge.*

throughout, however, in the drama of the handling of the paint; these paintings are actively created by the artist. In a sense, man or the drama of storytelling (with its implied narrator) is never far away, even in Homer's most barren landscapes; having begun as a genre painter and war correspondent, he never abandoned his interest in humanity. The crash of opposing armies marking battle scenes like *The War for the Union, 1862—A Cavalry Charge* (Figure 33) has been sublimated into natural forces.[27]

In *Sunlight on the Coast* (Figure 8), 1890, the first of his pure marines, Homer set out the elements he explored in later variations. Initially a trifle disconcerting, the close-up focus requires a moment or two for the viewer to determine the setting and time; all the ordinary clues are withheld. It is difficult to know at first whether the sunlight is supposed to be a momentary flash through the clouds or the slow withdrawal or onset of daylight. The title seems almost ironic. The sunlight barely pierces the darkness of the scene but transforms the backrush of one wave, which has covered half the shelf of rock, into a glimmering carpet of water. At this point all the elements of nature—earth, air, light, and water—merge into one.

The only sign of man is a steamship in the far distance which chugs toward the left, its stern very low. The wind blows the smoke ahead of it, into the thick fog creeping in from the left, so that the two may merge. Similar boats in the distance appear in

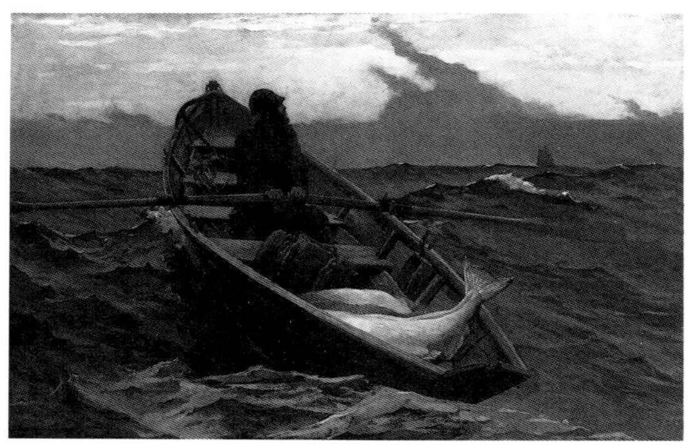

34. Homer. *The Fog Warning,* 1885.

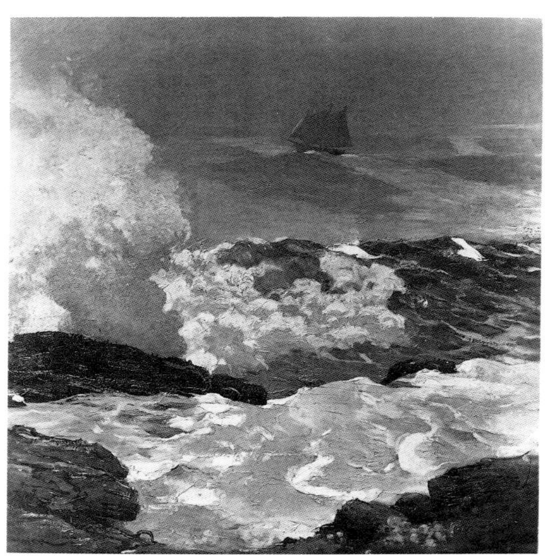

35. Homer. *On a Lee Shore,* ca. 1900.

several paintings, always with ironic undertones. In dramas such as *The Gulf Stream* (Figure 24) and *The Fog Warning* (Figure 34), they are ships that will not reach the harrowed men in the foreground, ships that will not react but will just sail on. The ships will never connect to the drama of the foreground; they represent everything human beyond the reach of the protagonists. In *Sunlight on the Coast* the steamer's presence, while less dramatic, seems to signify this same lack of connection between the picture's actor (here the observer) and the rest of humanity. In two of the last paintings in which such a boat appears, *On a Lee Shore,* 1900, and *Summer Squall* (begun in 1896 and completed in 1904), Homer dramatized the helplessness of the boat and the solidity of the rock (Figures 35, 36). But these rocks provide neither sure footing for the viewer nor a safe haven for the boat. In this case, the positions of relative security have been reversed: should the boat wish to land, it will not be able to safely.

The last pure marine to be completed, *Early Morning after a Storm at Sea* (Figure 20), turns the drama in a new direction. Gone is the forcefulness of the earlier years, particularly as seen in the two pictures begun at the same time: *Eastern Point* and *West Point* (Figures 18, 19). Now the transubstantiation of elements has been achieved in quiet. The storm is over; the night is done. It is uncertain what kind of day it will be: how strong the sun, how warm the air. We are suspended from time, in a realm of fancy.

The landscape *Cape Trinity, Saguenay River,* 1904 (Figure 37), shows a similarly quiet transformation, but this time worked inland. The painting, Homer's first of scenery in Quebec, indicates what he might have achieved if he had lived longer. Just as it took ten years for Prout's Neck to be expressed in oil paint, a similar length of time elapsed before the northern landscapes of the Canadian interior, which he had been depicting in watercolor since his first visit in 1895, finally worked their way deep enough into his soul. The work is unusually quiet, as is the landscape itself. On a river late at night the voice of the water is hushed but the least sound reverberates a hundred-fold. The dip of a paddle in the water, a small animal splashing can echo across the river, bouncing back against the cliff's face. Almost vaporized, the cliff's presence is felt more through the way it occludes light than

36. Homer. *Summer Squall,* 1904.

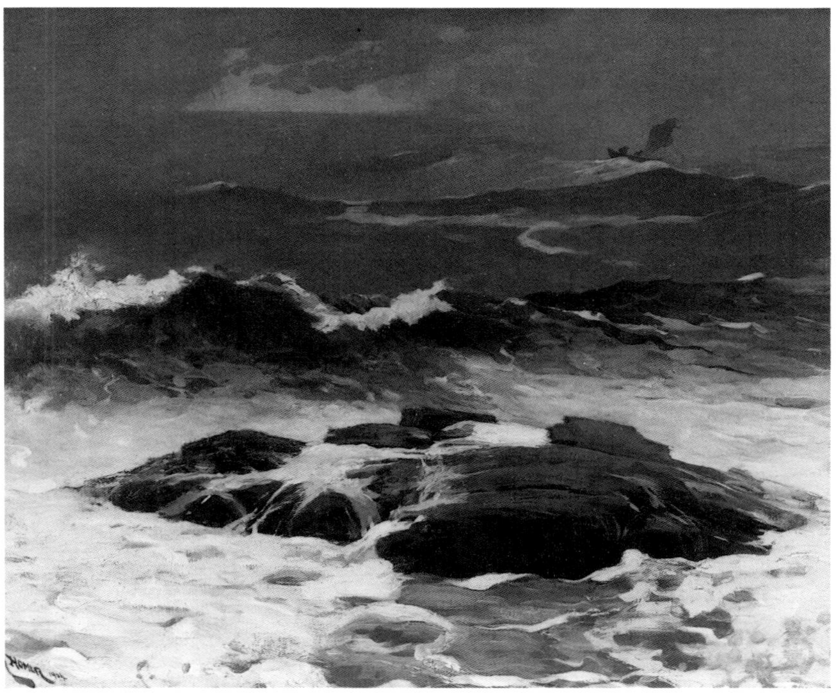

through any tangible presence. The line of the waves in *Early Morning* here appears inverted as banks of clouds across the top of the canvas. The cliffs bulk organically, not architectonically; everywhere there is a subtle, swelling rhythm. Responding to this environment, which seems so still, lacking in movement, Homer produced his most static late painting. We are at last enfolded by nature, not merely observing it. In these two paintings man rests quietly in the balance with nature.

His last completed painting is both less serene and more explicit. In *Driftwood,* 1909 (Figure 38), an almost square painting with rocks edging the foreground as in *Cannon Rock,* a man in an oil slicker stands on the rocks with his back to us, his way into the picture barred by the driftwood of the title, no small decorative flotsam but the trunk of a large tree. This tree marks the first time a thing of the land has been returned to it by the sea, albeit not safely, but indifferently spat out by the waves. In the distance to the left is another seafarer, an ocean liner. A trail of foam leads diagonally to it, against the movement of dancing spray in the foreground which lifts once, twice, up to the gull on the right. The ship heads in one direction; the gull in the other. This is a less violent statement of the elements of *Kissing the Moon* and *Right and Left* (Figures 31, 32): the boat and bird

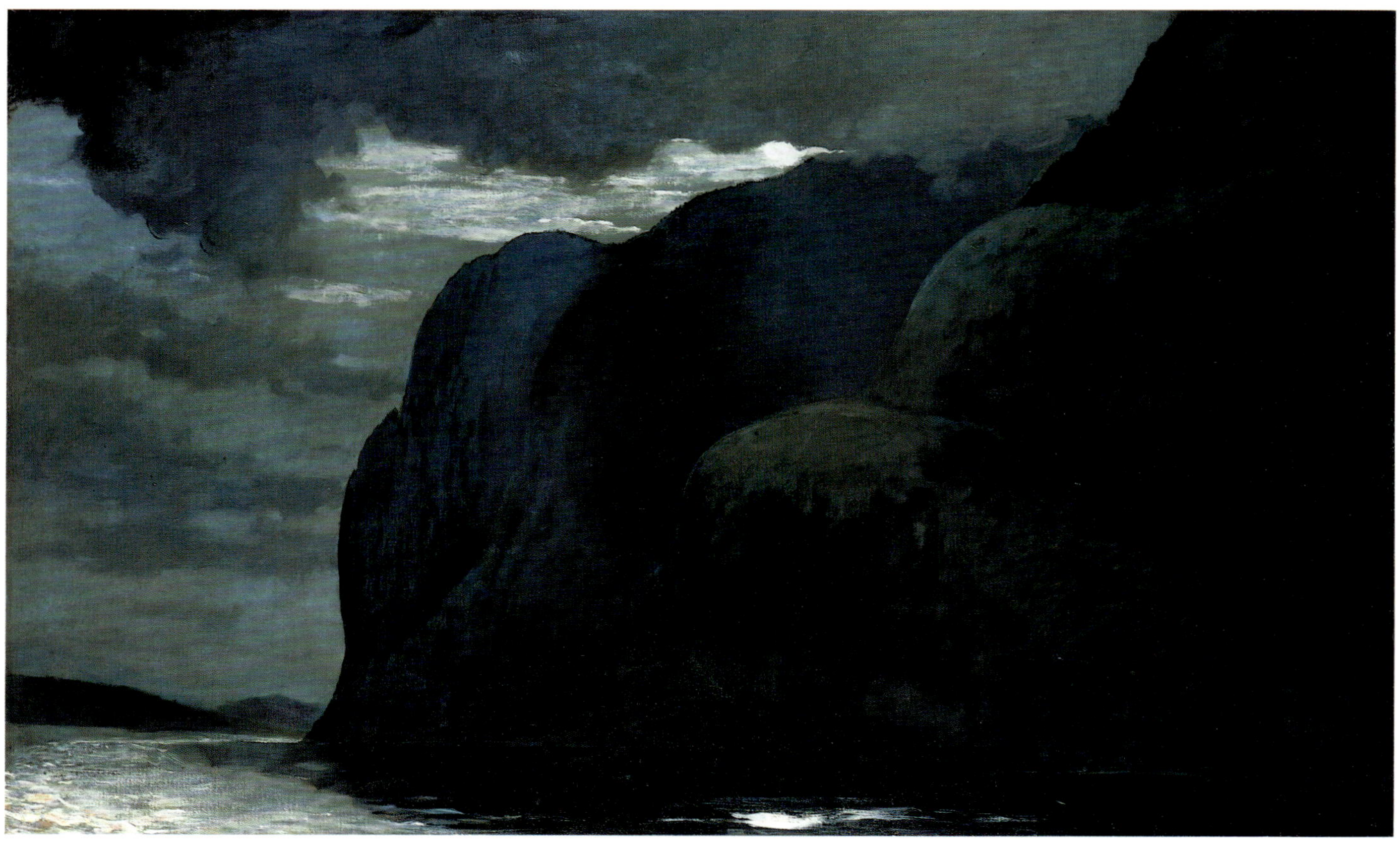

37. Homer. *Cape Trinity, Saguenay River,* 1904.

moving away from each other. Judging from the angle of his shoulders, the man appears to be looking at neither; rather he fixes his gaze on the spray, as in *Below Zero* (Figure 28), the area most obscure in the painting. He looks literally at nothing in the little time he has before he disappears into the devouring sea. To see clearly is its own reward.

Yet he does see something; we must imagine his eyes are open because we view the same scene he does. It is thus wise to balance this incipient nihilism against two other late paintings, *A Light on the Sea* (Figure 39) and *West Point* (Figure 19). The way that the dancing spray in *West Point* mimics the curving pose of the woman in *A Light on the Sea,* both in its form and placement in the canvas, has been remarked on repeatedly. It is as though her stolid bulk has been transmuted into something airy and graceful; that is to say, the water represents the positive union of land and ocean, man and nature, not just a blank screen of waves. The essential Homeric stance, where a lone figure defies the fate

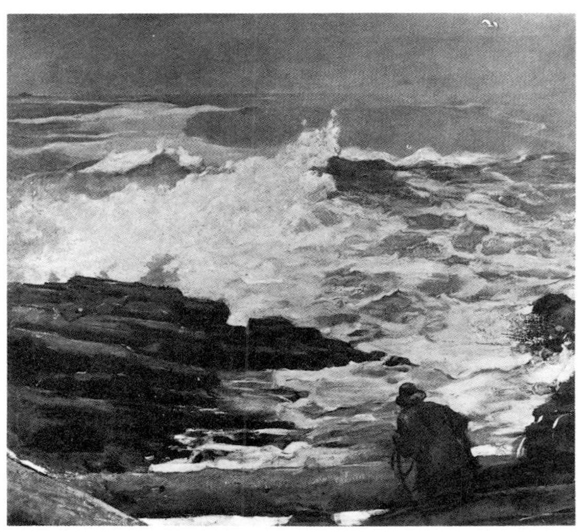

38. Homer. *Driftwood,* 1909.

39. Homer. *A Light on the Sea,* 1897.

of man in this world, has been transformed into an entirely natural drama.[28] This union of humanity and nothingness has been called mournful. Certainly it is not the fate many of us would seek, but that Homer allowed himself no false hopes, no illusions, should not be held against him.

It is significant that the last full figure completed by Homer is one of a woman. It is not extreme to say that she represents art, the muses, decorativeness, color. Homer was wedded to his art—an insubstantial marriage, perhaps, and one he took increasingly long vacations from toward the end of his life. Yet, at every point when he claimed to abandon his muse, he started painting again. As he wrote to Thomas B. Clarke, his most important patron, at the end of 1901, "Do not think I have stopped painting. At any moment I am liable to paint a good picture."[29] And he did.

Homer's unique strength lay in the way he pressed out to the farthest reaches of the wilderness and yet came home again. In the roughest subjects he found beauty, in the most old-fashioned of senses. He combined masculine and feminine qualities, hard realism and vaporous transcendence, speaking always in his own voice. This accomplishment, for the next generation of artists who followed him, served as a steadfast beacon.

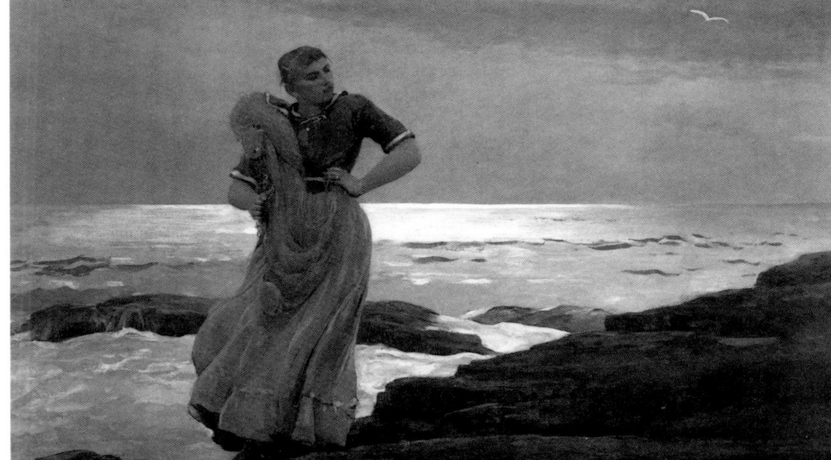

Maine and Marine Painting: Charles H. Woodbury and Frederick Judd Waugh

By the time Homer began painting his marine landscapes at Prout's Neck, Maine was already crawling with artists, accompanied by their mostly female hordes of students. Wrote one critic in 1892: "Every school-girl who dabbles in art now goes to Cape Ann and the coast of Maine for summer study; but it was Winslow Homer who discovered the riches of that new world."[1] This was not quite true; landscape artists from New York and Boston had been visiting Maine regularly from the early 1840s. The most famous early visitor was Thomas Cole, who was followed by many prominent landscape painters over the next fifty years. Maine offered the wilderness landscape in as pure a form as could be found on the East Coast—much of the state's interior was still untouched by forestry and its coast was sparsely settled at best. Artists were merely one group of nature lovers to visit the state; they joined scores of other tourists. Hotels were going up wherever steamships and railroads reached.

In the 1880s, as the Homer family began buying land on Prout's Neck, many others had similar ideas. The number of tourists and resorts catering to them mushroomed, and Maine became an easily accessible summer holiday area. With these vacationers came the first art colonies and artists who spent every summer there, rather than occasionally visiting on fact-finding missions. It was at this point that Maine became a popular and recognizable subject, but even then, it never presented a single, unified image.

For the most part, these summer residents—tourists and artists alike—saw a different state from the one Homer did. They were treated to a balmy atmosphere, far from the stifling city, to brilliant skies and to plentiful wild flowers that delighted the eye and scented the air. There were expensive resort hotels to frequent, where the mood was one of calm relaxation and expansive peace. Life slowed down and the scenery was correspondingly low

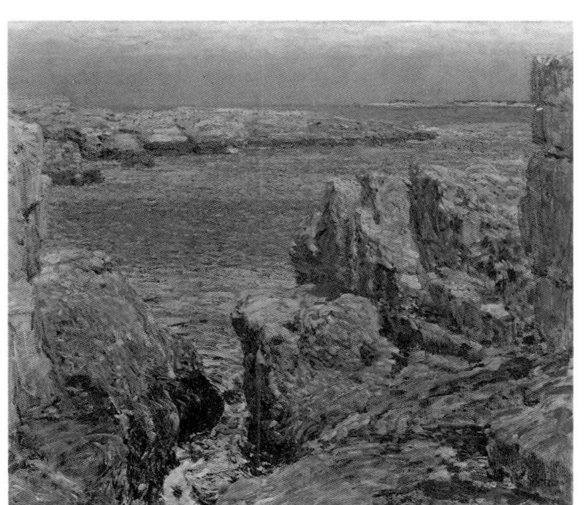

40. Hassam. *Coast Scene, Isles of Shoals,* 1901.

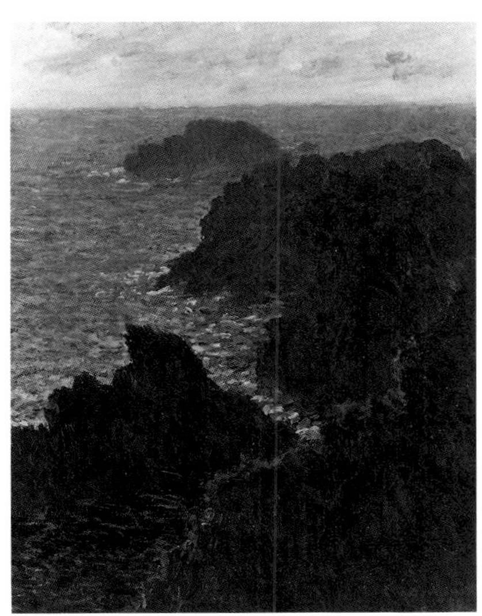

41. Monet. *Rocks at Belle-Isle (Rochers a Belle-Ile),* 1886.

and broad: the summer sea was the dominant note, not the rocky shore. The few times Homer painted summer residents in oils, in his first views of Prout's Neck, he showed them in unconventional settings: talking to a local tar as in *Cloud Shadows* (Figure 4), dancing in the moonlight as in *A Summer Night* (Figure 5), or even braving a storm of the kind visitors prefer to forget as in *West Wind* (see Figure 56). But most artists painted the summer scene in a gentler mood. Childe Hassam (1859-1935) was the genius of this subject in his paintings of Appledore, a magical spot filled with flowers and sunshine set amidst the Isles of Shoals, a few miles off the coast of Maine and New Hampshire (Figure 40). There, Mrs. Celia Thaxter entertained cultured guests with her stories and piano in the parlour.[2] For Hassam, the sea was a placid arena for light, the rocks merely shapes and color accents, and the ladies in white who might rest on them were always attended by their parasols. The influence of the paintings by Monet of Etretat (Figure 41) is obvious and remained powerful for those who followed Hassam's lead, such as Willard Metcalf (1858-1925), Edward Potthast (1857-1927), and many others. Homer despised such insipidity, calling the calm sea "that duckpond!"[3]

For those with Homer's sense of drama, there were places to explore other than Prout's Neck, which was not exceptionally rocky. Many areas could compete with an equal grandeur. Mount Desert to the north was the more dramatic coastal landscape that had been painted by Thomas Cole (1801-48) and Frederic Edwin Church (1826-1900); they were followed by Sanford Robinson Gifford (1823-80), Harrison Bird Brown (1831-1915), Alfred Thompson Bricher (1837-1908), William Stanley Haseltine (1835-1900), and many others.

Even those artists who might have wished to follow in Homer's footsteps could never do so precisely. Prout's Neck was already expensive. Artists having a taste for the dramatic but little money had to find other sites. Cheap summer rentals were located in less developed regions, although no place on the Maine coast remained unpainted by the turn of the century. Once an area had been discovered by too many people (as had Ogunquit, where Charles Woodbury led a school from the 1890s), the rents went up. For young people with families and practically no income, places like Appledore and Prout's Neck were out of the question; the dominant concern in the letters of George Bellows, Robert Henri, Rockwell Kent, and their friends was the summer cottage's rent.

Many nonetheless tried to paint at Prout's Neck: it was inundated by artists and art lovers beating a pilgrim path to Homer's door, generally to have it slammed in their faces. He had a reputation for scaring intruders off with a shotgun. A few enterprising ones actually got into his studio, only to have Homer resolutely avoid talking about art. On the other hand, when so inclined, he could be very generous. The Brush'uns, an amateur group in Portland which counted among its members the architect of Homer's house, were treated to a painting lesson. Leon Kroll, while still an art student, not only met the artist but also recorded the useful tips he received, and anecdotes from other artists survive.

If it could not be Prout's Neck or Mount Desert, there were other possibilities. The most satisfying for younger artists was Monhegan, twelve miles off the coast from Port Clyde. Monhegan possessed two advantages over other islands: it had dramatic headlands facing the open Atlantic and the locals were sympathetic to artists. The first meant that all the drama of the surf was readily available; the second, that artists were free from censure and obstruction. There were two inns on the island and a few rental cottages, but it was essentially undeveloped (and remains so today).

Monhegan had occasionally been painted as early as the 1850s.[4] In the 1880s an English watercolorist and photographer named S.P.R. Triscott (1846-1925) settled there, supporting himself in the summer months by selling photographs and drawings to visitors. Most of the more conventional marine painters of the day visited Monhegan at one point or another, but the island also attracted artists who had never painted a marine in their lives, but were simply seeking a summer away from the city in new and invigorating circumstances.

Robert Henri (1865-1929) was the first of the young New York artists to arrive, in 1903. He had been convinced to venture there by Edward Redfield (1869-1965), a Philadelphia painter and longtime friend. Redfield, with wife and children, was less mobile than Henri and so stayed on the mainland most of the time, sick from eating too many lobsters. When he did get to Monhegan, he discovered "Anywheres from 1 to 2 doz. embryo artists around the place," amidst the hundred visitors in two hotels.[5] Henri was entranced by Monhegan and seriously considered buying land on the island. His immediate response was a quick note to Redfield: "Great rocks—cant describe it—looks like foreign and dont [sic] —looks like Monhegan. powerful stuff ... its [sic] all there and builds down to the sea and surf in a mighty way. Variety." Henri expanded on his reactions to his family: "This is the real thing. I have never seen anything so fine ... and from the great cliffs you look down on a mighty surf battering away at the rocks ... or you can descend and get a side view of the cliffs from the lower rocks and then you can disappear from the sea in to the pine forests.... They are wild ... a little harbor shielded by a small island—simply a huge mass of rock. It is a wonderful place to paint—so much in so small a place one can hardly believe it."[6] Equally important to him were the people who lived there: "The character of the people here is certainly fine. They seem to be good honest pleasant kindly people ... as a rule natives and visitors live as a large happy family."[7]

Over the next decade, Henri inspired many of his friends and students to visit Monhegan, first Rockwell Kent (1882-1971) in 1905, George Bellows (1882-1925) and Randall Davey (1887-1964) in 1911, then William Hekking (1885-1970), Leon Kroll (1884-1974), Edward Hopper (1882-1967), and many others. All except Kroll returned; Kent even taught a summer class there in 1909. Students of Redfield and other artists, such as Eric Hudson (1864-1932), Jay Connaway (1893-1970), and Andrew Winter (1893-1958), carried on the tradition. There is still today a thriving art colony, which includes Jamie Wyeth, the third generation of Wyeths to summer in the area (his grandfather, N. C. Wyeth, stayed in Port Clyde on the mainland, which is connected to Monhegan by a daily ferry).

All reacted enthusiastically. Kent, in his first letter to Henri after arriving on the island reported: "This place is more wonderful and beautiful than you told me it was.... It seems to me now that I'd like to paint here always. I could sit all day in some of those holes under the headlands, watching the water and scared to death. I've never seen such terrible places as some of these crevases [sic]." He echoed Henri's response to the people: "I love the fishermen here. I never in my life saw such a fine kind-hearted set of people. I'd like to be one of them."[8]

The drama of Maine's coast to which these artists responded was a purely natural one. It evoked no stories, no Revolutionary battles, no heroic deeds or great tragedies, unlike the literary or historical associations of locations in New York or Massachusetts. A monotonous toll of wrecked ships could be counted but no single great disaster. The sea threshed its way through human life just as it ground at the shore, relentlessly and endlessly. No action of man could withstand it; one could only ride it out. The drama was a repetition of eternal friction rather than glorious action.

The natives had a similarly timeless and nonliterary quality. Going to Maine was a little like going to Brittany, or even Tahiti: it was a journey into simplicity and primitivism (however luxurious the hotel might be). Here were to be found "peasants," simple, plain-spoken honest folk, or the closest one was going to get to them in America, with the advantage that they spoke English, when they spoke at all. The impulse to redeem the enterprise of art through the honesty of its subjects—as though a kind of talismanic connection existed between the beings in the paintings and those who painted them, the one revivifying the other, with the picture merely a physical record of a metaphysical transaction—was endemic among artists at the end of the century. And Maine was a perfect location for this enterprise.

The values of the Maine coast—its moral or cultural associations—were those of simple virtues and facts: strength, solidity, unremitting struggle. Unlike the city of a thousand tales, the coast of Maine was host to only one drama: life and death. It is no coincidence that Frederic Church used his studies of the Maine coast to paint his large canvas *The Deluge;* the confrontation of sea and land at Mount Desert inevitably suggested the mythic Flood.[9] Other coasts might have different meanings. Images of a smooth, long curving stretch of a sandy beach might suggest Robert Frost's response in the poem "Devotion": "The heart can think of no devotion/Greater than being shore to the ocean." The sea itself, without reference to the coast, could be taken as an image of the mind, as Wordsworth had done at the end of *The Prelude.*[10] The type of coast depicted and the format of the painting tell us much about the artist's intended meanings.

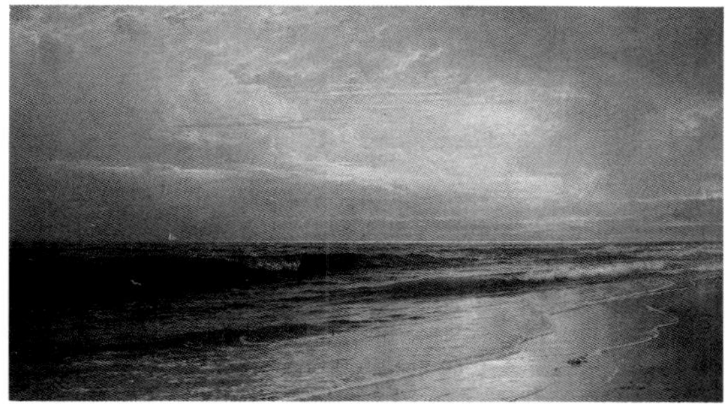

42. Richards. *On the Coast of New Jersey,* 1883.

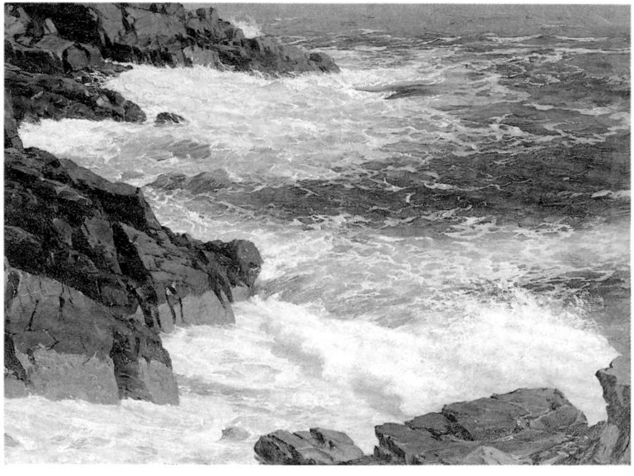

43. Church. *Rough Surf, Mount Desert Island, Maine,*
1850.

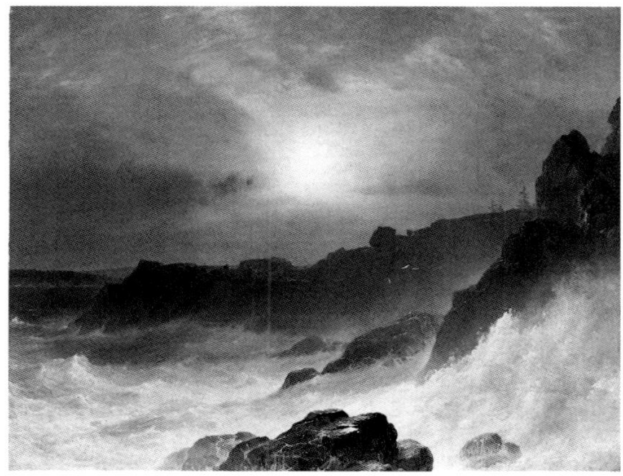

44. Church. *Coast Scene, Mount Desert,* 1863.

Marine painting flourished in America at the turn of the
century and was considered one of the most distinctive achieve-
ments of American art, a branch of painting in which American
artists outshone the Europeans.[11] Although a number of American
painters before the 1870s had specialized in marine painting, such
as Thomas Birch (1779-1851), John Frederick Kensett (1816-72),
and Fitz Hugh Lane (1804-65), marine painting was not recognized as a distinctively American mode until William Trost Richards (1833-1905), Alfred Thompson Bricher, William Haseltine,
and Thomas Alexander Harrison (1853-1930) came along. When
Harrison began winning awards in Paris for his enormous paintings of waves in the mid-1880s, American audiences sat up and
took notice.

For the most part, these men's paintings were panoramic and
quiet—images of timeless repetition on an evolutionary scale,
rather than of dramatic force, as in W. T. Richards' *On the Coast
of New Jersey,* 1883 (Figure 42). Distinctly different, Homer's
work had a stronger impact. After only a handful of marine
paintings, he immediately became the undisputed leader of the
school. Indeed, by the end of his life he was generally categorized
as a marine artist, the rest of his *oeuvre* almost forgotten.[12]

In locating Homer amidst other marine painters and paintings,
it is tempting to think first of what he shared with his fellow
artists. Often the physical situation itself prompted similar
compositions: either standing on the high cliffs looking down to
capture the drama of the surf or standing at the base of the cliffs,
their overwhelming verticality invariably blocking the sky. But
fundamental differences are clear. Church's sketches, such as
Rough Surf, Mount Desert Island, Maine, 1850 (Figure 43), often
anticipated the basics of Homer's Prout's Neck landscapes: surf
dramatically plunging over rocks and dominating the foreground
with only a touch of distance. These were sketches, however; the
major oil paintings that Church produced from these trips, such
as *Coast Scene, Mount Desert,* 1863 (Figure 44), were all much
more academically constructed, with a clear progression from
front to back or, failing that, a stable grid of horizontals and
verticals. And even in the sketches, Church seldom massed rocks
and water into the simple, large elements that Homer did, or
exploited as strong a diagonal in his compositions.

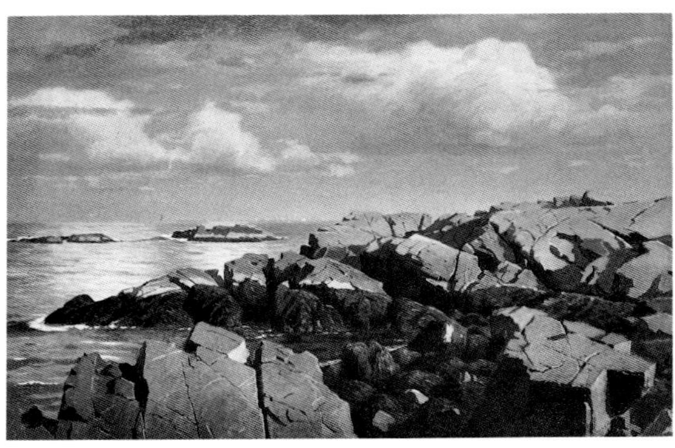

45. Haseltine. *After a Shower—Nahant, Massachusetts,* ca. 1862.

The same analysis may be applied to Hassam's work.[13] Both Homer and Hassam stared down on rocks that dominate the scene; both renounced the grand panoramas of the 1870s and 1880s. But in many fundamental ways Hassam was a good deal closer to Haseltine than he was to Homer (the debt to Monet has already been mentioned). In a sense the apparent difference between Hassam and Haseltine was simply one of viewpoint. Whereas Haseltine, in *After a Shower—Nahant, Massachusetts,* ca. 1862 (Figure 45), painted the profile of the rock in horizontal format, standing at some distance from it, Hassam stood on it, looking down, as in *Coast Scene, Isle of Shoals,* 1901 (Figure 40). The difference was one of traditional distance and modern immediacy, which created a certain drama of effect. But the significant mood had not really changed: in both landscapes the rocks were bathed in light, and atmosphere was considered with an acutely sensitive eye. The real action of the painting lay in the aesthetically minded observer's satisfied knowledge that he had witnessed something not all were privileged to see.

In contrast, Homer's dramatic sense placed the action in the objects: we stand back half afraid of the conflict we witness. While both Hassam and Haseltine saw the landscape in placid balance—held in check by an even envelope of light and atmosphere—for Homer, who wintered in those parts, the rocks and ocean were the real thing refashioned in a Realist material equivalent, a drama of thick paint and richly varied surface.

The painter most like him was probably Gustave Courbet (1819-77), whose work Homer must have studied closely. Courbet was famous for, among many other things, his depictions of waves (Figure 46). Not only Homer's pigment-heavy treatment of waves, but his hunting scenes appear dependent on the earlier artist's work. As already mentioned, a very specific comparison may be made between Homer's *Fox Hunt* and Courbet's *Fox in the Snow.* The similarities were generally noted by his contemporaries; as one wrote: "He is our Courbet."[14] Nearly all, however, added the point that Courbet's paintings of waves were static in comparison to Homer's.[15]

Closer to home, Homer also knew contemporary American marine painters personally.[16] William H. Downes, his friend and biographer, later asserted that Homer praised the younger marine

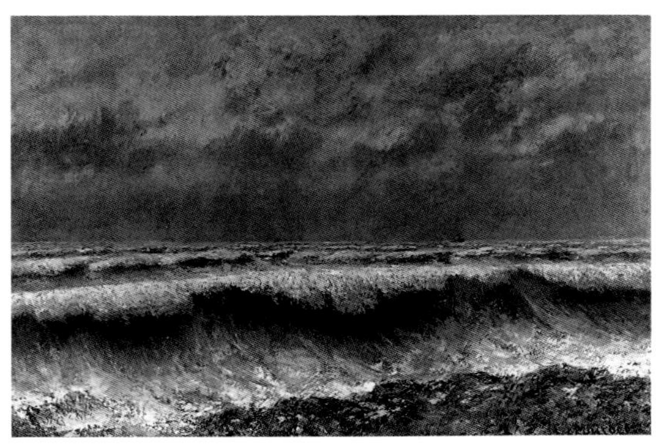

46. Courbet. *La Vague (The Wave),* 1870.

artists, calling them worthy successors.[17] In fact, Homer was generally placed at the head of the next generation of marine artists, as their teacher.[18] With Homer's advent on the scene, the panoramic look dissolved, and those not emulating the impressionists began to paint Homeric dramas of the sea. Among the ones called his closest followers were Charles Woodbury, Frederick Judd Waugh, and Paul Dougherty.

Charles H. Woodbury (1864-1940), born outside Boston, attended Massachusetts Institute of Technology, where he trained as an engineer, and took night classes at the Boston Art Club. After some illustration work for *Harper's* and other magazines, he made his first European trip in 1890, studying at the Académie Julian. His first big splash, so to speak, was with a painting entitled *Mid-Ocean,* 1894, based on his experience in crossing the Atlantic and modeled on the work of Harrison. After several visits to Maine, Woodbury built a studio in Ogunquit, where he worked for the rest of his life, gaining fame as a teacher.

Woodbury's work was academically impressionist in color and broken brushstroke, with an admixture of tonalist softness every now and then. Much of his work was devoted to the summer scene of Ogunquit: children and women swimming and boating, the seashore, attractive cottages and boats, and so on. *Mid-Ocean* demonstrated an occasional interest in sterner stuff—the drama of the high seas. Woodbury's pure marines, such as *October, Seascape,* ca. 1907 (Figure 47), were often almost abstract studies of the elements, generally just water with sometimes a bit of rock for the waves to dash against, an excuse not only for coloristic studies of light and atmosphere but also for fields of decorative design at their most elemental. Like Homer, Woodbury often employed a simple diagonal to construct his compositions. These were the paintings that reminded his contemporaries of Homer. The comparison is not as farfetched as it might seem when we remember the light palette of such canvases by Homer as *Coast in Winter* (Figure 48), which closely approaches Woodbury's normal pastel range.[19]

Frederick Judd Waugh (1861-1940) was born in Bordentown, New Jersey, the son of a prominent Philadelphia portrait painter. This family background and his training at the Pennsylvania Academy of Fine Arts under Thomas Eakins and Thomas Anshutz

47. Woodbury. *October, Seascape,* ca. 1907.

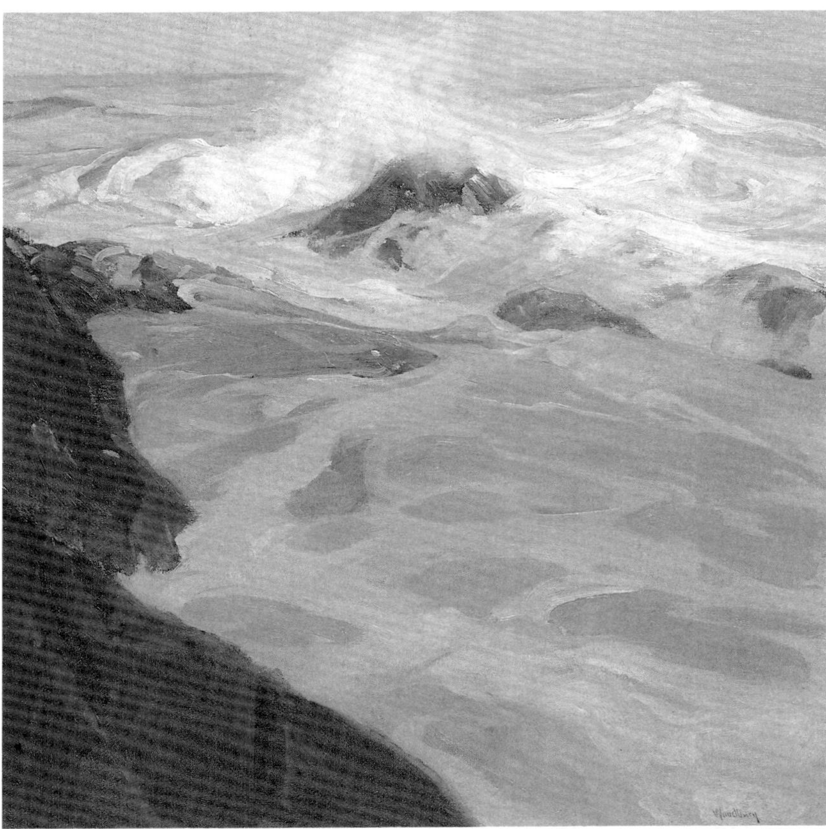

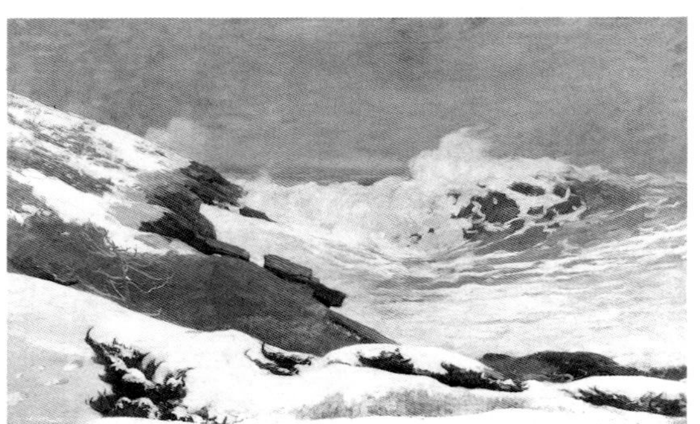

48. Homer. *Coast in Winter.*

gave Waugh a more professional grounding than any of his contemporary marine painters, as well as a much broader range of subjects and styles. Traveling widely, he worked abroad for many years, chiefly in England with British marine painters, before returning to the United States in 1907. He too worked on Monhegan Island in 1911 and 1914.[20]

Waugh explicitly denied being influenced by Homer, citing instead the model of such British marine painters as Henry Moore and Julius Olsson, whose work he had emulated well before his return to the United States in 1907. Only then did Waugh claim to have become aware of Homer's work. Nonetheless, in the minds of the public and critics, Waugh followed Homer.[21] Although seldom employing similar compositions, and using a much fussier technique and more colorful palette, Waugh's concentration on the surf booming off rocks and other dramatic effects of the sea placed him within Homer's reach. As one critic reacted: "[Although] his work has not the unpretentious technique of Homer's work, [both] are realistic, brutally frank."[22] Waugh also painted on Monhegan while George Bellows was there. In *Kelp-Covered*

49. Waugh. *Kelp-Covered Rocks,* 1923.

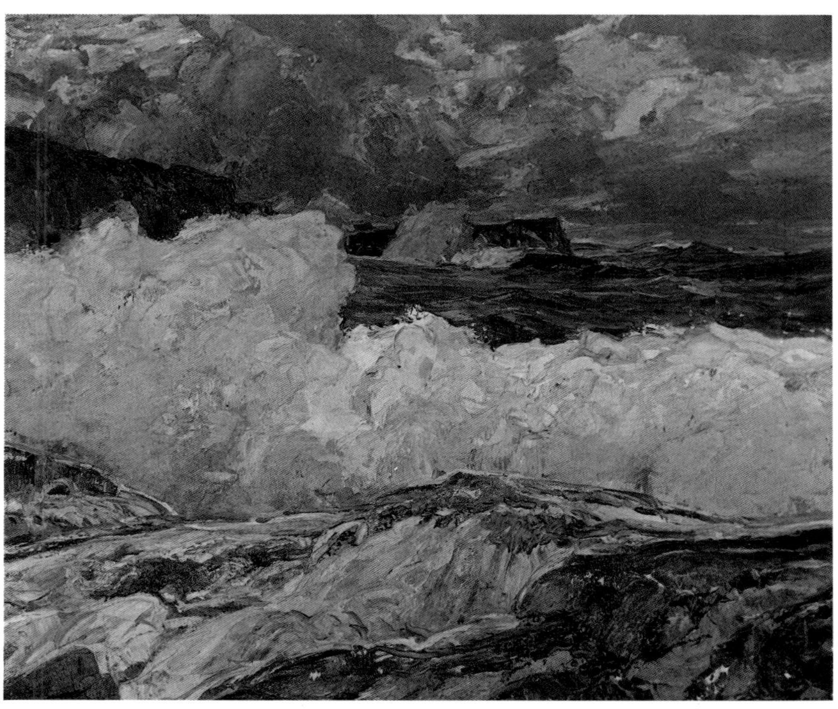

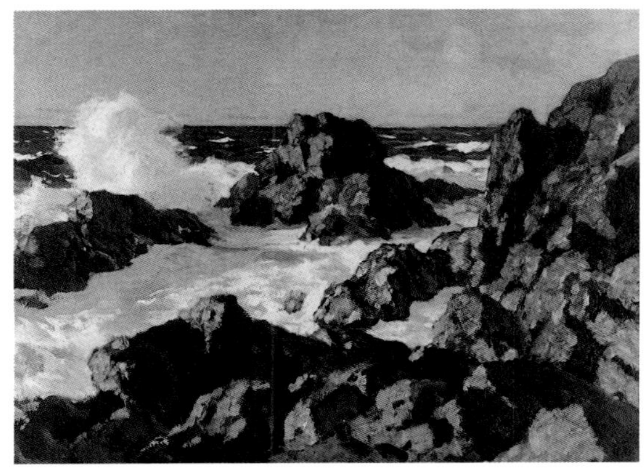

50. Dougherty. *Late Afternoon,* 1921.

Rocks, 1923 (Figure 49), for instance, Waugh's vigorous handling of the paint indicates a debt to Bellows as well as to Homer.

Paul Dougherty (1877-1947) was the youngest of the group. Born in Brooklyn and a graduate of the New York Law School, he studied in New York under Constantin Hertzberg and then in Europe. He returned in 1904, began summering in Maine, and quickly achieved a great reputation, having his first successful exhibition in 1906. As Leon Kroll rather sourly remembered: "Dougherty ... was supposed to be almost as good as Homer."[23] In a review of his work in 1906, a critic compared him to "blunt Walt Whitman" and, in words reminiscent of descriptions of Homer's work, commented on Dougherty's "virile sense of colour ... the strength of the sea, its motion and white turmoil as it dashes against a rocky shore."[24] In handling and color, paintings such as *Late Afternoon,* 1921 (Figure 50), resemble a rather over-heated and over-agitated version of Hassam, the delicate colors and touches of the brush of Hassam's Isles of Shoals paintings (Figure 40) grown hectic, hard, and matted. The waves and rocks are correspondingly heavier and more brutal, more like Homer.

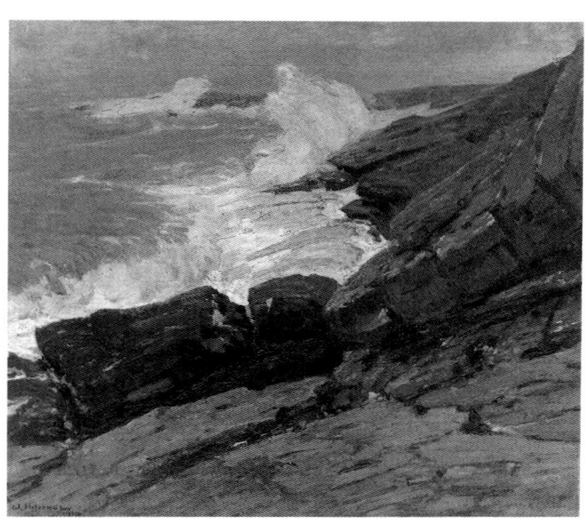

51. Ritschel. *Rocks and Sea, Monhegan,* 1914.

The willingness of the public to find Homer's influence in these rather different artists indicates the power of his example. It and Maine extended beyond the borders of those who dedicated their lives to that particular subject matter. Many artists tested Maine's waters before deciding to devote themselves to other themes. Henri, Redfield, and others seeking new challenges visited the coast and tried on Homer's style and subjects without being permanently altered by them. For a season, they might be hailed in the press as a follower of Homer, as Gifford Beal was in 1911.[25] William Ritschel (1864-1949) is one of the most interesting examples. Born in Germany and trained in Munich, he arrived in the United States in 1895 with a full command of fin-de-siècle international painterliness. Despite considerable gifts and the ability to render his choice of genres and subjects, Ritschel became a marine painter. He too went to Monhegan. His *Rocks and Sea, Monhegan,* ca. 1914 (Figure 51), demonstrates his mastery of Homer's idiom in the diagonal march of the foreground rocks and the central placement of the wave; but this was not an avenue that Ritschel followed very far. Within a few years he settled in Carmel, California, opting for more sunshine and color.[26] Evidently, Ritschel (like Woodbury, Dougherty, and Waugh) accurately gauged the nature of the market and settled on a steady, lucrative subject, adapting Homeric themes to the demands of a post-impressionist palette.

The continuing popularity of marine painting—whether panoramic in the 1880s and 1890s or more dramatic (along the lines of either Monet or Homer) from 1900 until World War I— prompts us to wonder, why? I suspect the reason has to do with the way marines, in their reduction of the natural world to its primal elements, acted as a conservative rendering of the impulses pushing more adventurous artists to abstraction: decorative composition and color could be handled in an essentially abstract manner while still remaining faithful to "reality."[27] The real ancestors of Mark Rothko's color-field paintings are the gigantic wave paintings of Waugh and Woodbury. But even within this context, Homer remained a distinctive figure: he never abandoned the dramatic physicality of the material world, its power to cause pain as well as pleasure.

Closely allied to marine painters in the way they played with potentially abstract interests at the same time that they pledged allegiance to the actual landscape were the artists who devoted themselves to painting snow. Much the same lineage may be discovered: a touch of Courbet and Whistler, with a dash of tonalism and impressionism. Winter scenes were also identified as peculiarly American, because of the climate.[28] Again, Homer had a commanding position. *Fox Hunt* was called "the embodiment of Winter," and his winter effects and moods were as much studied as the gentler ones of John Twachtman (1853-1902).[29] In this mode, Homer's followers were considered to be Edward Redfield, W. Elmer Schofield (1869-1944), and George Gardner Symons (1863-1930). Here, the similarities were less tangibly evident in composition, handling of paint, or even mood (Redfield and the others were never brutal), although such factors were occasionally mentioned by the critics. Rather, these artists were deemed to share with Homer a similar attitude toward the landscape, painting it without the prettiness of the impressionists or tonalists, but plainly, directly, in a supremely American manner.

The question of what were the distinctive American contributions to painting, seen in discussions of both marine painting and winter subjects, and the concern of artists like Ritschel to find the right genre with which to support themselves were hallmarks of the increasing self-consciousness overtaking American art in the last quarter of the century. For artists, critics, and the public, American art was measured constantly against a superior and foreign model.

After the Civil War American artists began to train in Europe in large numbers. Many had gone before the war, but in the 1870s not only a European tour but a stint in a foreign academy became *de rigueur*. These were the men of 1877 who so alarmed the old men of the Hudson River School and the National Academy, appearing like an invasion of European painters crowding the old folks off the exhibition walls in the same way that European paintings were crowding them out of the dealers' shops.[30] In one memorial tribute to Homer, the author remembered: "It became in the sixties the fashion, the necessity almost, for American students to go abroad.... 'When are you going?' 'This spring!' 'Lucky boy!'" Homer's decision to stay was called heretical.[31]

The young men went to Paris, Munich, or The Hague, and

sometimes all three; others continued to go to London. They returned armed to the teeth with technique, but had very little to say with it. Great dexterity in brushstroke, a hesitant acquaintance with the milder forms of impressionist color, and a taste for European genre formed their stock. Some preferred pure impressionism, in particular the suburban bucolics of Monet; others liked the Old Masters done up in the modern attitudes of Munich. Still others practiced a genteel aestheticism of quietly tonal landscapes, paying homage to what they believed Whistler to be all about.

The common thread through all their efforts was a concern for the decorative aspects of art: "Art for art's sake" in its least threatening forms.[32] As the Society of American Painters' objectives were described in 1877: "Art legitimately concerns itself only with the felicitous arrangement of color and line; ... its only proper aim is technical excellence and its only fit audience connoisseurs.... Art ... is decorative in its functions."[33] Color and texture, however treated, were their prime considerations. Anyone without a self-conscious mastery of technique was out in the cold. By and large, realist objectives of the kind that concerned Courbet and Manet had to wait for the Ashcan school to become popular: such objectives were too "modern" and smacked of French immorality. Jules Breton's peasants, pleasantly pasteurized, were preferred over Jean-François Millet's clod-like brutes.

Homer was by no means immune to these developments, although he had always been considered entirely his own man. J. Eastman Chase, a Boston dealer who knew Homer, claimed that the artist never mentioned styles, only specific pictures. Others testified to the complete lack of influence on him by other painters and his total unconcern for their work.[34]

Few remarks by Homer about art are recorded, but then few remarks of any kind escaped his lips for posterity. We know that he was a careful and self-conscious student of color throughout his life. Homer certainly went to New York City nearly every year and had opportunities to see the work of his contemporaries. The few comments he made about them, whether scathing or complimentary, indicate that he kept up with what they were doing. He served on several juries, and none of his fellow artists called him unknowledgeable. John LaFarge placed him, like his early contemporaries, as one who avidly studied the prints of the Barbizon

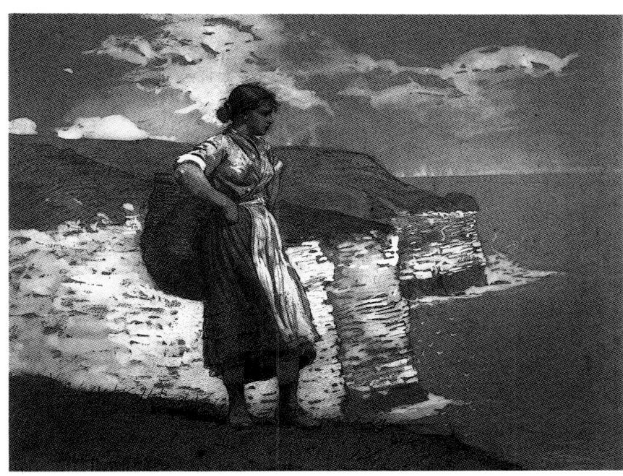

52. Homer. *Flamboro Head,* 1882.

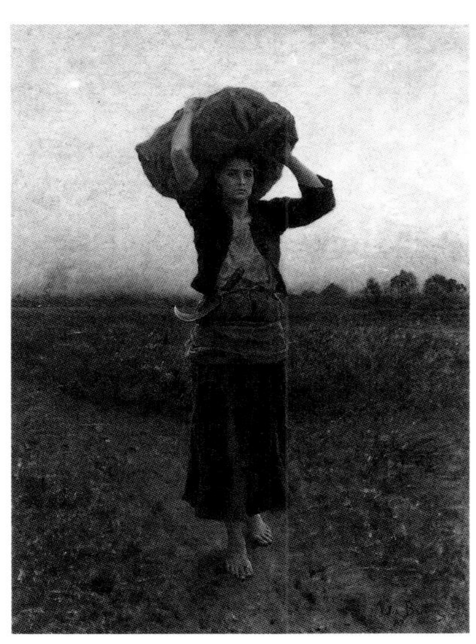

53. Breton. *The Shepherd's Star,* 1887.

school; Homer's interest in Courbet has already been noted. More recently, several scholars have suggested that the American knew Japanese prints, perhaps through his friend LaFarge, who was one of the first in this country to be interested in Japanese art.[35]

Homer's artistic self-consciousness may be demonstrated in a particular instance. During his visit to England, he closely studied contemporary British painting. In his watercolors, he began to practice a tight, hatched brushstroke to increase the sense of volume in his figures, a device used in British exhibition watercolors. Producing large-scale watercolors for the first time, Homer had undoubtedly studied the relevant models. It has often been noted that his figure type changed as well, as in *Flamboro Head* (Figure 52). At least one contemporary observer suspected the influence of London—not the work of other marine painters, of whom there were plenty producing quite similar subjects, but of Frederick, Lord Leighton and Albert Moore.[36] In other words, Homer again looked at the most appropriate artistic models to convey the sense of classic strength he sought for his figures. Not purely realistic studies of fisherwomen, they are rather self-consciously allied with the eternal work of the strong and noble. That he would be interested in a kind of classicism should not surprise us when we remember that the other great American realist, Thomas Eakins, was painting Arcadian themes at the same time. It is also salutary to be reminded that, despite his isolation in Cullercoats, Homer kept a sharp eye on London.

Homer continued to be interested in contemporary developments after his return to New York, as an examination of his paintings eloquently demonstrates. Not only was he aware of British painting, but he also looked closely at the work of Jules Breton and his American followers. The general situations and compositions—peasant women posed heroically against the sky—are similar, as are the palette and the manner of lighting the figure. The faces are seldom subjected to direct light so that they always look slightly gray, untouched by the light and surrounding atmosphere, and often backlit by the setting sun. *A Light on the Sea* (Figure 39) is only half a step from Breton's *The Shepherd's Star* (Figure 53), 1887.

Closer to home is the inescapable influence of James Abbott McNeill Whistler (1834-1903). Homer, just to be contrary, claimed

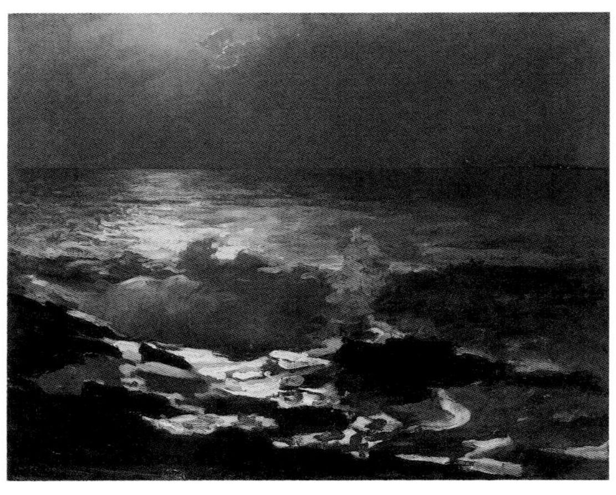

54. Homer. *Moonlight—Wood's Island Light,* 1894.

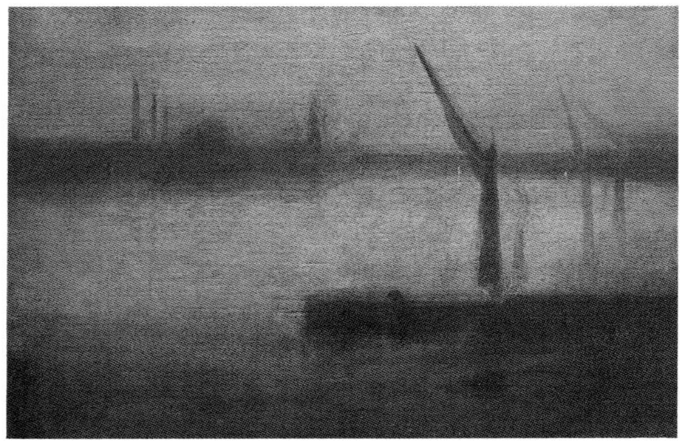

55. Whistler. *Nocturne—Blue and Silver—Battersea Reach,* 1870-75.

once not to know anything about the artist. But on another occasion, he remarked to John Beatty about Whistler: "His mother's portrait and Carlyle are important pictures, but I don't think those symphonies and queer things Ruskin objected to will last any great while." Homer's comments may be properly gauged in the light of his admission that he considered only twenty-five of his own paintings to be important.[37]

Despite Homer's disclaimers, it is impossible to conceive of his painting *Moonlight—Woods Island Light, Maine* (Figure 54), 1894, without his having seen some of Whistler's work. The monochromatic tonality and the way forms and the landscape situation are abbreviated almost to the point of abstraction betray the debt. And in little touches, such as the use of a dash of red to represent the distant lighthouse and also to dance on the surface of the gray paint, we see signs of Whistler's example, such as *Nocturne—Blue and Silver—Battersea Reach,* 1870-75 (Figure 55).

Homer's interest in an overall tone, and a rather gray, monochromatic one at that (Chevreul emphasized the importance of gray for setting off colors), placed him firmly within the context of artists like John H. Twachtman.[38] *West Wind* (Figure 56)—painted predominantly with tones of brown composed in large, almost unmodulated areas—is most like such Twachtmans as *Arques-la-Bataille,* 1885 (Figure 57). The smoky, cold, luminous quality, the specific reality of its atmosphere, however, is unmatched. Homer was conscious of the artifice of the effect, as he wagered LaFarge that he could paint such a monochromatic painting and sell it. Nor was *West Wind* an isolated exercise in tone: *Coast in Winter, The Artist's Studio in an Afternoon Fog,* and *Cape Trinity, Saguenay River,* are similar in intention. Homer's tonalist interests may be felt as well in the depicted light, which is generally diffuse, either because the sun cannot penetrate a thick cloud cover or because it is dawn or dusk. Also, in a surprising number of the Prout's Neck views, despite the bleakness of the land and the savagery of the waves, Homer paints the scene with refinement. Even in *Northeaster* (Figure 16), the line of the spume sinuously twisting on the advancing wave is decorative and elegant. At least one of his fellow artists, Henry Ward Ranger, felt these connections and considered Homer a tonalist.[39]

Homer took what he wanted from other artists and never felt

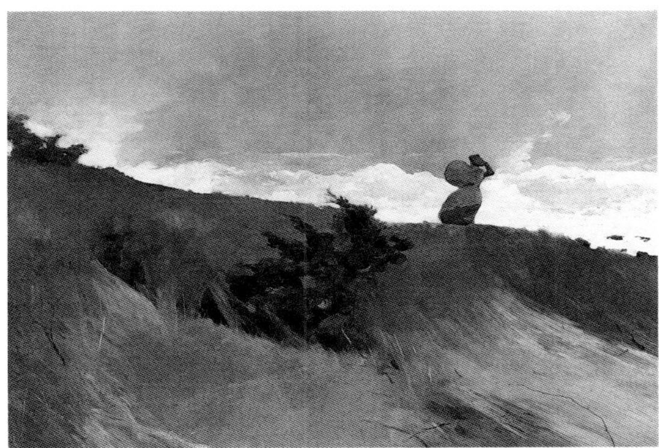

56. Homer. *West Wind,* 1891.

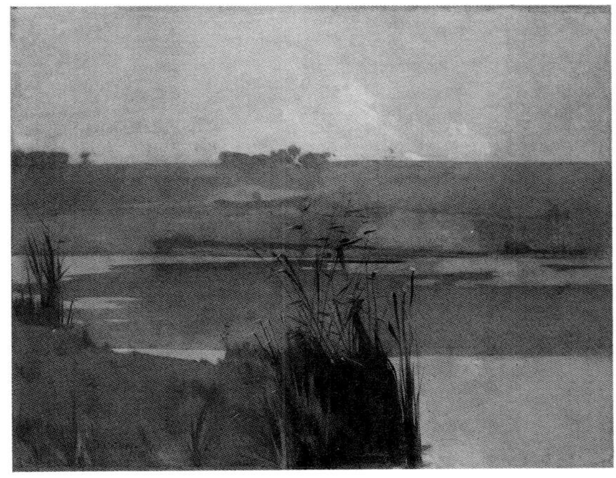

57. Twachtman. *Arques-la-Bataille,* 1885.

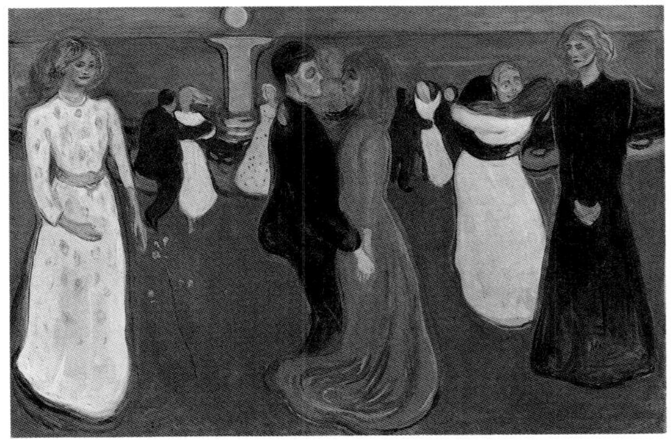

58. Munch. *The Dance of Life,* ca. 1899.

indebted to them. Textural manipulation was also an important aspect of late nineteenth-century painting. Aside from the pleasures of straightforward paint manipulation—where the thrill of the artist's dexterity was paramount—more calculated methods were often in vogue. One made popular by the impressionists was to prepare the ground with a loaded brush, painting the visible layers of color over an already textured surface. Homer occasionally experimented with this, as almost everyone did, but the virtuosity of his handling lay on the surface, not in such structural devices.[40] Less obviously textural was the habit of many painters to make the paint as matte as possible, by using an absorbent canvas and blotting the pigments to remove much of the oil.[41] Again, the device may be traced to the impressionists. This is something Homer never did, underlining his distance from artists like Monet and Camille Pisarro and all those who strove for purely decorative effects. Homer's paint texture almost always had some mimetic function. On the other hand, his understanding that light and color are one and the same is instinctively impressionistic.

The psychological element of Homer's narratives had affinities with northern symbolist painters. Several studies recently have pointed to a northern feeling characterizing much of the art of Scandinavia at the end of the century, and North America slightly later.[42] Similarities between *A Summer Night* and paintings by Edvard Munch (1863-1944) and others, such as Munch's *Dance of Life* (Figure 58), have been noted.[43] Regarded in the light of symbolist painting, the transformation of Courbet's *Fox in the Snow* into Homer's *Fox Hunt* is not just a matter of style, it also speaks to a deeper and darker alienation. Although both artists may be realists, realism in 1900 was a different animal from realism half a century earlier. Homer shared with such symbolist painters as Munch a sense that in the silence with which he surrounded himself and the figures of his creation, he spoke words and meanings known only to himself; that his very wariness of language acknowledged the way it invades privacy; that both the manner in which he lived and the nature of his subjects bespoke an urge that can only be called primitivist. But the kinship, like so much surrounding Homer, is something that we feel is instinctively right and instructive, but nothing we could ever prove. We cannot really imagine Homer looking at Munch. But the fact that we so insistently feel these connections is not a matter of wanting to bolster Homer's greatness by allying him with international and forward-looking movements; rather it is testimony to his immense genius. We suspect he came on these understandings of and convergences with European developments independently. Perhaps the comparable figure in American literature is not Walt Whitman, with whom Homer has always been compared, but Emily Dickinson: reclusive, old-fashioned in dress, gnomic in utterance, saying much by saying little in ways that seem ordinary but are utterly modern, and that reach far beyond the upstairs rooms to which she confined herself. But despite these connections, which seem evident to us, contemporary critics persisted in demarcating an impermeable barrier between Homer and his fellow artists. He was not to be permitted any outside influences. In their descriptions of his paintings, they sometimes seem blind, or perhaps self-blinded.

His audience insisted emphatically that he was no colorist. His colors were "crude" and "harsh," at best "rather neutral."[44] One critic, describing the streaks of red on the deck of the boat in *The Gulf Stream* (Figure 24), commented: "This scarlet spot recurs more than once, and is the more startling from its appearance in connection with a coldness and harshness of general tone that would of itself suggest a state akin to color-blindness."[45] In another instance, *Early Morning after a Storm at Sea* (Figure 20), which Homer called "the best picture of the sea that I have painted," was harshly attacked when first exhibited in 1903. One reviewer wrote: "The foam is not foam but vegetation of some strange, uncanny shape and color." Another added that the painting "represents a heaving sea of chalk and pink, with waves topped by bunches of wool, and the distant stretches of his ocean are illuminated milk." All these comments suggest that the painting was thought weak in color and action; everything was soft and pale. Both critics preferred *Cannon Rock,* a painting in which the rocks were jagged and the waves, as Homer described them, looked like broken crockery. What the critics were rejecting was the possibility that Homer's color could be beautiful.[46]

They insisted also that he was either indifferent to facture or that his paint-handling was deliberately brutal. He had no "refinements of handling."[47] None of the variety of touch we see plainly in the waves and foam of *Early Morning after a Storm at Sea* or *Maine Coast,* where rich impasto is balanced with scumbling and thin layers of color—a completely masterful and intelligent application of paint—was apparent to them: "His handling is vigorous but rude and even harsh and repellent."[48]

Sometimes even his compositions came in for criticism, or the pictures were considered entirely uncomposed. One contemporary thought: "In composition they were not remarkable—few of Mr. Homer's productions are noteworthy in that respect; he does not seem to care greatly for it."[49] His work was, in fact, "ugly." As one critic described his paintings in 1902: "[There is] not ... the slightest trace of mere decorative beauty either in composition or coloring.... His canvases are often frankly ugly ... his technique is strictly his own." Another underlined the point: "To the usual arts of picture-making ... he was oblivious."[50]

One typical statement sums up the rest. In Samuel Isham's influential history of American painting, published while Homer was still alive, that artist's work was described in these terms:

> *His color is strong and sure, sometimes a little harsh, but always true. The writers who confuse tone with values should study his works. The values are impeccable, not subtle, not over-refined, but sure...; of tone, however, of a pervading color note which draws the whole picture into a harmony there is no trace except in pictures like the "Lookout," where Nature has charged herself with the task of providing it. For this reason the pictures are not decorative in the generally received sense. They do not unite with a wall as an ornament on it apart from their meaning as pictures, as Inness' or Whistler's do. Time adds a certain mellowness, but they will always be windows opened in a wall rather than squares of brocade stretched upon it; they have none of the amenities of the drawing room, and you might almost as well let the sea itself into your house as one of Homer's transcripts of it.[51]*

Nonetheless, Homer was universally acknowledged one of the nation's best painters. Downes, his earliest biographer, established Homer's greatness on two grounds: he was the first truly

American painter, and he was a realist. In order to support his points, Downes exaggerated Homer's autochthonic nature: "Mother Nature [was] his only teacher.... He belonged to no school. He leaves no pupils, no followers."[52] Writing in 1911, Downes was both a friend of Homer's and spoke with some authority about his aims and, just as important, an understanding of the artist's audience. Homer's Americanness and his realism were the two important things taken up by those influenced by him, for despite Downes' strictures, Homer had followers.

Americanism and Realism

The terms contemporaries used most often to describe Winslow Homer were *big, virile, American,* and *real.* He had assumed a mythic character, becoming as it were the John Wayne of American painting. We have already seen how far from actuality this myth is, in so far as we are able to see Homer's paintings without preconceptions. But why was the myth created and what function did it serve? We can gain a clearer picture by examining the associations that condensed around these terms, defining them as much by what they rejected as by what they proposed about the nature of Homer's art. *Big* was opposed to *decorative, virile* was associated with the great outdoors, and both were balanced against *feminine,* the domestic, and interior spaces. *American* was set against *European,* of course, and the *real* was opposed to the *ideal* and the abstract. The oppositions could be, and were, extended further: power versus art, or strength versus refinement.[1] Finally, moral virtue might stand against culture, and democracy must stand up against aristocracy. And from there we rapidly plunge into the anti-intellectualism so much a feature of American life.

Such simplistic but comprehensive oppositions were bound to cause paradoxes. The fundamental one in looking at Homer was how to understand an art supposed to be artless, allied with everything opposing art. Blinding oneself to the sophistication of Homer's art necessitated misreading essential elements. But this misreading proved extremely creative for the next generation of artists because it enabled them to select from Homer's art whatever they wanted, and to ignore the rest. Seen only partially, Homer's late paintings spoke clearly to Bellows, Hopper, Hartley, and others.

The system of terms that bound Homer's work addressed a problem basic to American society at the end of the nineteenth century. These terms tried to define what it was to be an Ameri-

can in a world changing more quickly than could be compre-
hended. Robert Wiebe has characterized America in the last
quarter of the century as a group of island communities, hostile to
outsiders and bewildered about the nature of their own identity.[2]
The question of Americanness reached fundamental levels: what
was it to be native-born (or Anglo-Saxon), to be white, to be male,
even to be human in a world in which machines and nature both
loomed larger than any man (women, blacks, and foreigners were
seldom privileged to ask these questions). For Homer and his
generation, the question was inward directed and sometimes
paralyzing. A great number of creative figures in the period suffered nervous breakdowns in mid-career.[3] These were men in a
republic whose dream of national mission had been shattered by
the Civil War and had never really healed. Healing now seemed
impossible, the pastoral past irrevocably displaced by industry,
immigrants, corporations. As a sociologist exclaimed in 1905:
"Under our present manner of living, how many of my vital
interests must I entrust to others! Nowadays the water main is
my well, the trolley car my carriage, the banker's safe my old
stocking, the policeman's billy my fist."[4]

For the generation born well after the Civil War, the response
to this dissipation of a sense of self was an almost turbulent
energy. Action, almost any action, served as its own justification.
Whether sincere or not—and we may rightly question the depth of
feeling—for George Bellows and his fellows the energy was
directed outward. Robert Henri's certainty about his artistic
mission, for example, is astonishing, John Sloan's political activ-
ism unthinkable for an artist of Homer's generation. However
much the 1913 Armory Show undermined these artists' sense of
purpose, and World War I broke it, it is unwise to underestimate
their positiveness in the decade before the war. For the most part,
the image of Homer galvanized them into energetic painting,
which ignored Homer's own sense of alienation. The comments of
Sadakachi Hartmann (a friend of the archpriest of modernism in
America, Alfred Stieglitz) on Homer were typical: "It is extremely
seldom that we find an American artist who is also American by
nature." Hartmann attributed "the lack of rough, manly force, and
the prevailing tendency to excel in delicacy and subtlety of expression" to "the Anglomania and love of titles of our plutocracy....

Only men like Winslow Homer and Thomas Eakins have endorsed [the idea of strength].... Winslow Homer is an American by birth and nature."[5] Wrapped in the flag, Homer inspired their efforts to forge an American identity.

The critical term of approbation perhaps most frequently used was *big.* Reading it in sophisticated art criticism strikes our ear oddly today, partly because it is only one syllable and three letters long, and is not French.[6] But its flatness and heartiness is consonant with the dominant tone of criticism at the turn of the century: "The conception must be big ... before a picture can be classed as first-rate."[7] Others spoke of "bigness of feeling."[8] Homer painted with "big strong feeling."[9] His "pictures are big work; big in their sympathy with and comprehension of the subject of his study. They were succeeded by work that was even bigger...."[10]

Nor was the term limited to culture. As one historian has written: "Big business, big labor, big cities, big farms—all were quickly becoming the norm rather than the exception.... 'Capitalists ... talk of millions now as confidently as formerly of thousands.'"[11] Andrew Carnegie proclaimed that "the bigger system grows bigger men, and it is by the big men that the standard of the race is raised."[12] Bigness was not only a matter of industry, cities, and capital, it was also the most dramatic fact of American politics. At the end of the century, the United States turned itself into an imperial power, waging war against Spain in a theater ranging from Cuba to the Philippines. But imperialism and immoderate force disgusted and disturbed many. Henry James observed with revulsion in 1905: "the will to grow ... everywhere written large, and to grow at no matter what or whose expense." Earlier his brother William James had declared: "I am against bigness and greatness in all their forms, and with the invisible moral forces that work from individual to individual."[13]

The adjective *big,* by itself, had a double-edge to it. The big hero humanized and made non-threatening the impersonal immensity of industrial capitalism. Raised against giant factories, cities, mass movements, and hidden forces was the shadow of the big man, as if his actions could match or even overturn the demonic power of modern progress, a spurious hope. The essential aspect of such big men (embodied in mythic figures like Paul Bunyan and his brothers) was just that: they had no sisters or wives. Their virility was a self-contained absolute. They were hard, they spoke plainly, and their manners were simple and sometimes rough. Their thoughts and actions were direct and unpretentious. Homer and, by extension, his art were all these things: "Winslow Homer personifies the clearest type of fresh American virility.... Sober, earnest and full of movement, his pictures go direct to the point with originality of vision, and with that strange power of the big man.... He never becomes pretty, but ever remains direct."[14] Homer's work was seen as being "singularly devoid of mystery or sensuous seduction."[15] No soft feminine wiles marred his paintings.

His fishermen and his art were one: "Some painters have understood the dignity of labor and painted it ... So did Winslow Homer.... [His] art is not one of dreamy compassion, but of manly power, the beauty of man strong in will and muscle fighting the elements.... His figures, austere, virile, solid flesh, look as if they had sprung from his hands in one 'go.' Hence the powerful grandeur of 'All's Well.' As simple as his themes were his compositions; the latest style in technique meant nothing to him."[16]

Homer, as a big painter, was compared to other American heroes, and different aspects of his life evoked different myths. His career as a recluse recalled Henry David Thoreau, his red-blooded American themes invoked Walt Whitman, while perhaps it was his parsimony with words and dogged endurance that recalled Lincoln.[17] The most important fact of Homer's life was that he did not live in the city. Only alone in the land, recreating in some sense a pioneer existence, could he be truly American:

> *Many great human qualities come to their best in a life of comparative isolation. A big tree, an oak or elm, standing out in an open field, has a toughness of fibre, a spread of boughs and roundness of shape that are never seen in a tree that stands in the woods. So people get individuality by being much alone.... They acquire inflexibility of purpose by facing obstacles and conquering them. The pioneers of our country and the fathers of the republic were such men.... The country is the natural nursery of such qualities.[18]*

American men could never be found in the city, which was both increasingly dominated by immigrants and increasingly unreal in its fantastic pace and variety. The real American lived in the country, as he had always done. As one writer put it in 1886, the village was a place where "there are lives that do go on with apparently unbroken coherence.... Here the constantly overlapping continuity of the neighborhood existence helps to a keep a man's own thread of personality unbroken." In the city identity is disrupted, man is alienated even from his sense of himself. Not only is it impossible to be a true American, it is impossible to be oneself: "But when we once cut loose from geography, make friends and break with friends ... then how far backward over our days can the uninterrupted 'I' be said to extend?"[19] Thus, Homer's figures, such as the woman in *A Light on the Sea* (Figure 39), represented the continuities of human life with the eternal rhythms of the sea. Only in the country was a man whole and himself. Homer's strength derived from Prout's Neck, which was his native land (or close enough as to make no difference: his mother's people, after all, came from Maine). He "possess[ed] a heritage of virile, sturdy Americanism ... a direct and wholesome response to local environment."[20]

The American man, however, was neither passive nor quiet in his isolation; he was forceful, energetic, always in the doing and striving—even if it killed him, as it did John Henry driving steel. Speaking of Homer, one critic suggested that "no painter in this country has so aggressive an individuality, founded upon and justified by such superiority of individual force.... He is the only painter who has struck out a clear, clanging note, distinctively American."[21]

The Americanism attributed to Homer was obviously a product of that perennial pride and insecurity in being an American noted by all foreign visitors since the Revolution. It was as well a result of his own conscious exploration of nationalist themes.[22] But Americanism was also part of a much larger tendency in late nineteenth-century nationalism, the ubiquitous importance attached to place and race. In contrast to the dogma of traditional academic theory, the greatest artists, it was now believed, were those who reached the universal through the particularities of their homeland, who were true to the essential nature of themselves. Moreover, the terms in which this nativeness was expressed were not environmental but genetic. Bluntly, the characteristics were seen as racial: "The traits of a great artist are traits of race."[23] For an American, this meant truth to the nature of the American landscape and society, and the genuine expression of his racial (or national) characteristics. More specifically, it meant the expression by the New Englander of the facts of his native soil and character, as opposed to that of a New Yorker or Ohioan or Pennsylvanian. Even New England was divided into its different states and regions and cities: Bostonians contrasted to citizens of Amherst, New Haven to Hartford, *ad nauseam.* Typical of the extremity to which this racialism could be carried were Henry Adams' comments (which may be taken as slightly tongue in cheek, but only slightly): "The Pennsylvania mind, as minds go, is not complex; it reasoned little and never talked; but in practical matters it was the steadiest of all American types.... Albert Gallatin ... was, if American at all, a New Yorker, with a Calvinistic strain—rather Connecticut than Pennsylvanian."[24] Henry James, a more distant observer, found such facetiousness provoking. Surprised at many points by the change immigration had worked throughout the United States during his visit in 1904, he concluded: "What meaning ... can continue to attach to such a term as the 'American' character? ... The challenge to speculation ... is so intense as to be, as I say, irritating."[25]

Few art critics had such reservations, and most engaged avidly in the pursuit of the American character in art. The great fear was that, because of European training, most American artists were not truly American. Speaking of the generation of 1877, one contemporary wrote: "They no longer reflected the culture, the likes and dislikes of their compatriots as, in spite of foreign travel or training, the elder generation had done. They appeared almost as aliens."[26] These were the years when it became most difficult to discover any native qualities amidst the onslaught of artists "finished" in Europe. The very sophistication of these young artists told against them; their styles seemed over-refined, even effeminate. To dedicate oneself to the arts was difficult enough in America (as it is now), and that difficulty was being compounded by the threat of European dominance.

In contrast, Winslow Homer was "one more intensely American ... possessing no foreign training, showing no foreign influence, always himself."[27] One member of the public expressed his opinion forcefully in 1907: "There is one American, an old man, who stands out a giant among the degenerates of the age, more virile, more youthful than all the youngsters. Winslow Homer's *Gulf Stream* is one of the great modern pictures.... There is no decadence here, no conscious striving for color or brushwork. This masterpiece is honest, virile and rugged, yet not brutal. It is as American in character as Abraham Lincoln."[28]

To highlight his native qualities, he was often paired with Whistler, who represented everything Homer was not: sophisticated, expatriated, decorative.[29] But even the negative comments served to identify Homer as vigorous, manly, and authentically American. He was no limp-wristed artiste: "Much of Homer's brusqueness of manner found its way into his art. There is no grace or charm or polish about it. The manner of it repels rather than wins one."[30] On the positive side, Homer's work had that "intense human interest with much of that 'knowledge never learned in schools' so despised by our self-exiled Paris Americans."[31] One critic claimed that Homer would "address an aspiring young pupil who came to him for advice, especially in these days of imported Paris and Munich styles, when men's schools dispute the claims of Nature's school—when deft, dexterous, dashy, artificial effects are the ambition of so many studios" to go look at Nature.[32] In landscape painting specifically, Homer was contrasted with John Twachtman: "The river of modern American landscape painting flows down from Winslow Homer and John Twachtman—force and delicacy."[33] To admit that Homer might have shared qualities with Whistler and Twachtman would have diminished him.

A genuinely American artist like Homer could not at the same time be decorative or European (the two terms amounted to the same thing). Having fit him into one category, his audience could not conceive of his belonging to another. Almost single-handedly he embodied all the best hopes for successfully negotiating a way between provincial isolation and European sophistication. But to acknowledge that he had been influenced by European painting— that he had looked at it closely and responded to it deeply—would have threatened his almost mythic role. Homer, of course, did nothing to dispel the myth.

What critics wanted to see in Homer's work was naturalness, honesty, and simplicity, and that they found in buckets. For them, the strength of his art lay in his subjects, rendered without any artifice or artfulness: "He paints what he has seen; he tells what he has felt; he records what he knows."[34] One critic admitted difficulties in even thinking of Homer as a self-conscious artist:

It is this absorption in his subject that makes it so difficult to compare Homer with other artists... [It] is as if one left pictures for reality.... [It] is only by making a special effort that his very great artistic merits are recognized, his drafts-manship, his composition, his color, and even when that is done, the tendency is to revert again to the indwelling spirit, the love for the strong, free life of men who fight in the open air against man, beast or the elements, the life that his great namesake sang in the days before history. They are Homeric.[35]

The essential aspect of his late paintings was their forcefulness and simplicity. Thus, "When Winslow Homer's great swells roll in out of the fog ... we feel the awful, elemental force."[36] His sense of energy led to a disregard for picayune detail and a concentration on simple, large-scale elements: "It was the awful energy of such a scene that attracted him ... less the specific forms of rock and wave than the shock of their collision.... The effect depends upon some incredible simplification, both of the vision and of the creative act." His pictorial streamlining "instinctively attained classic form."[37] Simplification could also be seen as abstraction. Speaking of Homer's late paintings, one eulogist wrote: "In its final expression it rises to heights of abstract grandeur unap-proached by any other American painter, yet always and every-where it sounds the note of race and country."[38]

The style of a truly American work of art was the same as the character of its subjects: forceful, simple, and true. As one critic noted: "This truth of Homer's, this directness, this almost blunt naturalism, and, finally, this crisp spontaneity, are intensely American.... Even in his pictures of the sea, pictures of a gran-deur excluding thoughts of mere race."[39] The essence of American style was that it was realistic:

> *Winslow Homer* [was] *profoundly representative of the American spirit.... What is that spirit, in the domain of the fine arts? A spirit absolutely objective.... We have had a master of creative design like John La Farge, a master of taste and original decorative felicity like Whistler. But these and other highly individualized artists have done nothing to divert their countrymen from a kind of art primarily rooted just in technical rectitude wreaked upon truth. The American artist remains ... a man for whom the visible world exists."* [40]

The truth of this statement has generally been felt to be obvious. Homer has always been compared with the founders of European Realism, Courbet and Millet.[41] And among American artists, his comrade was Eakins, self-consciously a realist in most definitions of the term.

Certainly Homer's subject matter has a sometimes uncanny affinity to such icons of literary realism as Stephen Crane's *The Red Badge of Courage,* 1895, and "The Open Boat," 1897, which recall vividly the beginning and end of Homer's career—the first with its descriptions of Civil War battles, the second with its vivid story of shipwreck. And on the level of style, as the poet John Berryman has said about Stephen Crane, Homer was "deeply uninterested in manner" unlike nearly all of his contemporaries; in Homer, as in Crane, "the subject appears naked."[42] Deeper levels of affinity may be found with American literary realists in general. Eric Sundquist, for example, has noted that death seldom occurs in bed in the naturalist novels of Crane, Jack London, Theodore Dreiser, and others, "but in open boats ... in blinding fields of force, sudden traps of mysterious making. And they [die] ... by becoming bloated figures in which the human constantly threatens to detach and deform itself into the bestial [as we see in Homer's *Hound and Hunter*] or, at extremity, in which the human disappears completely into the beast [as in *Fox Hunt*]."[43] Lionel Trilling's famous remarks, that "in the American metaphysics, reality is always material reality, hard, resistant, unformed, impenetrable, and unpleasant," recall the language used by his contemporaries to describe Homer.[44]

Critics of Homer's generation liked to suggest that he simply painted what he saw: "Aggressive in disposition, he engaged in a bitter warfare against all conventionality, scorning alike all accepted schools, claiming that nature, studied from the standpoint of observation and discernment rather than that of intellectuality or sentiment, should be the only foundation of art."[45] This bellicose isolationism is as limiting a view, however, as for us to call him a Realist like Courbet or Eakins without qualifying the statement. As I have suggested, Homer may fruitfully be seen in the light of Whistler and tonalism, even aspects of symbolism. But there are more fundamental ways in which the label of realism, while it is certainly accurate, does not clothe Homer completely and even inhibits our understanding of the nature and extent of his influence. The relationship between reality and realism, as we analyze Homer's mythic presence in American painting, is more problematic than we thought. Nor is it easy to come to an understanding of how realist artists represent the reality they claim to depict so naturally and transparently.

In general, the works we might instinctively call most real in American art are those with the fewest people in them: *trompe-l'oeil* still lifes by John Frederick Peto (1854-1907) and William Michael Harnett (1848-92), and landscapes by members of the Hudson River school. American painting, no matter how you slice it, is incurably materialistic and realistic; no historian has seriously challenged this view in a century.

But the self-evidentiary nature of this definition for American painting has little to do with definitions of realism in other fields, particularly literature. Rene Wellek has defined realism as "the objective representation of contemporary social reality."[46] Although any critic today would quibble over the words *objective* and *representation* (claiming that the two terms cannot be yoked together, in that all representation is socially and ideologically coded, and that the first term probably doesn't exist anyway), none have problems with the last three. There is a consensus that Realist art in Europe (in both literature and painting) tended to focus on class relations; in American literature, on social relations. Both, in any case, dealt with people. The nature of Homer's realism, and of American painting in general, would seem to be very different.

In trying to understand his realism, it is worth looking at what the term might have meant in his own day. Several contemporary comments provide a starting point: "[Homer's] style is large and free, realistic and straightforward, broad and bold," wrote George Sheldon in 1879.[47] In 1910 Samuel Isham was more concerned with the veracity of Homer's representation, suggesting that Homer's paintings "were manifestly true. The conviction of their veracity, of their absolute reproduction of the thing seen, is overwhelming." He added, perceptively, "yet they never reproduce a subject as the spectator would have imagined it." That is, they add none of our conventional ideas of how a story should be told or presented, they lack "arrangement, ... prettiness.... This ignorance of or indifference to what other men have done before leads Homer to attempt things which have been generally accepted as impossible of representation."[48] Frank Jewett Mather, discussing the Ashcan school in 1916, defined a realist as "the artist who prefers discovering his beauty ready made in the world and when he has ambushed it lets it alone ... such an artist tampers as little as he may with his discovery, being content with it and seeking merely to report it clearly and sharply ... a tough minded lover of visual facts."[49]

Sheldon characterized realism as a kind of freedom "broad and bold," while Isham considered realism to be reticent, independent, plain, and factual. Mather (who belonged to a younger generation) saw it as almost ornery: it is what it is. For Mather, realism's very truthfulness to appearances asserts its independence of the viewer and even the maker: the work of art is a record of an object or person (seldom an event) in the way an election or murder is reported and read in a newspaper. Its virtues consist of its factuality, not the manner in which it tells the truth. And the truth it records is the world of the loner, the hunter. As a result, the more forbidding and desolate the struggle Homer recorded, the more sincere it would seem to an audience in 1916. This is what places the realism of Homer's late style in harmony with Crane's fictional world, not with the detailed society stories of William Dean Howells, the dean of American realist authors at the time, who was younger than Homer by only one year.

Of course, the realism of painting cannot be the same as literary realism: words and brushstrokes represent the world in different ways. The realism of painting is built into it at a much more apprehensible level. The letters and tickets apparently tacked onto the wall in Peto's *trompe-l'oeil*'s have a reality than no sophistry can take away from them. On the other hand, no artifact escapes the touch of the society to which it belongs. Many critics in the last few years have revealed the ways in which objects, the things we buy and sell, which are the meat of the consumer discourse shaping our culture, metonymically express the lives of those who use them. Gracing our days or riding our souls like succubi, artifacts infiltrate our lives and convince us that we cannot do without them. Nature herself and her creatures of wood and flesh, trees and animals, become ours to own; and entering into our economy, they seem to ape our souls. It is a good question as to whether we play Nature's Aeolian harp, or it plays us. Thus, even in the most "natural" of Homer's paintings, we are right to see the hand of man. After all, the basic act of realist painting is to be manifestly paint before it represents anything else; this is vividly true of the English painter John Constable, the French artists Courbet and the impressionists, and Winslow Homer. But even beyond that level of artifice, Homer's sailors, rocks, and surf are extensions of a self formed by a particular society and inevitably representing it. (They do, of course, also represent sailors, rocks, and surf.)

But knitting Homer's silent paintings into the social fabric of contemporary realist literature is not without difficulties. Traditionally the primary mode of American fiction has always been considered the romance, in which the "isolated hero embarks on a melodramatic quest through a symbolic universe unformed by networks of social relations and unfettered by the pressure of social restraints."[50] Realist fiction has been deemed at best marginal, at worst a total failure. The culture of American society has been too weak, threadbare compared to European, to sustain anything else. America has seemed to produce only two kinds of men, pioneers who struck out for the wilderness to clear the land and who moved on the moment another settler entered the same valley, or crass merchants who rejected all the airs of polite society. The one rejected social drama; the other was immune to it. Attempts by such realists as William Dean Howells and Theodore Dreiser to write about society cannot stand in the canon beside such romances as Mark Twain's *Huckleberry Finn*.

More recently, several critics have taken up the realist cause.

Others insist on suggesting that at the heart of every successful realist fiction lies a romance.[51] But all these debates obscure the basic generational shift among the writers who called themselves realists, and the historical event demarcating the faultline. The realism produced by authors born before the Civil War, such as Howells and James, is different from that produced by those born soon afterward, such as Crane, Frank Norris, and Dreiser. The first is a realism about the society of people; the latter is a realism about the matrix of forces and things in which an individual might find himself ensnared. These realisms, in turn, were conditioned by two developments. First, by the 1890s the long-buried trauma of the Civil War finally had worked its way to the surface (we are witnessing something similar today in Eastern Europe more than forty years after the end of World War II), permitting a return to the ideals of personal honor and valor. But just as Americans could begin to reassert their manliness, they felt the force of another war, which seemed to have been fought and lost without anyone realizing that the conflict was under way—the war that industrialization (with its two generals, technology and the corporation) was waging on the structures of American life. At a time when a long shadow might have departed, both society and the individual continued to be deformed and thwarted, whether in the eyes of an older conservative, such as James, or a younger rebel, such as Jack London. Despite all the postwar rhetoric about a return to a Jeffersonian society, the Civil War had permitted the money men and the government to get a grip on the lives of Americans that could not be shaken off. The first generation of realists saw themselves as working during the long drawn-out aftermath of the Civil War; only a few years later, the second generation felt themselves to be in the midst of burgeoning American imperialism and industrialization. In both cases, whatever the positive character of the fiction (a healing society, a forceful individual), a sense of injury vitiated the result. The older generation feared that society was hollow; the younger generation that the individual was trapped.

The words of a magazine editor writing at the turn of the century help us to bridge generational differences. The editor declared that he wanted a style of "homely realism," but modern conditions demanded writing "with more directness, more clearness, with greater nervous force." He noted, "Women can't write editorials, neither can feminine men," because such writing demanded stronger, more authoritative points of view.[52] In other words, by 1900, the need to be manly was even more imperative than before; the needs that realism addressed had changed as had the society it mirrored. What the editor unwittingly revealed is that under the impulse of business and politics, realism had become harder and even more sexually differentiated; it had moved beyond the description of polite society.

It is Homer's distinction that while he belongs to the same generation as Howells and James and for the first part of his career painted subjects similar to theirs, he transformed himself into a different kind of realist by the end of his career, one in harmony with the subjects and tone of the next generation. His early scenes, particularly the wood engravings of country schools, resorts, and farms, are recognizably about society, but his last works are grounded in things and nature.

The *big* and *virile* works of Homer's old age may be realistic and American, but not in any flat-footed version of "he just painted what he saw." Homer had a more complex relationship to the commerce of the world of things made and consumed, the immaterial forces of ideas and honor, and the transactions between men and women, the ultimate proving ground for explorations of power and physical sensation. More bluntly, Homer had plenty to say about business, politics, and sex. Although this is most obvious in his figurative and narrative paintings, given the unity of his *oeuvre,* we may sense it even in his most abstract work.

Since before the Revolution, the political entity "America" and the land "America" have been profoundly connected, the one the symbol or synecdoche of the other. When Homer stood on the Atlantic coast, looking east, it is important to understand that he stood not on the closed frontier to the west, which lay behind him, but on the sea's edge, the beginning of America. Homer not only looked out, he looked back—at an older order. Did he look out nostalgically, or with foreboding? Did he sense that all those Old World troubles were now washing up at his feet?

The Old World, in contrast to the New, spelled "man" and his troubles to Americans: cities, ruins, decay. Contemporaries of Homer's always noted his lack of not only urban subjects but even

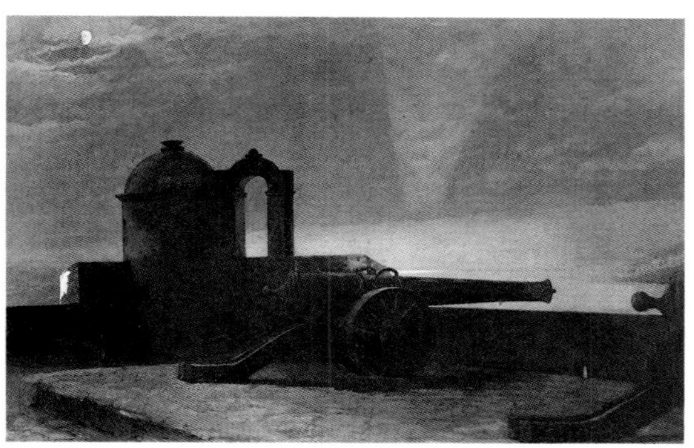

59. Homer. *Searchlight: Harbor Entrance, Santiago de Cuba,* 1901.

city types in his works.[53] The "gilded spread-eagleism" of the cities was contrasted to the "noble simplicity" of Homer.[54] In one late painting inspired by an historical event, however, we find the usual complexity and balance of his thought expressed on Old World political matters. In *Searchlight: Harbor Entrance, Santiago de Cuba,* 1901 (Figure 59), Homer painted his record of the Spanish-American war. No jingoistic paean to American imperial glory (as were the illustrations flooding the American press at the time, which recalled Homer's work in the Civil War), he focused not on the victorious American ships, which are evident only through the insubstantial light shining in the night sky, but on the hulking mass of the Spanish cannon. There is no easy identification of victor and enemy here: the cannon seems mute and seemingly impotent, but we stand on its side, not on the American side. As in *Inviting a Shot, before Petersburg, Virginia,* 1864, and more ambiguously in *Prisoners from the Front,* 1866, Homer's sympathies lay on both sides.

Writing soon after the Spanish-American War, Frank Norris argued that the Anglo-Saxon impulse was to conquer, but now that "the equation of the horizon" had been solved and marines had been sent to China, Americans would fight a different battle, "no longer War but Trade." Businessmen were to be the warriors of today, the new soldiers of fortune.[55] And Homer expressed himself just as ambiguously about this new corporate culture as he had about American military efforts. On the one hand, Homer himself was often taken as a businessman, especially by his fellow artists.[56] More the old-time Yankee trader than the modern corporate boardsman that the painter Cecelia Beaux imagined him to be, he once crankily muttered: "[Painting is] just like any other business.... It is spend one dollar and get back 33 1/3 cents." His letters to his dealers record his close attention to money matters, as do his real estate dealings on the Neck: "I want to know if you are still over-loaded with my pictures. I am waiting until some of them get settled for good—before I paint More."[57] Not surprisingly, he came from a family of businessmen.

Ostensibly, his rural subjects lay at the other end of the world from Wall Street. "Winslow Homer's art is not one which appeals to the cliff-dwellers of the great cities," wrote one critic in 1911.[58] But it was urban dwellers who bought his paintings. Homer's

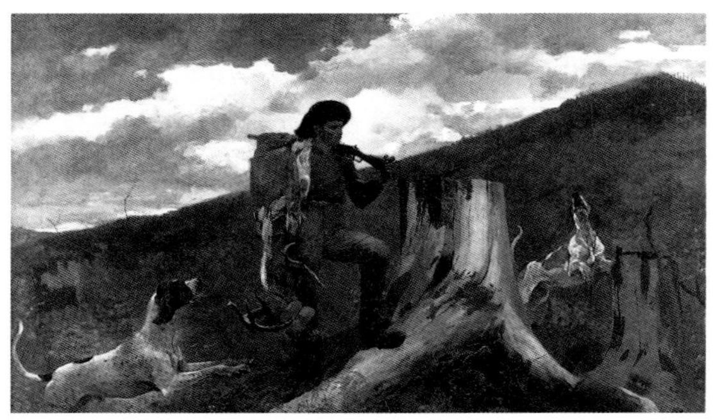

60. Homer. *Huntsman and Dogs,* 1891.

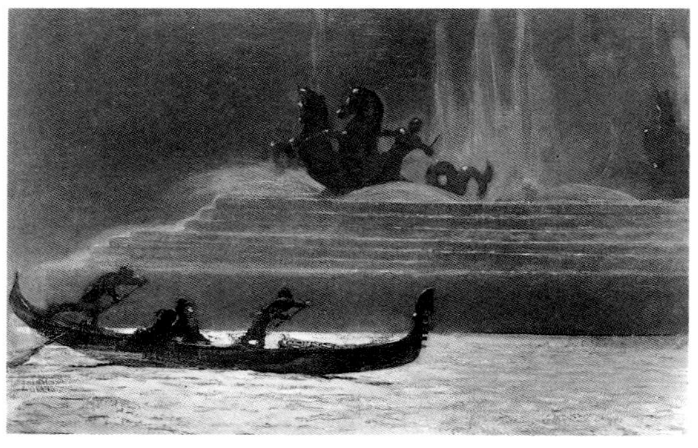

61. Homer. *Fountains at Night, World's Columbian Exposition,* 1893.

patrons were the businessmen who were often the other guests at the fishing lodges Homer frequented with his brother Charles. Homer's hunting paintings no doubt appealed to them by translating the pursuit of profit, the survival of the fittest, into nature's terms. It is only a small step from Norris' aggressive martial metaphors of struggle and fight to sport: corporations might behave like invading armies, but businessmen move more like hunters stalking their prey. Homer's response to the world of aggressive masculinity, characterized in this period by businessmen, may perhaps be found in his hunting pictures. As in *Searchlight: Harbor Entrance, Santiago de Cuba,* Homer's sympathies are difficult to divine. In *Hound and Hunter* and *Huntsman and Dogs,* 1891 (Figure 60), the killing of the deer seems senseless and cruel, the hunter repellent.[59] Yet Homer's comments on the paintings are flatly objective.

The world of business presented itself in a different guise in the White City of the World's Columbian Exposition in 1893 in Chicago, much praised as an enlightened example of business patronage. The White City was understood as an image of the ideal America, an America gigantic in scale, pure and bloodless in form, expressing the new corporate and consumer society of the country.[60] One of the greatest artistic attractions of the fair was the fountain by Frederick MacMonnies in the Great Lagoon in front of the Fine Arts Building, recorded by many photographers and painters. Homer painted it too, but at night, in monochrome, and close-up, capturing only a fragment of it. Rejecting the bombast, he focused on the irony of a Venetian gondola transporting two swooning maidens at night under the indifferent eyes of a plaster man. *Fountains at Night, World's Columbian Exposition,* 1893 (Figure 61), is a peculiar vision of Pygmalion in reverse. The only two other living beings, the gondoliers, fade into anonymity. The tail of the seahorse is contrasted with the "head" of the boat, reducing both to flat designs. For once the women are on the water, instead of bound to the land; but the male sea creatures they look at are plaster. All the references to romance and culture, the hallmarks of a successful European Grand Tour, are flattened and reduced, the color washed away to black and white. Here are Homer's ideas of love and art in Middle America, both of them impossible creatures in a consumer society.

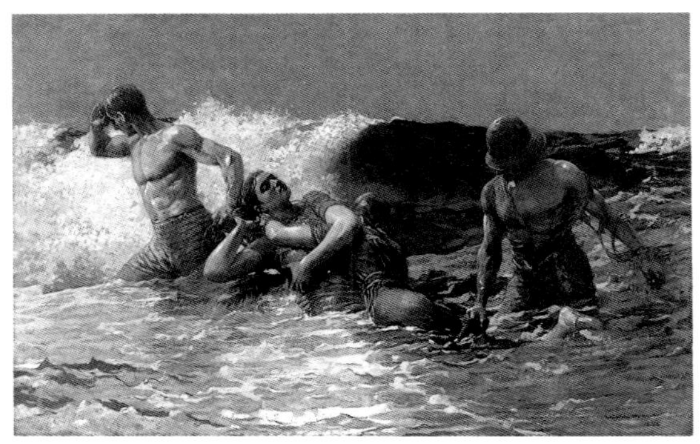

62. Homer. *Undertow,* 1886.

The relationship of businessmen to civilization preoccupied artists in the period. Howells' *The Rise of Silas Lapham* is the story of the son of a Vermont farmer, a paint manufacturer (like Charles Homer, Jr.), almost destroyed by his brush with the moral dilemmas of the city, business, and culture. Henry James, in *The American Scene,* remarked on the prevalence of businessmen frequently. At one point he observed that, as a businessman never hopes to be anything but a businessman, he has abdicated "the boundless gaping void of 'society'; which is but a rough name for all the other so numerous relations with the world he lives in that are imputable to the civilized being." This is the sphere of women.[61] James, like many other commentators, often pointed out the disparity between the sexes in America; not so much one of power but of other interests, separate spheres of action and thought. Homer felt this division strongly. In his own art it is almost impossible to find examples of love; the relations depicted between men and women are awkward at best. They touch only in moments of extreme crisis, as in *Lifeline,* 1884, and *Undertow,* 1886 (Figure 62).

The story of Homer's sexual uncertainties is by now well established, but it is worth rehearsing once again. Never one for painting domestic felicities in his youth, he still had a modest reputation for having undergone the normal number of affairs of the heart. After his return from England, however, men and women seldom unite in his major works. In his private life, the question of love and marriage seems never to have been raised again. Lloyd Goodrich has commented on the lack of sexual feeling in the women in Homer's late paintings: "Sexual emotion, that deep source of art, had been sublimated out of all recognition. The sensuousness on which all great art rests had remained undeveloped. To this sexlessness, typical of much American painting of the time, we can ascribe the externality of his art." Nearly every writer on Homer has tackled the question, but of course there can be no resolution to the question of his sexual interests or identity now.[62]

His asexuality is in fact an appropriate part of his myth. While the whiff of sex that surrounded Eakins and Whistler made them not only morally dubious (to the puritanical) but European, the lack of it around Homer simply confirmed his Americanness. One

of Eakins' attractions was just this taint of rebelliousness, a sign
of the urban nature of his art and training. But Homer represented another American ideal: the loner, the cowboy. In American culture, until very recently, one never wondered what cow-
boys did with themselves alone on the range. Their sexual nature
was swallowed up in the grander but less specific sensuality of
the wilderness. The same is true for Homer.

Nonetheless, there is a fundamental connection between
realism and sex. Evoke "dirt" in America and you have "smut,"
while cleanliness is next to godliness. These are difficult equations
for Americans who would like to have their cake and never get
their fingers sticky. European Realism at the end of the nineteenth century was notorious in this country for its reek of un-
clean lives, dirtied by their lack of washing and their sexuality.
One of the reasons why American realism always seems to slide
into romance—not the romance novel but the escape into
Nature—is just this desire to avoid sex. But feelings must be felt,
if life is to seem real: "Yearnings for the authentic, the natural,
the real pervad[ed] contemporary American culture," as a modern
historian has observed of turn-of-the-century America.[63] An
alternative to sex was suffering: only through hardship could real
experience break through the dispossessed self. A harsh reality
guaranteed truth of experience. Knowing other people could not
provide reassurances of reality in late nineteenth-century culture;
they were themselves the problem. Only in inanimate objects or
animals, or faraway people or primitive ones could authenticity be
recovered. Genteel American society offered no sense of reality
and had to be escaped, whether into rebellious bohemia or the
desolate shores of Maine.

Henri and Homer, New York and Maine: Robert Henri, Van Dearing Perrine, and George Bellows

In 1910, shortly after Homer's death, a large exhibition of recent American painting was held in Germany. Contemplating the national characteristics that might be perceived in the works, an English observer, Lewis C. Hind, wrote: "I think that a national American art will have to be something subtler than hustle and bustle and smoke-stacks.... Can we find in this exhibition any signs of a national American art? My answer is Winslow Homer.... His big, comprehensive work ... could have been painted no where but in America."[1]

The "hustle and bustle and smoke-stacks" to which Hind referred was the work of the painters called the Ashcan school, a group of realists in New York led by Robert Henri. Hind saw two competing locations for the claim of Americanness in American painting, the Ashcan's urban subjects and Homer's simple Maine landscapes. Whether or not one concurs with his final judgment, the fundamental difference between the two seems obvious. The Ashcan painters were a group of raucous Greenwich Village radicals, who delighted in upsetting their stuffy academic elders; their subjects were crude, vulgar, and devoted to describing the exhilarating variety and seeming chaos of the people, streets and buildings of New York City. What could be further from Homer's spare, unpeopled scenes?

At another level, too, Hind's distinction makes sense. For most viewers, Homer's late paintings seem a natural evolution from his earliest works, in a career that not only stretched back before the Civil War but was always firmly anchored in mid-nineteenth century traditions. The Ashcan painters, on the other hand, both proclaimed their debt to European Realists, especially Edouard Manet, and their courageous defiance of previous American standards of good taste in subjects and style. They saw themselves as revolutionaries. While in the light of the Armory Show of 1913 and the real avant-garde of Marcel Duchamp, Pablo

Picasso, and Henri Matisse, they may now seem pretty tame, we have been willing to grant them their independence from their American heritage. As a result, Homer seems never to have arrived in the twentieth century and the Ashcan school exists in a little island of fame, cut off from both the nineteenth and the twentieth centuries.

In fact, all the Ashcan painters began painting while Homer was still alive and continued to paint long after the close of the Armory Show. Their careers overlapped not only with each other but also with many of the artists we like to call modernists today. When George Bellows, one of the youngest Ashcan painters, died in 1925, it seemed to most discerning critics a great tragedy. He had negotiated his course through the temptations of European fashions, assimilating what he needed from them, and seemed well on the way to new and greater successes as a modern painter. To observers in New York in the 1930s, surrounded by social realists and American scene painters, abstraction (and its attendant "-isms") probably looked like an interesting and historically valuable aberration.[2] Even Picasso had abandoned it. We would disagree with them, having, we think, a greater historical perspective. But in the first years of the twentieth century, before the battle lines were clearly drawn, Winslow Homer had much to say to many young artists.

The Ashcan school included Robert Henri, John Sloan, George B. Luks, William Glackens, Everett Shinn, and George Bellows in most accounts. These artists were friends, shared similar subjects, and found themselves attacked together in the press. Another group popular among art historians, The Eight, included the artists Henri chose to exhibit with in 1908: Sloan, Luks, Glackens, and Shinn, as well as Maurice Prendergast (1859-1924), Arthur B. Davies (1862-1928), and Ernest Lawson (1873-1939). Both these fellowships were largely accidental in nature, due to the fortune of similar age and joint participation in exhibitions more than any strict similarity of style or subject matter. Moreover, the Ashcan school and The Eight are only two of several temporary coalitions, but they are the two art historians and critics have most often chosen to discuss. At the turn of the century, there were a great many artists who tried their hand at painting New York City in all its newness and shocking vitality, any of whom might have been candidates for inclusion in the Ashcan school if their personalities, friendships, or ages had been a little different. Robert Henri was the real connection between the artists of both the Ashcan and The Eight, in both cases, as well as among the artists discussed in the next chapters. Luks and Sloan were his fellow students and rebels from Philadelphia; Van Dearing Perrine was a friend in New York; Rockwell Kent, Edward Hopper, and Bellows were Henri's students; and Leon Kroll was a friend of Bellows. Situated in the center, Henri was teacher, catalyst, rebel, and prophet.

Born in 1865 in Nebraska, Henri's early life offers the stuff of melodrama. His father, John Jackson Cozad, was a real estate speculator who founded Cozad, Nebraska. Henri lived there until 1882, when his father shot a man during an argument. The family fled east under new identities: Robert Henry Cozad became Robert Earl Henri. The spirit of the Wild West never seems to have left Henri, which goes a long way toward justifying his individualism and rebelliousness.

For a long time Henri worked within the conventional path of fame, training first at the Pennsylvania Academy of Fine Arts, then at the Académie Julian in Paris, before winning entrance to the Ecole des Beaux Arts. With the purchase of a landscape painting by the French government in 1899, the year before Homer's *A Summer Night* was bought, he felt assured enough of his future to move to New York City and aggressively pursue a career as a painter and teacher. In 1903 he was elected to the Society of American Artists and in 1905 to the National Academy of Design, which since its founding in 1825 had led the artistic efforts of the city. Henri was soon a member of the National Academy's annual jury, avidly promoting the fortunes of young and adventurous painters (who were also his students). Within a very few years, however, he felt stifled and insulted by the conservatism of the National Academy and began exploring alternative ways of exhibiting the work of his friends.

Although there had been breakaway groups in the past, including the Society of American Painters in 1878, with the arrival of Henri the number of independent exhibiting groups and exhibitions quickly increased. He organized his first group show in 1904, at the National Arts Club, and in 1907 formed The Eight.

Their first exhibition was held in 1908 and toured the country, causing a stir. In 1910, with Sloan, Henri organized the Exhibition of Independent Artists. Rockwell Kent organized another independent exhibition the next year, and two years later the Armory Show opened, this time without Henri having a leading role. In little more than a decade, the almost monolithic character of the New York art world was permanently fragmented.

These exhibitions were to Henri an expression of his commitment to young artists. Having first begun teaching in New York in 1900, by 1902 he was sharing the New York School of Art with William Merritt Chase (1849-1916) but by 1908 Henri had his own school. Looking back at the period, it seems that nearly all the major artists of the next generation studied with him and remembered him fondly: from Edward Hopper and George Bellows to such avant-garde artists as Patrick Henry Bruce (1880-1937). In teaching, Henri stressed freedom and individuality: technique was something to express oneself with, not a thing in itself. The variety of styles found among his students testifies to his success.

Equally important was the society he formed around himself. His friends shared a sense of brotherhood, opposed to the National Academy's policies and united in their rebelliousness and sense of unconventionality. Early in his studio days in Philadelphia, and then again in Paris, Henri had had the habit of holding weekly studio parties, a practice he continued in New York. His conviviality marked the whole group.[3] They were constantly in and out of each others studios. They played games and jokes; the spirit of student days and bohemia never left them.

They were also, for the most part, denizens of Greenwich Village, whether they lived there or not. The Village was a mecca for disaffected but idealistic youth the country over. It had a mythological presence far greater than its size; SoHo today is a pale imitation. The Village was a recreation of the Parisian artist's bohemian Montmartre, filled with little cafes complete with political radicals. Free love was in the air, whether practiced or not. They applauded the dancer Isadora Duncan madly and listened to the anarchist Emma Goldman. Their politics were all more or less socialist or anarchist. John Sloan, inspired perhaps by his wife Dolly, was the most dedicated. He was an editor of *The Masses,* a left-wing magazine with a sense of humor; most of the

other artists were contributors. In contrast to the alienation felt
by European anarchists and socialists, however, Village radical-
ism had an almost simple optimism. Not insignificantly, all these
artists were native-born Americans, and several were from
midwestern or rural areas.

Like any small group their relationships varied; friendships
heated up and cooled off. The bonds formed in one summer
together in Monhegan might be loosened the next, when some
went to Ogunquit and others Gloucester. They were also competi-
tive. Rockwell Kent had an immediate success with his first
exhibited work in 1904 and again in 1907 with his first one-man
show. Many aspects of Bellows' early work show Kent's influence.
But in a few years, Bellows' more enduring and overwhelming
success set him apart slightly from Henri and Sloan, as well as
removed him thoroughly from Kent's influence.

There were other differences as well, of temperament and age.
The oldest in the group discussed here were George Luks (1866-
1933) and John Sloan (1871-1951), Luks being one year younger
than Henri. Van Dearing Perrine (1869-1955), whom Henri met in
New York after he moved there in 1900, was also of their generation. Rockwell Kent (1882-1971), George Bellows (1882-1925),
Edward Hopper (1882-1967), and Leon Kroll (1884-1974) belonged
to the next generation; three of them, remarkably enough, had
been born in the same year. All were trained in New York; all
were students of Henri, except for Kroll, who became close friends
with Bellows in 1910 and soon fell within Henri's orbit.

In one sense, this gathering of artists is as arbitrary as any
other, such as the Ashcan and The Eight. The Eight at least had
one show together: the only time all these artists—along with a
hundred others—exhibited in the same place was the Armory
Show. Like The Eight they had no single unifying style, no
manifesto, no organization. Unlike the Ashcan, not all of them
explored the city as subject. What they did share was a sense of
rebellion against authority and an awareness that their art lay
outside the limits of the National Academy.

While lacking a common name, they were united by a common
dilemma. They were American artists seeking to distinguish
themselves from their forebears but unwilling to look to their
contemporaries in Europe. The previous generation or two had

seen whole cadres of young American painters swallowed up by European schools only to emerge years later as native sons no longer. On the other hand, they knew that they could not allow themselves to lapse into provincialism. They were ambitious and vigorous; they wanted to depict real life as they saw it around them. They wanted nothing intervening between themselves and their sense of the brash new world they lived in. Neither across the Atlantic nor in the galleries at home was there much to guide them; their path had few signposts.

Among them only one had seriously trained in Europe, Robert Henri, the teacher or leader of nearly half the artists in this exhibition. And yet he was the strongest advocate of Americanism, of being true to himself. While he traced his artistic heritage primarily to Manet and Courbet, he also recognized Eakins and Homer, as well as Whistler.[4] But of this trio of Americans, Whistler was too decorative, and hardly interested in real life as it was lived, while Eakins seemed mainly a portraitist. In any case, the latter's work, although well known to the Philadelphians in the group, was hardly recognized by the New Yorkers until his memorial exhibition at the Metropolitan in 1917. Of the three, Homer was the most accessible and most comprehensive.[5] It is their response to Homer that differentiates this group of artists from their fellows.

From the 1890 exhibition of four paintings by his dealer in New York, Homer's work was almost continually before the public in temporary exhibitions of one kind or another. Moreover, the Pennsylvania Academy had purchased *Fox Hunt* (Figure 29) in 1894. The Carnegie Institute in Pittsburgh acquired *The Wreck* in 1896, while *The Lookout—All's Well* entered the collection of the Museum of Fine Arts, Boston in 1899. *On a Lee Shore* (Figure 35) was bought by the Rhode Island School of Design in Providence the year after it was painted, in 1901. Five late works were acquired by museums in 1906: in Washington, *A Light on the Sea* (Figure 39) entered the Corcoran and *High Cliffs* (Figure 15) entered the National Gallery; in New York, the Metropolitan bought *The Gulf Stream* (Figure 24) and received *Cannon Rock* (Figure 17) and *Searchlight: Harbor Entrance, Santiago de Cuba* (Figure 59). *Northeaster* (Figure 16) was acquired by the Metropolitan in 1910 (although it had been on deposit since 1908), followed shortly by *Maine Coast* and *Moonlight—Wood's Island Light* (Figures 23, 54). Paintings by Homer were reproduced in every study of American art and frequently appeared in magazines.[6] There were very few Homers that were not available, in one form or another, to his public.

As a result, many artists looked at Homer and some, like Frederick Judd Waugh and William Ritschel, might be said to have imitated him. In one sense, Homer's presence and his influence was pervasive: a model of artistic integrity for a multitude of painters. As any young artist's work gained in boldness, he would often find himself compared to Homer.[7] But Henri and his students may be singled out for the intensity of their encounter with both Homer's paintings and his myth. A major reason why these artists were attracted to Homer was their commitment to the ideal of big, strong, American painting. Henri, who praised Homer frequently in his teaching from an early date, claimed that: "[Winslow Homer] had such a sense of proportion that his work would hold a business man straight. He gives the integrity of the oncoming wave. The big strong thing can only be the result of big strong seeing."[8]

It was just this strength of seeing that interested Henri most, not the strict representation of reality or light effects, but the artist's reaction to the world. As he said, in connection with Homer's profoundly local paintings of Prout's Neck: "It is not so much the actual place or the immediate environment; it is personal greatness and personal freedom which any nation demands for a final right art expression."[9] Henri wanted the effect of nature, not its record: "[Critics] have not learned yet that the idea is what is intended to be presented and the thing is but the material used for its expression."[10]

What Henri transmitted to his followers was an urgency to place themselves in correct and strong relationship to themselves. That is to say, style and school came last, heart and character came first. This position was a world away from the interest in technique preoccupying Whistler and his followers; it also has none of the irony and complexity of European modernism. Henri had a naive faith that what we see is what we get, what we know to be true must be true—about both people and painting. In effect, Henri placed himself above all styles. To him, the men who followed cubism and other such movements were simply giving themselves over to yet another school. Such styles should be one more ingredient in the pot, strong enough to flavor it perhaps, but surely not the whole meal.

Homer's influence was easily recognized by Henri's audience. While other artists might infrequently be compared to Homer, Henri and his friends were continually measured as artists against Homer's example. John Van Dyke, a conservative critic, lamented the influence:

> *Unfortunately, much of Homer's barbarism of the brush lives after him while his splendid vision and stubborn character are in danger of being interred with his bones. He himself has become a tradition, a master to be imitated, for though he founded no school and had no pupils, a great many young painters in America have been influenced by his pictures....* [They are] *painting with the crude color and gritty brush of Homer, thinking thereby to get something strong.... We are now asked to admire this or that because it is "real" or "just as I saw it," or "absolutely true."[11]*

Others, seeing exactly the same thing, regarded it more positively. As one critic wrote in 1915: "'Character,' rather than 'charm' and 'prettiness,' as the chief condition of art, gave rise to the so called New York School of painting more than a decade ago. Not that this was a new thing in American art. Winslow Homer had already been painting for many years his rugged canvases of fishermen and the sea, and these have been acknowledged to be more purely native in spirit than anything that had been done up to his time." The artist held most responsible for this New York School was Henri, and the strength of his art lay, as it had for Homer, in his nature as an American: "Through [Henri's] democratic humanism, his exclusion of feudal themes, and his vigorous mental attitude and faith he is an American. He is more American than Whistler, less than Winslow Homer."[12] So close was the association that Henri invited Homer to join his group of independent artists in 1906.[13]

But the connections do not lie simply at the level of generalized similarities of something so insubstantial as spiritedness, or

Americanness. In nearly every case, specific similarities in composition or subject matter link these artists to Homer. For some, such as Sloan, Homer was an influence at a critical point, but not one that permanently marked their art; for others, Homer was a guiding light. Bellows simply said: "Winslow Homer's my particular pet."[14]

Most of these artists tried to meet Homer on his own ground, literally or figuratively. Only Kroll seems to have had the temerity to stalk him to his den in Prout's Neck and record the encounter.[15] George Luks, who spent several seasons painting marines during the early 1920s, worked at Cape Elizabeth, Maine, in 1922, only a few miles from the Neck. The proximity suggests that this may have been an act of emulation or competitiveness (as it so often was with Luks). The others went to Monhegan Island off the coast of Maine. The person responsible for inspiring them to go there and confront the heritage of Homer on his own turf was Robert Henri.

During the first years of his career, it was clear that Henri was undecided as to whether he would make his mark in landscape or portraiture. His first success was with city landscapes of Paris. At his dealer's urging he transferred the theme to New York, painting many views of the city. Only later did portraiture overtake this interest, although he continued to paint landscapes throughout his career.

Nonetheless, Henri's city pictures were the foundation for the landscape paintings of his friends and followers, leading them ultimately to Homer's threshold. At first glance it is difficult to see any connection between these city pictures and Homer's views of Prout's Neck. Unlike Homer's intensely felt, rare monumental productions, Henri's paintings such as *Snow in New York,* 1902 (Figure 63), have the quality of quick sketches. To some extent they were simply another genre for him to practice. Edward Redfield's comments in a letter to Henri illuminate a common attitude toward them: "The River stuff has been so successful that I have about made up my mind to tackle some of the river and harbor stuff in NY city.... I certainly think the stuff is in NY to paint."[16] Later Henri's quest for characters and types to paint led to a similarly programmed picturesqueness, as he hunted for interesting natives all over Europe and America: Dutch, Irish,

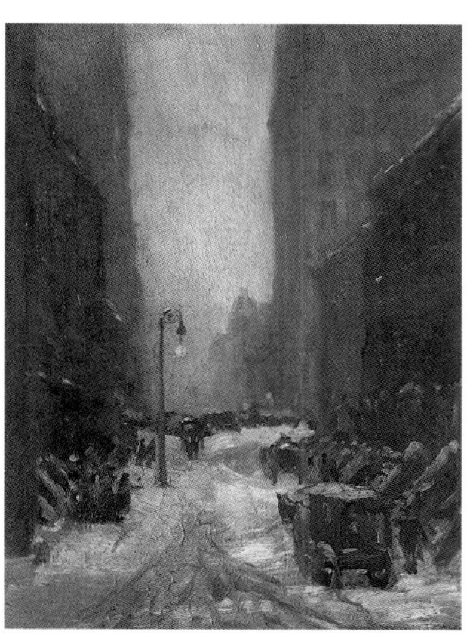

63. Henri. *Snow in New York,* 1902.

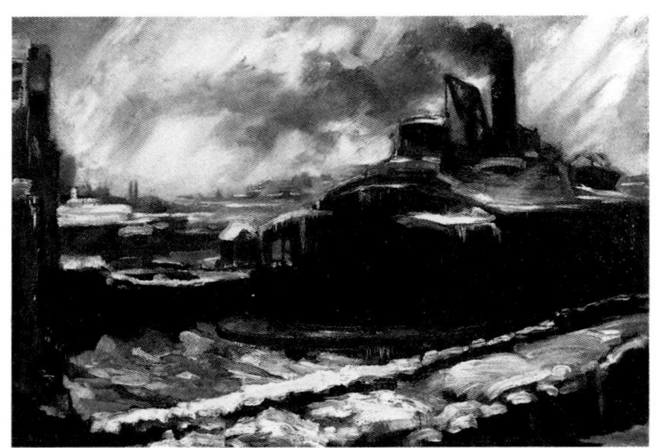

64. Sloan. *Ferry Slip, Winter,* 1905-1906.

and Spanish peasants; gypsies in Europe and America; and native Americans. Despite this element of calculation, his landscapes were seen as lively: "His works are full of the spirit of life, of the great struggle of nature, and the power of moving forces.... All his canvases have the sparkle and vitality of living matter."[17]

But Henri also approached an important idea in his urban views: the dynamism of modern city life. As Bruce Chambers has written, "Henri's subject is the idea of the city energized and in flux," not a record of urban variety and life.[18] Henri's students and followers seized the idea with greater vigor and carried it further; for example, John Sloan and George Luks both painted dramatic views of New York (Figure 64).[19] Two artists in particular made such scenes central to their work: Van Dearing Perrine managed to find a natural wilderness adjacent to New York City, while George Bellows saw the working technology of the city as a kind of natural force.

Born on the raw prairie of Kansas in 1869 and orphaned in childhood, Perrine's early life was a appalling saga of destitution. Determined to become an artist, in 1896 he moved to New York and studied at the Cooper Institute and the National Academy of Design. In 1902 he moved to the foot of the Palisades, where he lived until 1922, making that landscape his special territory. After his marriage in 1911, he became more interested in theories of color. He began to paint brightly flecked canvases of children playing amidst flowers and trees, reflecting the growth of his family. In 1931 he became an Associate of the National Academy. Perrine seems to have taught for much of his later career and died in obscurity in New Canaan, Connecticut.[20]

The Palisades are a geological wonder, which despite almost two centuries of quarrying and dynamiting, still retain (at a distance) their pristine nature and their power to astonish. Great, sheer cliffs of basalt on the New Jersey side of the Hudson, they line the shore opposite Manhattan. The Palisades are only a short boat ride away from Manhattan, but few sensible New Yorkers make the trip. Perrine, both country-born and country-minded, found in his little shack at the base of the cliffs as rugged and remote an environment as Prout's Neck—worse, because he had no summer resort next door. The natives, Hudson rivermen, were every bit as colorful and rustic as Maine fishermen, entirely

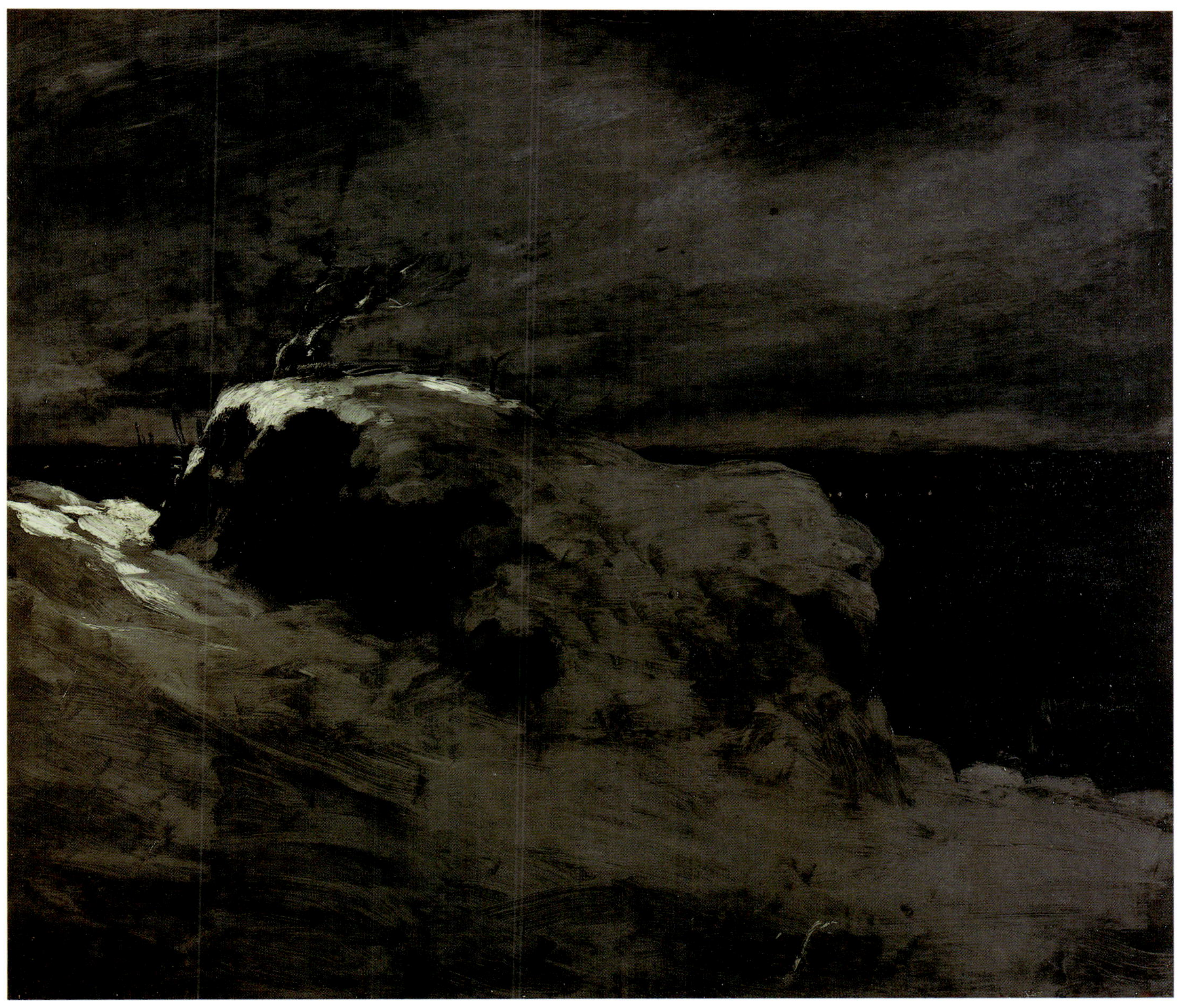

65. Perrine. *Bleak Winter,* ca. 1905.

untouched by the big city across the river. Perrine lived like an impoverished hermit (although friends visited frequently), achieving a life much like the myth of Homer's, only more severe because it was real. He wrote of the Palisades: "Their bigness— immensity—ruggedness appealed to something in my own nature. I tried to use the cliffs as symbols of the vast stubborn struggle of life, the immense grind, the immense upheaval, the eternal and silent combat that is typified by these crags that have pitted themselves against the elements and wrestled with the glaciers."[21]

He summed up his philosophy: "Life is contention.... Great obstacles afford great conquest and nature never elects a coward."[22]

Bleak Winter, ca. 1905 (Figure 65), is typical of the work he achieved there. Manhattan has sunk into oblivion in the distance, enveloped in darkness. In the foreground only a stump of a boulder can be seen, drifted over with snow, one small weedy tree struggling above it. The subject and the composition have been reduced to their simplest terms. The paint itself has a Whistlerian tonality, but without small touches of color and texture to relieve the moody spread of somber blue. Little is known about the development of Perrine's style, but his earliest works must have been equally bold. As early as 1899, a critic declared: "For a reckless sincerity in the matter of eyesight, Mr. Perrine would seem to lead, especially in his land and sea work. His largest marine, 'The River in Winter,' was one of the best marines seen in this city for many a day. Winslow Homer would have made a cold, crude monstrosity out of the subject. This man has conquered the proposition at every point."[23]

Henri and Perrine knew each other well during Henri's first years in New York. Not all of Henri's city scenes concentrated on the bustle of the street and buildings; he too could be pastoral amidst the city (although he went no farther than the docks in one direction and Central Park in the other). The similarities between these works and Perrine's suggest an influence running from one to the other—but in which direction it is impossible to tell. Henri's *Snow in Central Park,* 1902 (Figure 66), shares with Perrine's *Bleak Winter* several important elements.[24] In both the bustle of Manhattan is removed to the far background. The foreground has a tonal simplicity and breadth: a single downward sweep of snow, interrupted in Henri's painting only by a few trees, in Perrine's by the boulder. Both evoke a memory of Homer's *Sleigh Ride* (Figure 27). In this case, it is unlikely that either could have known Homer's painting; the similarity arises from the knowledge both artists had of Homer's works, with both moved by the same impulse in front of a similar motif.

George Bellows differs from Perrine in nearly every respect. Born in 1882 in Columbus, he attended Ohio State University, where he was active in a fraternity and athletics. Turning down a career as a professional baseball player, Bellows left at the end of his junior year and went to New York City in 1904. Having taken every art class offered at Ohio State, he learned to become an artist in the New York School of Art. His teacher was Henri.[25]

Bellows' progress was extraordinary. Within two years, he began painting city scenes that rivaled his teacher's. He very quickly learnt to use Henri's slashing brushstroke to convey a sense of a much more substantial energy than Henri's often almost nervous touch. Bellows' city scenes are similarly more dramatic. Not surprisingly, the excavation of Pennsylvania Station in 1907, which was numbered among the great engineering feats of the day, led to one of his most impressive works.

Pennsylvania Station Excavation, 1909 (Figure 67), is the last of several studies of the great pit. Under an extraordinarily blue sky, dark featureless buildings hulk around the great pit out of which a gout of steam rises.[26] In this amphitheater, the giant cranes seem dwarfed: despite being a man-made artifact, the scale of the excavation suggests only natural forces at work. Bellows has transposed Homer's drama of sea opposing land into the city. Instead of water grinding away the rock, with the two forces meeting in the crash of a wave, Bellows gives us an excavation undermining the buildings looming over it, the action of the bulldozer made visible as steam so that the earth seems to escape skyward as vapor.

Bellows was not alone in naturalizing the structures of the city, although more than any other he turned the urban landscape into an elemental, natural one. The central symbol of the city was the skyscraper, which was regarded not merely as a sign of technological progress but was personified as an American male. As one reviewer said of Henri and his followers: "All are men who stand for the American idea. It is the fashion to say the skyscrapers are ugly. It is certain that any of the eight will tell you 'No, the skyscraper is beautiful. Its twenty stories swimming toward you are typical of all that America means, its every line is indicative of our virile young lustiness.'"[27] In a telling comparison, the philosopher George Santayana contrasted the American Will with the American Intellect: one resides in the skyscraper, the other in "a neat reproduction of the colonial mansion." The reference to decorative, old-fashioned styles in art was deliberate. Santayana added: "The one is the sphere of the American man;

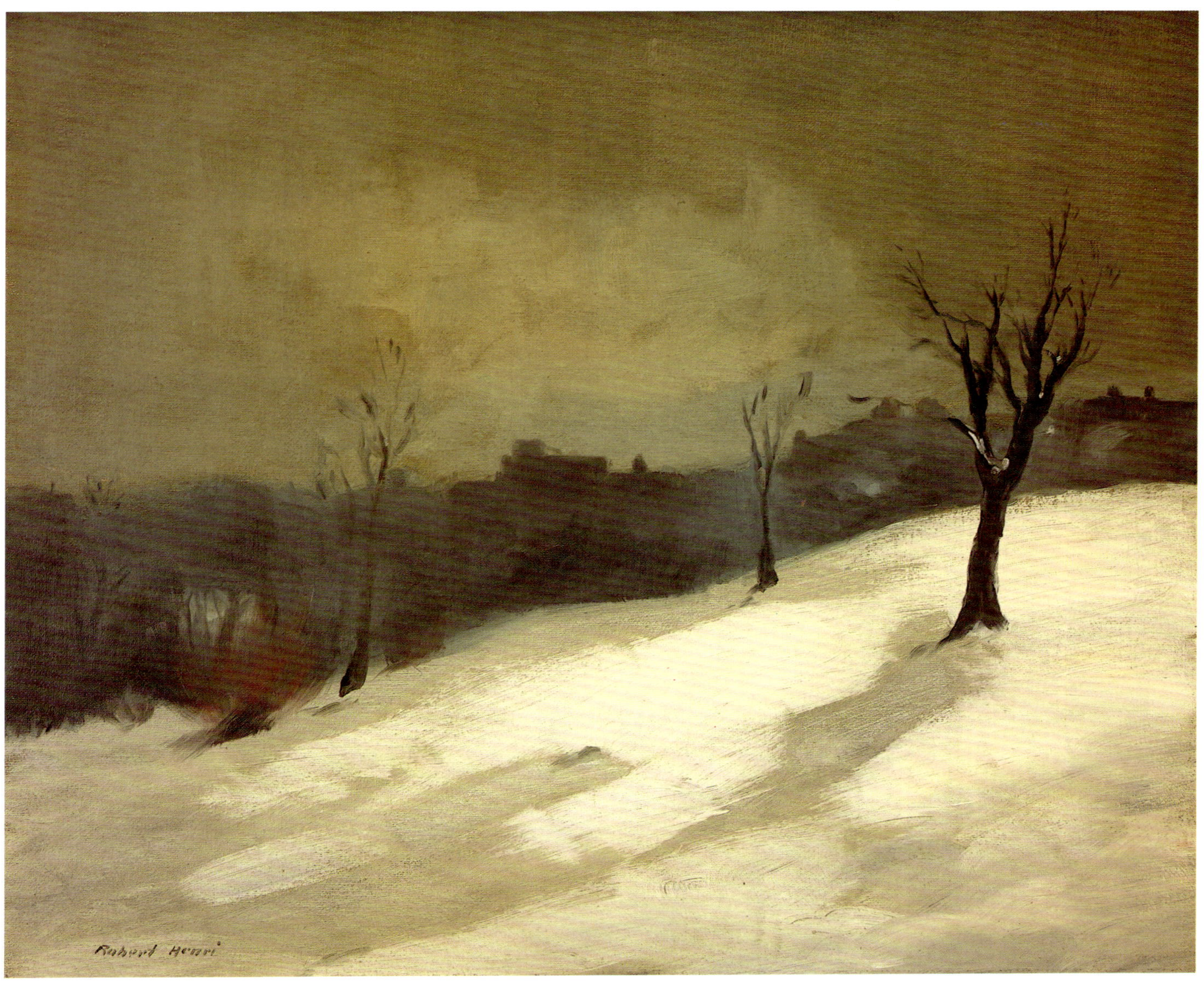

66. Henri. *Snow in Central Park,* 1902.

the other, at least predominantly, of the American woman. The one is all aggressive enterprise; the other is all genteel tradition."[28] To carry these metaphors to their conclusion, the skyscraper (the symbol of the modern city) was the epitome of manliness, which—we know from other contexts—is crude, vigorous, a pioneer in the wilderness; the real American man above all belongs to the great outdoors. Within this locus of masculinity could also be found the art of Winslow Homer. The leap from the drama of Prout's Neck to the drama of the new engineering

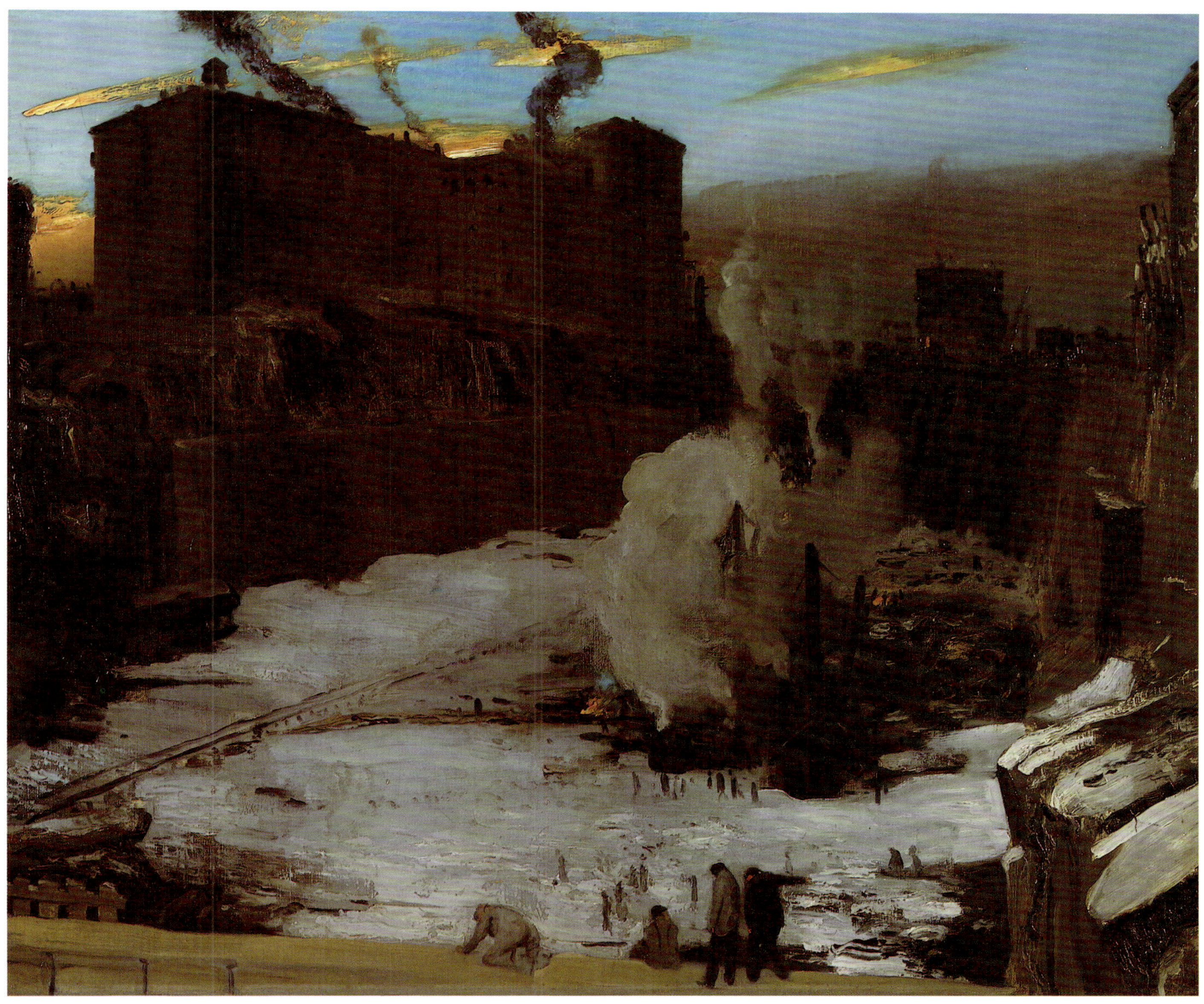

67. Bellows. *Pennsylvania Station Excavation,* 1909.

marvels of Manhattan was instinctive and natural for Bellows, a virile artist painting manly subjects.

Lewis Hind, despite misgivings, articulated the connection clearly, on seeing paintings by Homer and Bellows together for the first time in Berlin in 1910: "Something of Winslow Homer's force I find in the work of George Bellows, in his *Bridge* arching the indigo water, rough, frank, original, true, a large sketch, a quick impression that has been left as seen, not worried into an exhibition picture."[29] The key word is *force.* The single most

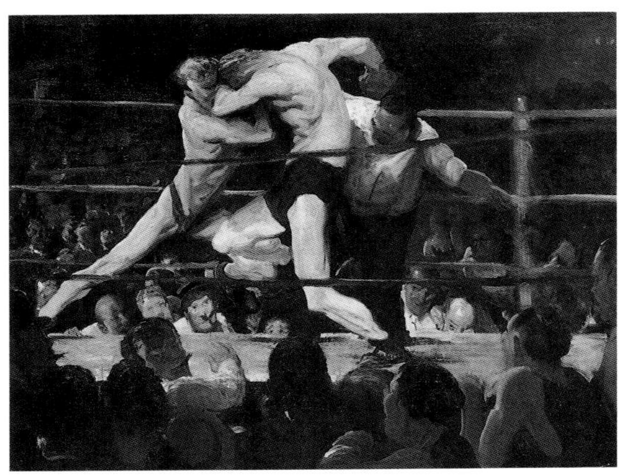

68. Bellows. *Stag at Sharkey's,* 1909.

69. Bellows. *Polo at Lakewood,* 1910.

important point of similarity was Bellows' vigor and interest in dynamic action. As other critics wrote: "Bellows ... is primarily an artist of energy," "He was in love with force," and "A typical American, loving dynamics above all things, as most Americans of the moment do ... sharing the widespread American love of action."[30] The drama of opposing forces—the fundamental action of Homer's marines—also attracted Bellows to sports, as it had drawn Homer to hunting subjects. *Stag at Sharkey's,* 1909 (Figure 68), and his other boxing pictures are the most famous examples: two brutal men, pitted against each other like animals, battling with evenly matched force in a fight with no victors. Less brutal were the next sporting pictures he completed, a series of polo matches observed on the estate of Jay Gould. In *Polo at Lakewood,* 1910 (Figure 69), the element of landscape has been introduced and the action somewhat dispersed. The horses and riders of the two teams roll against each other like waves, cresting in a peak of mallets thrashing down at the ball, the horses almost colliding in the force of the encounter. The spectators are safely shepherded behind the rail; in the sky, rain clouds lower. Both in its essential, headlong action and its pictorial construction, the painting seems inspired by Homer's works such as

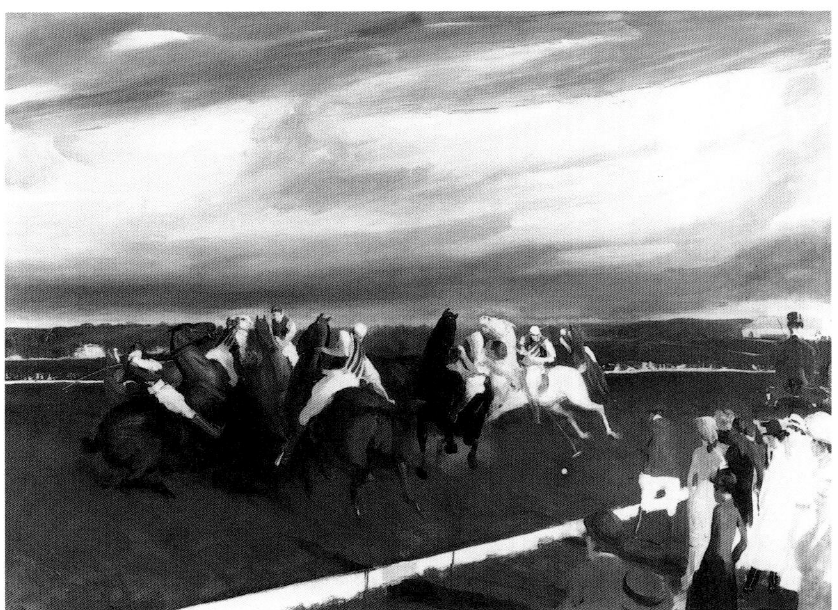

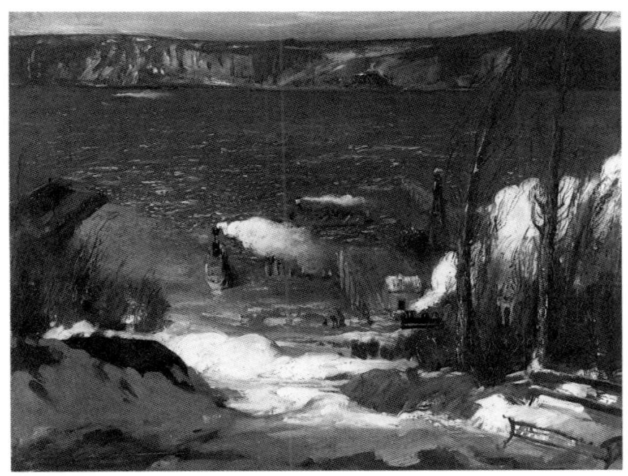

70. Bellows. *North River,* 1908.

Northeaster (Figure 16). In both, the foreground slices the picture plane at a diagonal while the waves churn and break beyond, under dark skies.

One further point of comparison with Homer was also evident in the first pictures of New York and its environs: Bellows loved winter. Writing to a friend one year he complained: "There has been none of my favorite snow. I must allways [*sic*] paint the snow at least twice a year."[31] While scenes of winter were popular with many artists, Bellows seemed to attack snow differently.[32] *North River,* 1908, and the other paintings of the Hudson, such as *Winter Afternoon (Riverside Park, New York City),* 1909, and *Blue Snow, the Battery,* 1910 (Figures 70-72), were singled out for praise because of their strength.[33] The space and the forms in them are simple and large; no sinuous curves, only straight, clean blocks of river, paths, and snow. Winter is not made pretty; it is striking. The snow is hard and bright; the sun etches the shadows distinctly blue.

Henri achieved a similar sense of drama in his landscapes consistently only for a short period, and not in New York. For him the connection with Homer's work was made much more obviously, in Maine.[34] After his first one-man exhibition in New York,

71. Bellows. *Winter Afternoon (Riverside Park, New York City),* 1909.

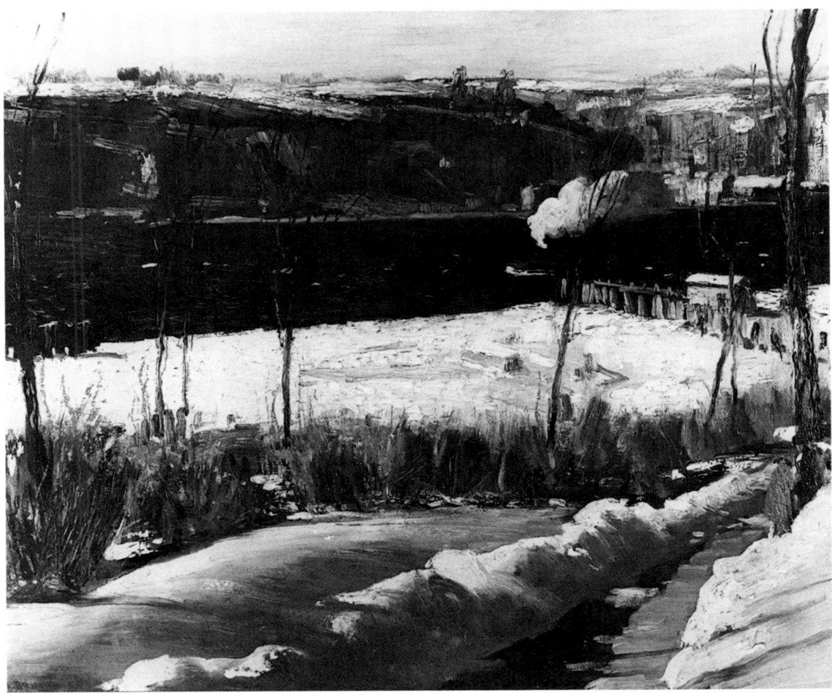

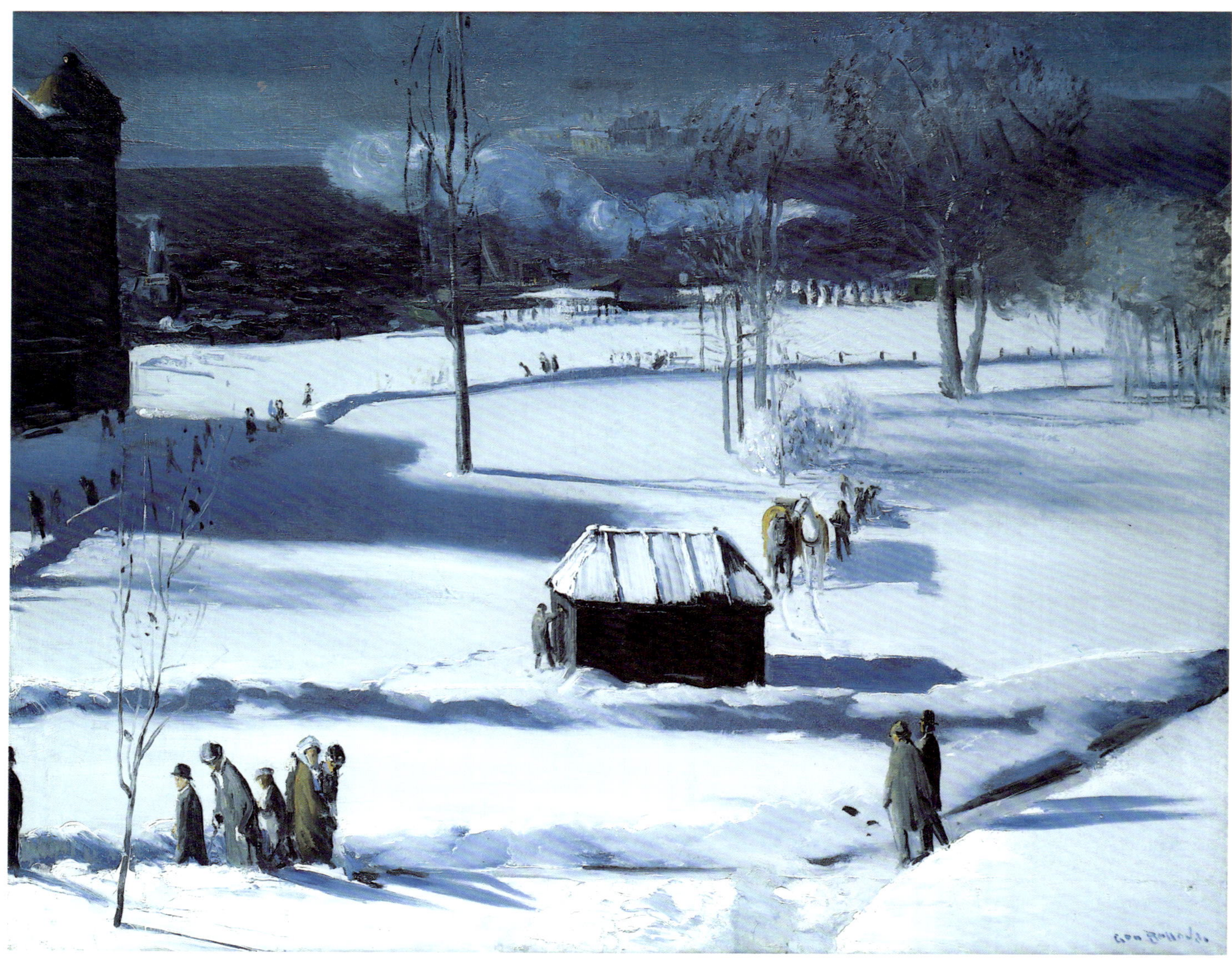

72. Bellows. *Blue Snow, The Battery,* 1910.

in which he hoped to reproduce the success of *La Niege* by including similar urban scenes of New York, Henri had gone to Walnut Creek in western Pennsylvania to spend the summer with his wife near her family. For the first time he spent an extended period painting the rural American landscape. Although primarily a farming area, the massive hills and the uninterrupted expanse of the sky (as well as the quantity of storms that seem to have passed overhead that summer) led him to confront nature on a grand scale. With no activity on the ground to distract him, and no buildings to detract from the drama of the sky, he confronted the forces that Homer had painted. The next summer Henri went

73. Henri. *Rolling Sea,* 1903.

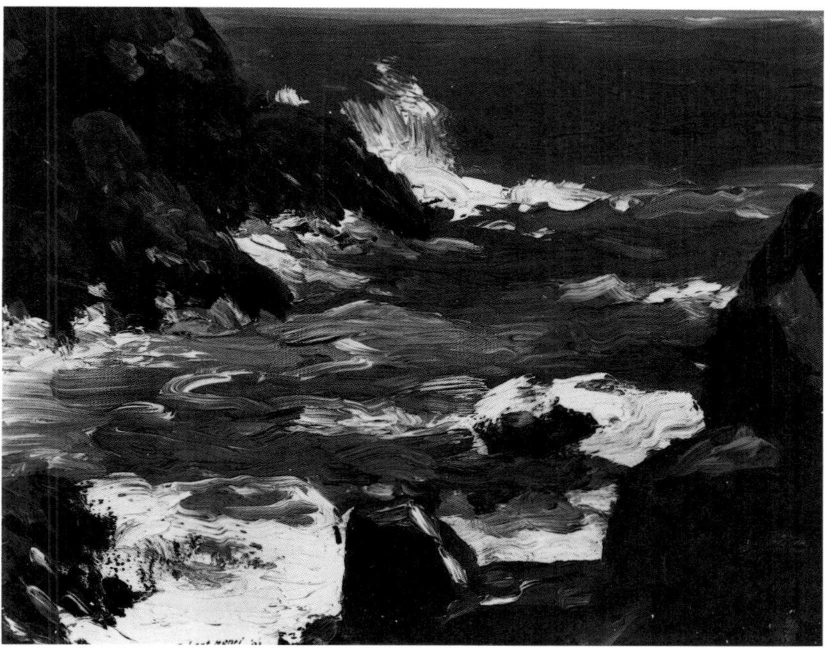

to Maine, to Boothbay Harbor and Monhegan Island.

On Monhegan he seems, as always, to have defined specific motifs that he pursued assiduously: he ignored the boats for the most part but painted the woods in the heart of the island. His primary subject, however, became the rocks at the base of the cliffs on the east side. In a letter to his mother, Henri wrote "Yesterday the surf was real Monhegan and we got a lot of sketches that I think good surf pictures."[35] Homer's influence was inescapable and deliberately explored. *Rolling Sea* (Figure 73), typical of the small panels he painted, is obviously Homeric.[36] Henri wrote later: "Look at a Homer seascape. There is order in it and grand formation. It produces on your mind the whole vastness of the sea, a vastness as impressive and as uncontrollable as the sea itself. You are made to feel the force of the sea, the resistance of the rock; the whole thing is an integrity of nature."[37]

The change was noted immediately. In an article entitled "Six Impressionists, Startling Works by Red-Hot American Painters," the critic for *The New York Times* wrote: "Mr. Henri has some bold marines and landscapes, thick in impasto, such as 'Cliff and Sea' where the water is intensely alive, while the rocks are characterless."[38] After his second trip to Monhegan, another reviewer commented:

"The paintings are all done with the utmost simplicity ... gathering up and representing the essentials of character in people or nature.... And all of this bigness of effect and beauty were [*sic*] accomplished in a series of very small paintings."[39] Although Henri was obviously proud of them—reproducing *Rocks and Sea* in an article he wrote[40]—he did not develop these Homeric subjects very far, devoting most of his time thereafter to the exploration of character in people. His students, however, did.

Henri's Students and Friends: Rockwell Kent, George Bellows, Leon Kroll, George Luks, and Edward Hopper

The first of Robert Henri's students to follow him to Monhegan was Rockwell Kent, in June 1905. Henri himself returned in 1911, with Bellows and Randall Davey, two more pupils. In later years scores more visited, establishing an art colony which to this day evokes the spirit of its founders in depictions of the wild surf and imposing cliffs.

Rockwell Kent came from a family that had arrived in America in the seventeenth century, spreading from New England to Ohio. He was born in New York, his father dying only a few years later. Growing up in genteel poverty, he and his family were dependent on the haphazard generosity of relatives. Although proud of his American roots and family background, at the same time Kent ferociously defended his independence from them.[1]

Entering Columbia University in 1900 to study architecture, Kent soon discovered he wanted to be a painter instead. He had spent several summers studying with William Merritt Chase at Shinnecock, Long Island, and in the spring of 1902, entered Henri's night class at the New York School. By the end of the year Kent had given up architecture. During the summer of 1903 he studied with Abbott Handerson Thayer (1849-1921) in Dublin, New Hampshire. Becoming close to the whole family, a few years later Kent married Thayer's niece.

The most important decision of Kent's career—striking out on his own to Monhegan—was made because of Robert Henri. Kent spent the best part of the next six years there, including several winters, working as a carpenter and lobsterman. He built houses for himself and his mother (separated by half of the island), and his own studio. He became one of the islanders as much as possible (even to the extent of getting Janet, a fisherman's daughter, in the family way). And he painted furiously. Furthermore, Kent's stay on Monhegan set the pattern for his life. Every few years he would escape from his family by going north, to the most

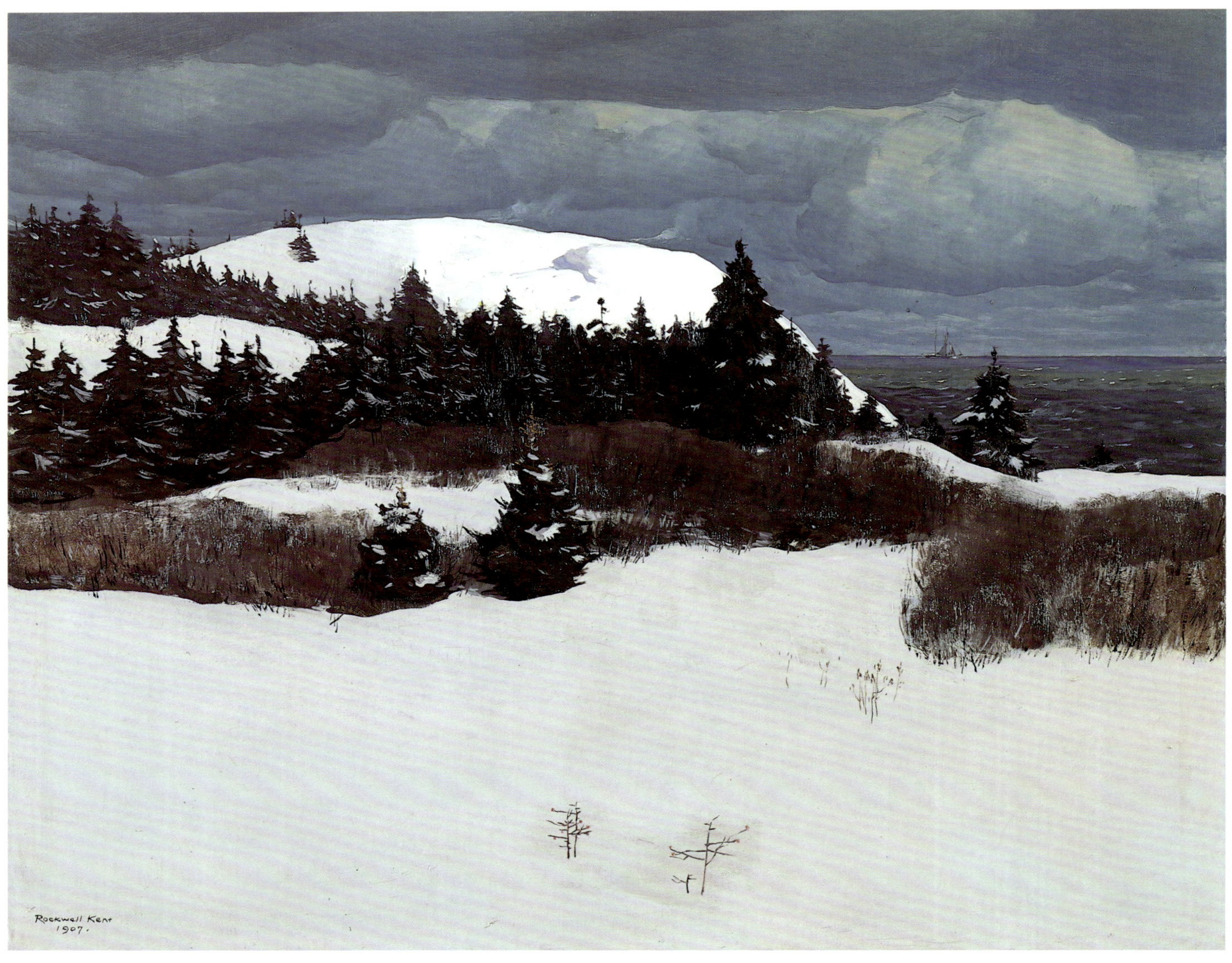

74. Kent. *Maine Coast,* 1907.

isolated communities he could find: Newfoundland, Alaska, Labrador, Greenland (or to the extreme south, Tierra del Fuego). There he would insinuate himself into the lives of the natives and paint, returning to New York with stories and a fund of images and paintings, staying until the need to escape grew strong again.

The first exhibition of his Monhegan landscapes was held in 1907. It won rave reviews from critics and artists. Both Sloan and Bellows responded favorably. Sloan wrote in his diary: "These pictures are of immense Rocks and Seas in fair weather and in winter. Splendid big thoughts. Some like big prayers to God. I enjoyed them to the utmost and accept them as great. I'd like to

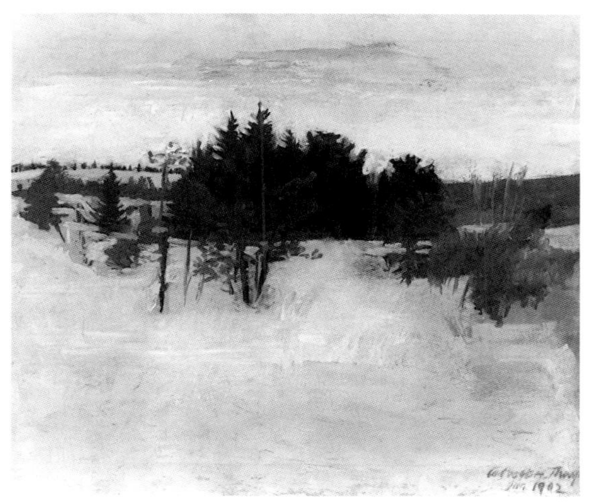

75. Thayer. *Winter Landscape,* 1902.

buy some of them." And Bellows said: "Each [of Kent's paintings] is for itself. They are not decorations for a wall but works of art, expressions of powerful ideas which have not the least thing in the world to do with decorating the home."[2] Over the years the critics agreed. Kent had a "big grip on essentials. But rough paint, crude paint, very rough paint!"[3] Another wrote: "I find, too, something elementally American in Rockwell Kent's *Evening on the Coast of Maine,* the blue-white snow rightly seen, the whole picture a big, simple statement."[4] The adjectives were the same as those applied to Homer, and before long the comparison was made explicitly: "Henri's students are producing results—big results—many of them. One young man, Rockwell Kent, is already doing shorescapes and marines that are being favorably compared with the paintings of Winslow Homer, our greatest living delineator of the life of the open."[5] In fact, Kent seems consciously to have emulated Homer, in both his life and his paintings.[6] His strenuous pursuit of seafaring adventures and solitary vigils in frozen wastes would seem to be an extreme version of Homer's retreat to Prout's Neck.

Despite being a devoted student of Henri's during this period, Kent was never strongly influenced by his style. Kent's work always had a crisp edge to it, with his brushstroke respecting the limits of large, simple forms, which in turn were arranged primarily as flat planes rather than dynamic, space-producing forces. He once wrote: "What in the world has happened to mankind that *soft*—soft lines, soft colors, soft effects—means excellence?"[7] His early paintings often revealed Thayer's influence. For example, *Maine Coast,* 1907 (Figure 74) (painted from his studio window on Monhegan looking toward Whitehead, one of the two large cliffs on the east side of the island), was derived from Thayer's views of the area of Mount Monadnock (Figure 75). But Kent's response to Monhegan also reveals the effect of Winslow Homer's works.[8]

Unlike Henri, who carefully selected a variety of picturesque subjects to paint at Monhegan, Kent concentrated on two quintessential Homeric themes: winter and the fisherman. *Maine Coast,* while most like Thayer stylistically, also has several touches of Homer about it. Besides its bleakness and lowering skies, which give the landscape a forcefulness alien to Thayer's aesthetic, a specific decorative note seems lifted from *Fox Hunt* (Figure 29):

76. Kent. *Blackhead, Monhegan,* ca. 1909.

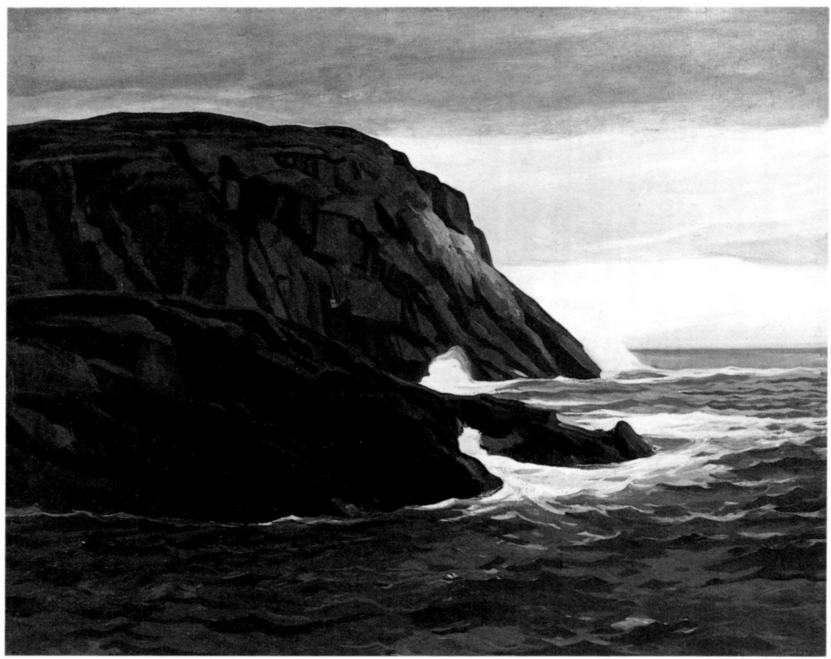

the red twigs in the foreground could be a direct quotation of the red berries and stems in Homer's painting. Kent's *Blackhead, Monhegan,* ca. 1909 (Figure 76), recalls such paintings as *High Cliffs* and *Coast of Maine,* in their perspective and reduction of the landscape to large simple forms. In *Toilers of the Sea,* 1907 (Figure 77), with its single fisherman straining at the oars of the dory, Kent seems to remember the lone fisherman of *The Fog Warning* (Figure 34). In nearly every instance, however, Kent has deemphasized the drama. The colors are stronger and brighter, and there are few touches of broken color.

Like Bellows, Kent's winter scenes have a brilliant zest, as though he had rolled back the clouds over Homer's snowbound and foggy coasts. Kent loved the dazzle and hardness of light reflecting off pure white snow. *Snow Fields (Winter in the Berkshires),* 1909 (Figure 78), makes these differences with Homer clear. While in Homer's *Below Zero* two figures mutely ponder the scene, in Kent's painting a family plays joyfully in the snow. Although the figures, two women and four children, with two dogs dashing about them, may depict his neighbors and family, it is possible that they reflect Kent's wishful thinking. At the time he painted *Snow Fields,* he had just married Kathleen Whiting. He later wrote: "So loving [the Berkshire landscape], loving the glare of sunlight on the snow, loving the blue shadows, loving the forms that cast them and the deeps of space their blue reflected, loving that world in sunshine and under clouds, loving all the world and life and Kathleen, I painted."[9] But, although full of love for her and his home, Kent still had not given up his affair with Janet on Monhegan. The winter landscape has the special clarity of a vision, untroubled by nagging realities; Kent seems to project two happy families onto his canvas, with himself as husband and father of both, in a burst of confidence after his honeymoon. The somber materials of Homer's world have been turned on their head through the power of love.

In later years, after Kent had left Maine far behind and even as his style hardened under his infatuation with the art of William Blake, the Homeric influence abided. For many years pictures of fishermen and the women waiting for them on the shore dominated his *oeuvre. Driftwood Alaska,* 1919 (Figure 79), is perhaps the most symbolically dramatic example, in which the stoic waiting fisherwoman found in Homer's paintings now recoils in grief from the wreck.[10]

The poles of Kent's art were his passionate identifications with the North and with the working class. He ennobled hard labor and suffering in his art, identifying class struggle not with the urban proletariat but with the honest peasant. In this, as in so many other ways, Kent's loyalties were romantically inspired. In 1904 he became a Socialist and remained a dedicated member of the party for the rest of his life. On his way to Newfoundland in 1910 (leaving his wife and children behind with the Sloans), he wrote to John and Dolly Sloan: "I changed my personality from that of a cultured young tourist to the rough and ready type of American working-man. And right there is the experience. For the first time in my life I have been able to play that role successfully. They're really a foreign people here, a good crowd and friendly." He added, describing a trip into a coal mine, "I have planned to come back here some day and get a job underground. It is an experience that I covet."[11] The simultaneous self-abnegation and self-glorification inherent in these impulses, along with the asceticism and denial of physical comfort dominating much of his life, were all trials of his manhood. Kent faced the harshest nature alone, as one of the people, without any of the defenses

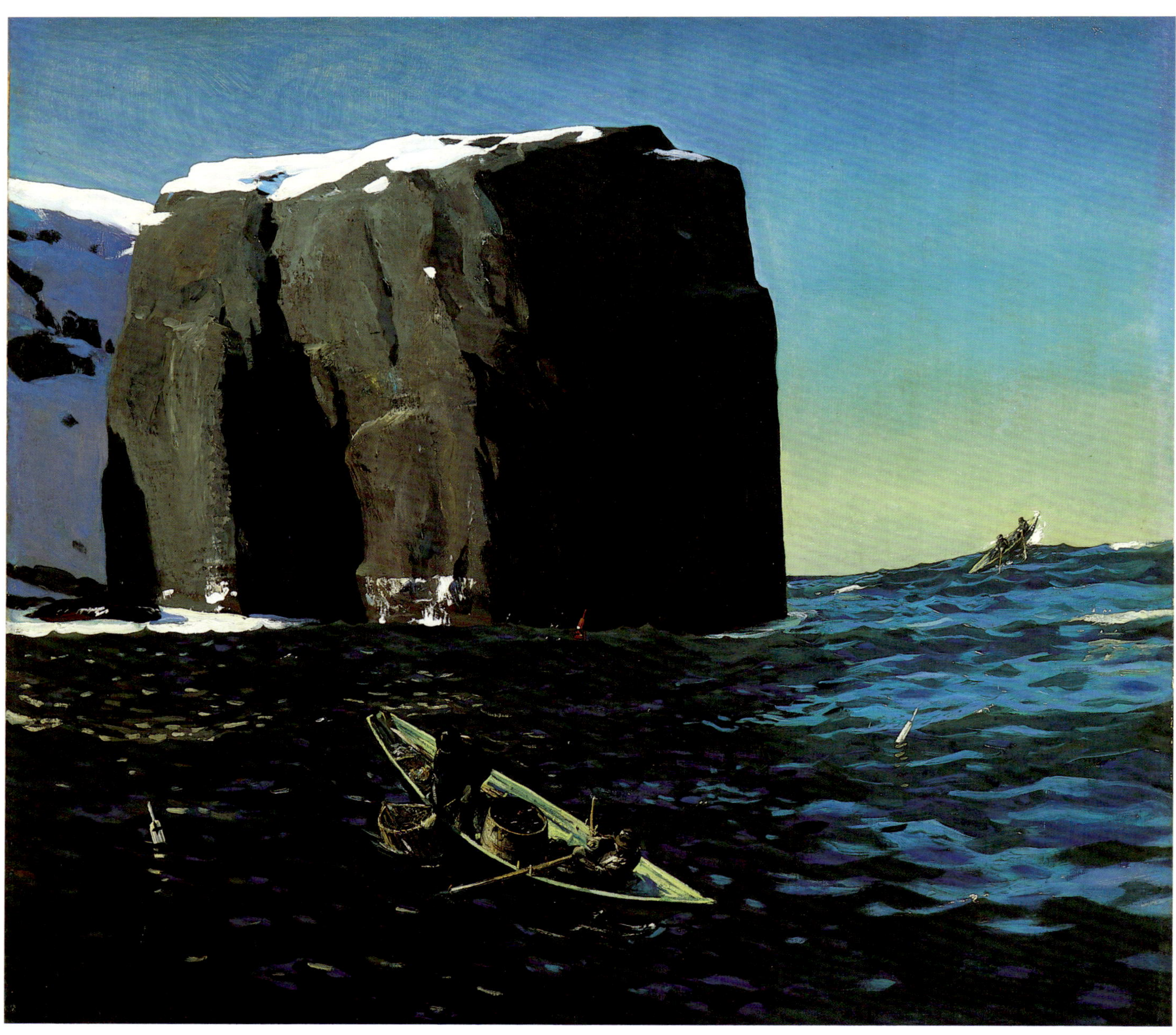

77. Kent. *Toilers on the Sea,* 1907.

and artifices of civilization to ameliorate the conditions of his life. To an almost frightening degree, Kent carried out the mythic quest of isolating himself in a forbidding landscape to confront nature on her terms, a quest exemplified in Homer's art (if not quite in his life).

Bellows followed Kent to Monhegan as soon as Kent had left for the far north. He arrived with Robert Henri and Randall Davey in July 1911. While the other two worked slowly and

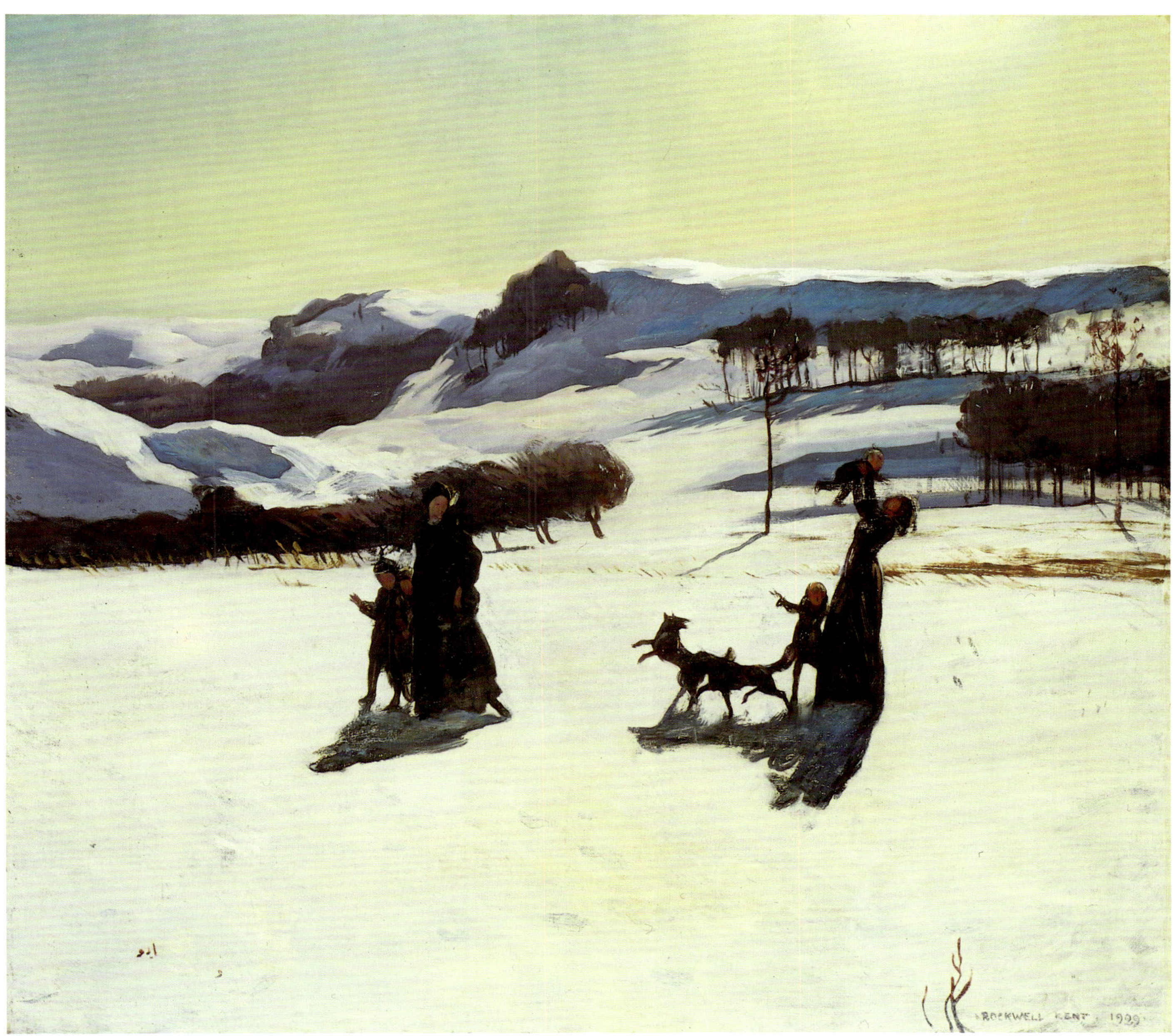

78. Kent. *Snow Fields (Winter in the Berkshires)*, 1909.

fitfully, Bellows completed thirty panels and twelve canvases in an immense release of energy during his first sustained period of pure landscape painting. Like Henri and Kent before him, Bellows was ecstatic at the variety of the landscape and the drama of the surf. "This is the most wonderful country ever modeled by the hand of the master architect," he wrote his wife Emma. "The island is only a mile wide and two miles long, but it looks as large as the Rocky Mountains."[12] However, unlike Henri and Davey,

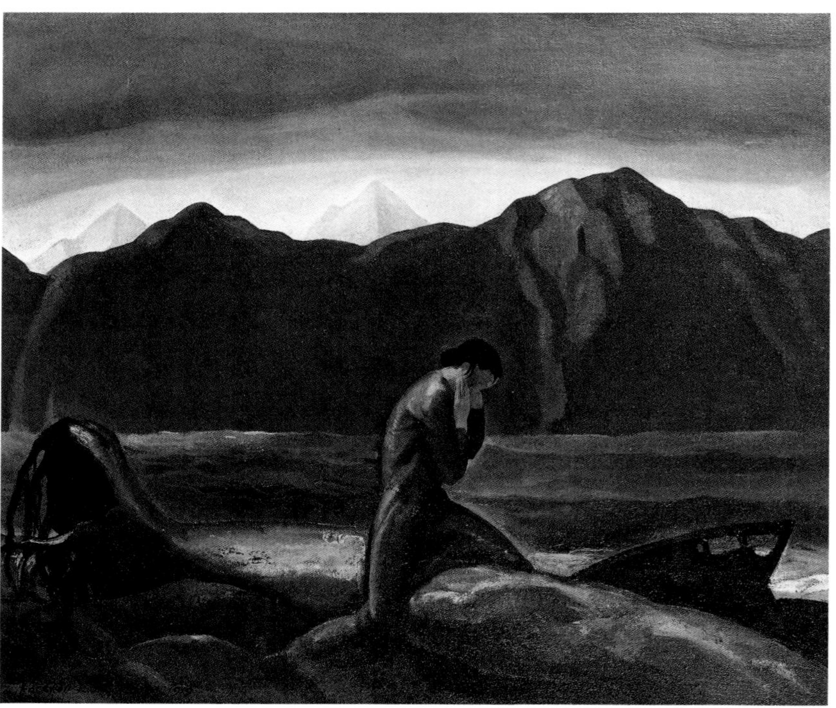

79. Kent. *Driftwood, Alaska,* 1919.

Bellows focused wholeheartedly on the ocean, not the land.

Bellows arrived in Monhegan with his absent wife very much on his mind. He had been married less than a year before, and Emma was nearly ready to give birth. Placed before the expanse of the ocean, his libidinous nature opened up. He compared the island to Montauk, where they had honeymooned the year before; and his thoughts returned to Emma with great intensity: "In your condition the thing I've got for you will endanger your life. I am virulent strong, brimming with the sturdy North. and I've got it bad." In a more romantic mood he imagined himself with her:

> *If you were with me we could tramp the wild places all day and night and be alone together again; and sit by the sea in the night wind; and watch the moon lay a silver carpet over the ocean. We could slip over the velvet covered rocks down at the Sea's brink and watch the waves reach for us, and you could laugh at me for being timid and afraid of those crystal green hands which are so clean and cold. And everything I spoke to you would be about love and beauty and love again and the greatness of this nature which is in*

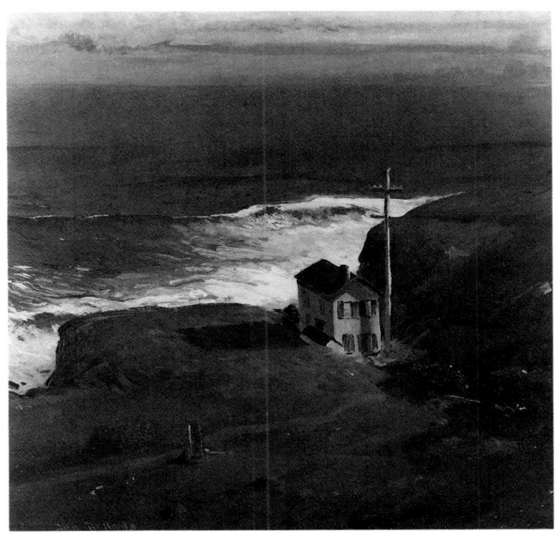

80. Bellows. *Shore House,* 1911.

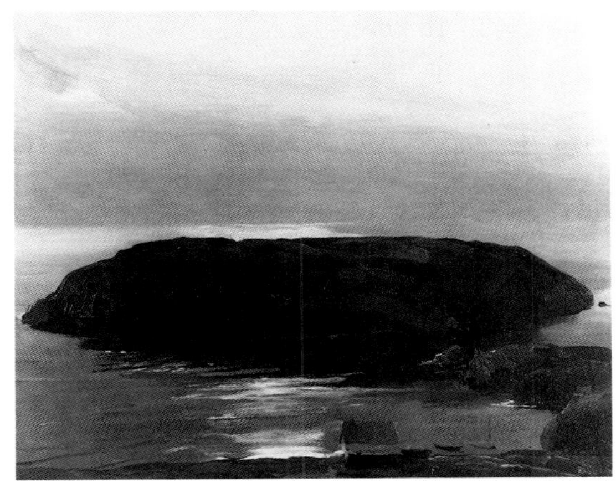

81. Bellows. *An Island in the Sea,* 1911.

us. We two and the great sea and the mighty rocks greater than the sea, and we two greater than the rocks and sea. Four eternities.[13]

In this daydream, Bellows pared his life to its essentials: he and Emma, and the world of nature, four Eternities and four Verities. The progress and situation were significant in Bellows' imagination, moving from the two of them to the threatening sea, then to the solid land, and finally back to them. He personalized the sea, and expressed some sexual anxiety (the little green hands are siren hands, and Emma laughs at him), but ultimately, as he worked his way through the fantasy, he returned to certainty: the rock and the pair of them.

Three further texts may be adduced to delineate further Bellows' personalized fascination with the ocean. In a letter to Henri during his second visit in 1913, Bellows presented himself in a misogynist mood. He feminized nature and art, and disowned both. He complained of being surrounded:

by that hag of a sea, ... low crone of a wind, ... capricious inconstant coquette of a light, and that indelicate wanton of a breeze.... I sickened of these insidious feminine seductions—yawned and came back home. Yes, since 'Art' has enthralled, she's begun to treat me as inconsiderately as if I were her lawful husband.... Gee! this wedded life is awful! I sometimes regret not having received the legal sanction of the National Academy, as then I would have a certificate. or an N.A. or something.... You're right about that "native nymph of Monhegan"—there aint no such person.[14]

The advance and retreat of his emotions toward womankind were also expressed in his paintings. In *Shore House,* 1911 (Figure 80), the work commemorating his honeymoon on Long Island, he painted a lonely cottage by the sea; in *An Island in the Sea,* 1911 (Figure 81), which he painted as a pair to *Shore House,* the cottage has been replaced by a small island: the house has now been put out to sea, isolated completely from the land.[15] The island Bellows depicted is Manana, which lies a few feet off the

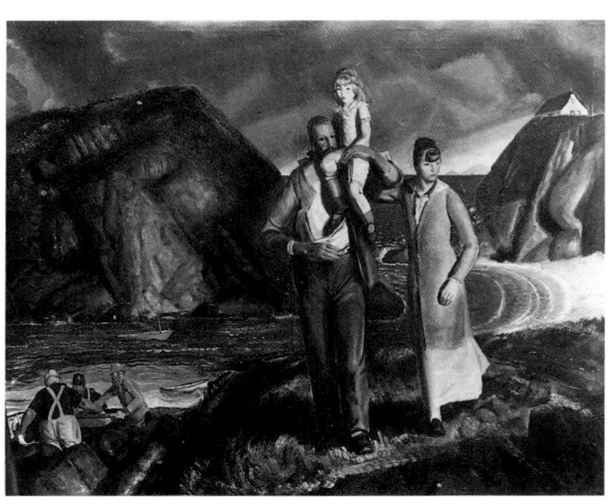

82. Bellows. *The Fisherman's Family,* 1923.

harbor of Monhegan (it can also be seen in Kent's *Winter, Monhegan Island,* 1907; see Figure 104); Bellows has exaggerated its smallness, displacing it into the ocean, to enhance the effect of isolation and alienation. The symbols of his matrimony have been rendered inconsequential before the timelessness of the sea.

On the other hand, Bellows' ultimate statements of man's relationship to the sea were much more positive. In *The Fisherman's Family* (first painted in 1914, destroyed in 1919, and repainted in 1923), he depicted himself, Emma, and their daughter on Monhegan as heroic figures (Figure 82). Naturalized as a fisherman's family, they are both at home on the island and standing above it, dominating the sea that threatens to eat away the land. Another painting, *The Fisherman* (Figure 83), done on the West Coast during a visit to Carmel in 1917, is almost his last statement of man's relation to the ocean. At the edge of the rocks and the waves, a situation where Homer either painted no one or placed the figures well back from the water, Bellows painted a man, his feet planted firmly, his back arched, pulling up out of the water, withstanding those forces tearing at the land as though he were the land itself come to life and resisting. In contrast, in *A Light on the Sea* (Figure 39), Homer's last juxtaposition of the heroic figure and the sea, the woman is a passive and ambiguous figure. As in any comparison with Homer, Bellows seems almost loud in his assertion of certainty. That is why such paintings as *Shore House* and *An Island in the Sea* are so remarkable, because they expose uncertainty. It is significant that it should be marriage and the ocean that made him experience doubt.

Bellows' immediate and enduring response, however, was much more typically straightforward. Excited always by displays of energy, the power of the ocean as it smashed against the rocks and base of the cliffs of Whitehead and Blackhead seems to have driven him almost to a frenzy of activity. Scores of panels of the water and the rocks flowed from his brush. He proudly recorded the numbers his second season: 135 canvases and panels.

Bellows' full-scale paintings from his first season on Monhegan, in 1911, are a more careful summation of the island, where it is obvious that he was trying to step around the example of his predecessors as much as he was painting Monhegan. *Evening Swell,* 1911 (Figure 88), is obviously circumscribed by

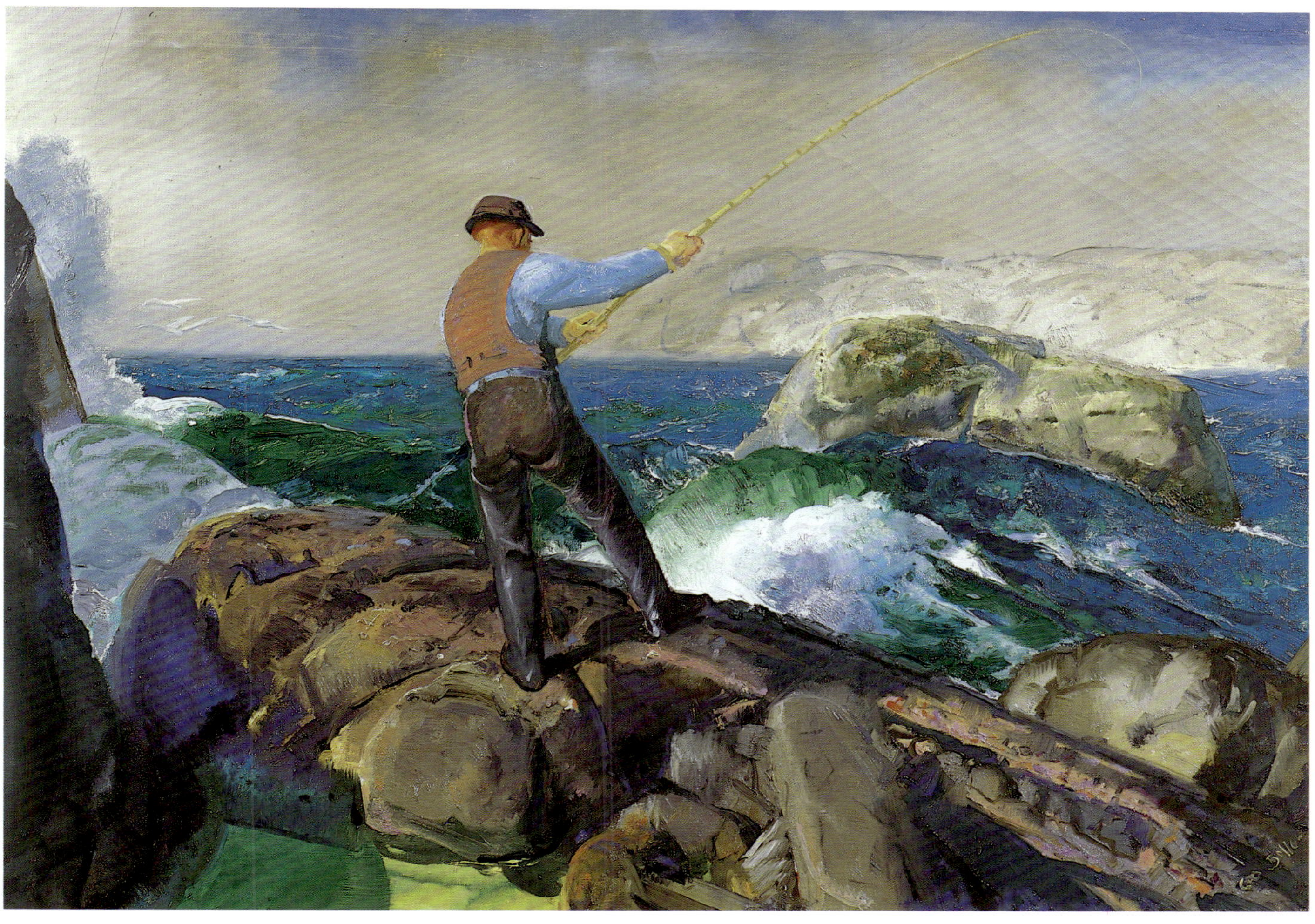

83. Bellows. *The Fisherman,* 1917.

Bellows' memory of Kent's *Toilers on the Sea* (Figure 77). In contrast, *The Sea,* 1911 (Figure 89), is imbued with the memory of such Homer paintings as *Summer Squall* (Figure 36). By 1913 Bellows' response was much more direct and powerful. Kent's careful brushstroke and decorative value contrasts were forgotten, as Bellows wrestled with the ocean and his true master, Homer. The paintings of Monhegan by Kent and Bellows both have simple forms, but where Kent tried to create a sense of volume through contrasts of value, Bellows simply energized the masses of rocks and water through his brushstrokes. *Churn and Break, Green Breaker, Tumble of Waters,* and *From Rock Top, Monhegan* (Figures 84-87) are only a small sampling from 1913. Again and again, Bellows returned to the Homeric situation of a wedge of rock and the water boiling over it, an "invocation to energy and

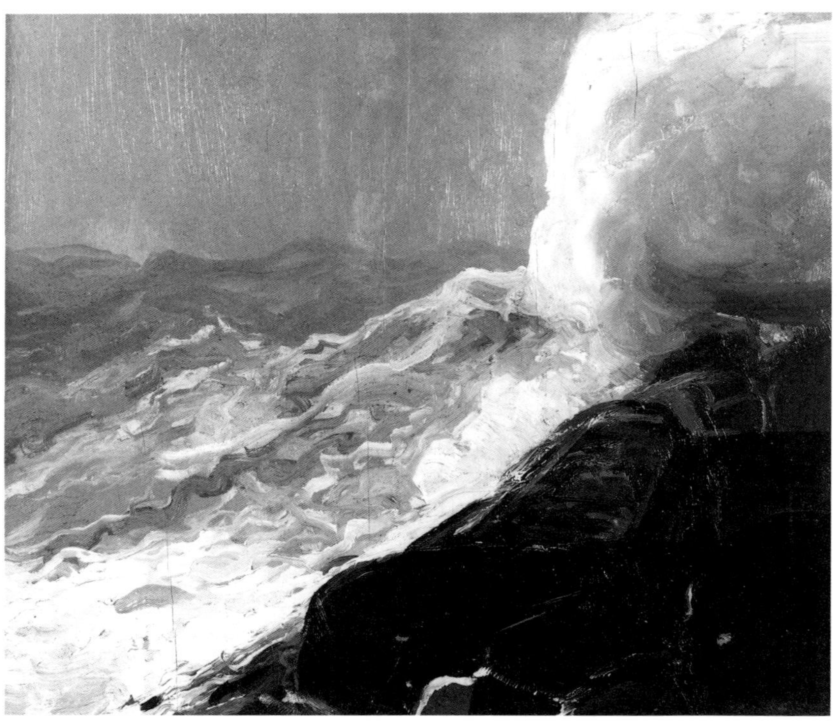

84. Bellows. *Churn and Break,* 1913.

action,"[16] painting it obsessively under changing light and at different angles. Few large paintings resulted from these sketches; experiencing and recording the furious surf seems to have been sufficient in itself.

Although Bellows depicted the forcefulness of the waves vigorously, unlike Kent he made no attempt to live as stormily or prove his manhood by testing the waters himself. The most dramatic experience Bellows had on the ocean came after leaving Monhegan for the last time. In 1916 he and his family stayed in Camden, Maine. One day, as they were all out in a small boat with Leon Kroll, a sudden squall came up, and Bellows beat a hasty retreat to the shore. To hear him tell it, it was a narrow escape: "I painted the thing as an epic of terrific nature and tried to express the fear of it all."[17] The painting title, *In a Rowboat,* 1916 (Figure 90), however, is relatively undramatic. Bellows has pulled his punches, skirting the danger to his family. Instead of rendering the drama of Homer's *The Fog Warning* (Figure 34), the painting is closer to *Cape Trinity, Saguenay River* (Figure 37), the certainty of the shore holds the boat comfortably in its visual field. The composition of the hulking cliff which occupies half the

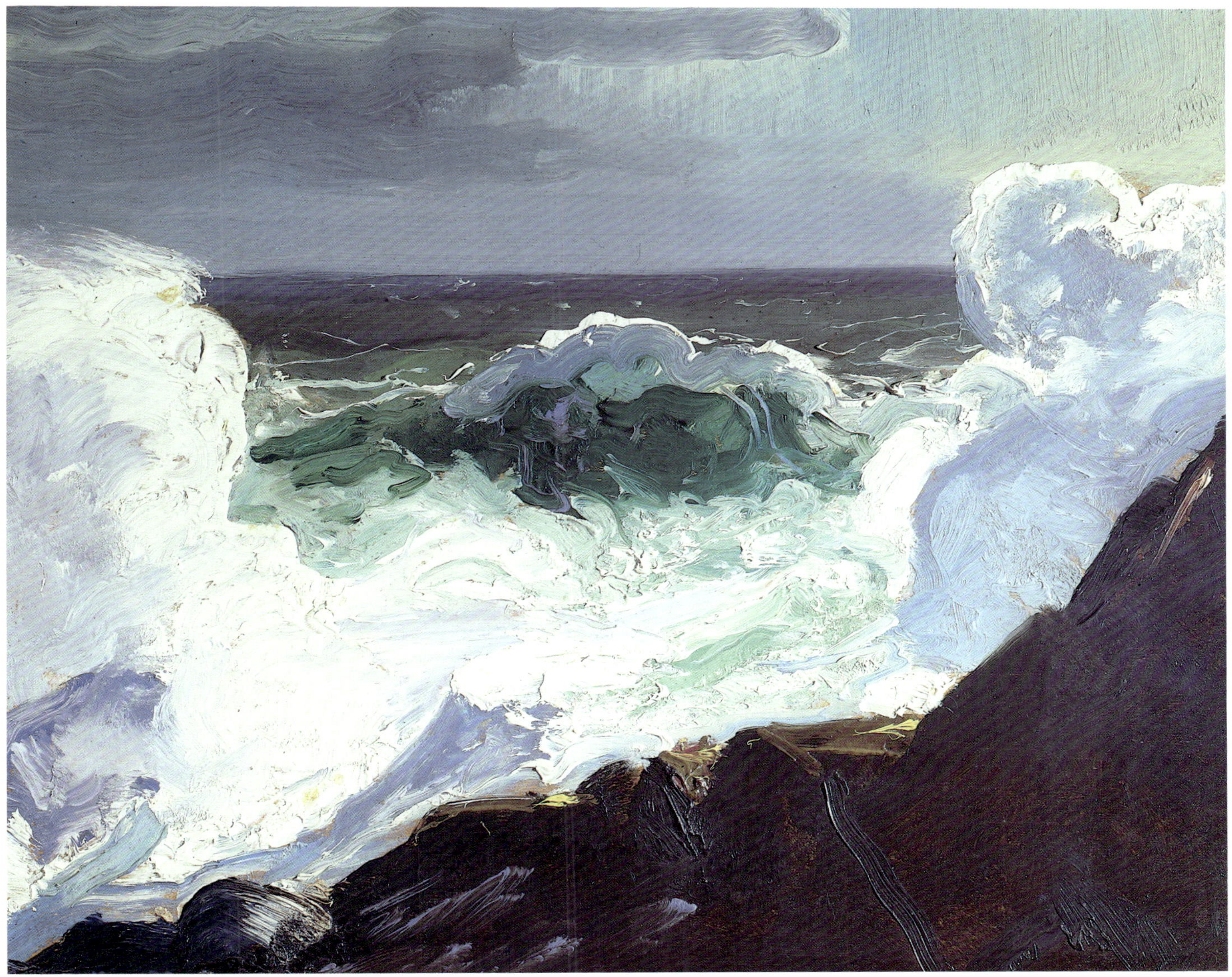

85. Bellows. *Green Breaker*, 1913.

pictorial field is remarkably close to *Cape Trinity*. Although Homer certainly didn't invent the type, his formulation of the composition had some influence: the large, soft forms of the Cape are repeated again in the hills at Camden. Whether or not Bellows could have seen the Homer, the repetition indicates a similar sensibility of form and paint handling.

The critics saw the presence of Homer in Bellows' Monhegan paintings immediately: "Our first impression, in looking at a gallery full of rather diverse pictures, some harking back to Winslow Homer [is that] Mr. Bellows has been spending some time on the rocky Maine Coast, and no doubt the same things

86. Bellows. *Tumble of Waters,* 1913.

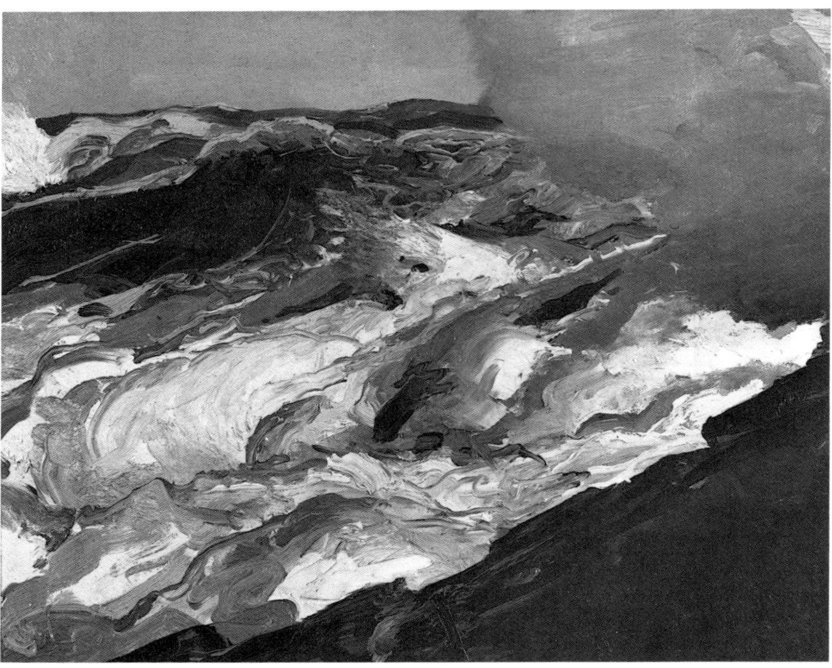

which operated on Winslow Homer's mind have operated on his. Two sketches of fishermen pushing a red-bottomed dory into rough waters are so strangely suggestive of Homer that they seem to be an experiment doing a thing just as Homer would have done it."[18] Another commented: "[Bellows] excites in his broadly brushed virile (Winslow) Homer-(ic) oils [*sic*]. Following in

87. Bellows. *From Rock Top, Monhegan,* 1913.

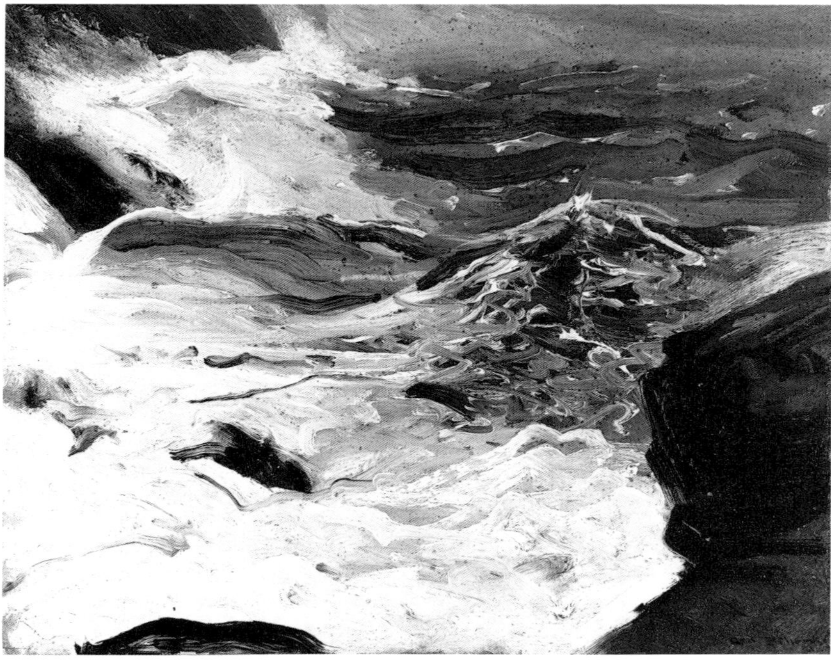

88. Bellows. *Evening Swell,* 1911.

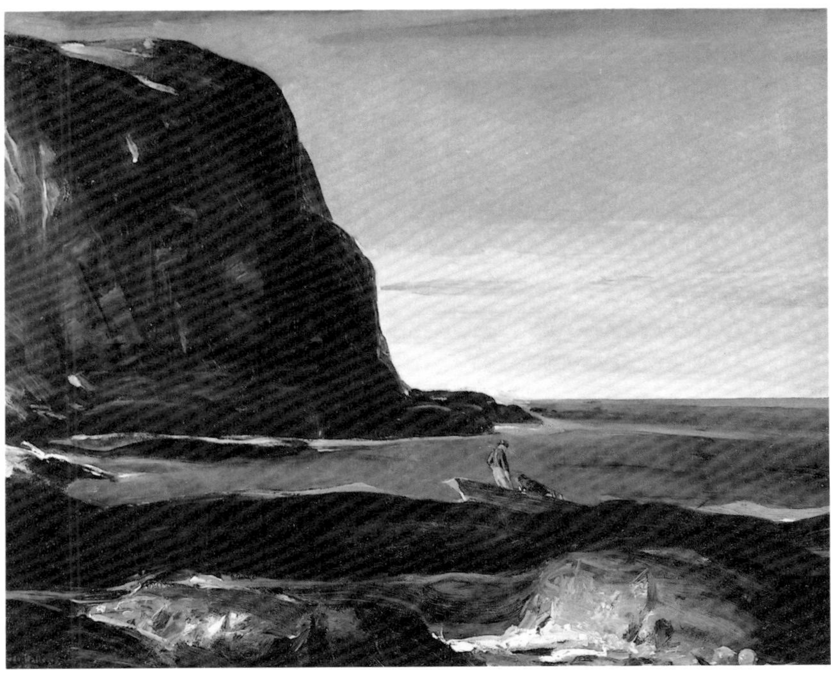

Winslow Homer's footsteps Bellows, like Rockwell Kent, has translated with crude color, oftentimes, but it seems to the writer, with remarkable strength and sympathy, the scenery, the sea and the humans of the stern and rockbound Maine Coast." The critic found the same "gripping quality" in Bellows' landscapes of the North River in winter.[19] In fact, critics had seen the connections

89. Bellows. *The Sea,* 1911.

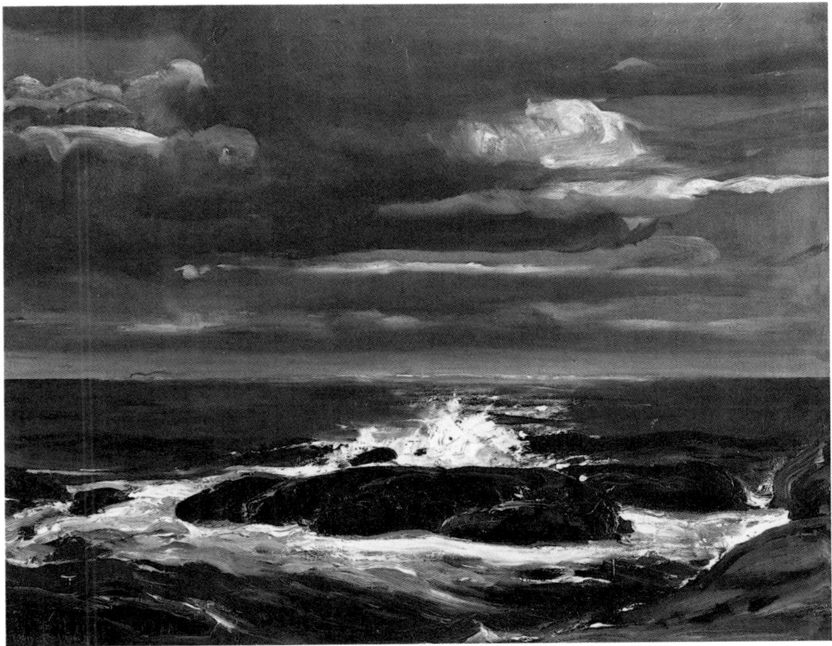

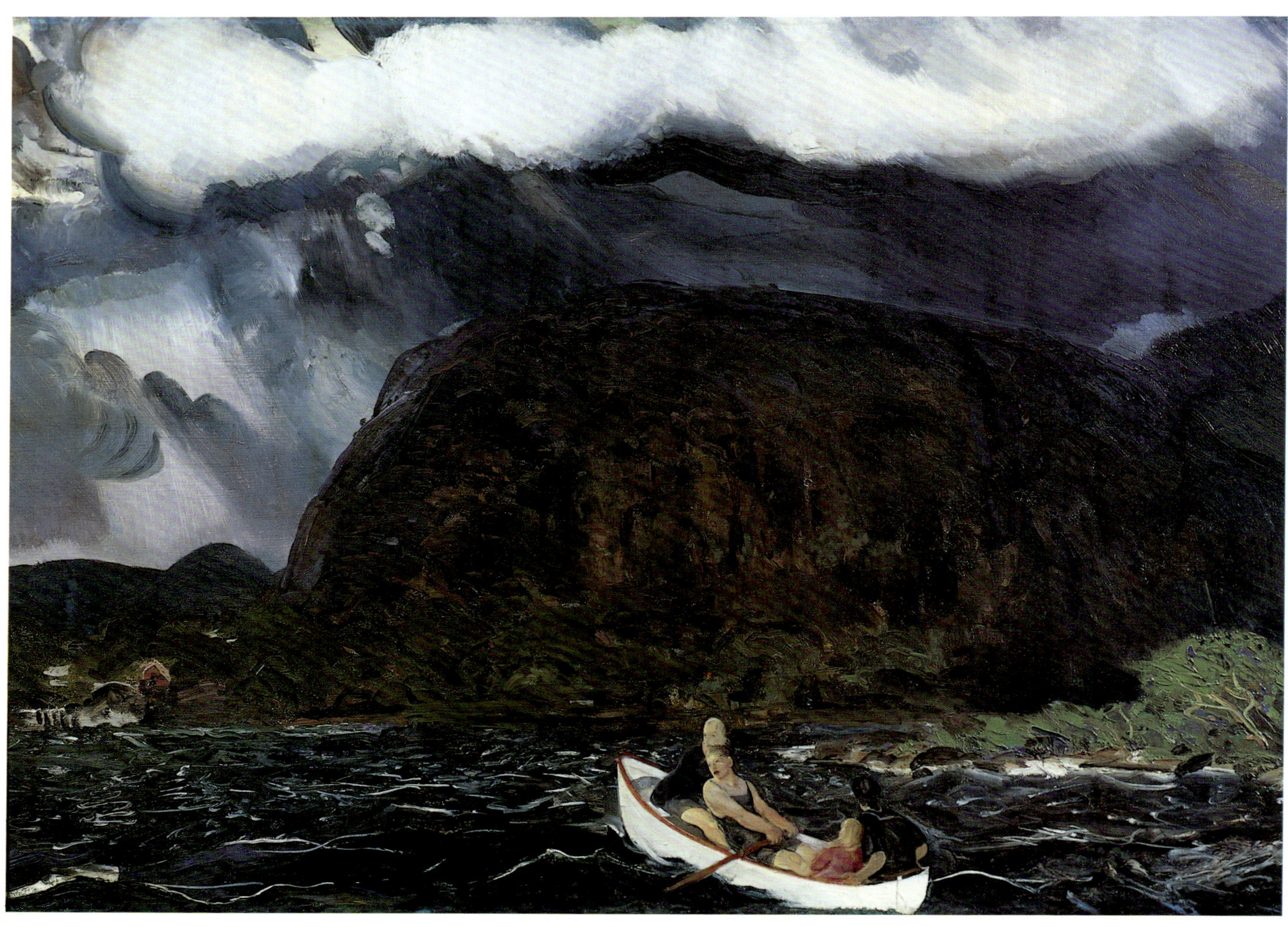

90. Bellows. *In a Rowboat,* 1916.

with Homer from Bellow's earliest work, as they had with Kent. They used the same language: Bellows' work was virile, big, strong, real, and American.[20] In words recalling descriptions of Homer's work, one wrote: "[Bellows'] purpose in painting a picture is not to ornament wall paper, but to generate power."[21]

Bellows' early death in 1924 prompted an outpouring of tributes, which endeavored to sum up his contributions. His chief eulogist, Frank Crowninshield, used (unconsciously but fittingly) a hunting metaphor to describe Bellows' aim as an artist: "A Painter's only preoccupation, when the hunt is on, is to meet his game fairly, appraise it correctly, ask no favors of it—and come

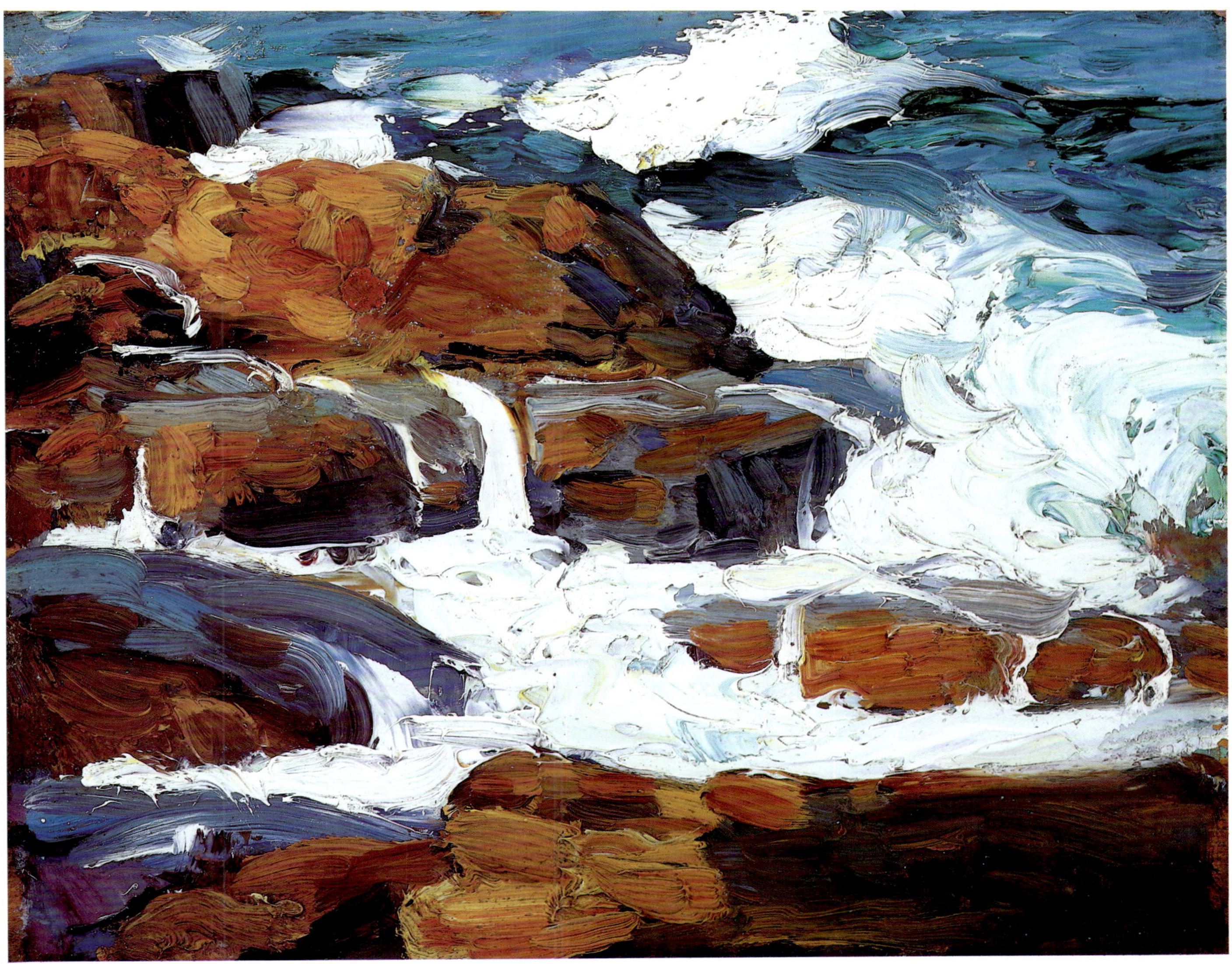

91. Kroll. *Breaking Surf, Prout's Neck,* 1907.

home with a full bag."[22] The conservative critic Royal Cortissoz made the implicit comparisons with Homer explicit in his memorial. After describing Bellows' ancestry and asserting that his Americanism came in his blood, he compared him to Eakins, Homer, and J. Alden Weir (1852-1919), another landscape painter, in contrast to Whistler and Chase: "These recall you to what is most American in our native art—its fresh, unspoiled character, its invincible raciness. With the differences that individuality imposes Bellows is of their line." Then, comparing Bellows' "New York wharf rats" with "Homer's Maine fishermen," Cortissoz concluded that Bellows "painted what he saw because it

92. Kroll. *Monhegan Landscape,* 1913.

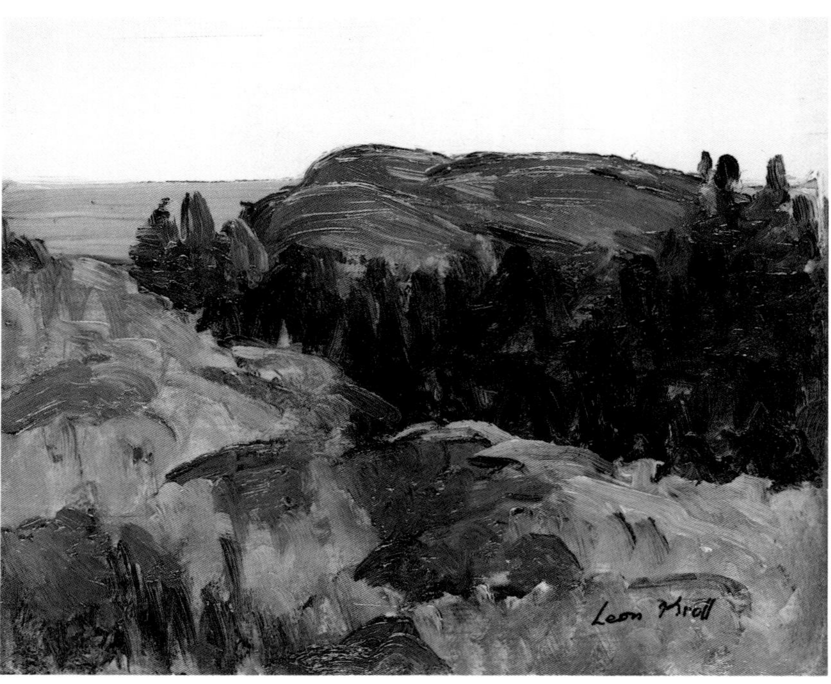

was there and because it roused the gusto in him.... American traits of breadth, simplicity, sincerity, and blunt truth which Bellows drew from the soil."[23]

Bellows' and Kent's Maine paintings rendered Homer's influence anew to an eager public, which included many artists. Leon Kroll, primarily a figure painter, during the first two decades of the twentieth century was, like so many others, entranced by the possibilities of painting New York City and was drawn into the orbit of Henri and his students. Kroll had once spent a summer painting on Prout's Neck, where Homer himself had looked over his sketches and given him advice. One of the young artist's sketches from that summer survives, *Breaking Surf, Prout's Neck,* 1907 (Figure 91). The paint is more buttery than Homer's, but the vigor of the brushstroke and the cropped view of the rocks suggest Homer's spirit. Following Bellows to Monhegan in 1913, Kroll painted the Maine Coast once more. His sketches there, such as *Monhegan Landscape* (Figure 92), are almost indistinguishable in their handling from Bellows'—except that, despite the advice of Homer himself, few show waves. Homer had told him to "stick to figures and leave rocks for your old age," advice Kroll seems to have taken.[24] Soon after the second Monhegan summer, Kroll developed a much more classical and restrained manner. While remaining close friends with Bellows, the effect of Homer and Bellows was momentary. Painting beside Bellows also affected Henri. His sketch *Gray Sea* (Figure 93), which dates from 1911, the summer he and Bellows worked together on Monhegan, is sonorously vigorous in a way that *Rolling Sea* (Figure 73) from 1903 is not. Despite its quiet gray tones, so reminiscent of Whistler, the panel has the sharp tang of salt to it, unlike the less atmospheric earlier works. *Surf and Rocks* (Figure 94), also from 1911, manages to evoke both Bellows' wild energy and Homer's simplicity.

Although evidently never visiting Monhegan, George Luks felt the need to emulate the work of Bellows more strongly, if just as briefly. Luks was born in Williamsport, Pennsylvania, to well-educated Central European parents.[25] He tried various art schools in Philadelphia and Europe, but by and large trained himself. Working for the *Philadelphia Press* in 1894, he got to know the crowd of newspaper artists who were friends with Henri. Luks arrived in New York City in 1896 and began exhibiting his paintings regularly in 1903, under the guidance of Henri. The rejection of Luks' submission to the spring exhibition of the National Academy in 1907 prompted Henri's first feud with the institution and his decision to organize The Eight.

Luks was frequently belligerent and erratic in his behavior, as well as exceptionally imaginative and often hilariously comic. With his personal problems and outsized ego his career and painting were uneven, sometimes guided more by a spirit of competitiveness than by any strong sense of commitment. His early work consisted largely of studies of street urchins and the poor, but also includes several strong urban landscapes. His subject matter and technique were always exaggeratedly vigorous and cruder than that of Henri's and other members of the Ashcan school. Nonetheless, the artist earned the same accolades and epithets: "Above all, Luks is an American.... Under the urge of commercial activity those conditions are produced which should provide the inspiration for a great, virile, vital and abiding art."[26] In the 1920s, seeking to enlarge his range (and perhaps find new audiences), he went to Nova Scotia and then Maine, painting fishing scenes and marines. Visiting Cape Elizabeth, near Portland and Prout's Neck, in 1922, Luks claimed to love Maine

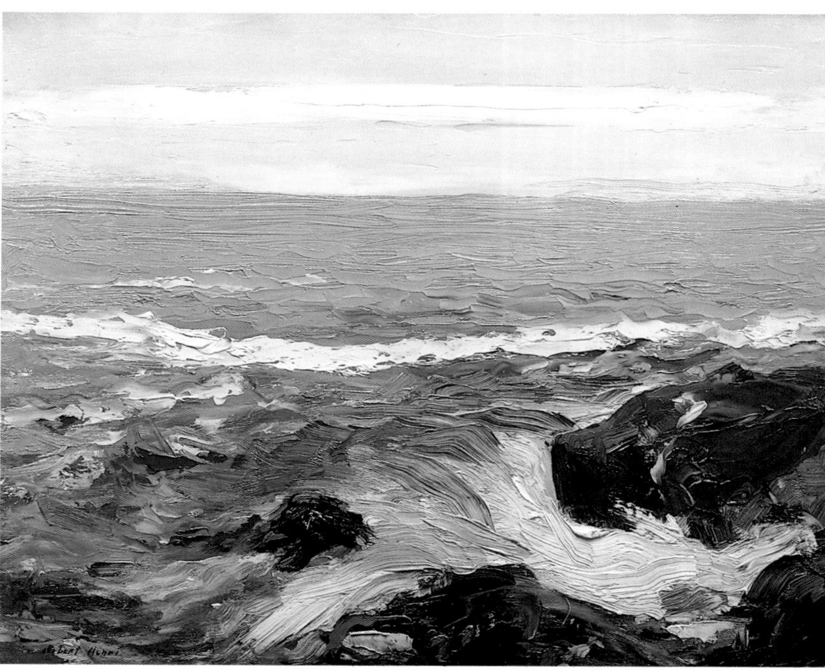

93. Henri, *Gray Sea,* 1911.

(although he does not seem to have visited again), finding not only that the rocks were dramatic but the people American. He told the local Portland paper: "Maine has it all over them, here you have that wonderful gray that is found only in such a climate as that of Maine, and your rocks and shores are so rugged and bold that they make other rocks and shore seem pretty and puny

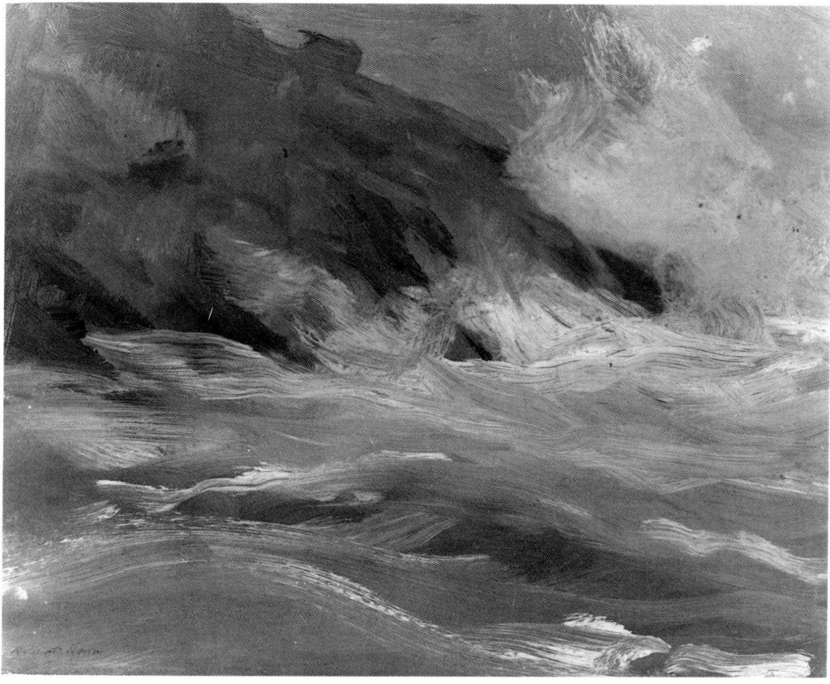

94. Henri. *Surf and Rocks,* 1911.

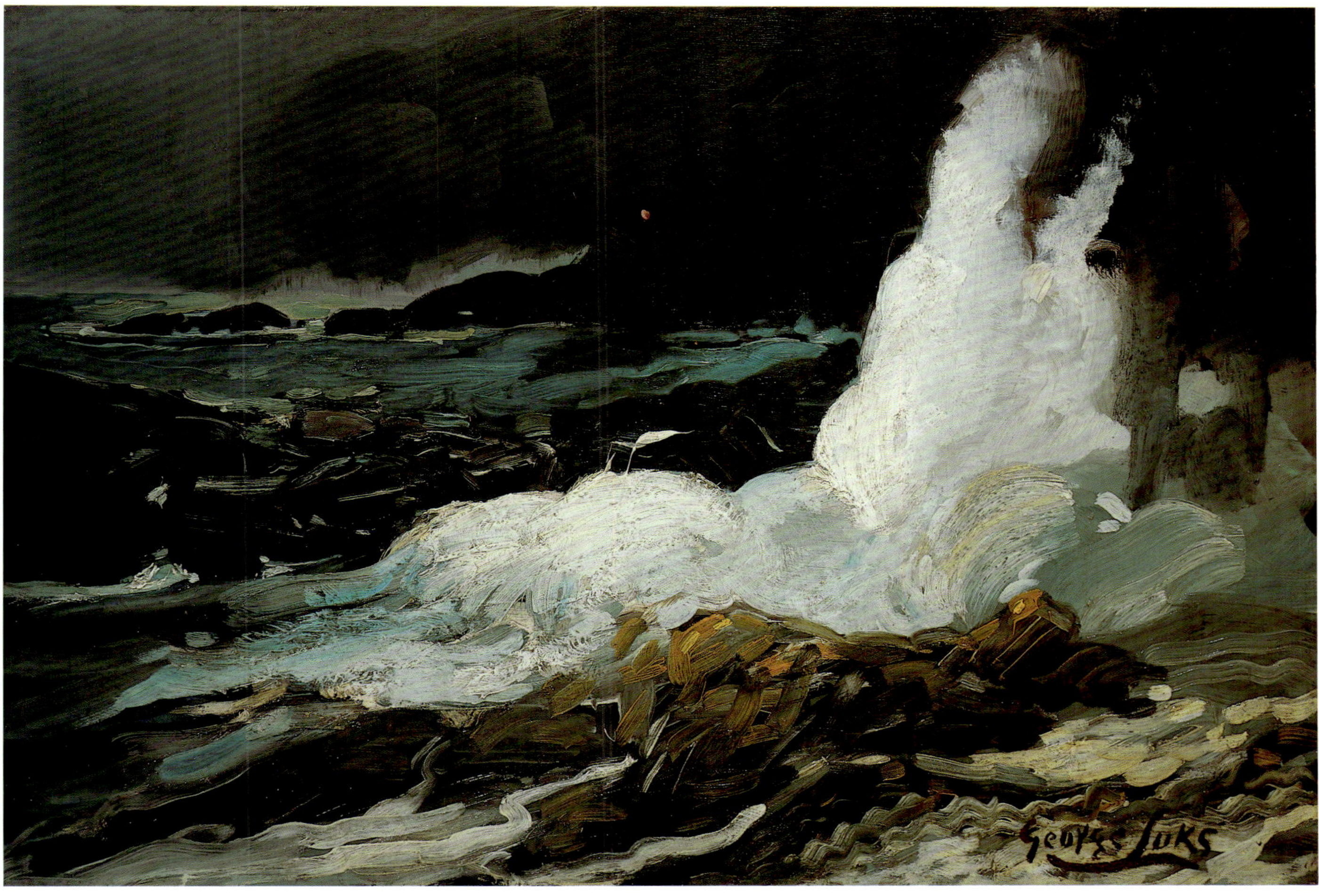

95. Luks. *Great Waves (Coast of Maine),* 1922.

in comparison, and your characters, there are real American types here."[27]

In these works, the influence of both Homer and Luks' Ashcan friends is strong, particularly Bellows' Monhegan paintings from 1911 and 1913, with their similar compositions, stormy seas, and vigorous brushwork. *Great Waves (Coast of Maine),* 1922 (Figure 95), may be compared to Bellows' *Green Breaker* (Figure 85), although the somber palette recalls Homer's overcast paintings.

Luks' Maine marines were seen with the same eyes as Bellows'. Reviewers found that "the surfaces are too often painty, crude," but Luks is "a virile, imaginative painter."[28] Comparisons with Homer were also inevitable: "The canvases in the current show ... were inspired by the Maine coast, that artists' haven made famous in the paintings of Homer. And Luks has registered in his own way the same bold ruggedness, the warring of sea and rock, and the occasional fishing dory that kept the master brush of Homer at work for so many years.... He makes us sense the ponderous strength of the rocks with the splashes of flaming color, their dark silhouettes and jagged teeth."[29]

Another artist influenced by Bellows' work on Monhegan was Edward Hopper, also a classmate from Henri's school. Hopper was born in Nyack, New York, in the same year as Bellows and Kent.[30] Like them, his family was English in origin and had lived for generations in America. He studied at the New York School with Henri from 1900 to 1906, and visited Paris three times between 1906 and 1910. After returning to America, Hopper got off to a very slow start. For many years, like other Ashcan school painters, he supported himself through commercial illustration, not achieving any recognition as a painter until an exhibition of his watercolors at the Brooklyn Museum in 1923. Thereafter his fame grew rapidly, so that by 1933 he was the subject of a one-man exhibition at the Museum of Modern Art. But nothing affected the simple, reserved patterns of his life: he lived in the same apartment for 54 years, even after his marriage in 1924.

During those years of exile, Hopper spent several summers in Maine. In 1914 he went to the artists colony at Ogunquit; in 1916 he visited Monhegan, returning for the next several summers. Few other artists joined him: George and Emma Bellows had abandoned the place because of fears of German submarines; only the Henris visited in 1919.

Hopper was a remarkably stable artist; the matter and style of his art was formed during this period in which he painted very little, and barely changed during his long career. The oil sketches (and few completed paintings) from these early years may be divided into two large groups: the Parisian sketches and paintings, which Hopper always regarded fondly and frequently exhibited before 1923, and the sketches he made during the summers after he returned from Paris, which build to a crescendo at Monhegan.

The paintings he produced in Paris perversely revealed his Americanness. He ignored the avant-garde and called himself an impressionist because he bathed landscapes in light; but he never translated that light into an atmosphere rendered with rich and varied paint textures. Moreover, his subjects and compositions had an almost defiantly prosaic quality to them; they were flat-footed, deliberately so. The Henri brushstroke was subdued into something plain and strong; the kinetic energy of the "slashing stroke" was replaced by an almost sculptural solidity of planes and masses. The mature Hopper was already manifest, despite the foreignness of the subjects. Something similar had happened a few years earlier to Van Dearing Perrine who, visiting Venice, sketched not the Grand Canal by which he sat but his memory of the Palisades. For Perrine, going to Europe confirmed his true location, America. Paris had the same effect on Hopper.

In Monhegan Hopper produced no finished oils: since no one wanted to buy them, there was no point in painting them. But the oil sketches are abundant. Like Bellows and the others, he seems to have been inspired by the landscape of the island. Like Bellows again, Hopper concentrated on the water and rocks, exploring different configurations and weather conditions. *Waves Crashing on Rocks, Monhegan; Rocky Shore and Sea, Monhegan;* and *Rocks and Waves* (Figures 96-98), each show similar scenes under different weather and light. In *Waves Crashing on the Rocks, Monhegan,* the day is cold and gray and there is a touch of red in the rock (Homer's device to enliven the cold color harmonies). In *Rocky Shore and Sea, Monhegan,* the light is strong and the contrasts great, with bold brushstrokes used in the waves. In *Rocks and Waves* (Figure 98), the rocks are tawny but the sea is

96. Hopper. *Waves Crashing on the Rocks, Monhegan,* ca. 1916-19.

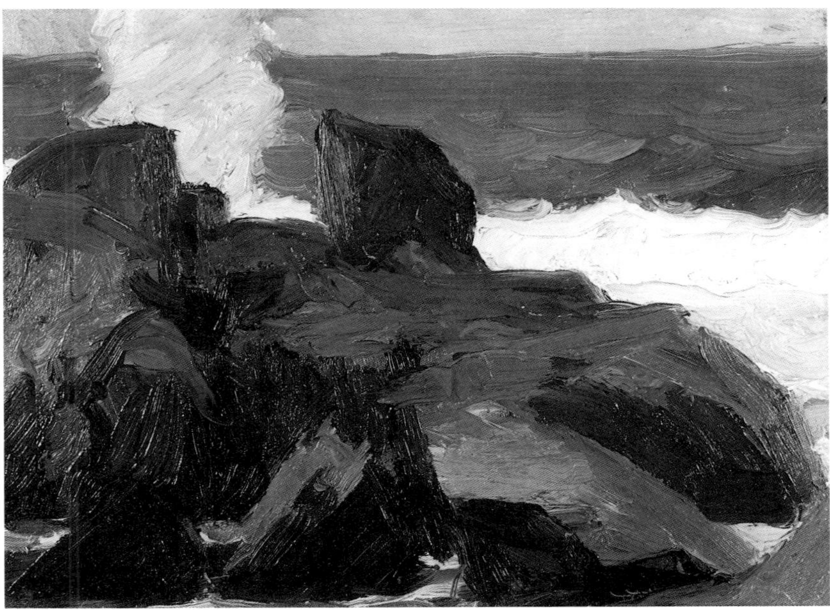

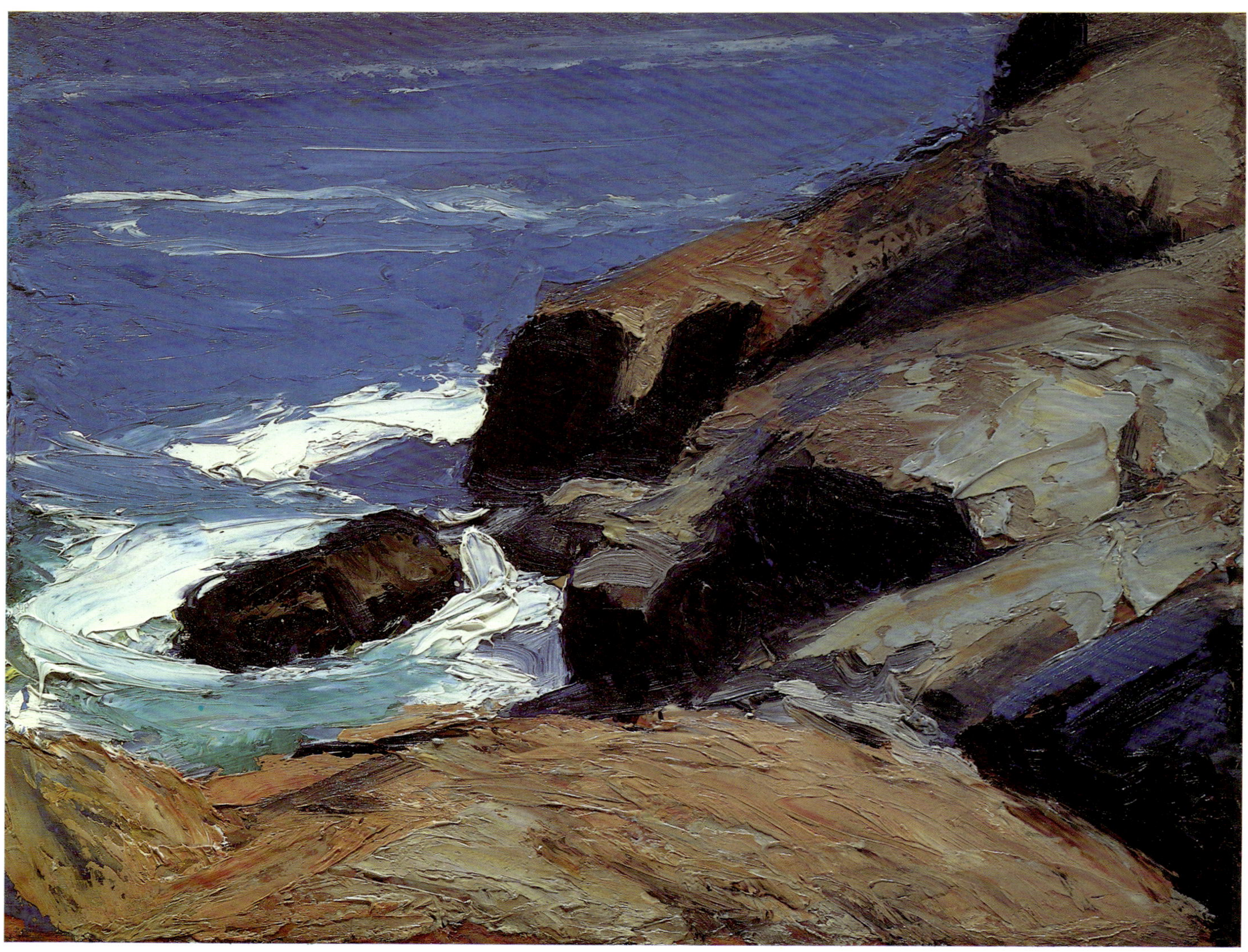

97. Hopper. *Rocky Shore and Sea, Monhegan,* ca. 1916-19.

cold. Hopper has employed typical devices from Homer's seascapes, beyond the extreme closeup found in all three. In the first there is a spume of spray; in the second, the sliding wedge of rocks; in the third, the row of teeth of the Maine Coast.

Like Homer and Bellows, confronted by the elemental display of force of primary water and rock, Hopper reduced his compositions to their simplest parts. *Rocky Projection at the Sea* (Figure 99) is simply a forceful protrusion of rock; the emphasis is on the thrust of it, not on its volume or surface. This concentration on energy, not matter, leads Hopper as close to abstraction as he ever got; these are also the paintings in which he came closest to describing

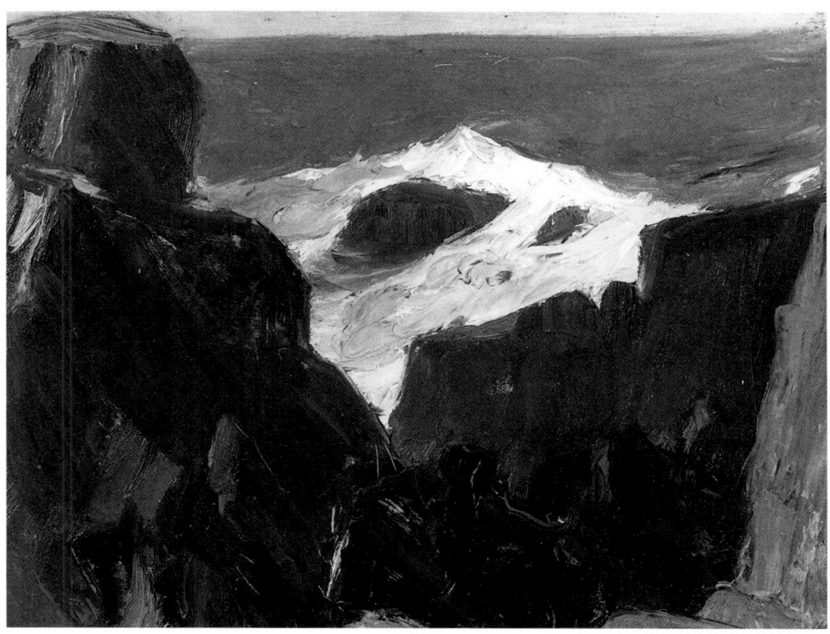

98. Hopper. *Rocks and Waves,* ca. 1916-19.

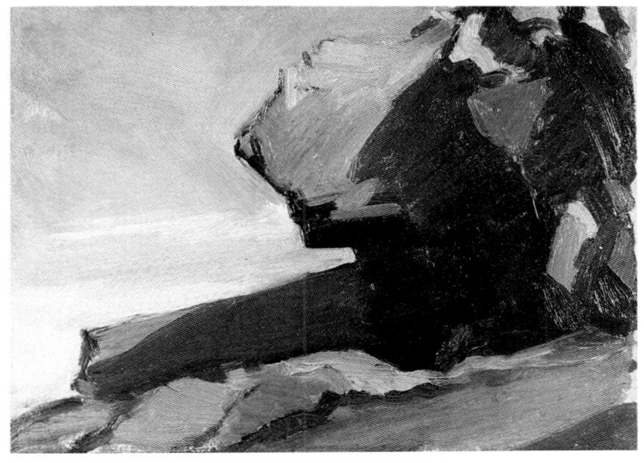

99. Hopper. *Rocky Projection at the Sea,* ca. 1916-19.

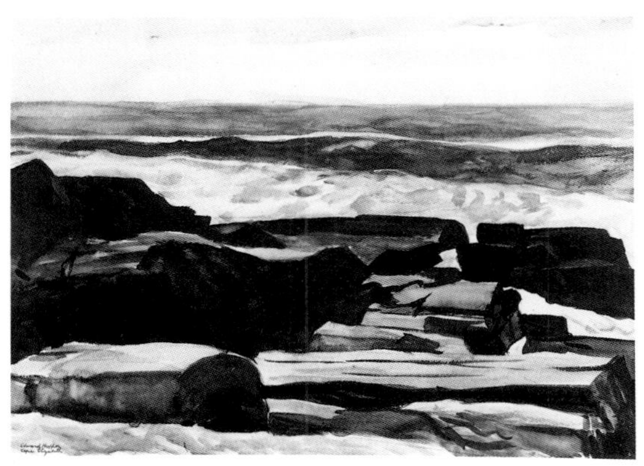

100. Hopper. *Foreshore—Two Lights,* 1927.

the energy of the natural world, rather than its static presence.

Hopper never developed these Monhegan sketches into finished oils, partly because he did not return to oils seriously until after the success of his Brooklyn exhibition in 1923. Thereafter, Hopper's experience of Homer was revealed for the most part in watercolors, such as *Foreshore—Two Lights,* 1927 (Figure 100), not in his oils. But even where similar compositions and subjects may be found, Hopper rarely attained such forceful expression of the momentary flux and chaos of nature as on Monhegan. Never again did he construct so dynamic a composition as *Rocky Projection* (in later works, the drama lies in the perspective, not in the projection of solid mass at the viewer). As with so many other artists, it was the confrontation with Homer's heritage on his own ground that inspired Hopper. When he did return to pure landscape in his oils, it was years later and in a very different region.

In 1930 he and his wife, Jo, summered on Cape Cod, near South Truro. They built a house there in 1934 and for the rest of their lives returned to spend summers amidst the rolling dunes and large, sun-washed skies of the Cape. For the most part Hopper depicted the structures he found nearby—houses, lighthouses, cottages—but in his first years he occasionally painted landscapes wiped clean of human presence.[31] In *The Camel's Hump,* 1931 (Figure 101), he employed his typical composition, a horizontal stretch along the front of the canvas, an empty stage with the action taking place behind it. *Camel's Hump* still retains something of Homer's seascapes about it, the ridges rolling like great slow waves. Everything has been simplified and made massive; we feel the weight of the forms, the waves have petrified, the sky has been cleared. Homer's marines have turned to stone.

After 1923, when Hopper's watercolors were exhibited, his reputation quickly solidified and hardly varied, much as his style and essential subjects remained unchanging until his death in 1967. His work was forcefully, simply American. As one writer exclaimed: "What vitality, force and directness.... His work has become synonymous for racial quality in contemporary American painting.... The truth of the matter is that Edward Hopper likes his native environment for all its faults and crudities. He likes it because it is native and has the courage to be itself."[32]

Comparisons with Homer were inevitable, and often made in connection with his watercolors: "Edward Hopper is perhaps the one nearest to the direct line of Homer's succession."[33] The terms of the comparison were clear. Hopper was, first of all, a realist of things, not people. He had "a broad style of solidly defined forms and bright clear color which is closely related to the objective vision of Winslow Homer."[34] The simplicity of his style was an aspect of his manhood and his American aversion to other men's styles. He was a loner: "His is a masculine landscape art as contrasted with the feminine one of the impressionists. In its strength and its deep feeling for the earth, it reminds one of a realist older than impressionism, Courbet.... Hopper's art has an unusually direct relation to reality, owing less to other art than that of most painters. This directness is almost naive, giving him the courage to paint aspects of the real world that a more conventional painter would consider non-artistic."[35] Hopper also lacked decorative beauty (and hence, sexual affect): "[Hopper is] a man who has always been stubbornly American, in both technique and subject matter.... His major weakness, on the other hand, seems to arise from a certain Puritan disdain of the more sensual aspects of painting—beauty of texture and charm of color.... Although Hopper's essential realism and stark statement of fact strike one with great force."[36] As a fellow realist painter, Charles Burchfield, said: "His art seems to have had few antecedents and, like most truly individual expressions, will probably have no descendants.... In him we have regained that sturdy American independence."[37] These critics might have been describing Homer only a generation before.

Hopper himself, while he acknowledged his distrust of contemporary modernist painting as "purely decorative," did shy away from assertions of his Americanness. He claimed to have simple, humble goals: "My aim in painting has always been the most exact transcription possible of my most intimate impressions of nature.... The trend in some of the contemporary movements in art ... appears to lead to a purely decorative conception of painting.... The question of the value of nationality in art is perhaps unsolvable."[38] Like Homer, he preferred silence.

Hopper's stance—a distrust of European modernism and a desire for a direct expression of his response to nature—was shaped primarily by Robert Henri. As a critic wrote in 1908: "The question as stated by the radicals is, Shall there be an American art—an art that dares paint New York for instance. Shall the American art school displace the schools of foreigners.... Henri leads the new group of radicals ... in a new and distinctive movement toward Americanism."[39] The art of Henri's students was as independent as America itself. Giles Edgerton wrote the same year in an article entitled "The Younger American Painters: Are They Creating a National Art?": "In America we have already produced our own type of men inevitable from a civilization crude without tradition. Paris may no longer set our fashions; we think for ourselves along all these lines of national development." He concluded: "A man *must* paint best what he feels and knows and understands best, and if he paints the life that he thrills in answer to, he puts upon canvas conditions that have developed him into the racial type he is.... There are no great varieties of theories among these men, rather one very manifest and definite purpose to paint *truth* and to paint it with strength and fearlessness and individuality."[40] Another critic added "The younger American painters are so strong, so virile, so muscular—let us say—that instinctively they lean toward the painting of things in a big, broad constructive manner."[41] In other words, these artists "just paint the way they see things every day."[42]

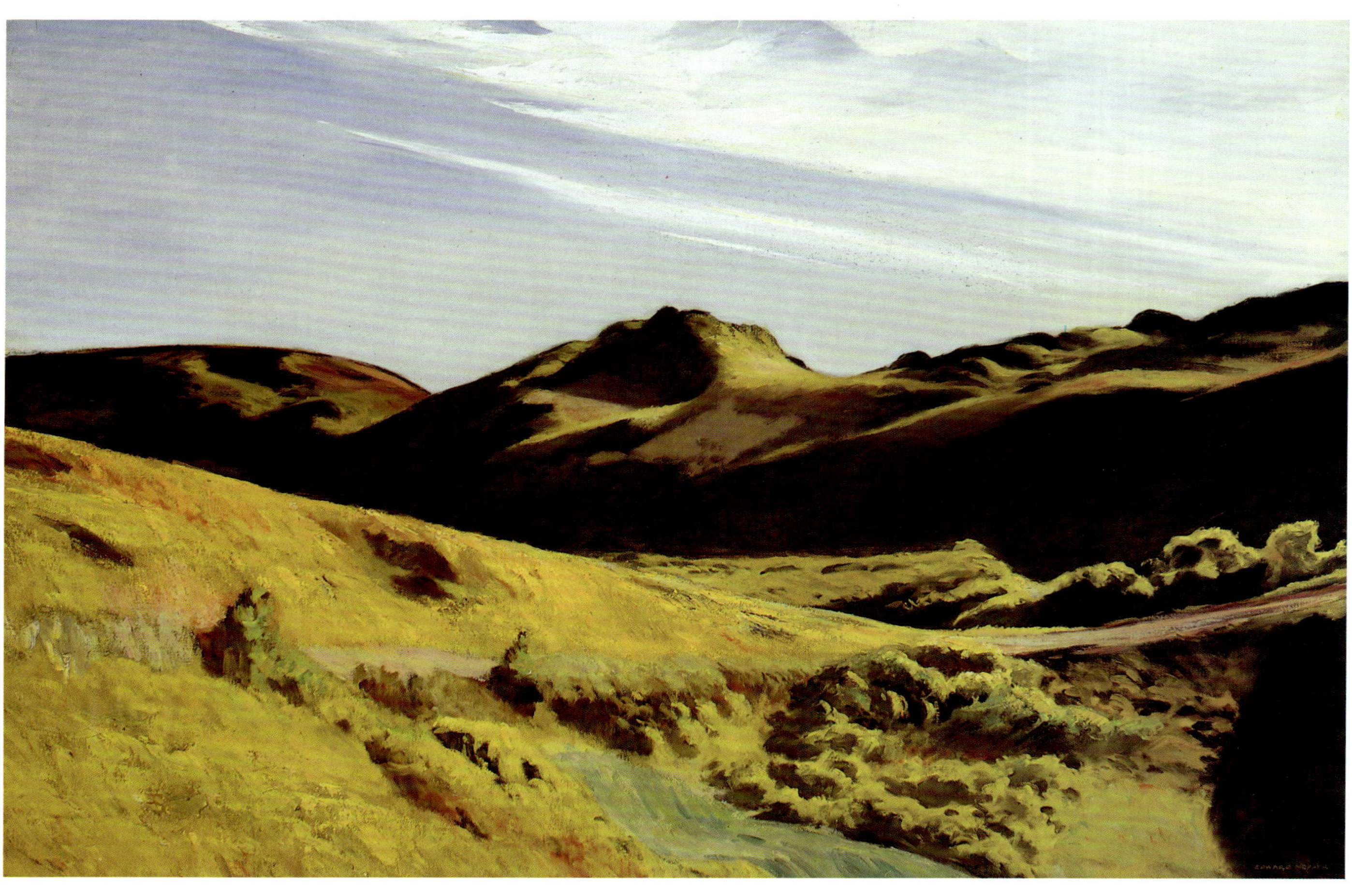

101. Hopper. *The Camel's Hump,* 1931.

Henri guided them all to consider Homer, both the paintings themselves and what the man and his work represented, and to refashion him. Rockwell Kent adopted the myth of Homer's character most directly, living a Homeric existence in northern wastelands among heroic fishermen and painting them. Edward Hopper understood Homer's isolation as alienation, not heroism, and made it his own. George Bellows responded to Homer's energy and modeled his paintings on Homer's brushstroke and compositions, translating that energy into new situations.

Despite individual differences in their responses, these artists shared some generational similarities. The screen through which they saw Homer was one constructed in the early twentieth-century, in an America radically different from the one that had shaped Homer. In a fundamental manner, the American charac-ter had changed. As a study of the popular press has shown, the heroes of the Progressive Era, the decade before World War I, were politicians; during the 1890s they had been businessmen.[43] The bombastic Theodore Roosevelt, walking softly but carrying a big stick, is the exemplary figure. The manhood of this generation differed greatly from the stoic hardness of Homer. And it is important to remember that the foundation of their art was self-consciously based on character, as it never was for modernists: they painted out of themselves to reflect their own nature. Their art mirrors their self-perception.[44] It is also relevant that nearly all were native Americans, only Luks and Henri came from recent immigrant families; the rest had lived in New England and New York, or the first stepping off place for the Midwest, Ohio, for generations.

Bellows epitomized this new American. Of his work, one eulogist wrote: "This rankness, this swaggering gusto in a world of raw savors would seem, to the plain American, comfortably remote from the rarefied atmosphere of highbrow art. Here was an art that had what [Bellows] would characterize as 'the punch.' But along with the punch, the American likes to see things done with an impressive air of performance: a President smashing trusts with a big stick, a 'Giant' pitcher with a pretty wind-up and a 'fade-away ball.' When all is said, the genius of George Bellows resides in this: his power to evoke on canvas a world stirring with a mysterious energy."[45] The simplicity of these attitudes was dangerously close to childishness; the result was often an almost intolerable boyishness. The letters and other writings of these artists convey a hearty simplicity that seems alarmingly naive. Quite literally, these were boy scout years: the Boy Scouts of America were launched in 1910. The excursion into nature attained an overtone of sporting fun and nationalist need that it had never had with Homer. As the American leader of the Boy Scouts wrote: "This is a time when the whole nation is turning toward the Outdoor Life, seeking in it the physical regeneration so needful for continued national existence."[46]

The fears of softness in American men—soft bodies and degenerate morals (related to fears of soft style)—which prompted the founding of the Boy Scouts and other similar movements after 1900, were to be put to rest in encounters with the wilderness. But Nature (traditionally feminine) led paradoxically to the world of women. "The physical regeneration so needful for continued national existence" which men of this generation found outside the city also took them to physical self-expression.[47] Mastery of the body, rediscovered in manly adventure in the wild, led quickly to sex, despite cold showers, bad food, and hard ground. For the most part, these artists were all married and extolled the virtues of healthy sex. They played the cowboy role during the summer months and then returned to the city and their families. The raw forces of nature were, for the most part, happily contained. Only Hopper seems to express anxiety about relationships in his art and life (and it is for this reason that he seems to have dwelt on themes of isolation).

But boy scouts have to grow up, and sometimes a harsher reality intrudes. All these artists finally confronted nature on her own terms, an unsettling experience for which a lifetime of campfire songs provided little preparation. All, at some time in their careers, felt the need to re-erect Thoreau's cabin on Walden Pond, to find some isolated place where in the contemplation of nature they might find themselves. But the way they proceeded was very different from the manner in which earlier American artists had taken up the task. *A Home in the Wilderness,* 1866 (Figure 102), the work of the Hudson River painter Sanford Gifford (1823-1880), may be taken as a typical example of a mid-nineteenth-century expression of the theme. For Gifford, the cabin sits comfortably in the landscape, in harmony with a wilderness that is controlled and shaped to some extent by man. The water is a smooth, untroubled lake, sheltered within a bower of mountains. Men may venture out on it, but they return to the wife and child who happily greet them: like the landscape, the family is also in harmony. For these later artists, such accord was not so easily attained, and to be isolated in nature was often threatening. Nor was this simply because they are essentially urban painters—Gifford had lived just as comfortably in New York City as they did.

Nevertheless, when Robert Henri painted a similar theme, in his *Storm Tide,* 1903 (Figure 103), there is not one house, but a huddle of them. Too social to live alone, these people withstand the elements in groups. The small figure of a woman can be dimly seen beside her doorway, adding a little touch of human drama to the scene; but she waits alone, the men have disappeared. The

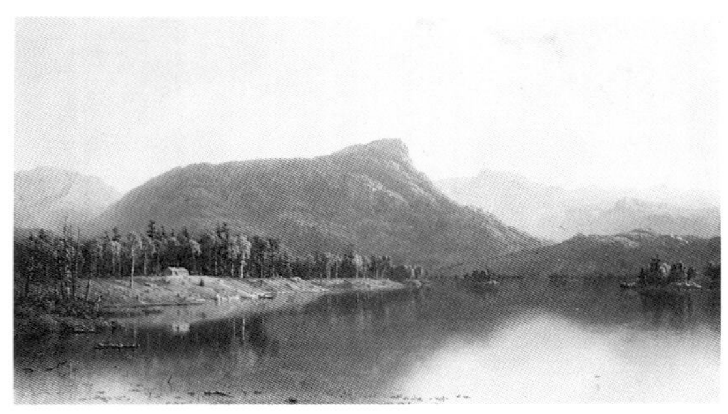

102. Gifford. *A Home in the Wilderness,* 1866.

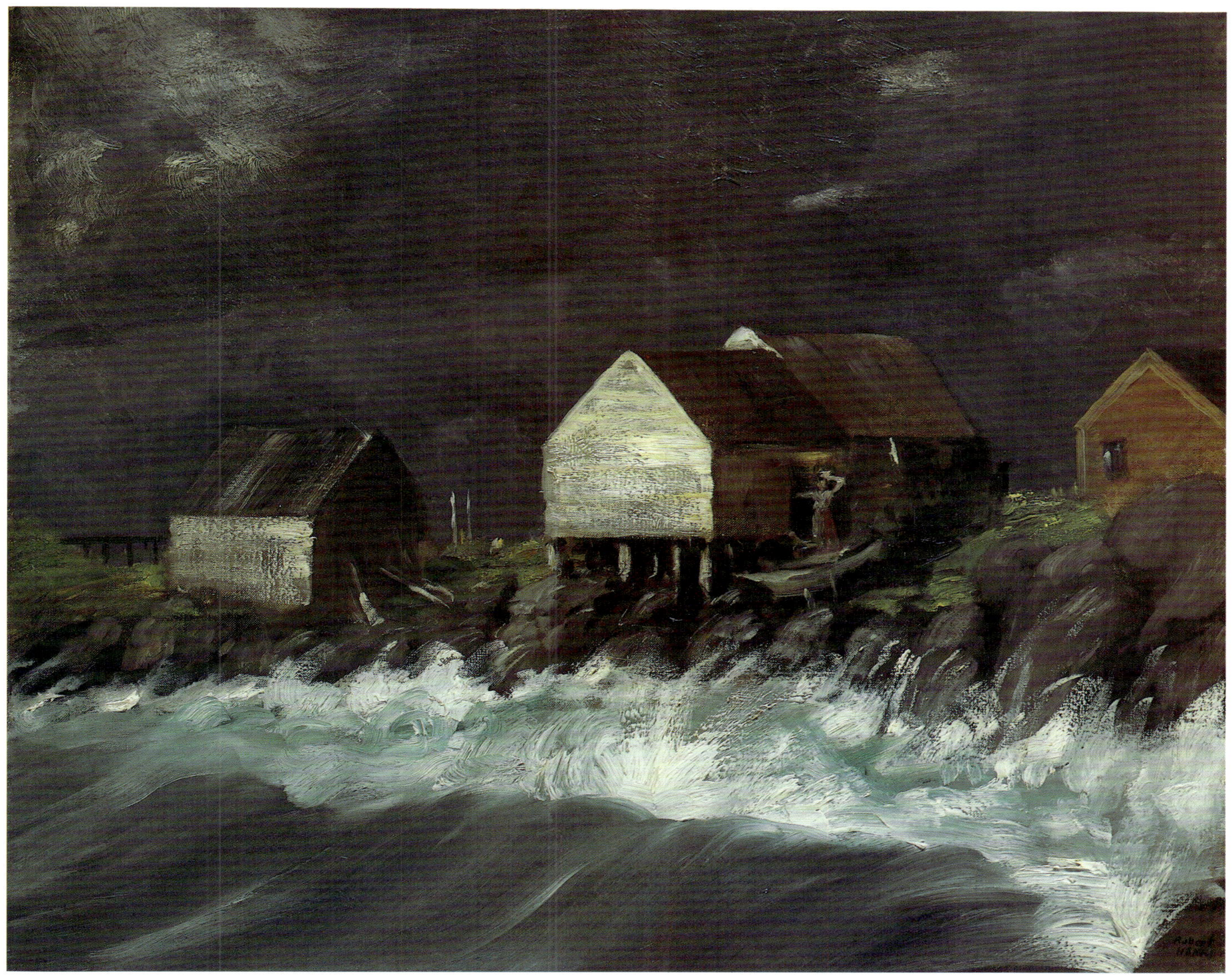

103. Henri. *Storm Tide,* 1903.

surf threatens to carry all trace of man away before it. Henri described the painting as a "gray storm effect, breaks of light, ragged clouds in sky above bank of heavy leaden sky. Houses struck by brilliant light, electric color to green surf."[48] Others responded to the drama of the scene with equally vivid language: "Look at the painting that he shows here of an ocean beating a surf of jade against cabins on stilts and be shocked if it be in your temperament to be shocked. He has the ideas of a man, the strongest that agitate the world of today."[49]

At first sight, Rockwell Kent's *Winter, Monhegan Island,* 1907 (Figure 104), is as bleak a winter scene as one could hope for.[50]

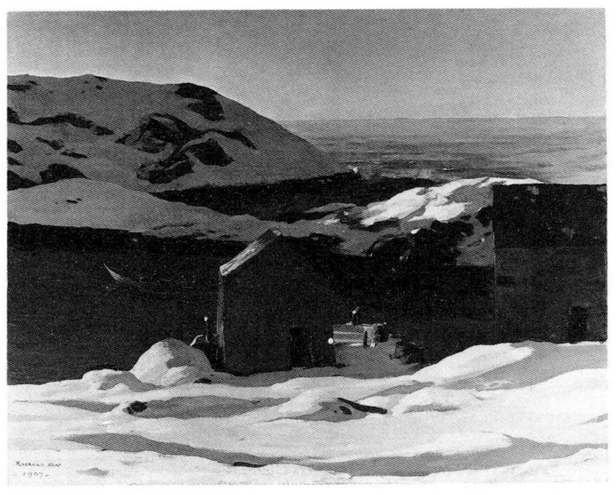

104. Kent. *Winter, Monhegan Island,* 1907.

The boat is a chip of wood on a cold sea; the lone box of the shed seems so frozen as to be an ice-cube; the brilliant blue and white of the snow (an effect which Bellows appropriated for his winter scenes) has leached all human warmth from the structure. In Kent's words, the fishing houses on Monhegan "evok[ed] in their dilapidation those sad thoughts on the passage of time and the transitoriness of all things human so dear to the artistic soul."[51] But a closer look reveals that the shed is balanced by another to the right; the fishing boat is hospitably sheltered from the open sea by a spit of land extended from the shore to the island. It helps to know that Kent painted the scene from the warmth of the dining room of the island's chief hotel. Kent's lonely house exists within a community of social relations, much as in Henri's *Storm Tide;* nature freezes the village, not a hermit's cell. Only Bellows and Hopper truly dwelt in Thoreau's cottage—Bellows once only and Hopper without a pond at his door.

Bellows' *Shore House,* 1911 (Figure 80), like so much in his *ouevre,* was painted in reaction to a specific event. He had just spent the last few months madly at work preparing a townhouse in Manhattan for Emma and himself. It was to be his new home in every way, the first house that he had lived in for more than five years, other than his parents' place. Emma and George had married in late September and went to Montauk, at the farthest tip of Long Island, for their honeymoon, not far from George's relations in Sag Harbor. The little white house in *Shore House* stands for that new home, experienced first in its purest form here on his honeymoon (the essence of marriage). This ideal home is the country cottage so dear to American culture, where he and Emma will find their "Blue Heaven." It represents all that is good and holy in the state of matrimony, blessed by the cross standing over it. The house signals the end of the city in Bellow's mind, the end of the urban adventure, of free love in the Village. Now he and his wife will form the nuclear family, immune from outside influence, sufficient unto themselves. We know from Bellows' love letters to Emma, as well as their subsequent life, that theirs was an ardent (if argumentative) marriage. But at this moment, the jaws of the land seem to close in on the house, as though to crush it like a walnut; the telephone pole dangles above it pathetically. Beyond rests the sea, representing every obdurate otherness, that which resists all our efforts to order our lives and reduce the chaos of existence. The precarious position of the house and its lack of solidity signal Bellows' uncertainty about sex and family. As one perceptive observer wrote: "[The] cottage on a seashore has a loneliness and desolation that is depressing."[52]

In contrast to Bellows, the house in nature is one of Hopper's fundamental subjects. But depicting structures even more solid than those painted by the other three, Hopper faced a more insubstantial and intransigent intruder: sunlight. His isolated buildings, like the house beside the tracks in *Hills, South Truro,* 1930 (Figure 105), speak always of the fact that man is never at home in nature. His solitary figures are always sheltered by buildings, whether sitting on their front steps or standing in their bedrooms with the windows open. In *Cape Cod Morning,* 1950 (Figure 106), the woman greets the new day with her arms braced and her jaw set as though the sun will blast her back into the shadows behind her. Nature, however welcome, seems alien to Hopper: it always lies uncomfortably outside.

Homer, on the other hand, in his mature work almost never showed man facing nature from the security of a house. In *Below Zero* (Figure 28), for example, his men venture outside with only animal skins on their backs. Far from their habitation, they confront nature directly, without society or human structure. The only time Homer painted his own home, in *The Artist's Studio in an Afternoon Fog,* 1894 (Figure 107), he de-humanized it. Not only Homer's studio but his father's house and an outbuilding are ranged against the dull sky, the sun vainly trying to beat through the fog. All three are seen, not as artificial structures on the land, but as outgrowths of it. They form part of the band of shadow which is the far ground, bonded into a neutral brown, as much an outcropping of rock as the tree. They become the crests of waves, no more houses where men live than the blank shore in front of them. Homer revealed to the next generation (who made of it what they could) that to be at home in nature was not to be a "transparent eyeball," experiencing nature without physical sensation, nor by a small pond in the woods, as the Transcendentalists would have had it, but standing on the shore buffeted by the wind and waves. The revelation was sometimes an uncomfortable one.

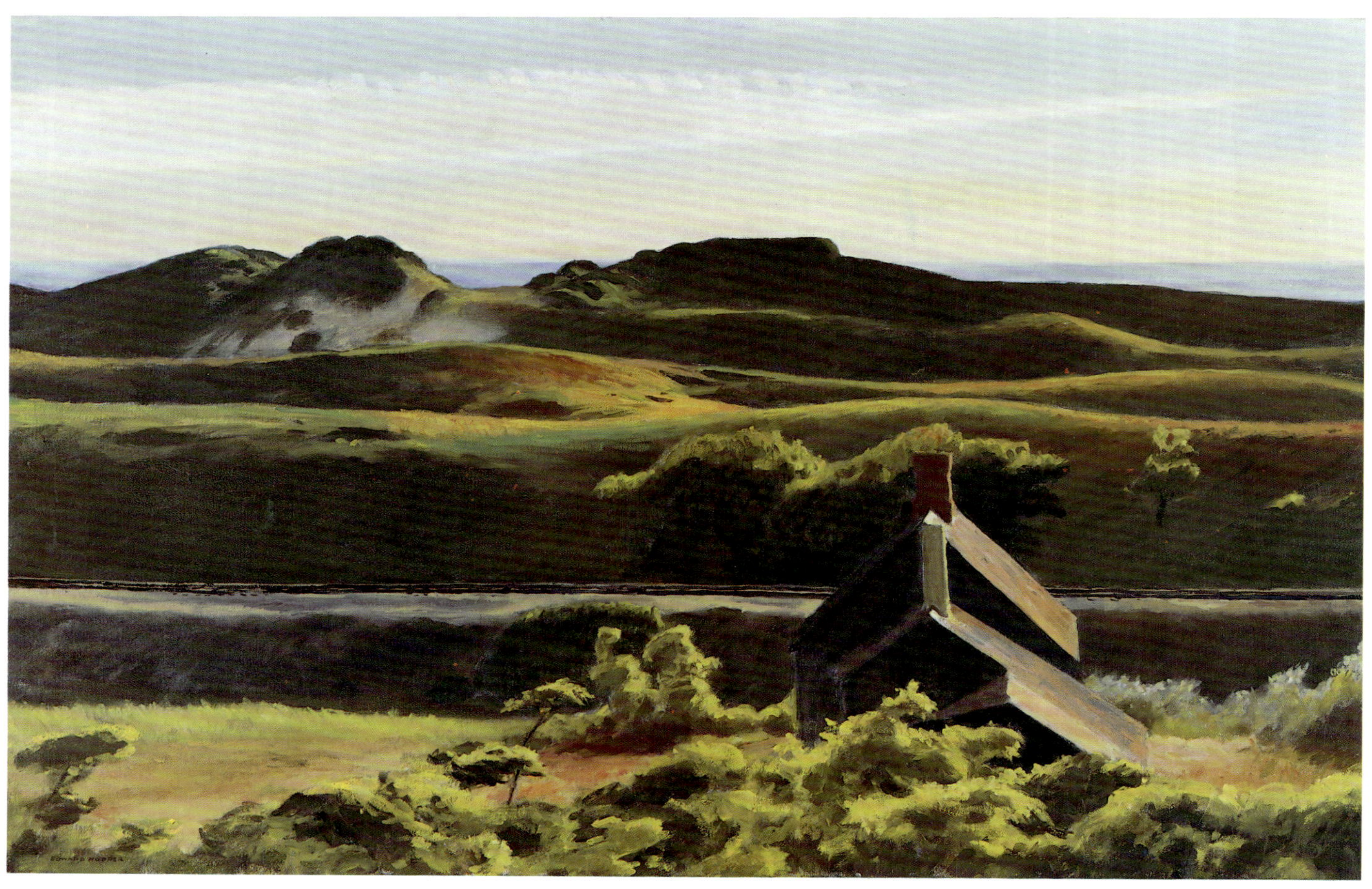

105. Hopper. *Hills, South Truro,* 1930.

Homer's paintings were the product of old age—experience, worn love, bitterness, endurance. He faced death in these works, as none of these younger artists did. Theirs was the work of brash youth. For Homer, the rocks were the end of a voyage, a voyage conducted on land which led from war, society, and the city, to the farm (man and nature in harmony), the woods, and boats (man alone in nature), to nature herself. These landscapes mark a limit reached, a conclusion. The Ashcan painters returned him to the world of men. What Bellows did definitively—and the others

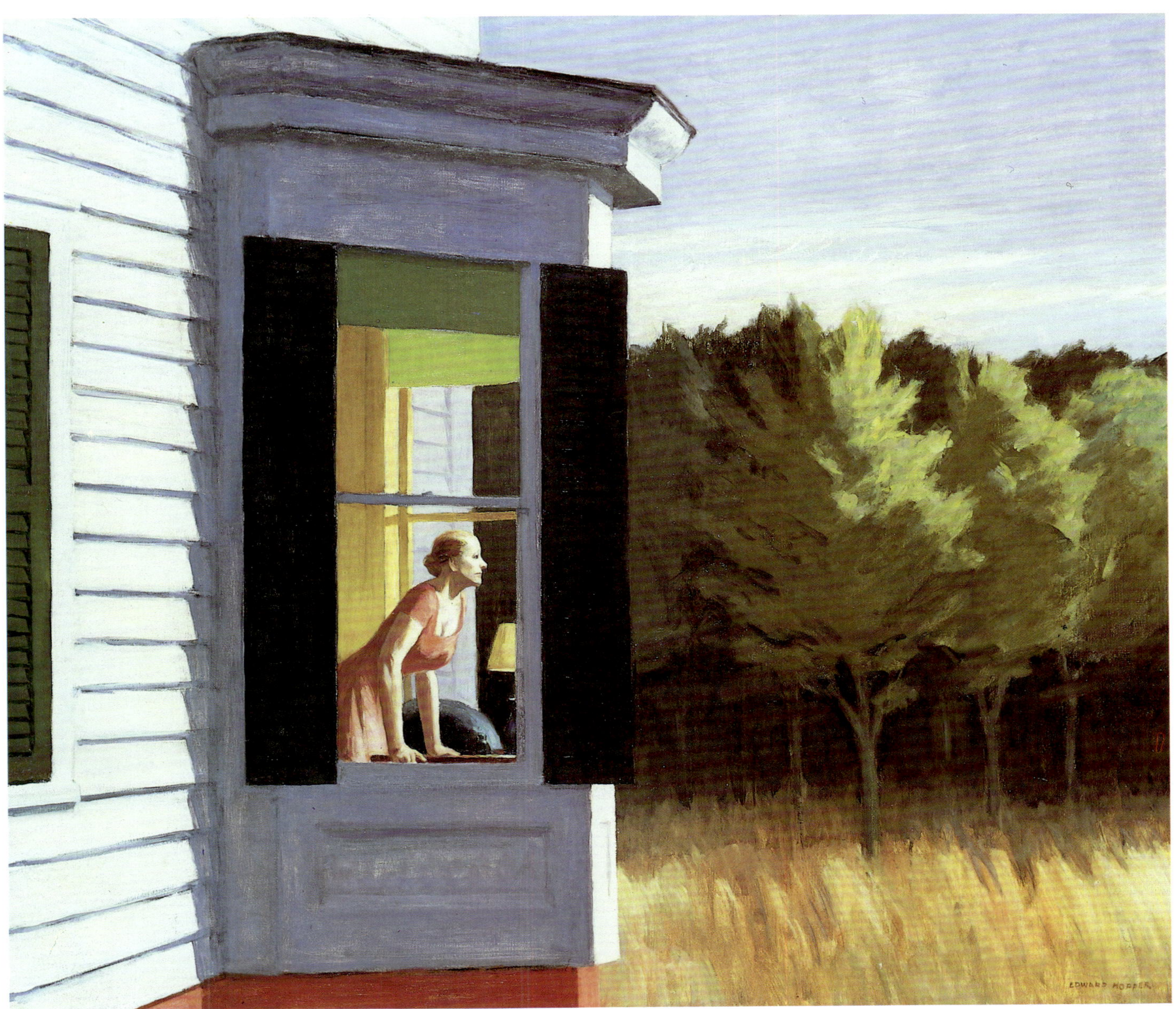

106. Hopper. *Cape Cod Morning,* 1950.

to a lesser extent—was to break the mold of seeing Homer solely as a marine painter. Instead of viewing Homer as a great full stop, they saw him as foundation on which to build. Reacting to him most completely on his own territory, in the end they naturalized him on theirs, each in their own way.

Robert Henri wrote of his own art: "The work of art is not a finality.... It is engaged in the full play of its own existence."[53] This sense of becoming, rather than being, is fundamental to all

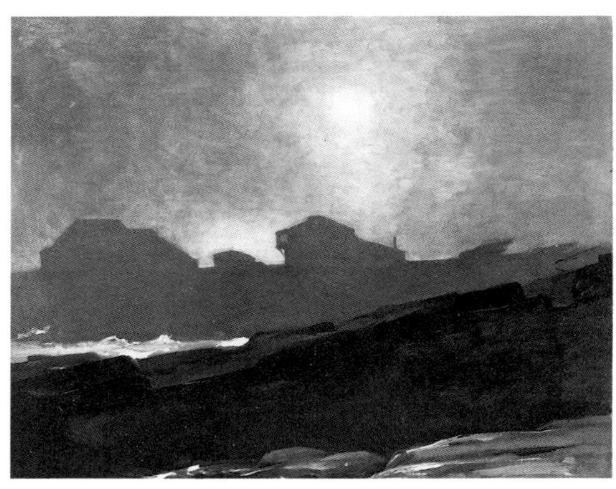

107. Homer. *The Artist's Studio in an Afternoon Fog,* 1894.

these artists' approach to reality. Even in Hopper, whose art is without movement, the tension between the clarifying nature of the light and the stolid structures, which look as though they shelter mysteries they do not want revealed, is dynamic. Whether in Bellows, where the energy is all on the surface, or in Hopper, they all suggest the secret that things are not what we suppose them to be, that what we see is just a surface beneath which lies everything else. This is the core of their realism—a realism not social or class-bound as in literature but one that is about the way material things contain meanings. Clement Greenberg has said of Homer that his "presumably matter-of-fact vision, like that of Stephen Crane, another 'literal' realist, would, when directed out of doors, usually alight on something that moved dramatically, were it but waves or a leaping fish."[54] This moving wave or fish is just that: an assertion that the meanings of the world are not metaphors—symbols we create and read out of the books of experience we write ourselves—but are things that force themselves on our attention.

After the Armory Show: John Sloan, Newell Convers Wyeth, John Marin, and Marsden Hartley

Abrupt and sometimes cataclysmic change staggered Europe and America after 1910. World War I shifted the earth under everyone's feet, killing off an era and leaving the few survivors wandering in a wasteland. Begun in 1914 with an assassin's bullet in a European backwater, by 1917 the conflict had engulfed the United States. During the intervening years, men seemed slowly to lose their reason, until all the old certainties were unrecognizable. Every field of life was touched by tremors announcing a new order, American art no less than any other. The Armory Show, which had preceded the war by one year, altered the terrain of the American art world ineradicably, or so it has always seemed.

Beginning with the idea of trumping all previous independent exhibitions, a group of artists even younger and more rebellious than Henri began to organize the biggest show ever, with the idea of admitting foreign artists as well as American. Calling themselves the Association of American Painters and Sculptors, they included both members of Henri's circle and artists connected with Alfred Stieglitz and his gallery "291," which represented the more adventuresome tastes of France and Germany. The group was led by Arthur B. Davies as a result of some bickering and maneuvering between different factions, which left Henri out in the cold (Stieglitz himself deliberately kept his distance). The show opened at the 69th Regiment Armory, on Lexington Avenue and Twenty-Fifth Street, in February 1913 and included nearly 1,300 works of art. During the three-week run, over 80,000 people crowded through its doors. Nearly one third of the show was the work of Europeans, including the latest work of the Parisian avant-garde; these garnered the most press attention, most of it ludicrously unfavorable. Perversely, these artists also made the biggest impression on the cognoscenti: of the 174 works sold, 123 were by foreigners.[1]

Important as the eye-opening first extensive appearance in New York of the latest happenings in France, the show also offered a revised history of modern art that quickly became orthodoxy and only recently has suffered revision. Giving an historical perspective on the current avant-garde, the show began with the work of Eugene Delacroix and other early nineteenth-century French artists: modernity began with the school of Paris and ended with it, with only one or two exceptions. All other national schools were cast into shadow, which would have surprised the many internationally successful late nineteenth-century Italian, Dutch, Spanish, Austrian, German, British, and Scandinavian artists. In the Armory Show's accounting, few older American artists made the grade. Homer was not one of them (Eakins was also excluded). Only Albert Pinkham Ryder (1847-1917), the visionary eccentric whose work was so popular with artists seeking a romantic heritage in American painting, was included in the exhibition.

The advent of modernist art in the United States is usually dated from the Armory Show. The way had been prepared by Alfred Stieglitz and his gallery "291," where as early as 1908 works by Henri Matisse and Pablo Picasso could be seen. In conventional histories it is taken for granted that the sight of so many cubists, Fauves, and their ilk in the show ended forever the dominance of the Ashcan school on the left of the mainstream of American art. Compared to Picasso, Matisse, and Duchamp, Henri and his students were revealed to be stale and rather conservative. The battles they had fought with the National Academy of Design might as well have taken place in the previous century for all the relevance their victories seemed to have to what was going on at that moment in Paris. But, of course, things were not so simple. Bellows, in particular, but certainly Henri, Kent, Luks, and Sloan, were all well-enough established to continue receiving favorable press notices and, more significantly, to be bought by collectors and museums.

However, for several years it did seem that every artist in New York wanted to be "modern" (a term variously defined). But few more than flirted with cubism and abstraction, and most soon renounced Parisian influence. For every rebellious young artist who lost himself in Paris after the war, there was another who quickly came home, weary of the destruction and weight of the past. The critic Henry McBride declared in 1921: "I like Paris, too,... but I think the time has come when it is no longer necessary for a first-rate American to go there."[2] Others continued to express a stronger resentment against Europe. As Thomas Craven said of Bellows after his death: "He is important to the young American; he has demonstrated that it is possible for a man to paint without addressing himself to the fads and philosophies of the Continent. With his keen sense of subject-matter and his faith in the American environment, he has indicated the road which our artists must travel in order to deliver themselves from European masquerade and create something in their own right."[3] By the 1930s, although Steiglitz and his artists were still working, most other artists had followed this reactionary advice. The dominant mode was nationalist, regionalist, and realist, with figures cast in a more classical style, or even an historicist adaption of earlier styles. Thomas Hart Benton is the most famous example: he tried out cubism in Paris but then deliberately adopted a figure style based on sixteenth-century Italian mannerism. His later position was extremely abusive of foreign influence and modernist abstraction. But perhaps it is just as fair to see his development and that of other American artists, including Bellows, in line with the development of an artist so "modern" as Picasso, who by 1920 had returned to painting large and impressive classical figures.

Just as the Armory Show had demoted most earlier American artists, many now returned to favor. It was a sign of the times that the Museum of Modern Art organized a show in 1930 devoted to that trinity of late nineteenth-century American artists— Eakins, Homer, and Ryder—and devoted a one-man show to Edward Hopper in 1933. Actually, in spite of a non-appearance in the Armory Show, Homer was never out of favor and continued to influence both realists and modernists.[4] He had achieved classic stature. Lewis Mumford, writing in 1931, declared his generation's interest in the art of the 1890s was the inevitable result of the grandfather law, but added that, more profoundly, both periods were similarly "post-war."[5] Ironically, another war ended the decade.

By and large, the members of Henri's circle reacted to the Armory Show by experimenting with formal elements of design more consciously, as though modernism had released them from the need to see formal qualities as merely decorative. For example, Vincent van Gogh had revealed that color for its own sake could be a direct and strong experience, rather than purely ornamental and aesthetic. Henri and his students pursued Jay Hambidge's "dynamic symmetry" and Hardesty Gillmore Maratta's color system, two home-grown theories developed in response to the European challenge.[6] Staunchly American, however, they rejected any long-term influence from such shallow Continental fashions. A year later Bellows, for example, felt: "Having got what I can out of the modernist movement for fresh spontaneous pure color I am now turning my attention to the 'Secrets of the Old Masters.'"[7] Later, he wrote to John Beatty, the Director of the Carnegie and Homer's friend: "Whatever in 'Modern Art' is most worthy ... seems to me to be an instinctive or a conscious search for funda- mental principles of abstraction."[8] After a few years' flirtation with outrageously strong color and stronger brushstrokes, he became more sedate, "old-masterish." The preoccupation with form engendered by his encounter with modernism led to monu- mental, rather static figures, with brushstrokes confined within their contours, ending much of the spontaneity and dynamism of his earlier paintings of New York and Monhegan.

World War I and the Armory Show seem to have sent another member of the Ashcan school out of both New York and the school altogether. John Sloan, who had been Henri's right hand man for a decade, now began to change in every aspect. Growing up in Philadelphia, Sloan had begun working at the age of sixteen, attending art schools, including the Pennsylvania Academy, at night.[9] He considered himself primarily a newspaper artist and a printmaker, and it took both time and pressure for him to start painting and leave Philadelphia for New York in 1904, the last of Henri's friends to do so. In many of Henri's independent exhibi- tion efforts during the next few years, Sloan played the trusted second-in-command; he was good at getting things done. Sloan and his wife Dolly were also extremely political. A devoted mem- ber of the Socialist party, he ran for the State Assembly twice, in 1910 and 1915, on the Socialist ticket (he did not win). He was also an editor of *The Masses,* which consumed much of his time during the prewar years.

During World War I, artists who had called themselves Social- ists faced a difficult dilemma: whether to support the war fever or deride it. Bellows, for example, became quite partisan, producing an overly dramatic series of lithographs denouncing German war atrocities (in which he competed with Goya's *Disasters of War* for graphic horror). Sloan, in contrast, declared himself a pacifist, an act of great courage and conviction at the time. Increasingly alienated from his associates during these years, he apparently retreated from the upheaval of politics and war, looking for ways out of what must have been a distressing position.

All along Sloan had had much less success than the others as a painter, despite a prolific output and exhibition record. He did not sell his first painting until 1913, nearly twenty years after he had begun. His subjects were almost entirely urban—scenes of people in New York streets and restaurants; always he saw people and places together, seldom painting either landscapes in which figures were subsidiary or single character studies. Unlike others in Henri's circle, once he had arrived in New York he almost never ventured beyond its limits to paint, partly because the city was his subject and life, and partly because he couldn't afford to.

Sloan had been invited to join Henri on Monhegan in 1911, along with Davey and Bellows. Although Sloan must have wanted to go, and had admired Kent's first paintings of Monhegan, he had declined because it was just too expensive.[10] Beginning in 1914, however, he began to summer in Gloucester, Massachusetts, returning there for the next four years. He continued to depict scenes full of people and the life of the village but also painted his first landscapes devoid of the human presence, using simple titles such as *Black and Yellow Rocks* (Figure 108). This departure from his usual habits excited the interest of his friends. Writing late in the summer of 1915, Henri told him that he had heard "great landscapes are being done in the Sloan shop.... I sh'd like to see the pictures."[11]

The first summer in Gloucester Sloan painted ninety canvases, in a great release of energy; his record the following summers was as good. Beginning in 1915, he painted a series of pure landscapes devoted to the rocks and water, to the exclusion of nearly everything else. In them, Sloan adopted the by-now classic posture of standing at the water's edge and looking down at his feet. *Fassett's Cove, Purple Rocks and Green Sea,* and *Red Rocks, Quiet Sea, no. II* (Figures 109-111) are examples of the most extreme concentration of form and content.

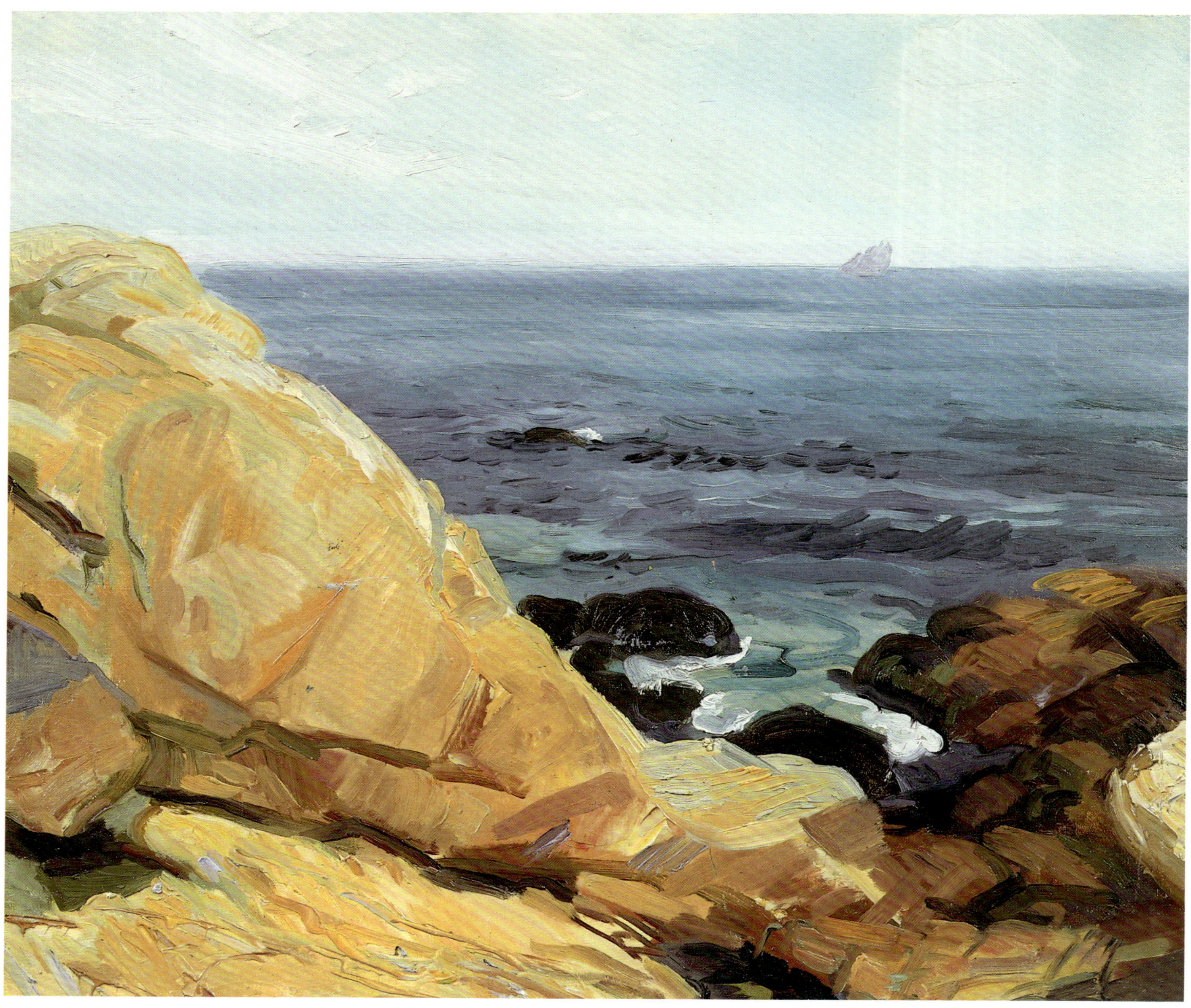

108. Sloan. *Black and Yellow Rocks,* 1917.

During his summers in Gloucester, Sloan's response to the European paintings in the Armory Show was quite evident. The strength of his brushstroke reveals a debt to van Gogh, the color to van Gogh and Paul Gauguin, the sense of weighty form to Cézanne. Years later Sloan recalled the Armory Show: "I consciously began to be aware of the technique of art: the use of graphic devices to represent plastic form. While I have made no abstract pictures, I have absorbed a great deal from the work of the ultra-moderns."[12] For the first time, in the Gloucester land-

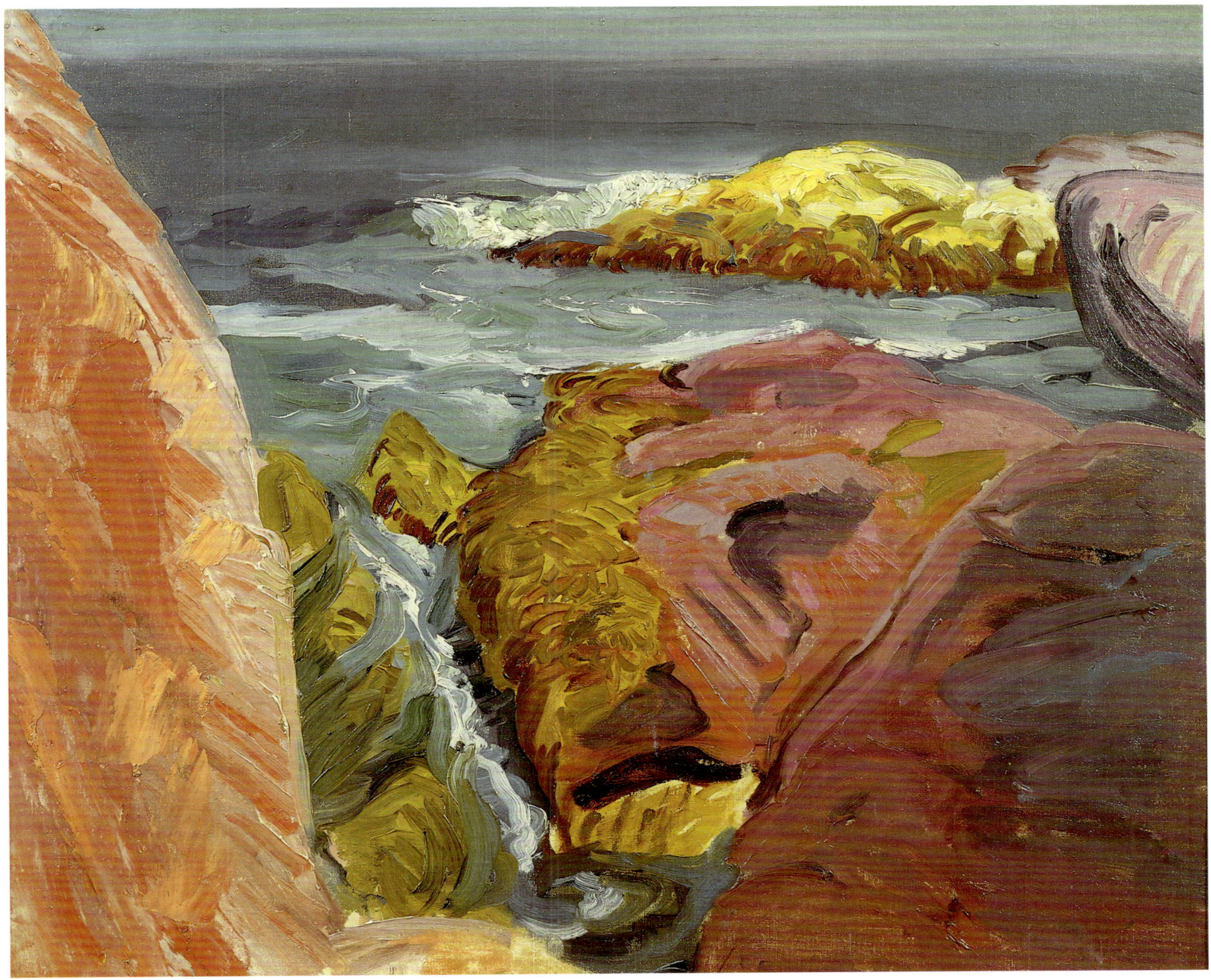

109. Sloan. *Fassett's Cove,* 1915.

scapes, Sloan began to think of formal issues; he played with color as an independent entity, instead of simply part of the object or person he was interested in painting. He began to consider how to convey mass in a two-dimensional pictorial surface, instead of seeing the surface naively as a screen on which to project the scenes he drew. He began to consider the classical concerns of balance, symmetry, dynamism, as primary elements in a picture instead of accidental benefits accruing from having seen his subject precisely.

110. Sloan. *Purple Rocks and Green Sea,* 1916.

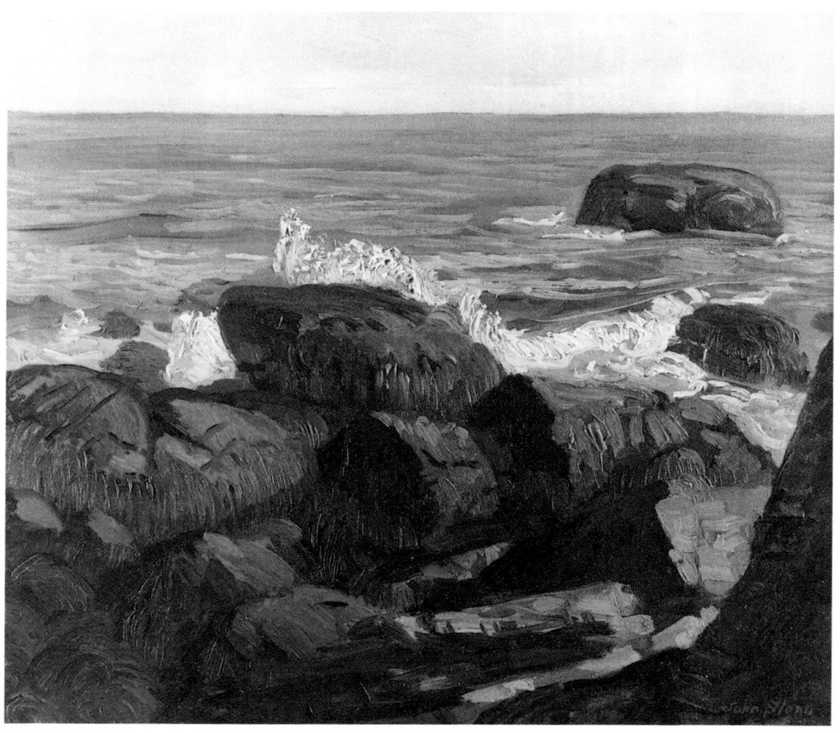

But his landscapes also had resonances closer to home, with the work of Bellows and Homer. Indeed, the similarities between Bellows' paintings at Monhegan and Ogunquit and Sloan's at Gloucester are striking. Using the same palette designed by Maratta, the color harmonies of their landscapes from 1915 through 1917 are often identical. Moreover, facing similar subjects, their compositions sometimes echo one another. For instance, Sloan's *Fassett's Cove* (Figure 109), 1915, anticipated Bellows' *The Fisherman* (Figure 83), 1917. Both artists, in order to achieve a sense of the land as a solid anchor against the undermining sea, proceeded by placing a great vertical shaft of rock to the left and smaller rocks to the lower right, reaching into the surf. Sloan's painting is a full-scale sketch, Bellows' is a finished work. One is painted in a warm harmony of salmons and yellows, the other, in an acidic palette of blues, purples, and greens. But the formal conceptions and response to the subject are identical.

In *Red Rocks, Quiet Sea, no. II* (Figure 111), 1916, Sloan used Homer's classic device of the diagonal wedge of rock. Sloan's *Red Rocks* is Homer's *Northeaster* (Figure 16), but with Homer's passionate, surging sea formalized into strong color contrasts. In *Purple Rocks and Green Sea* (Figure 110), 1916, Sloan adopted

Homer's device of a line of rocks in the foreground from paintings like *Maine Coast* (Figure 23). Here again, Sloan translated and simplified Homer's drama into a quieter statement where the energy of the scene lies in the pure color.[13] Drawn to Homer's works, Sloan also worked hard not to be controlled by them.

Sloan's decision to explore his responses to the Armory Show in landscape painting was hardly surprising, given that the works most engaging his interest were landscapes by Cézanne and van Gogh; their paintings had revealed to him "that landscape could be a magnificent source of exciting subject matter."[14] Nonetheless the choice of subjects so close to the work of Bellows and Homer indicated a strong desire to Americanize their foreign influence and betrayed an anxiety about the power of Europe. Landscape painting also constituted neutral ground in another sense: in painting the rocks and sea, Sloan could turn his back literally on the politics of New York City and the rest of the world, which were getting increasingly arduous. Where before his espousal of Socialist causes had been uncomplicated by factionalism, by 1916 he was forced to resign from *The Masses* in a dispute about editorial policy; the magazine was becoming more hard-line politically while he grew less. A few years later, he resigned from the Socialist party altogether. In his later art, Sloan adopted a bizarre, pseudo-Renaissance device of linear marks to denote form and a technique of tempera glazes. His subjects grew equally retardataire: nudes and portraits. But in the first moment of questioning his art, under the strain of both artistic and political events in Europe, he turned to the subjects of Winslow Homer, a bulwark against a sea of troubles.

While Homer was a temporary palliative for Sloan, for others he remained a guiding light during the troubled years ahead. Buffeted by tides of non-representational art, many artists continued to paint seascapes in the manner of Homer (as they do to the present-day). For other conventional artists, a dash of Homer could invigorate and inspire. One example is Newell Convers Wyeth (1882-1945), who was exactly the same age as Kent, Bellows, and Hopper. An illustrator all his life, toward the end of his career Wyeth got the hankering to be taken more seriously. He bought a house in Port Clyde, the small village from which the ferry departs for Monhegan Island, in 1920 and finished renova-

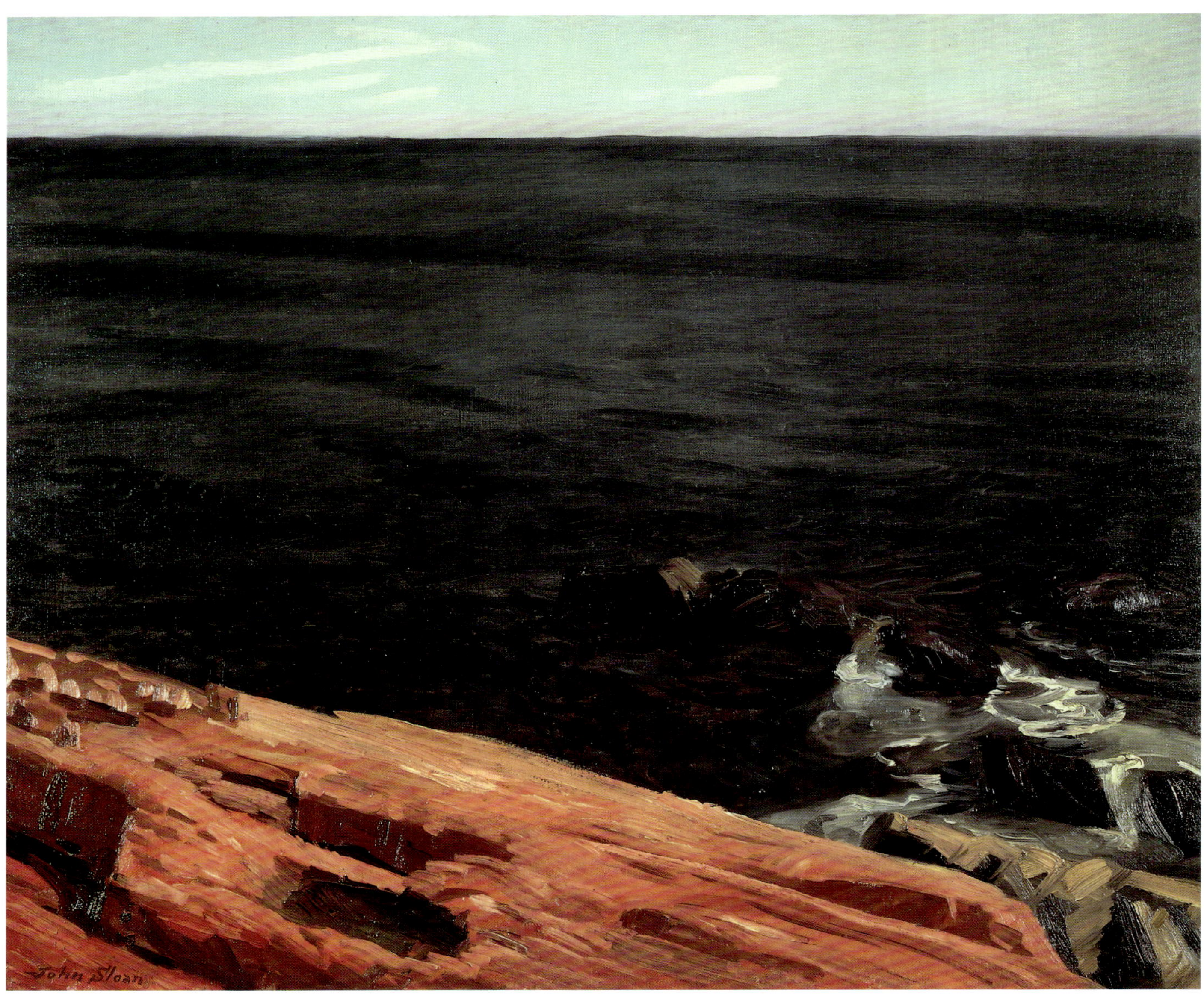

111. Sloan. *Red Rocks, Quiet Sea, no. II,* 1916.

tions in 1930. Settling in, he named the house "Eight Bells," after Homer's painting of the same name, and hung a reproduction of the painting in the living room. Inspired both by Maine and Homer, Wyeth began to paint "the sterner aspects of life and living on that robust coast," wanting "something bigger" than his earlier work.[15] He produced variations of both Homer's fishing paintings and his marines. In one work, *Portrait of a Young Artist,* ca. 1930 (Figure 112), Wyeth captured both the heritage of Homer and his own hopes for the future. The painting shows the young Andrew Wyeth, N. C. Wyeth's son, who had just begun his

112. N. C. Wyeth. *Portrait of a Young Artist,* ca. 1930.

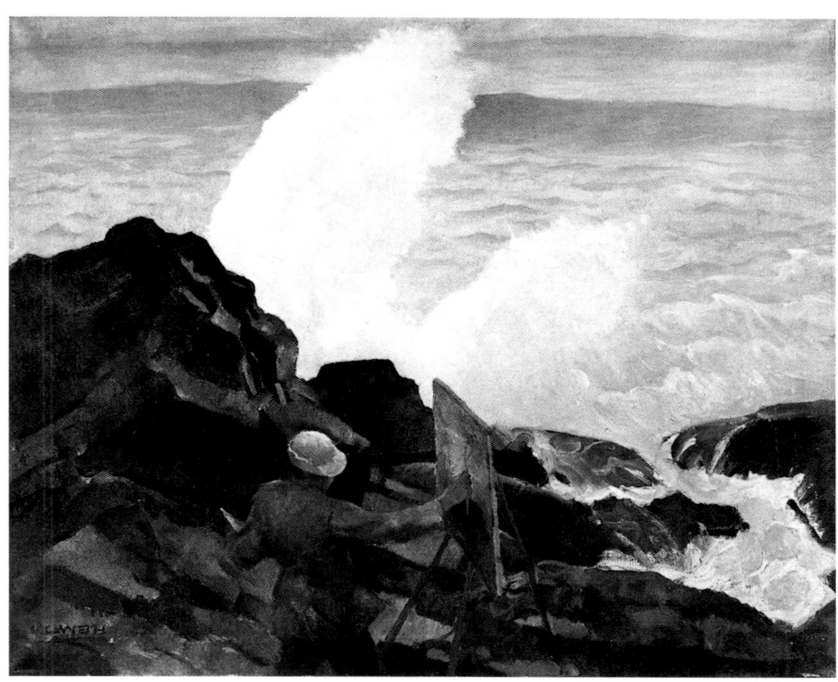

career as a serious artist, standing before his easel on the shore and painting the sea. The setting is quintessential Homer: a diagonal foreground of rock and scrub vegetation, and a great spray of a wave cresting over the artist's head. The setting and, more particularly, the spume, which acts like the wings of a guardian angel protecting the destiny of the young man, express both the content of the artist's work and its essence: simple, direct, and real. N. C. Wyeth's painting could not have been more prophetic: if any single artist today may be reckoned as following in Homer's footsteps it is Andrew Wyeth.

In this accounting modernism seems to have lost to the realist counter-attack very quickly. But, of course, it was not so. Modernist painters, after the Armory Show, continued to paint; their work was bought and defended. Socially and spiritually the divisions between them and many of the artists of Henri's circle were not very deep: Max Weber, for example, was George Bellows' first choice for the show of American painting organized in France in 1920. For the artists of Steiglitz's circle and others involved in the modern movement, Homer exerted a powerful attraction.[16]

The artist and patron Hamilton Easter Field, for example,

admired and collected Homer at the same time that he championed modern art.[17] Field ran an art school in Ogunquit, which catered to young and adventurous art students. He and his students scampered over the rocks of one side of the bay, daringly painting nudes and primitive landscapes, while Charles Woodbury and his ladies toiled on the other side. Students enrolled in Field's school included Yasuo Kuniyoshi, Stefan Hirsch, and Lloyd Goodrich (our foremost Homer scholar); other artists who were attracted to Ogunquit because of his presence were Bernard Karfiol, Marsden Hartley, and Maurice Sterne. Like N. C. Wyeth, Field "revered the nobility and grandeur which he felt was innate in these Maine natives."[18] And he, like so many others, felt the need for a national art based on American traditions. Writing in 1920, he stated: "We should not allow ourselves to be drawn away from the task we have before us of creating a national tradition by sympathies for schools of art which are natural products of an over-ripe culture."[19]

Other supporters of modernism were inspired by Homer. Henry McBride, recalling his early years as a critic, wrote: "In those days Winslow Homer was my religion (and still is)."[20] In the pages of *Camera Work,* Steiglitz's own journal, Charles Caffin and Edward Steichen, among others, praised Homer's work.[21] Even in the midst of a discussion of cubism, Homer's name could pop up. Arthur Jerome Eddy, in *Cubists and Post-Impressionism,* the first book published on the subject in America, in 1914, described Homer using much the same language employed by Kenyon Cox, the archenemy of avant-garde painting, in his book *Winslow Homer* published the same year. Eddy wrote: "Take, for instance, the strongest things by Winslow Homer; the strength lies in the big, elemental manner in which the artist rendered his impressions in lines and masses which departed widely from photographic reproductions of scenes and people."[22] Eddy, along with nearly every other critic, was concerned about the nature of American art; as always Homer filled the role of the quintessential native, the one who stood up against foreign domination. As Eddy explained:

What is happening in America? Exactly what might be expected in a young, vigorous and virile country ...

American-Impressionism, or, more generically, Virile-Impressionism.... [American artists] have painted not the surfaces of things but the substance—in short, they were Cézanne-Impressionists as distinguished from Monet-Impressionists. For instance, Winslow Homer was a great and true Impressionist, but he had nothing in common with the Neo-Impressionists, and little in common with Monet. He had, however, a great deal in common with Cézanne.... He was, in a sense, the greatest of American-Impressionists—he was a Virile-Impressionist.... It was inevitable that Impressionism in America should follow along virile and substantial lines rather than along nervous and superficial; it is the way the country is built.[23]

The two modernist artists who most keenly felt Homer's influence and who were often compared to him are Marsden Hartley and John Marin; both were members of Stieglitz's circle and both worked in Maine. Despite temperamental differences, they have often been paired together like oil and vinegar; Marin the blithe spirit, Hartley the tortured soul. Gail Scott has characterized them most acutely, noting that Marin's seascapes are mostly water, Hartley's largely rock.[24] Their responses to Homer express the same distinction.

John Marin (1870-1953) was born in Rutherford, New Jersey, and intended to become an architect.[25] He did not study painting until he was nearly thirty, when he took classes at the Pennsylvania Academy. In 1904 he enrolled at the Art Students League in New York and the next year sailed for Paris, where he stayed for four years, mixing with avant-garde artists. On his return in 1909, he met Stieglitz and had his first exhibition at "291" in 1910. His work betrays the influences of the latest French styles—fauvism, cubism, and futurism—absorbed and translated into his own terms, in watercolor. His subject was Manhattan, portrayed in a dynamically fragmented style. Done at the same time as Bellows' paintings, Marin's watercolors were their antithesis in style, but similar in feeling: both artists were concerned with portraying the city as a force of nature.

John Marin first visited Maine in 1914, at the age of forty-four, and spent nearly every summer there for the rest of his life,

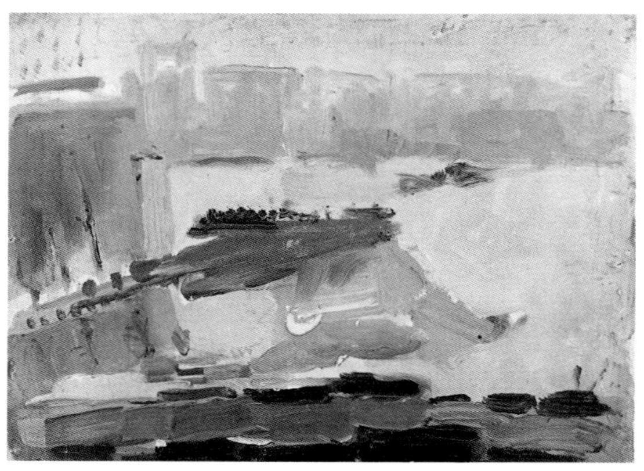

113. Marin. *Weehawken Grain Elevators* (from the series: *Weehawken Sequence),* ca. 1916.

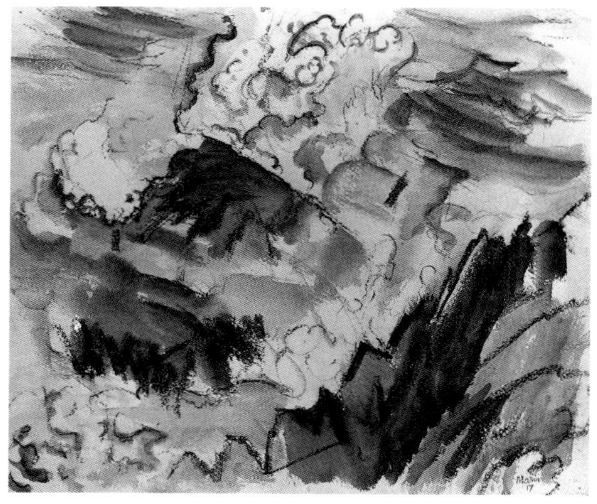

114. Marin. *Study of the Sea,* 1917.

buying a house at Cape Split in 1934. His first reactions were strong: "This is one fierce, relentless, cruel, beautiful, fascinating, hellish, and all other ish'es, place."[26] Almost his first act was to buy an island: "I am strong on houses and islands—the ocean can (go) nuts." But as he stayed longer on the Maine coast, the sea claimed him more completely; he later exclaimed: "Here the sea is so damned insistent that houses and land things won't appear much in my pictures."[27]

His first watercolors of Maine seem almost Chinese meditations on the delights of pine trees, granite, and small islands. In 1917, however, the watercolors done in Small Point on Casco Bay, near Portland, show Homer's influence strongly: many are closeups of the rocks, with a great clump of granite to one side in the foreground, another rock a few feet off in the water, surrounded by water and pounded by a wave. The significant artistic event intervening between these two perceptions of Maine was his series of views of Weehawken, his childhood home, painted in 1916. In *Weehawken Grain Elevators* from the *Weehawken Sequence* series (Figure 113), for example, the jetty thrusts energetically into the river. Both water and dock emerge out of heavy, energetic oil paint. The energy in the medium and motif is direct here, not expressed indirectly as the lines of force and vision characterizing his earlier urban views. In these paintings the energy resides materially in the thing itself, not in the manner in which it is seen. Like Bellows, Marin was prepared for Maine and Homer by his experience of the dynamism of the city. The connection to Bellows may be taken further. Marin's watercolor *Study of the Sea,* 1917 (Figure 114), for example, is reminiscent of Bellows' oil sketches of only a few years before, which Marin could well have seen in New York.[28]

In 1928 Marin began to paint extensively in oil for the first time since 1916, a change explained only, it seems, by a desire to face a new challenge: he was fifty-eight years old. *Rocks and Sea, Small Point, Maine* (Figure 115), painted in July 1931, is one of the first of these oils. The painting heralds a new sense of energy and power in Marin's work, in which the use of the heavier and more plastic medium of oil suits the newly aggressive encounters of sea and rock, the waves attacking the shore with great ferocity.[29] This conjunction of medium and subject, with its obvious

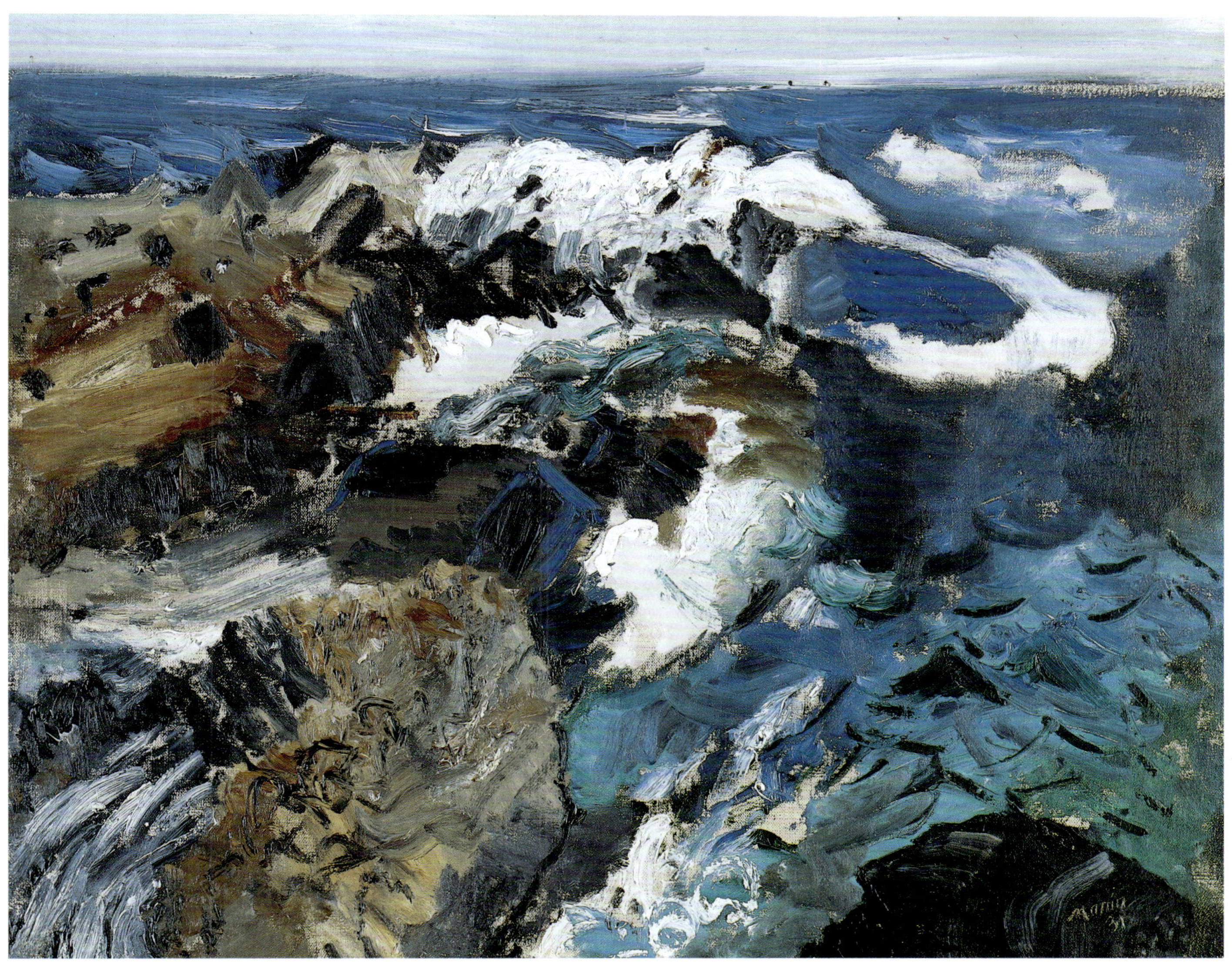

115. Marin. *Rocks and Sea, Small Point, Maine,* 1931.

debts to Winslow Homer, continued for several years, reaching a climax in works even more explicitly Homeric, such as *Wave on Rock,* 1937 (Figure 116). Here, the sea even more violently bursts into the center of the canvas, breaking on hard, dark stones. One rock projects into the middle of the maelstrom, reminding us (probably deliberately) in its shape and placement of Homer's *Cannon Rock* (Figure 17).

Marin's new dynamism in handling oil paint coincided with a fresh emphasis in his attitude toward his craft and to nature itself. Both became more explicitly sexualized, perhaps not surprising in a man confidently facing his mid-sixties. The summer of

1931 he called "unforgettably lovely, unforgettably beautiful." His biographer tellingly adds: "Even the sea was benign: coy, womanly, smiling."[30] Marin wrote to Stieglitz in July, reflecting on the nature of his task in tones both eager and crudely pragmatic:

> *Yes, I'll have it that painting is a* Job—*a* Job *in paint—and I am afraid that in the crazed desire to be modern—to have ideas—to be original—to belong to the tribe* intelligentcia [sic]—*we have gotten away from the paint job which is a* lusty thing ... *and I almost feel like saying "what you have to say don't amount to so much"—but the* lusty *desire to splash about—submerge oneself* [sic] *in a medium—you might come up to surface with something worth while—Oh there be phases and phases still more—but at the present I sing to the LUSTY.*[31]

Marin disassociated himself from European modernist painters; he contrasted their work with the "lusty" job he did, where the medium of oil itself was made voluptuous.

The next summer he continued in the same vein, regarding nature even more sexually, as he had the act of painting:

> *Old Mistress—Maine ...*
> *she's lovely ...*
> *with an unforgettable loveliness—an unforgettable beauty*
> *—Turns masculine—borders big and mighty—against—the big and mighty Atlantic*
> *Tremendous shoulders to brace against his furious brother...*
>
> *Maine makes or breaks...*
> *—A painter man—here—if-of-her breed or her adoption—must needs conform—*
>
> *The sea—it's the sea*
> *The rock-ledge—it's the rock-ledge....*
> *Trees—bushes—all—all—all themselves of themselves—of their belonging—*
> *This insistence of being themselves—painter man—This dominance—painter man—This objective subjecting*

itself—going through you compels—painter man—all your lustiness—penetrates—to the marrow.[32]

Appropriating Homer's power and granite-like confidence as well as his motifs, Marin took on a new, sensualized strength and life, surprising most of his critics. He had always been known as a watercolorist, treasured for his lightness of tone and touch. Normally his vision sparkled, delighting the viewer. Marin did not bear down heavily but had an irrepressible independence of voice. Despite the exuberant modernism of his art, his very freedom redeemed him. Ultimately, Marin was basically a "meat and potatoes" guy, an American artist.[33] Through the mastery displayed in his watercolors, as well as his Maine subject matter, he had always warranted comparison with Homer but lacked Homer's gravity and sober realism.[34] Marin was like the Maine weather, not the solid rock. As the collector Duncan Phillips observed: "John Marin blows through the world of modern art like a strong bracing wind from the sea ... [and] an apprehension of the elemental which transcends school and dogma."[35]

Marin's oils forced critics to reconsider the seriousness of his vision, not always kindly. The rare reviewer who did appreciate Marin's oils interpreted them darkly: "The somber tone of a mature vision, the resigned peace after tragedy is to be felt in [them]. The painting is austere, passionate, strong, as majestic as the watercolors but somehow sterner."[36] Today we grant their maturity but see little tragedy in them; they seem rather to display a love of energy for itself, as his work always had, only now expressed in the viscosity and drag of oil paint. Marin never lost his light-heartedness, as the rest of his later oil paintings demonstrate. Marin's return to Homer in the 1930s empowered him to paint in oil, but he never explored Homer's depths. Marin is the rare painter who gathered from Homer energy but disregarded Homer's morbidity (with the possible exception of his *Wave on Rock*).

Both in character and painting, Marsden Hartley (1877-1943) was a more complicated figure than John Marin.[37] Hartley was born and died in Maine, and always considered himself a native of the state, but he spent most of his life beyond its borders. His first training took place in Cleveland, where his sisters lived, but by

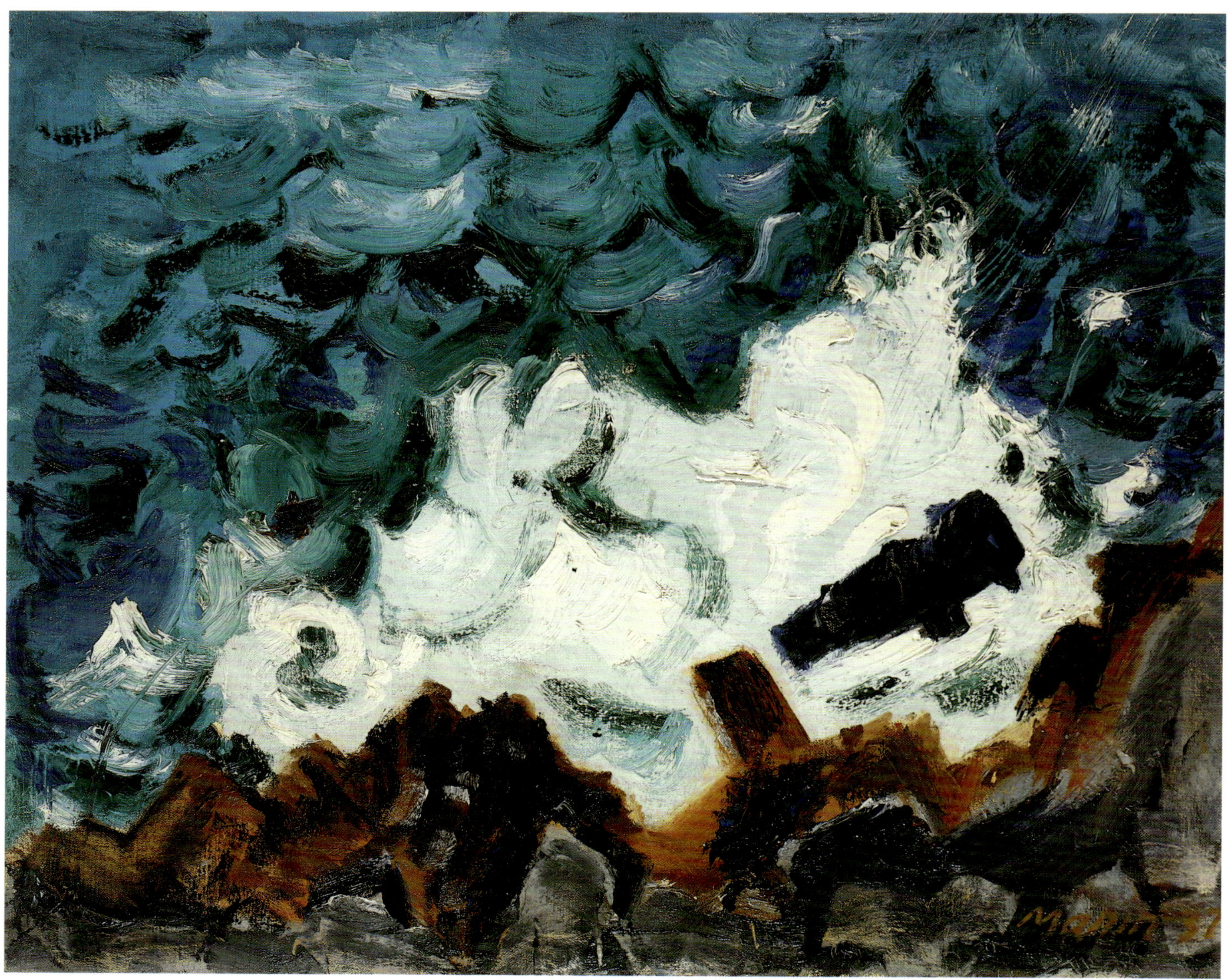

116. Marin. *Wave on Rock,* 1937.

1899 he was in New York City, at the Chase school. The next year Hartley transferred to the National Academy of Design, where he studied for four years, spending his summers in Maine. There or in New York City he became acquainted with Socialism, later becoming a friend of John Reed (although, like Marin, politics never seem to have concerned him greatly). In 1909 Hartley had his first one-man show at "291," but by this time he had also been befriended by the Prendergasts and Glackens, members of The Eight. For the next twenty years, with the interruption of World War I, Hartley spent most of his time in Europe. During a stay in Berlin before the war, he painted his first important non-representational paintings; until that point he had been primarily a landscape painter. In the years that followed the war, his style and subject matter oscillated among a variety of options, always returning to landscape.

Hartley's response to nature was at first earnestly mystical, in a good transcendental fashion. He wanted to feel intensely the presence of a nature in which his own self could be submerged. Nature, for Hartley, was always tied to the particular character of a place, but at the same time, he wanted to universalize his experience. Unlike Marin, who was also concerned with place, Hartley did not deal in energy and flux, but in hardness, certainty, and power. Although he might wish to swim freely in the ocean of natural sensation, at the same time he feared losing his own identity. The pattern of his life reveals the contradictions he felt: in the city he pined for the country; stuck in the countryside he regretted the loss of friends and urban pleasures.

Perhaps the foundation of his divided experience of life was the interaction of his sexuality and his family history. His mother had died when he was eight. His father then left him in the care of relatives and moved to Cleveland with Hartley's sisters. Hartley followed some years later, but the damage had already been done. The barrenness of his upbringing, the lack of love expressed toward him, made him tend to withdraw from any expression of love himself. For the rest of his life, "family" consisted of relationships that might be close for awhile, but that sooner or later half-dissolved, as Hartley would move on or become reclusive. The problem was compounded by his homosexuality, which made the expression of intimate love socially nearly impossible. Other homosexual artists of the time managed to maintain long-term relationships with lovers, but most of them lived in cities, in Europe, and few were as lacerated by their family history as Hartley. Only in Berlin did he seem to have had a wholly successful social and sexual life, and the war ended that catastrophically.

In spite of the problematic nature of his sexuality and its acceptable expression, Hartley nonetheless sexualized his art. He recalled his first interest in art: "I began somehow to have curiosity about art at the same time when sex consciousness is full developed and as I did not incline to concrete escapades I of course inclined to abstract [ones] and the collecting of objects which is a sex expression took the upper hand."[38] Later in life he expressed his concern about masculinity in art, as did most male American artists, irrespective of sexual preference. Surrealism attracted his disgust: "You will never make me believe those pictures were not done by a woman."[39] Painters must be fully men: "I want the whole body, the whole flesh in painting. Renoir said that he painted with all of his manhood, and is it not evident."[40] And of the American *trompe-l'oeil* painter William Harnett Hartley wrote, "There is no knowing how Harnett would have done flowers as I have seen none if he did them, but quite likely his maleness was interested in a masculine sense of truth and volume."[41] Masculinity was associated, for Hartley, with realism and solidity.

Some of Hartley's greatest paintings were prompted by the death of close male friends. His series of the German officer paintings, his most monumental pre-war paintings, elegized the death of Karl von Freyburg, his intimate friend. Three other deaths prompted profound responses. In 1932 Hart Crane, another homosexual artist, committed suicide by jumping overboard when returning to the United States from Mexico. Hartley had just gotten to know him and responded to the loss with the painted elegy *Eight Bells Folly: Memorial to Hart Crane,* 1933. Two years later Hartley found himself in Nova Scotia, boarding with a fisherman's family. Hartley adopted the Masons in his imagination as his own family: he, the outside spectator; they, the center of the universe. He had begun to write a long narrative inspired by them, when the two sons, Donny and Alty, whom Hartley idealized as embodiments of masculine vitality and wholeness, drowned in a sudden storm in September 1936. Shattered, Hartley abandoned Nova Scotia and the next year painted *Northern Seascape—Off the Banks* (Milwaukee Art Museum).

Despite this record of loss and flight, his heart was centered in one place. However much he might have hated it, and deserted it, Maine claimed him. Paul Rosenfeld acutely observed in 1924: "Some day, perhaps some day not so far distant, Hartley will have to go back to Maine. For it seems that flight from Maine is in part flight from his deep feelings."[42] Concerned as he was with the character of men and Maine, the terms in which Hartley finally identified himself with Maine, in his 1937 essay "On the Subject of Nativeness—a tribute to Maine," were not surprising. Characterizing the land and the people as one, Hartley declared the people of Maine to embody "simple, unaffected conduct ... that hardiness of gaze and frank earnestness of approach which is typical of northerners." They are "the type of hard boned sturdy beings, [who] have the direct simplicity of these unique and original places." Almost inevitably, he described Winslow Homer as a typical "Maine-iac." Hartley concluded: "This quality of nativeness is colored by heritage, birth, and environment, and it is therefore for this reason that I wish to declare myself the painter from Maine."[43]

In his requisitioning of Maine, Hartley also sought artistic ancestors. The two most important were Ryder and Homer, representing the two sides of the state: the romantic pull of nature and the reality of the struggle for life. Ryder was the love of Hartley's youth, a painter to whom he returned in several moments of stress, in need of inspiration. But Homer was an artist for Hartley's old age, when he knew to the marrow of his bones what Homer had to say about life and death.

For years Hartley had been writing about Homer. While recognizing his limitations (his frozen emotions, his lack of imagination), Hartley acknowledged his strengths: "In Winslow Homer we have yankeeism of the first order... You are held by him constantly to the bold and naked theme, and you are left to wander in the imagination only among the essentials of simple and common realism."[44] Hartley felt the power of Homer's footing in Maine: "He was essentially on the ground, and wanted to paint the very grip of his own feet on the rocks. He wanted the inevitability put down in recognizable form."[45] And Homer was masculine and direct. Hartley concluded his essay: "[*The Gulf Stream*] has the powers of Jack London and of Conrad in it. Homer was intense, vigorous, and masculine. If he was harsh in his characteristics, he was one who knew the worth of economy in emotion. He was one with his idea and his metier, and that is sufficient."[46]

Hartley's first paintings of Maine, done while he was a student in New York, were the antithesis of Homer's. Hartley painted the mountains as great impassive forms on which the clouds, storms, and colors of the autumn played as on a screen, a reassuring objectification of the sacred emotions of love and awe that the

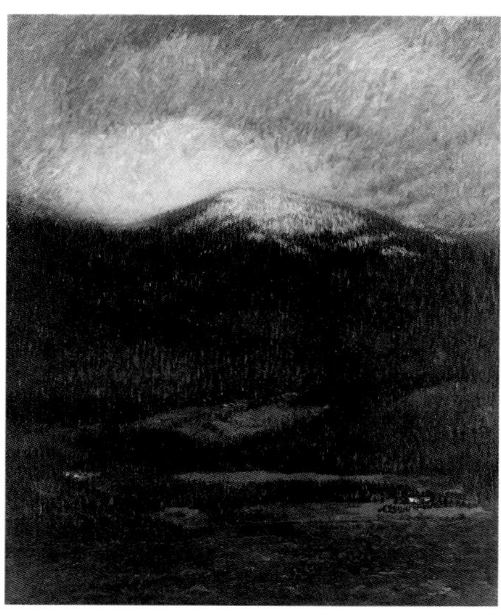

117. Hartley. *Autumn Lake and Hills,* 1907.

scene aroused in him (Figure 117). He did not begin to paint the coast and the ocean until after visits to Dogtown (near Gloucester, Massachusetts) and Nova Scotia. When he finally did return to Maine in 1937, he did so in the company of Death, filled with mourning for the dead boys, Donny and Alty Mason.[47]

Marin also helped bring Hartley back to Maine. That fall, Hartley wrote an essay for a show of Marin's work at the Museum of Modern Art, in which he discussed "my native land of Maine which I am always being told about by one good painter, this being Marin." The show included Marin's *Rocks and Sea* (Figure 115), which was reproduced in the catalogue. While Hartley was in New York at the end of 1936, the Whitney Museum had an exhibition marking the centennial of Homer's birth. In August, only a few months before, Hartley had written of his pride "that Homer's inspiration and his sense of dramatic nature were derived chiefly from my own native rocks, at Prout's Neck, Maine."[48] In April 1937 Hartley wrote "On the Subject of Nativeness—A Tribute to Maine" for an exhibition of his work at the gallery An American Place only months from his sixtieth birthday. Finally, in the summer of 1937, Hartley arrived in Maine, "for exactly this reason and no other, I returned to its tall timbers and its granite cliffs—because in them rests the kind of integrity I believe in and from which source I draw my private strength both spiritual and esthetical."[49]

Hartley's independent existence of the 1920s ended with the Depression, and repatriation to America became a journey to his roots in many ways. But the return to his past came at a time when his past was being stripped away from him. In going back to Maine, he found himself like Homer on a rocky shore facing an ocean that ate the land out from under him. If the land stood for permanence, then the ocean represented time and destruction: the loss of loved ones and the onset of old-age. Moreover, during these years World War II was gaining momentum until it at last enveloped America in 1941. Hartley's isolation was only compounded by the renewed destruction in Europe (initiated again by the Germany which had once claimed his heart) and by the tumultuous war preparations on the domestic front.[50] Only his powers as an artist resisted: his late work triumphantly withstood all the ravaging of his daily existence.

In the end he found another family, the Youngs, in Corea, Maine. Accounts of his last illness are pitiful. Confined to his bed, he could not bear to be left alone and forced himself down to the kitchen to share their company. Finally, unable to care for him, the Youngs sent him to a hospital, despite his pleading to stay and begging them not to let anyone else touch him. He died a day later, alone.

The manner of his death makes his essential loneliness apparent, but we feel the lack of human warmth, of human touch, in all of Hartley's last work. Like Homer, he faced the end of life by himself, with just the sea in front of him and the bare rock at his feet. The sea, author of his most tragic loss, became the central image of his art. He once said that Ryder was "the only great painter of the sea in the whole range of painting at any time ... he gave not only the majestic appearance of the sea but he gave it its tragic and merciless inner power."[51] But now, painting the North Atlantic for the first time in Maine, the inspiration of Winslow Homer's work became crucial.

Northern Seascape—Off the Banks, 1936-37, was a memorial to the young Masons. It was Hartley's first seascape, although elements of the sea had appeared in his work for years. In this painting two sailboats drift under a clouded sky; in the foreground great, granite teeth forbid their landing: they threaten to thresh the water to shreds, and the lives borne by the sea. As Hartley wrote:

> *"I'll have them both," said raging sea*
> *and took these lovers to his water strategy.*[52]

Memories of Ryder's work have been noted in Hartley's painting, as well as Homer's *The Gulf Stream* (Figure 24). But Ryder's oceans never engage the shore; they are dramas of mid-ocean. Although the shapes of Hartley's clouds and boats are reminiscent of Ryder, the painter's viewpoint in the painting is closer to Homer's *Summer Squall* or *On a Lee Shore,* or even *Maine Coast* (Figures 36, 35, and 23). The murderous conjunction of rock and wave held Hartley's attention. He equated the sea and death frequently in his poems of this period: "Stiff tone of death / in every wave / what more can wave have / save perhaps a little

118. Hartley. *Off the Banks at Night,* 1942.

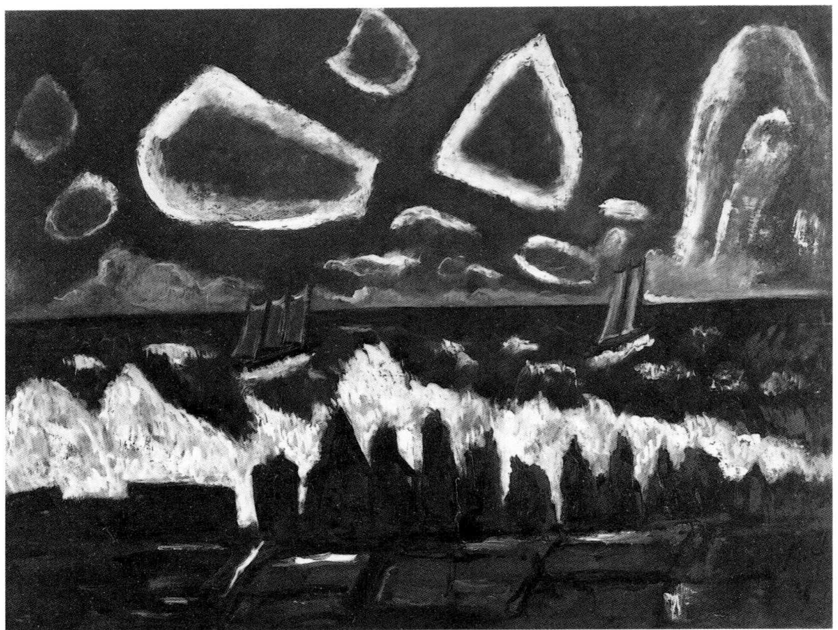

love."[53] That equation and the image of the shore studded with teeth like the jaw of a shark captivated him for many years, as he continued to mourn the Masons' death. His last book of poems, *Seaburial,* 1941, restates the theme, as does one of his last paintings: *Off the Banks at Night,* 1942 (Figure 118), a more savage version of *Northern Seascape.* The deep fissure in his life—the love he felt but could never hope to see returned to him, with which so many of these paintings resonate—was never healed. In every way his restatement of Homer's theme is harder and more tragic; the balance in which Homer finally rested Hartley had to fight to maintain.

Hartley wrote admiringly of Homer's sea paintings: "The crashing of the waves after a storm at sea, upon the jagged shores, no one has ever done just that, he has made the sea even more 'life-like' than Courbet the great French realist."[54] Certainly it was in paintings of the battle of water and land that Hartley became most Homeric. *The Spent Wave, Indian Point, Georgetown, Maine,* 1937-38 (Figure 119), one of several versions of the subject, is dominated by a diagonal mass of rock reminiscent of Homer's *High Cliffs, Coast of Maine* or *Coast of Maine* (Figures 15, 14).[55] But the water has invaded the land: the rocks could almost be barrels or logs tossed by the surf onto the shore.

All sense of stability has been lost, and the few trees in the upper right of the composition are about to be swept out to sea. In *Evening Storm, Schoodic, Maine,* 1942 (Figure 120), the foreground has been stabilized and flattened, but the wave has grown more massive.[56] This is Homer's *Northeaster* modernized, made even more elemental and more powerful.[57] Gone are any decorative niceties. The time is night; the weather is stormy. Human hopes and fears have been rendered irrelevant.[58] Homer, in his last work *Driftwood* (Figure 38), interposed a single human figure between the land and the ocean. Hartley dispenses with even that gesture. Nonetheless, *Evening Storm* is not tragic but immensely heartening. Time may do its worst to man, but seen through the artist's eyes, wind and wave advance and recede eternally.

Writing "Dry Salvages" from *The Four Quartets* as Hartley was painting *Evening Storm,* the poet T. S. Eliot also explored man's place within nature's sphere, using the sea for his metaphor.[59] Describing "the granite teeth" of the shore, "the ragged rock in the restless waters, ... the sudden fury" of the storm, and "the drifting wreckage," Eliot acknowledged the power of nature, even when "unhonoured, unpropitiated by worshippers of the machine." "The river is within us, the sea is all about us," Eliot explained. Concerned with "the intersection of the timeless with time," he concluded that we "are only undefeated because we have gone on trying." Facing the same worshippers of the machine, Henry Adams' decision "to live two separate lives" a generation earlier has now been narrowed to Eliot's simple advice: "Fare forward, voyagers." Hartley and Eliot, both working in the midst of the horrors of World War II, found a measure of peace "between two waves of the sea."

Homer's American identity in his late works is a narrow space between realism and abstraction inhabited by large and forceful forms, a familiar territory for American artists, from Jackson Pollock and Franz Kline to Eric Fischl and many others. As Hartley and Marin both demonstrated, American artists have been reluctant to ignore the call of nature, tied ineluctably to their own bodies.

The transcendentalist Henry David Thoreau reflected on his experience of nature descending from the peak of Mount

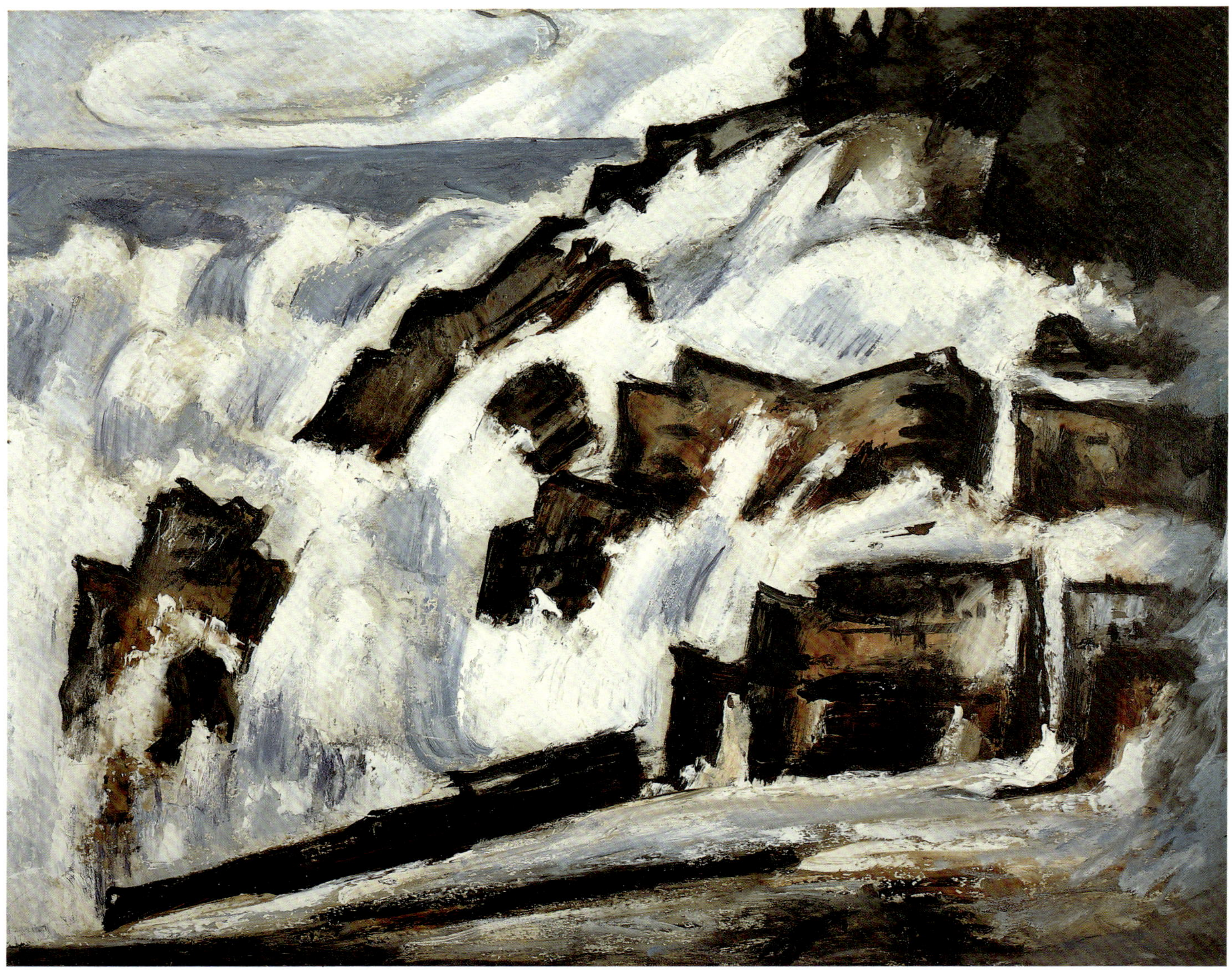

119. Hartley. *The Spent Wave, Indian Point, Georgetown, Maine*, 1937-38.

Katahdin, Maine, in 1846: "I stand in awe of my body, this matter to which I am bound has become so strange to me. I fear not spirits, ghosts, of which I am one,—*that* my body might,—but I fear bodies, I tremble to meet them. What is this Titan that has possession of me? Talk of mysteries!—Think of our life in nature,—daily to be shown matter, to come in contact with it,—rocks, trees, wind on our cheeks! the solid earth! the *actual* world! the *common sense! Contact! Contact! Who* are we? *where* are we?"[60] American artists have seldom abandoned this common-sense affinity for solid matter, nor an awe of their own physical being. The American poet Robert Frost, of the same generation as Sloan and Hartley, characterized his search for a truer reality

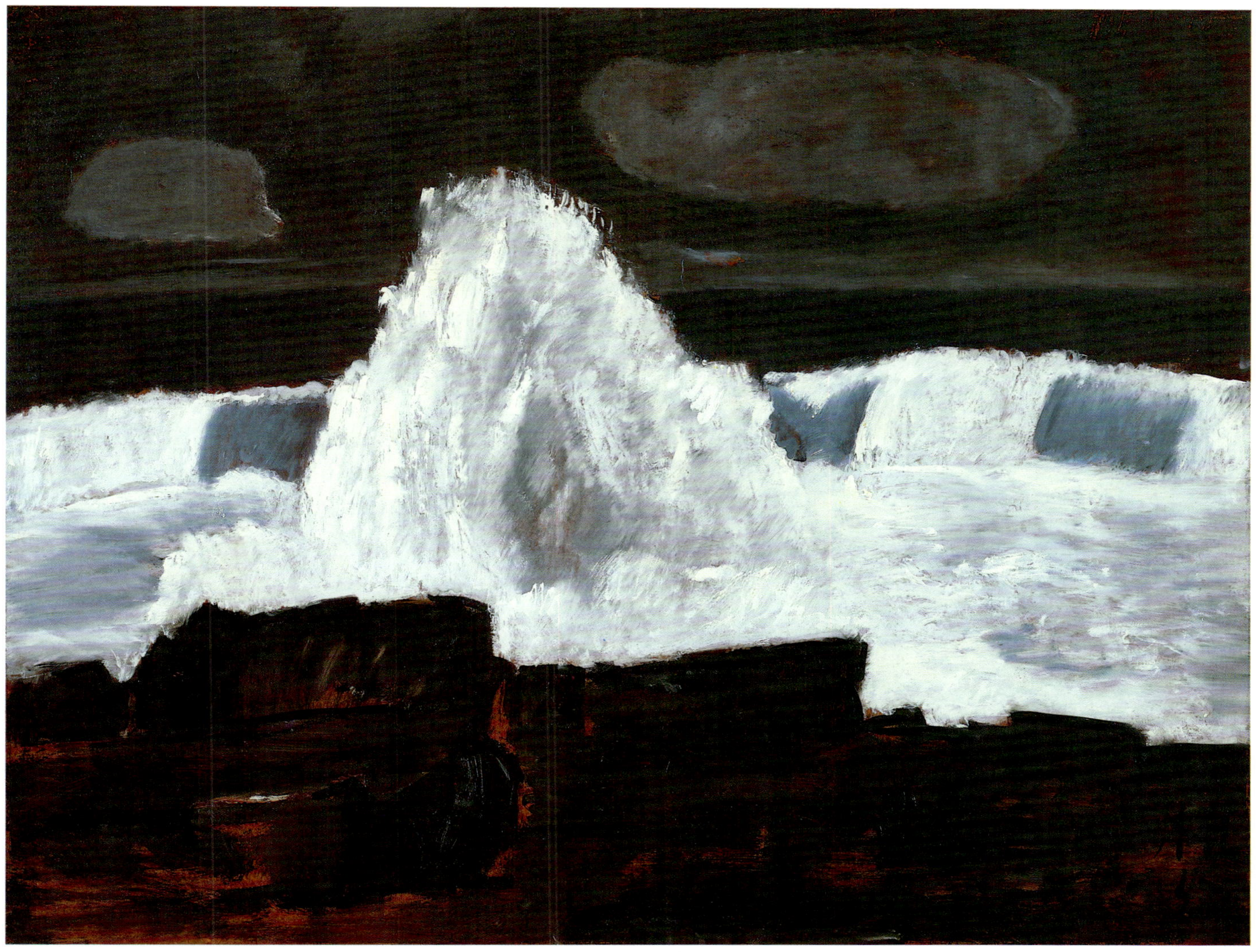

120. Hartley. *Evening Storm, Schoodic, Maine,* 1942.

beyond the veil of appearances in a peculiarly American fashion when he described seeing through water: "Truth? A pebble of quartz? For once, then, something." While the philosopher seeking reality may wonder at this confusion of truth with matter, the artist is more direct. Like Thoreau, Frost wanted contact, but more harshly. In "To Earthward" he wrote:

> When stiff and sore and scarred
> I take away my hand
> From leaning on it hard
> In grass and sand,

The hurt is not enough:
I long for weight and strength
To feel the earth as rough
To all my length.

The reality of the world in American art, felt in the scars the land leaves on the body, lies through a gate guarded by Winslow Homer (with Thomas Eakins). Not merely through emotion or sensation, certainly not through people, nor through the recording of things, but through nature do American artists experience reality and refashion it. Increasingly, in this century, they have wanted to feel more strongly the weight and substance of the world. Homer, more than any other painter at the end of the nineteenth century, found ways to make nature solid and real on his canvases. His success showed the way for the next generation. Robert Henri surely had Homer's work in mind when he wrote: "By solidity I mean the employment of bulk as a factor of expression. Forms interacting with forms. The weight and density of the sea. The bulk and hard resistance of rock.... It's a question of the life within."[61]

List of Captions and Photograph Credits

Measurements are given in inches; height precedes width. The paintings in the exhibition are marked with an asterisk(*) in the listing below; those also reproduced in color have two asterisks (**).

Frontispiece. Peter Juley. *Winslow Homer at Prout's Neck,* 1908. Photograph. Archives of American Art, Photographs of Artists I, Smithsonian Institution, Washington, D.C. Copyright Smithsonian Instition.

**Figure 1. Winslow Homer (1836-1910). *Rocky Coast,* ca. 1883-1900. Oil on canvas, 14 x 27-1/8. Wadsworth Atheneum, Hartford, Conn., Ella Gallup Sumner and Mary Catlin Sumner Collection, 1945.1. Copyright Wadsworth Atheneum.

Figure 2. Winslow Homer. *Weatherbeaten,* 1894. Oil on canvas, 28 x 48. Portland Museum of Art, Maine, Bequest of Charles Shipman Payson, 1988. Photograph: Del Cargill.

Figure 3. Winslow Homer. *Watching the Breakers: A High Sea,* 1896. Oil on canvas, 24 x 38-1/4. Canajoharie Library and Art Gallery, Canajoharie, N.Y., Photograph: LeBel's Studio, Canajoharie.

Figure 4. Winslow Homer. *Cloud Shadows,* 1890. Oil on canvas, 24-1/2 x 28. The Spencer Museum of Art, The University of Kansas, Lawrence, William Bridges Thayer Memorial Collection, 28.1781.

Figure 5. Winslow Homer. *A Summer Night,* 1890. Oil on canvas, 30-3/16 x 40-1/8. Musée d'Orsay, Paris. Photograph: Documentation Photographique de la Réunion des musées nationaux, Paris.

Figure 6. Winslow Homer. *The Wreck,* 1896. Oil on canvas, 30-3/8 x 48-5/16. The Carnegie Museum of Art, Pittsburgh, Pa., Purchase, 96.1.

**Figure 7. Winslow Homer. *Winter Coast,* 1890. Oil on canvas, 36 x 31-5/8. The John G. Johnson Collection, Philadelphia Museum of Art, J 1004.

Figure 8. Winslow Homer. *Sunlight on the Coast,* 1890. Oil on canvas, 30-1/4 x 48-1/2. The Toledo Museum of Art, Gift of Edward Drummond Libbey, 12.507.

Figure 9. Winslow Homer. *Prout's Neck Surf, Looking Toward Old Orchard,* 1883. Watercolor, 13-3/8 x 19-5/8. Addison Gallery of American Art, Phillips Academy, Andover, Mass. Photograph: Andover Art Studio, Andover.

Figure 10. Winslow Homer. *Prout's Neck, Breakers,* 1883. Watercolor, 14-7/8 x 21-5/16. The Art Institute of Chicago, Ill., Mr. and Mrs. Martin A. Ryerson Collection, 1933.1247. Copyright The Art Institute of Chicago.

Figure 11. Claude Monet (1840-1926). *Grainstack at Sunset near Giverney,* 1891. Oil on canvas, 28-7/8 x 36-1/2. Museum of Fine Arts, Boston, Juliana Cheney Edwards Collection, 25.112.

Figure 12. Claude Monet. *Grainstack in Winter,* 1891. Oil on canvas, 25-3/4 x 36-3/8. Museum of Fine Arts, Boston, Gift of Misses Aimée and Rosamond Lamb in Memory of Mr. and Mrs. Horatio A. Lamb, 1970.253.

Figure 13. Winslow Homer. *In the Mountains,* 1877. Oil on canvas, 24 x 38. The Brooklyn Museum, Dick S. Ramsay Fund, 32.1648.

*Figure 14. Winslow Homer. *Coast of Maine,* 1893. Oil on canvas, 24 x 30. The Art Institute of Chicago, The Arthur Jerome Eddy Memorial Collection, 1931.505. Copyright The Art Institute of Chicago.

Figure 15. Winslow Homer. *High Cliffs, Coast of Maine,* 1894. Oil on canvas, 30-1/8 x 38-1/4. National Museum of American Art, Smithsonian Institution, Gift of William T. Evans, 1909.7.29.

**Figure 16. Winslow Homer. *Northeaster,* 1895. Oil on canvas, 34-3/8 x 50-1/4. The Metropolitan Museum of Art, Gift of George A. Hearn, 1910 (10.64.5).

Figure 17. Winslow Homer. *Cannon Rock,* 1895. Oil on canvas, 39-1/8 x 39-1/8. The Metropolitan Museum of Art, Gift of George A. Hearn, 1906 (06.1281).

Figure 18. Winslow Homer. *Eastern Point,* 1900. Oil on canvas, 30-1/4 x 48-1/2. Sterling and Francine Clark Art Institute, Williamstown, Mass., 6. Copyright Clark Art Institute

Figure 19. Winslow Homer. *West Point, Prout's Neck,* 1900. Oil on canvas, 30-1/16 x 48-1/8. Sterling and Francine Clark Art Institute, Williamstown, Mass., 7. Copyright Clark Art Institute.

**Figure 20. Winslow Homer. *Early Morning after a Storm at Sea,* 1902. Oil on canvas, 30-1/2 x 50. The Cleveland Museum of Art, Gift of J. H. Wade, 24.195.

Figure 21. Winslow Homer. *Deer Drinking,* 1892. Watercolor, 14-1/16 x 20-1/16. Yale University Art Gallery, New Haven, The Robert W. Carle Fund, 1976.36. Photograph: Joseph Szaszfai, Yale University Art Gallery.

Figure 22. Winslow Homer. *The Fallen Deer,* 1892. Watercolor, 13-3/4 x 19-3/4. Museum of Fine Arts, Boston, Charles Henry Hayden Fund, 23.443.

**Figure 23. Winslow Homer. *Maine Coast,* 1896. Oil on canvas, 30 x 40. The Metropolitan Museum of Art, Gift of George A. Hearn, in memory of Arthur Hoppock Hearn, 1911 (11.116.1).

Figure 24. Winslow Homer. *The Gulf Stream,* 1899. Oil on canvas, 28-1/2 x 49-1/8. The Metropolitan Museum of Art, Wolfe Fund, 1906. Catharine Lorillard Wolfe Collection (06.1234).

*Figure 25. Winslow Homer. *To the Rescue,* 1886-1907. Oil on canvas, 24 x 30. The Phillips Collection, Washington, D.C., 0922.

**Figure 26. Winslow Homer. *Moonlight on the Water.* Oil on canvas, 14-3/4 x 31-1/2. Los Angeles County Museum of Art, Paul Rodman Mabury Collection, 39.12.10.

**Figure 27. Winslow Homer. *Sleigh Ride,* ca. 1893. Oil on canvas, 14-1/16 x 20-1/16. Sterling and Francine Clark Art Institute, Williamstown, Mass., 771. Copyright Clark Art Institute.

*Figure 28. Winslow Homer. *Below Zero,* 1894. Oil on canvas, 23-13/16 x 27-15/16. Yale University Art Gallery, New Haven, Conn., Bequest of George Roberts, B.A. 1905. Photograph: Joseph Szaszfai.

Figure 29. Winslow Homer. *Fox Hunt,* 1893. Oil on canvas, 38 x 68-1/2. The Pennsylvania Academy of the Fine Arts, Philadelphia, Joseph E. Temple Fund, 1894.4.

Figure 30. Gustave Courbet (1819-77). *Fox in the Snow,* 1860. Oil on canvas, 33-3/4 x 50-5/16. Dallas Museum of Art, Foundation for the Arts Collection, Mrs. John B. O'Hara Fund, 1979.7 FA. Copyright Dallas Museum of Art.

*Figure 31. Winslow Homer. *Kissing the Moon,* 1904. Oil on canvas, 30 x 40. Addison Gallery of American Art, Phillips Academy, Andover, Mass.

*Figure 32. Winslow Homer. *Right and Left,* 1909. Oil on canvas, 28-1/4 x 48-3/8. National Gallery of Art, Washington, Gift of the Avalon Foundation, 1951.81.

Figure 33. Winslow Homer. *The War for the Union, 1862—A Cavalry Charge.* Wood engraving, 13-1/2 x 20-5/8. *Harper's Weekly,* July 5, 1862. The Cleveland Museum of Art, Purchase from the J. H. Wade Fund, 42.1258.

Figure 34. Winslow Homer. *The Fog Warning,* 1885. Oil on canvas, 30 x 48. Museum of Fine Arts, Boston, Otis Norcross Fund, 94.72. Copyright Museum of Fine Arts, Boston.

Figure 35. Winslow Homer. *On a Lee Shore,* ca. 1900. Oil on canvas, 39 x 39. Museum of Art, Rhode Island School of Design, Providence, Jesse Metcalf Fund, 01.003.

*Figure 36. Winslow Homer. *Summer Squall,* 1904. Oil on canvas, 24-1/4 x 30-1/4. Sterling and Francine Clark Art Institute, Williamstown, Mass. Copyright Clark Art Institute.

**Figure 37. Winslow Homer. *Cape Trinity, Saguenay River,* 1904. Oil on canvas, 28-3/4 x 48-3/4. The Regis Collection, Minneapolis, Minn.

Figure 38. Winslow Homer. *Driftwood,* 1909. Oil on canvas, 24-1/4 x 28. Private collection.

*Figure 39. Winslow Homer. *A Light on the Sea,* 1897. Oil on canvas, 28-1/4 x 38-1/4. The Corcoran Gallery of Art, Washington, Museum Purchase, Gallery Fund, 07.3. Copyright Corcoran Gallery of Art.

Figure 40. Childe Hassam (1859-1935). *Coast Scene, Isles of Shoals,* 1901. Oil on canvas, 24-7/8 x 30-1/8. The Metropolitan Museum of Art, Gift of George A. Hearn, 1909 (09.72.6).

Figure 41. Claude Monet. *Rocks at Belle-Isle (Rochers a Belle-Ile),* 1886. Oil on canvas, 28-1/2 x 23. The St. Louis Art Museum, Gift of Mr. and Mrs. Joseph Pulitzer, Jr., 218.1975.

Figure 42. William Trost Richards (1833-1905). *On the Coast of New Jersey,* 1883. Oil on canvas, 40-1/4 x 72-1/4. The Corcoran Gallery of Art, Washington, Museum Purchase, 83.6. Copyright Corcoran Gallery of Art.

Figure 43. Frederic Edwin Church (1826-1900). *Rough Surf, Mount Desert Island, Maine,* 1850. Oil on paper mounted on wood, 12-1/2 x 16-1/4. Private collection. Photograph: Courtesy Berry-Hill Galleries, New York.

Figure 44. Frederic Edwin Church. *Coast Scene, Mount Desert,* 1863. Oil on canvas, 36-1/8 x 48. Wadsworth Atheneum, Hartford, Conn., Bequest of Mrs. Clara Hinton Gould. Copyright Wadsworth Atheneum.

Figure 45. William Stanley Haseltine (1835-1900). *After a Shower—Nahant, Massachusetts,* ca. 1862. Oil on canvas, 14-7/8 x 23. The Brooklyn Museum, Gift of Mrs. Helen H. Plowden, 48.197.

Figure 46. Gustave Courbet. *La Vague (The Wave),* 1870. Oil on canvas, 24 x 36. Phoenix Art Museum, Gift of the Louis Cates Fund, 59.87.

*Figure 47. Charles H. Woodbury (1864-1940). *October, Seascape,* ca. 1907. Oil on canvas 27 x 27. Collection National Academy of Design, New York City.

Figure 48. Winslow Homer. *Coast in Winter.* Oil on canvas, 28-5/16 x 48. Worcester Art Museum, Worcester, Mass., Theodore T. and Mary G. Ellis Collection, 1940.60. Copyright Worcester Art Museum.

*Figure 49. Frederick Judd Waugh (1861-1940). *Kelp-Covered Rocks,* 1923. Oil on canvas, 22 x 26. Maier Museum of Art, Randolph-Macon Woman's College, Lynchburg, Va.

Figure 50. Paul Dougherty (1877-1947). *Late Afternoon,* 1921. Oil on canvas, 26-1/2 x 36. Indianapolis Museum of Art, Gift of the Friends of American Art, 22.2. Copyright Indianapolis Museum of Art.

Figure 51. William Ritschel (1864-1949). *Rocks and Sea, Monhegan,* 1914. Oil on canvas, 30 x 40. Collection National Academy of Design, New York City.

Figure 52. Winslow Homer. *Flamboro Head,* 1882. Watercolor, 17-1/2 x 24. The Art Institute of Chicago, Mr. and Mrs. Martin A. Ryerson Collection, 1933.1240.

Figure 53. Jules Breton (1827-1906). *The Shepherd's Star,* 1887. Oil on canvas, 40-1/2 x 31. The Toledo Museum of Art, Gift of Arthur J. Secor, 22.41.

Figure 54. Winslow Homer. *Moonlight—Wood's Island Light,* 1894. Oil on canvas, 30-3/4 x 40-1/4. The Metropolitan Museum of Art, Gift of George A. Hearn in memory of Arthur Hoppock Hearn, 1911 (11.116.2).

Figure 55. James A. McNeill Whistler (1834-1903). *Nocturne—Blue and Silver—Battersea Reach,* 1870-1875. Oil on canvas, 19-5/8 x 30-1/8. Courtesy Freer Gallery of Art, Washington. Copyright Smithsonian Institution.

Figure 56. Winslow Homer. *West Wind,* 1891. Oil on canvas, 30 x 43-1/2. Addison Gallery of American Art, Phillips Academy, Andover, Mass.

Figure 57. John Twachtman (1852-1902). *Arques-la-Bataille,* 1885. Oil on canvas, 60 x 78-7/8. The Metropolitan Museum of Art, Purchase, 1968, Morris K. Jesup Fund (68.52).

Figure 58. Edvard Munch (1863-1944). *The Dance of Life,* ca. 1899. Oil on canvas, 49-3/8 x 75. Nasjonalgalleriet, Oslo.

Figure 59. Winslow Homer. *Searchlight: Harbor Entrance, Santiago de Cuba,* 1901. Oil on canvas, 30-5/8 x 50-1/2. The Metropolitan Museum of Art, Gift of George A. Hearn, 1906 (06.1282).

Figure 60. Winslow Homer. *Huntsman and Dogs,* 1891. Oil on canvas, 28 x 48. Philadelphia Museum of Art, The William L. Elkins Collection, 1891, E'24-3-8.

Figure 61. Winslow Homer. *Fountains at Night, World's Columbian Exposition,* 1893. Oil on canvas, 16 x 25. Bowdoin College Museum of Art, Brunswick, Maine, Bequest of Mrs. Charles S. Homer, Jr., 1938.2.

Figure 62. Winslow Homer. *Undertow,* 1886. Oil on canvas, 29-13/16 x 47-5/8. Sterling and Francine Clark Art Institute, Williamstown, Mass., 4. Copyright Clark Art Institute.

Figure 63. Robert Henri (1865-1929). *Snow in New York,* 1902. Oil on canvas, 32 x 25-3/4. National Gallery of Art, Washington, Chester Dale Collection, 1954.

Figure 64. John Sloan (1871-1951). *Ferry Slip, Winter,* 1905-1906. Oil on canvas, 21-5/8 x 31-3/4. Hirshhorn Museum and Sculpture Garden, Smithsonian Institution, Washington, Gift of Joseph H. Hirshhorn, 1966, 66.4607.

**Figure 65. Van Dearing Perrine (1869-1955). *Bleak Winter,* ca. 1905. Oil on canvas, 35 x 42. Private collection. Photograph: Courtesy Graham Gallery, New York.

**Figure 66. Robert Henri. *Snow in Central Park,* 1902. Oil on canvas, 26 x 32. Collection of Mr. Elie Hirschfeld, New York.

**Figure 67. George Bellows (1882-1925). *Pennsylvania Station Excavation,* 1909. Oil on canvas, 30-1/4 x 38-1/4. The Brooklyn Museum, A. Augustus Healy Fund, 67.205.1. Photograph: Philip Pocock.

Figure 68. George Bellows. *Stag at Sharkey's,* 1909. Oil on canvas 36-1/4 x 48-1/4. The Cleveland Museum of Art, Hinman B. Hurlbut Collection, 1133.22.

*Figure 69. George Bellows. *Polo at Lakewood,* 1910. Oil on canvas, 45-1/4 x 63-1/2. Columbus Museum of Art, Museum Purchase: Columbus Art Association Purchase, 11.1.

Figure 70. George Bellows. *North River,* 1908. Oil on canvas, 32-7/8 x 43. The Pennsylvania Academy of the Fine Arts, Philadelphia, Joseph E. Temple Fund, 1909.2.

*Figure 71. George Bellows. *Winter Afternoon (Riverside Park, New York City),* 1909. Oil on canvas, 30 x 38. Collection of the Norton Gallery of Art, West Palm Beach, Fla., 49.1.

**Figure 72. George Wesley Bellows (1882-1925). *Blue Snow, The Battery,* 1910. Oil on canvas, 34 x 44. Columbus Museum of Art, Museum Purchase: Howald Fund, 58.35.

*Figure 73. Robert Henri. *Rolling Sea,* 1903. Oil on wood, 7 x 9-1/2. Collection of Mr. and Mrs. Arthur G. Altschul. Photograph: Nathan Rabin, New York.

**Figure 74. Rockwell Kent (1882-1971). *Maine Coast,* 1907. Oil on canvas, 34-1/8 x 44-1/8. The Cleveland Museum of Art, Hinman B. Hurlbut collection, 1132.22.

Figure 75. Abbott Handerson Thayer (1849-1921). *Winter Landscape,* 1902. Oil on canvas, 29-3/8 x 34-7/8. Collection National Academy of Design, New York City.

*Figure 76. Rockwell Kent. *Blackhead, Monhegan,* ca. 1909. Oil on canvas, 34 x 44. Colby College Museum of Art, Waterville, Maine, Gift of the Phillips Collection, Washington, 64-P-10.

**Figure 77. Rockwell Kent. *Toilers on the Sea,* 1907. Oil on canvas, 38 x 44. The New Britain Museum of American Art, Conn., Charles F. Smith Fund, 1944.1. Photograph:E. Irving Blomstrann.

**Figure 78. Rockwell Kent. *Snow Fields (Winter in the Berkshires),* 1909. Oil on canvas, 38 x 44. National Museum of American Art, Smithsonian Institution, Washington, Bequest of Henry Ward Ranger through the National Academy of Design, 1981.73.

*Figure 79. Rockwell Kent. *Driftwood, Alaska,* 1919. Oil on canvas, 27-1/2 x 33-1/2. Collection of Joseph M. Erdelac, Cleveland.

Figure 80. George Bellows. *Shore House,* 1911. Oil on canvas, 40 x 42. Collection of Rita and Daniel Fraad.

Figure 81. George Bellows. *An Island in the Sea,* 1911. Oil on canvas, 34-1/4 x 44-3/8. Columbus Museum of Art, Gift of Howard B. Monett, 52.25.

Figure 82. George Bellows. *The Fisherman's Family,* 1923. Oil on canvas, 38 x 48. Location unknown. Photograph: Courtesy of the Estate of George Bellows and H. V. Allison Galleries.

**Figure 83. George Bellows. *The Fisherman,* 1917. Oil on canvas, 30 x 44. Berry-Hill Galleries, New York.

*Figure 84. George Bellows. *Churn and Break,* 1913. Oil on panel, 17-3/4 x 22. Columbus Museum of Art, Gift of Mrs. Edward Powell, 48.53.

**Figure 85. George Bellows. *Green Breaker,* 1913. Oil on wood, 15 x 19-1/2. Collection of Remak Ramsey.

*Figure 86. George Bellows. *Tumble of Waters,* 1913. Oil on wood, 15 x 19-1/2. Collection of Robert A. Mann.

*Figure 87. George Bellows. *From Rock Top, Monhegan,* 1913. Oil on wood, 15 x 19-1/2. Chris Huntington.

*Figure 88. George Bellows. *Evening Swell,* 1911. Oil on canvas, 30 x 38. Berry-Hill Galleries, New York.

*Figure 89. George Bellows. *The Sea,* 1911. Oil on canvas, 34 x 44-1/8. Hirshhorn Museum and Sculpture Garden, Smithsonian Institution, Gift of Joseph H. Hirshhorn, 1966, 66.439. Photograph: Lee Stalsworth.

**Figure 90. George Bellows. *In a Rowboat,* 1916. Oil on canvas, 30-3/4 x 44-1/4. Collection of the Montclair Museum of Art, Montclair, N.J., Gift of Mr. and Mrs. H. St. John Webb, 64.37.

**Figure 91. Leon Kroll (1884-1974). *Breaking Surf, Prout's Neck,* 1907. Oil on wood, 8-1/4 x 10-5/8. Collection of Robert Dance, New York. Photograph: Scott Bowron Photography, New York.

*Figure 92. Leon Kroll. *Monhegan Landscape,* 1913. Oil on panel, 8-3/4 x 10-3/4. Bowdoin College Museum of Art, Brunswick, Maine, Museum purchase, Hamlin Fund, 1970.79.

**Figure 93. Robert Henri, *Gray Sea,* 1911. Oil on panel, 11-3/4 x 15. Collection, Glen Echo Farm, Virginia. Photograph: Courtesy of H. V. Allison Galleries, New York.

*Figure 94. Robert Henri. *Surf and Rocks,* 1911. Oil on board, 11-7/8 x 15. Memphis Brooks Museum of Art, Memphis, Tenn., Bequest of Isaac L. Myers, 61.221.

**Figure 95. George Luks (1866-1933). *Great Waves (Coast of Maine),* 1922. Oil on wood, 24-1/8 x 36-1/8. Hirshhorn Museum and Sculpture Garden, Smithsonian Institution, Gift of Joseph H. Hirshhorn, 1966, 66.3162. Photograph: Lee Stalsworth.

*Figure 96. Edward Hopper (1882-1967). *Waves Crashing on the Rocks, Monhegan,* ca. 1916-19. Oil on board, 9 x 13-1/2. Collection of Whitney Museum of American Art, New York, Josephine N. Hopper Bequest, 70.1313. Photograph: Geoffrey Clements, Staten Island, N.Y.

**Figure 97. Edward Hopper. *Rocky Shore and Sea, Monhegan,* ca. 1916-19. Oil on board, 9-9/16 x 13. Collection of Whitney Museum of American Art, New York, Bequest of Josephine N. Hopper, 70.1311. Photograph: Robert E. Mates Studio, New Jersey.

*Figure 98. Edward Hopper. *Rocks and Waves,* ca. 1916-19. Oil on composition board, 9-5/8 x 13. Collection of Whitney Museum of American Art, New York, Josephine N. Hopper Bequest, 70.1308. Photograph: Geoffrey Clements, Staten Island, N.Y.

Figure 99. Edward Hopper. *Rocky Projection at the Sea,* ca. 1916-19. Oil on composition board, 9 x 12-7/8. Collection of Whitney Museum of American Art, New York, Josephine N. Hopper Bequest, 70.1310. Photograph: Geoffrey Clements, Staten Island, N.Y.

Figure 100. Edward Hopper. *Foreshore— Two Lights,* 1927. Watercolor, 13-5/8 x 19-7/8. Collection The High Museum of Art, Atlanta, Henry B. Scott Fund Purchase, 1959. Photograph: Jerome Drown.

**Figure 101. Edward Hopper. *The Camel's Hump,* 1931. Oil on canvas, 32-1/4 x 50-1/8. Munson-Williams-Proctor Institute Museum of Art, New York; Edward W. Root Bequest.

Figure 102. Sanford Robinson Gifford (1823-1880). *A Home in the Wilderness,* 1866. Oil on canvas, 30-1/2 x 54-1/2. The Cleveland Museum of Art, Mr. and Mrs. William H. Marlatt Fund; The Butkin Foundation; Dorothy Burnham Everett Memorial Collection; and various donors by exchange, 70.162

**Figure 103. Robert Henri. *Storm Tide,* 1903. Oil on canvas, 26 x 32. Collection of Whitney Museum of American Art, New York, Purchase, 31.242. Photograph: Robert E. Mates Studio, New Jersey.

Figure 104. Rockwell Kent. *Winter, Monhegan Island,* 1907. Oil on canvas, 33-7/8 x 44. The Metropolitan Museum of Art, George A. Hearn Fund, 1917 (17.48.2).

**Figure 105. Edward Hopper. *Hills, South Truro,* 1930. Oil on canvas, 27-3/8 x 43-1/8. The Cleveland Museum of Art, Hinman B. Hurlbut collection, 2647.31.

**Figure 106. Edward Hopper. *Cape Cod Morning,* 1950. Oil on canvas, 34-1/4 x 40-1/8. National Museum of American Art, Smithsonian Institution, Washington, Gift of the Sara Roby Foundation, 1986.6.92

Figure 107. Winslow Homer. *The Artist's Studio in an Afternoon Fog,* 1894. Oil on canvas, 24 x 30-1/4. Memorial Art Gallery of the University of Rochester, New York, R. T. Miller Fund, 41.32.

**Figure 108. John Sloan. *Black and Yellow Rocks,* 1917. Oil on canvas, 20 x 24. Kraushaar Galleries, New York.

**Figure 109. John Sloan. *Fassett's Cove,* 1915. Oil on canvas, 26 x 32. Kraushaar Galleries, New York.

*Figure 110. John Sloan. *Purple Rocks and Green Sea,* 1916. Oil on canvas, 20 x 24. Bowdoin College Museum of Art, Brunswick, Maine, Bequest of George Otis Hamlin, 1961.68.

**Figure 111. John Sloan. *Red Rocks, Quiet Sea, no. II,* 1916. Oil on canvas, 26 x 32. The Regis Collection, Minneapolis, Minn.

*Figure 112. Newell Convers Wyeth (1882-1945). *Portrait of a Young Artist,* ca. 1930. Oil on canvas, 32 x 40. Collection of the William A. Farnsworth Library and Art Museum, Rockland, Maine, 63.1285.

Figure 113. John Marin (1870-1953). *Weehawken Grain Elevators* (from the series: *Weehawken Sequence),* ca. 1916. Oil on canvas board, 10 x 14. Kennedy Galleries, Inc., New York.

Figure 114. John Marin. *Study of the Sea,* 1917. Watercolor and charcoal, 16 x 19. Columbus Museum of Art, Gift of Ferdinand Howald, 31.231.

**Figure 115. John Marin. *Rocks and Sea, Small Point, Maine,* 1931. Oil on canvas, 22-1/16 x 27-15/16. The Cleveland Museum of Art, Norman O. Stone and Ella A. Stone Memorial Fund, 56.361.

**Figure 116. John Marin. *Wave on Rock,* 1937. Oil on canvas, 22-3/4 x 30. Collection of Whitney Museum of American Art, New York, Purchase, with funds from Charles Simon and the Painting and Sculpture Committee, 81.18. Photograph: Geoffrey Clements, Staten Island, N.Y.

Figure 117. Marsden Hartley (1877-1943). *Autumn Lake and Hills,* 1907. Oil on canvas, 30 x 25. University of Nebraska, Lincoln, F.M. Hall Collection, Sheldon Memorial Art Gallery.

*Figure 118. Marsden Hartley. *Off the Banks at Night,* 1942. Oil on masonite, 30 x 40. The Phillips Collection, Washington, 0890.

**Figure 119. Marsden Hartley. *The Spent Wave, Indian Point, Georgetown, Maine,* 1937-38. Oil on panel, 22-1/2 x 28-1/2. Columbus Museum of Art, Museum Purchase: Howald Fund II, 1981, 81.13.

**Figure 120. Marsden Hartley. *Evening Storm, Schoodic, Maine,* 1942. Oil on composition board, 30 x 40. Collection, The Museum of Modern Art, New York. Acquired through the Lillie P. Bliss Bequest.

Notes

Introduction

1. See Lloyd Goodrich, *Winslow Homer and the American Watercolor Tradition* (New York: MacMillan Company, 1944).

2. Despite being few in number, Homer's later paintings were so frequently reproduced during the period covered by this exhibition that to list the reproductions would be a thankless task. The exhaustive entries in Natalie Spassky's *American Paintings in the Metropolitan Museum of Art,* vol. 2, *A Catalogue of Works by Artists Born between 1816 and 1845* (New York: Metropolitan Museum of Art, 1985), give a good idea of the popularity of Homer's work, as do the listings in *The Index of Twentieth Century Artists,* vols. 1-4, nos. 1-7 (New York: Research Institute of the College Art Association, 1933-37). I have noted in the text or notes the few instances where I have not located an easily accessible contemporary reproduction or exhibition of a specific painting by Homer. These instances are limited to small works given or sold to friends, or left in Homer's studio after his death (such as *Moonlight on the Water, Sleigh Ride,* and *Rocky Coast*). Otherwise, all of Homer's finished oils were exhibited or reproduced either before his death or shortly thereafter.

3. John Sloan, *Gist of Art* (New York: American Artists Group, 1939), p. 3.

4. John Rummell, *Aims and Ideals of Representative American Painters* (Buffalo, N.Y.: E. M. Berlin, 1901), p. 106.

5. Kenyon Cox, *Old Masters and New, Essays in Art Criticism* (New York: Fox, Duffield and Company, 1905), p. 147. Sadakichi Hartmann wrote: "We excuse the false notes in his flesh tints, his awkward linear beauty, his neglect of values, his crude key of colours...." *A History of American Art,* 2 vols. (Boston: L. C. Page and Company, 1901), vol. 1, p. 199.

6. For a brief discussion of how Americanness could be defined in contrast to Europeanness, especially in the context of Homer, see H. Wayne Morgan *New Muses: Art in American Culture 1865-1920* (Norman, Okla.: University of Oklahoma, 1978), p. 64.

7. See Donald Kuspit, "19th-Century Landscape: Poetry and Property," *Art in America* 64, 1 (January-February, 1976): 70-71.

8. Royal Cortissoz, *American Artists* (New York: Charles Scribner's Sons, 1923), pp. 122-23.

9. Clement Greenberg, *Art and Culture: Critical Essays* (Boston: Beacon Press, 1961), p. 186.

10. Our interest in sex and art is nothing new. In an essay entitled "Sex in Art," George Moore states: "all art that lives is full of sex ... that concentrated essence of life which the great artist jealously reserves for his art, and through which it pulsates." *Modern Painting* (London and Felling-on-Tyne: The Walter Scott Publishing Company, [1893]), pp. 227-28. A recent exhibition has explored Homer's interest in the antagonistic relationship between men and women in his earliest oil paintings: David Park Curry, *Winslow Homer, The Croquet Game,* exh. cat. (New Haven: Yale University Art Gallery, 1984).

Chapter One: Winslow Homer

1. While Homer may have abandoned the world of art, it did not forget him. He served on juries for the Carnegie International in Pittsburgh and rejected many more offers to serve. Invited to join "The Ten" in 1898, he turned them down, writing: "I am reminded of the time lost in my life in not having an opportunity like this that you offer ... but I am too old for this work and I have already decided to retire from business at the end of the season. So you see that I cannot join you at even this most cordial invitation—and admiring as I do all of you." Although his letter is dated January 20, on January 9, 1898, *The New York Times* reported the group as "Eleven Painters," because of the group's certainty that Homer would join them. Patricia Jobe Pierce, *The Ten* (Concord, N.H.: Rumford Press, 1976), pp. 25-26.

2. Quoted in William Howe Downes, *The Life and Works of Winslow Homer* (Boston: Houghton Mifflin Company, 1911), p. 234.

3. For example, his friendship with the Portland, Maine, architect John Calvin Stevens was sealed with the gift of *The Artist's Studio in an Afternoon Fog,* 1894, which he gave in return for Stevens' design and help in building a house in 1901. Earle G. Shettleworth, Jr., and William David Barry, "'Brother Artists' John Calvin Stevens and Winslow Homer," *Bowdoin* 61, 4 (Fall 1988): 16-19.

4. Lloyd Goodrich, *Winslow Homer* (New York: MacMillan Company, 1944), p. 194.

5. Quoted in Downes, *Life and Works,* p. 167.

6. Ibid., pp. 167, 228.

7. See Gordon Hendricks, *The Life and Work of Winslow Homer* (New York: Harry N. Abrams, 1979), pp. 12-13.

8. Winslow Homer to Charles Homer, Jr., February 21, 1895, Homer papers, Bowdoin College Museum of Art, New Brunswick, Me.

9. Quoted in Goodrich, *Homer,* p. 104.

10. Ibid., p. 218.

11. Ralph Waldo Emerson, "The Young American," 1844, in *Nature: Addresses and Lectures* (Boston and New York: Houghton Mifflin and Company, 1903), p. 365.

12. T. J. Jackson Lears, *No Place of Grace: Anti-Modernism and the Transformation of American Culture 1880-1920* (New York: Pantheon Books, 1981), p. 309. John Wilmerding also draws an analogy between Adams and Homer in "Winslow Homer's 'Right and Left,'" in *Studies in the History of Art,* vol. 9 (Washington: National Gallery of Art, 1980), p. 85.

13. Quoted in Goodrich, *Homer,* p. 224.

Chapter Two: Prout's Neck

1. *Undertow* had been completed at the end of 1886 and first exhibited in 1887. Though much admired, it did not sell. Homer then turned his attention to making etchings after his major works of the previous five years. Not until *Undertow* was sold in the summer of 1889 and the success of his watercolor exhibition in February 1890, did he again pick up his oil paints.

2. "The exhibition ... is sure to be appreciated by the many painters and amateurs who admire Mr. Homer's work—and this is equivalent to saying everybody—everybody who knows art from 'shop' at least." *Evening Post,* January 21, 1891, Homer clippings book, p. 81, Bowdoin College Museum of Art.

3. Goodrich, *Homer,* p. 210.

4. Philip C. Beam makes a similar point discussing Homer's working method. *Winslow Homer at Prout's Neck* (Boston: Little, Brown and Company, 1966), pp. 147-48.

5. Although the models were probably local girls, Maude Googins Night and Clara Sanborn, the pictures were taken as images of resort life. See Downes, *Life and Works,* p. 157; and Alexandra R. Murphy, *Winslow Homer in the Clark Collection* (Williamstown, Mass.: Sterling and Francine Clark Art Institute, 1986), p. 66.

6. After coming back from England, he had painted both men and women. The paintings of women were often criticized and several were repainted much later. However, his male heroics sold well. In painting tender but strong fisherwomen, he competed with several other artists, while as a painter of heroic men in action, he was unmatched. Having been dubbed a painter of the weak and disenfranchised—children, blacks, and shepherdesses—he was now preeminently a painter of men.

7. One could point out scores of others. *The Morning Bell,* ca. 1872 (Yale University Art Gallery), is an example where the same diagonal appears, not as a substantial rock but as a rickety wooden bridge. This compositional type has sometimes been considered evidence of the influence of Japanese design on Homer; but many other examples may be found in western art.

8. The curling spray is an addition to the painting, made just before Homer sent it out in 1900. See the entry in Spassky, *Am. Paintings in the Metropolitan,* pp. 471-75.

9. William H. Gerdts has firmly linked this square format to European and decorative sources. "The Square Format and Proto-Modernism in American Painting," *Arts Magazine* 50, 10 (June 1976): 70-75.

10. This was noted by contemporary observers: "His vision does not look toward far horizons; the passion of the subject is hemmed around by sullenness; its violence concentrated upon some focal point, immediately near." Charles H. Caffin, "American Painters of the Sea," *The Critic* 43, 6 (December 1903): 551.

11. Quoted in Goodrich, *Homer,* p. 220.

12. See Kristin Hoermann, "'A Hand Formed to Use the Brush,'" in Marc Simpson, *Winslow Homer Paintings of the Civil War,* exh. cat. (San Francisco: The Fine Arts Museums of San Francisco, 1988).

13. Curatorial files, Cleveland; Goodrich, *Homer,* p. 174.

14. *Leon Kroll: A Spoken Memoir,* ed. Nancy Hale and Fredson Bowers (Charlottesville: University Press of Virginia, 1983), p. 13.

15. See Helen A. Cooper, *Winslow Homer Watercolors,* exh. cat. (Washington: National Gallery of Art; New Haven: Yale University Press, 1986), figs. 161-168, 173-179.

16. The sense of balance I find in Homer's works has been sensitively explored by John Wilmerding in his essay on *Right and Left,* when he describes the "yin-yang interlocking of the bright and active with the dark and passive—first seen in the explicitly masculine-feminine interplay of *The Life Line.*" "Homer's 'Right and Left,'" p. 72.

17. Homer painted the subject once more in oil: *Watching the Breakers,* 1891 (Thomas Gilcrease Institute of American History and Art, Tulsa, Oklahoma).

18. Potter Palmer referred to the painting as "Buffalo Girls" in a letter to Homer, December 23, 1890; Homer called it "my Moonlight," in a letter to C. Klackner, December 10, 1890, Homer papers, Bowdoin College Museum of Art.

19. *Boston Herald,* ca. 1894, Homer clippings book, p. 92, Bowdoin College Museum of Art.

20. Christopher Reed, "The Artist and the Other: The Work of Winslow Homer," *Yale University Art Gallery Bulletin* 40, 3 (Spring 1989): 69.

21. One commentator notes: "In this, the largest of his paintings, Homer at the age of fifty-seven contemplates his own death." Theodore E. Stebbins, Jr., et al., *A New World: Masterpieces of American Painting 1760-1910,* exh. cat. (Boston: Boston Museum of Fine Arts, 1983), p. 337. See also Henry Adams, "Mortal Themes: Winslow Homer," *Art in America* 71, 2 (February 1983): 112-26, esp. 112-16; and Thomas Hess, "Come Back to the Raft Ag'in, Winslow Homer Honey," *New York Magazine,* June 11, 1973, p. 75.

22. In Courbet's *Fox Caught in a Trap,* 1860 (Matsukata collection, Japan), another possible source, the fox twists and fights against its fate. See also Murphy, *Homer in the Clark Collection,* p. 12.

23. See also Wilmerding, "Homer's '*Right and Left*,'" p. 72.

24. *Right and Left* is apparently not Homer's title, but one approved by him. Downes, *Life and Works,* p. 245

25. Simpson, *Homer's Paintings of Civil War,* p. 181.

26. As Homer said to a young student, "Do figures, my boy. Leave rocks to your old age. They're easy." Leaving aside his typical humor, Homer, by contrasting rocks and people, effectively equated the two as equivalent objects. Kroll, *A Spoken Memoir,* p. 13.

27. I am grateful to Stephen Wicks for suggesting this comparison.

28. See Simpson's remarks on *Inviting a Shot before Petersburg, Virginia,* in his *Homer's Paintings of Civil War,* pp. 181, 185; Carol Troyen's in Stebbins et al., *A New World,* p. 339; and Jules D. Prown's in "Winslow Homer in His Art," *Smithsonian Studies in American Art* 1, 1 (Spring 1987): 31-45.

29. Homer to Clarke, December 20, 1901, Winslow Homer papers, Archives of American Art, microfilm 2814, 661.

Chapter Three: Marine Painting

1. *Philadelphia Telegraph,* October 1892, Homer clipping book, p. 87, Bowdoin College Museum of Art. Ralph W. Carey stated the common view when he introduced the work of Gifford Beal: "Few, if any, external influences have made themselves more potently felt in American art than the geographical one exerted by the coast of Maine. There is something characteristically American typified by these rugged, rocky shores and the endless, tumultuous surge of the ocean waves upon them, which has been the inspiration of some of our greatest and most truly national paintings." "Some Paintings by Gifford Beal," *The International Studio* 44, 17 (August 1911): xxix.

2. See Susan C. Faxon, Alice Downey, and Peter Bermingham, *A Stern and Lovely Scene: A Visual History of the Isle of Shoals,* exh. cat. (Durham: University Art Galleries, University of New Hampshire, 1978).

3. Quoted in Goodrich, *Homer,* p. 135.

4. For example, Aaron Draper Shattuck's *Whitehead Cliffs—Monhegan Island, Maine,* 1858, reproduced by Roger B. Stein, in *Seascape and the American Imagination,* exh. cat. (New York: Clarkson N. Potter, Inc., and the Whitney Museum of American Art, 1975), fig. 90.

5. Redfield to Henri, August 14, 1903; and Henri to family, July 12, 1903, Henri papers, Beinecke Library, Yale University, New Haven, Conn.

6. Henri to Redfield, n.d. (July 12, 1903?); Henri to his family, July 12, 1903, ibid.

7. Henri to his family, August 25, 1903, ibid.

8. Kent to Henri, July 12, 1905, ibid.

9. Franklin Kelly, *Frederic Edwin Church and the National Landscape* (Washington, D.C.: Smithsonian Institution Press, 1988), pp. 37-38.

10. For example, Anna Seaton-Schmidt calls Woodbury's pictures of the sea "psychological" placing him "among the great interpretive artists of our time." "Some American Marine Painters," *Art and Progress* 2, 1 (November 1910): 7. Charles Caffin, citing Homer and others, once wrote, "It is only when one ... cuts himself off from the mad whirl of materialism and communes with the vast life of the Universal and Impersonal, as typified in the ocean, that a picture is made which stirs one's soul" (quoted by Geraldine Wojno Kiefer, "Alfred Stieglitz and Science, 1880-1910" [Ph.D diss., Case Western Reserve University, 1989], p. 335).

11. See W. H. De B. Nelson, "The National Academy of Design: Winter Exhibition," *The International Studio* 51, 204 (February 1914): clxxxiii. In this review of the annual exhibition at the National Academy of Design, the author cites William Ritschel and Paul Dougherty, and adds: "There is no field of art where the American artist is so thoroughly competent as marine painting." See also Frank Jewett Mather, Jr., *Modern Painting: A Study of Tendencies* (New York: Henry Holt and Company, 1927), pp. 178-79, who claimed: "Indeed our marine painting ... has perhaps maintained a higher level of inventiveness than our landscape painting generally." And William Howe Downes, "American Painters of the Sea," *The American Magazine of Art* 23, 5 (November 1931): 361.

12. For example, Lewis C. Hind, a British author, wrote: "This American is the greatest painter of the sea in art history." *Landscape Painting from Giotto to the Present Day,* vol. 2 (London: Chapman and Hall, Ltd., 1924), p. 140.

13. Homer visited Appledore and would have known Hassam's paintings. Downes, *Life and Works,* p. 195.

14. Mather, *Modern Painting,* pp. 171, 179.

15. In comparing him to Courbet, another reviewer said Homer had "a power to represent matter in motion which Courbet did not possess." "The Fine Arts: Four Paintings by Winslow Homer," January 1891, Homer clippings book, p. 75, Bowdoin College Museum of Art.

16. For example, William Bixbee and Charles Woodbury. Goodrich, *Homer,* pp. 104, 211.

17. Downes, "Am. Painters of the Sea," p. 374. In typical fashion, Homer jokingly indicated that he knew everybody copied him: "All I care for is to have it shown to the public before it is stolen by Art students." Letter to Knoedlers, January 4, 1903, quoted in Goodrich, *Homer,* p. 176.

18. Arthur Hoeber thought that: "to the art student he is and long has been a genuine inspiration" ("Winslow Homer, A Painter of the Sea," *The World's Work* 21 [February 1911]: 14009). Other critics concurred: "Since Winslow Homer found the ocean a source of artistic inspiration many of our artists have followed in his train" (Lorinda Munson Bryant, *American Pictures and Their Painters* [New York: John Lane, 1917], p. 247). See also Downes, "American Painters of the Sea," p. 374.

19. Woodbury "gives the sweep of the blue ocean water ... with something of the freshness and breadth of Homer if without his grandeur," according to Samuel Isham (*The History of American Painting* [New York: MacMillan Company, 1910], p. 462). Arthur Hoeber agreed that the successful painter of the sea must "be in full accord with its elemental quality, its soberer as well as its more attractive aspects. One felt this in the work of the late Winslow Homer and one feels it unmistakably in the work of Charles H. Woodbury ... though his color sense is far more delicate" ("Charles H. Woodbury, N.A., A Painter of the Sea," *The International Studio* 42, 168 [February 1911]: lxxi-lxxii). See also William Howe Downes, "The Ideas of a Marine Painter," *Art and Progress* 4, 1 (November 1912): 761.

20. During 1914 Monhegan celebrated the tercentenary of Captain John Smith's landing with an exhibition of works by eighteen artists living there that summer. Waugh and Bellows were on the selection committee. George R. Havens, *Frederick Judd Waugh American Marine Painter* (Orono, Me.: University of Maine, 1969), p. 134.

21. Ibid., p. 193. The similarities raise the intriguing possibility that Homer's works influenced British marine painting, possibly through the advocacy of Lewis Hind.

22. Eugen Neuhaus, *The History and Ideals of American Art* (Stanford: Stanford University Press, 1931), pp. 300-301

23. Kroll, *A Spoken Memoir,* p. 15. Bayard Boyesen stated: "[Paul Dougherty's] work demands attention with something of the same insistence and power which Mr. Homer's canvases attain" ("The National Note in American Art," *Putnam's Monthly Reader* 4, 2 [May 4, 1908]: 135-36). Boyesen was a summer resident of Monhegan and knew Kent; it is likely that he met Dougherty at the same time. Another critic wrote: "Two marines ... are the important pictures of this exhibition and they come from Winslow Homer and Paul Dougherty" (Arthur Hoeber, "The Winter Exhibition of the National Academy of Design," *The International Studio* 30, 120 [February 1907]: cii). See also Bryant, *Am. Pictures,* p. 247.

24. S.H. "Studio-Talk," *The International Studio* 30, 118 (December 1906): 180. Neuhaus also comments on his "broad and virile style" (*History of Am. Art,* p. 303).

25. Carey, "Paintings by Beal," pp. xxix-xxx. Duncan Phillips later concurred, commenting that Beal "owes more to Winslow Homer than to any artist and carries on his tradition of self-reliant and impassioned realism, romantic in spite of itself" (*A Collection in the Making* [Washington, D.C.: Phillips Memorial Gallery, 1926], p. 66). Frederick W. Kost is compared to Homer by Caffin in "Am. Painters of the Sea," p. 556.

26. The work of Ritschel, Dougherty, and others who visited the West Coast confirms Bellows' exclamation from San Francisco: "This place is exactly like Maine" (Bellows to Henri, August 7, 1917, Henri papers, Beinecke Library). Ritschel was commented on favorably by Caffin: "His work is very masculine" ("Am. Painters of the Sea," p. 558).

27. For example: "Mr. Whistler may call one of his small canvases of the open sea a symphony in blue or gray or catalogue it by any other fantastic name he chooses; but the fact remains that his few touches of the brush give us not only the form and color of the sea, but suggest to us the great ocean tossing after storm—rolling moodily under gray skies. The painter intended that such a meaning should be suggested." John C. Van Dyke, *The Meaning of Pictures* (New York: Scribners, 1903), p. 145.

28. Isham discusses snow painters (*History of Am. Painting,* pp. 440 ff.). Both Bryant (*Am. Pictures*) and Neuhaus (*History of Am. Art*) devote chapters to the subject. See also Deborah Shotner, "Twachtman and the American Winter Landscape," *John Twachtman: Connecticut Landscapes,* exh. cat. (Washington, D.C.: National Gallery of Art, 1989).

29. Isham, *History of Am. Painting,* p. 354.

30. Isham recalled that after the Civil War "the succeeding generation of artists departed for Europe almost in a body.... They accepted European standards of workmanship and also to a great extent European tastes and interests" (*History of Am. Painting,* p. xvi). He added: "[For] the American student on his return ... his ambition as well as real feeling directed him to more purely artistic qualities, to refinement of drawing, beautiful color, skillful handling" (ibid., p. 367).

31. Henry Reuterdahl, "Winslow Homer, American Painter: An Appreciation from a Sea-Going Viewpoint," *The Craftsman* 20, 1 (April 1911): 8.

32. Virgil Barker, speaking of late nineteenth-century painting, declared that "art for art's sake" was really "technic for technic's sake." *A Critical Introduction to American Painting* (New York: William Edwin Rudge for the Whitney Museum of American Art, 1931), p. 36.

33. Quoted by Wanda M. Corn, *The Color of Mood: American Tonalism 1880-1910,* exh. cat. (San Francisco: M. H. De Young Memorial Museum and California Palace of the Legion of Honor, 1972), p. 12.

34. J. Eastman Chase thought: "Homer was less influenced by others and by what others had done than any artist—any man, I may as well say—as I have ever known. He was a rare visitor to public galleries and exhibitions. When there his attitude was that of a detached and unprejudiced observer. Names meant little or nothing to him. He looked at any picture for precisely what it might have to say to him—the name of the painter, whether great or small, was of equal indifference. He was not accustomed to speak of a 'Corot' or a 'Turner': it was the picture, pure and simple, that interested or did not interest him. His comment was as you would suppose, fresh, original, penetrating, and free from art jargon" ("Some Recollections of Winslow Homer," *Harper's Weekly* 54 [October 22, 1910]: 13). On the other hand, James Thomas Flexner has stated: "It was surely no coincidence that this transcendent American master was an exact contemporary of France's transcendent masters, the Impressionists. Certainly Homer was helped to the heights by subtle assimilation" (*History of American Painting,* vol. 3, *That Wilder Image* [Boston: Little, Brown, 1962], p. 333).

35. La Farge noted: "Lithographs from these men came into our market and affected many of us. Mr. Winslow Homer was a student of these things, and has ... been largely made by them." Quoted by Suzanne Lafollete, *Art in America* (New York: Harper and Brothers, 1929), p. 179; Stebbins et al., *A New World,* p. 340.

36. John C. Van Dyke, *American Painting and Its Tradition* (New York: Charles Scribner's Sons, 1920), p. 100.

37. See Beam, *Homer,* p. 205; quoted in Goodrich, *Homer,* pp. 210, 213.

38. Michel Eugene Chevreul pointed out that: "All the primary colors gain in brilliancy and purity by the proximity of grey" (*Principles of Harmony and Contrast of Colors,* trans. Charles Martel, 3rd ed. [London: Bell, 1872], p. 82).

39. Although this may be taken with a grain of salt: Henry Ward Ranger seems to list everyone as a tonalist. Ralcy Husted Bell, *Art-Talks with Ranger* (New York: G. P. Putnam's Sons, 1914), p. 12.

40. Ranger discussed his experiments with a "loaded canvas [which] I hoped would give an appearance of vigour. But the big, vigourous brushmarks of the loading usually cropped up in the picture at the wrong place." Ibid., pp. 106-107.

41. Ranger recalled that with "a new theory that a 'flat' surface gave the effect of more air than a shiny one, there came a desire on the part of some painters to make their pictures look like pastels." Ibid., p. 74.

42. The less overtly symbolic Scandinavian painting was well known in this country at the time. The Norwegian Fritz Thaulow, for example, was a member of the Carnegie International Jury in 1897, and his role in popularizing paintings of winter subjects was remembered for years. See Neuhaus, *History of Am. Art,* p. 279; Roald Nasgaard, *The Mystic North: Symbolist Landscape Painting in Northern Europe and North America 1890-1940* (Toronto: University of Toronto in association with the Art Gallery of Ontario, 1984).

43. Stebbins et al., *A New World,* p. 335, n. 6.

44. Isham, *History of Am. Painting,* p. 355; Hartmann, *History of Am. Art,* vol. 1, pp. 197, 199; Cox, *Old Masters and New,* p. 146.

45. Kenyon Cox, "The Art of Winslow Homer," *Scribners* 56, 3 (September 1914): 384.

46. Goodrich, *Homer,* pp. 175, 177; 171.

47. Frank Jewett Mather et al., *The American Spirit in Art* (New Haven: Yale University Press, 1927), p. 75. See also Cortissoz, *Am. Artists,* p. 123.

48. Kenyon Cox, "Some Phases of Nineteenth-Century Painting, Part I, Naturalism in the Nineteenth Century," *The Art World* 1, 5 (February 1917): 320.

49. George Williams Sheldon, *American Painters* (New York: D. Appleton and Company, 1879), p. 25. See also George Williams Sheldon, *Hours with Art and Artists* (New York: D. Appleton and Company, 1882), p. 138.

50. Frederick W. Morton, "The Art of Winslow Homer" *Brush and Pencil* 10, 1 (April 1902): 40 (Morton's words closely echo M. G. Van Rensselaer's summation in "An American Artist in England," *Century Illustrated Magazine* 27 [November 1883]: 20); Frank Mather et al., *Am. Spirit in Art,* p. 75. Kenyon Cox agreed: "No great painter had ever less amenity or less care for the purely decorative and aesthetic elements of art" ("Phases of Nineteenth-Century Painting," p. 320). So did Christian Brinton who found his work "often prosaic or frankly ugly" ("Winslow Homer," *Scribner's Magazine* 49 [January 1911]: 9).

51. Isham, *History of Am. Painting,* pp. 355-56.

52. Downes compared him specifically to Velázquez, the quintessential realist figure for the nineteenth century, one with a pedigree and without the vulgarity and rebelliousness of Courbet. *Life and Works,* pp. 4-6.

Chapter Four: Americanism and Realism

1. Henry F. May, *The End of American Innocence: A Study of the First Years of Our Own Time, 1912-1917* (New York: Alfred A. Knopf, 1969), p. 45.

2. Robert H. Wiebe, *The Search for Order 1877-1920* (New York: Hill and Wang, 1967), p. xiii.

3. We should perhaps conclude that Homer's trip to Cullercoats, England, in 1880 and his subsequent change in direction were the product of some sort of breakdown. See May, *End of Am. Innocence,* p. 77.

4. Quoted in Lears, *No Place of Grace,* p. 34.

5. Hartmann, *History of Am. Art,* vol. 1, pp. 190 ff.

6. We still use the term when we speak of getting the "big picture" or the "big idea," but not in sophisticated journals.

7. Nelson, "N.A.D.: Winter Exhibition," p. clxxxiii.

8. Caffin, "Am. Painters of the Sea," p. 548.

9. Robert Henri, *The Art Spirit* (Philadelphia: J. B. Lippincott Company, 1923), p. 279.

10. Charles H. Caffin, *The Story of American Painting* (New York: Frederick A. Stokes Company, 1907), p. 234. And, as another critic added: "Grandly Homer saw the big things.... He saw things big, he had something of his own to say, and his ways shaped themselves" (Reuterdahl, "Homer: An Appreciation," p. 17).

11. David Shi quoting Senator John Sherman writing in 1866, in *The Simple Life: Plain Living and High Thinking in American Culture* (Oxford: Oxford University Press, 1985), p. 154.

12. Andrew Carnegie, "Popular Illusions about Trusts," 1900, quoted by Nell Irvin Painter, *Standing at Armageddon: The United States 1877-1919* (New York: W. W. Norton, 1987), p. 94.

13. Quoted in Shi, *The Simple Life,* pp. 155, 158.

14. H.St.G., "Winslow Homer," *The Critic* 46, 4 (April 1905): 323. In one book Mather noted: "His art is mostly bones ... but it is direct, virile and masterly" (*Modern Painting,* p. 178). In another place he also wrote: "It is a male art and often a raw art" (Mather et al., *Am. Spirit in Art,* p. 75). William H. Goodyear summarized the public perception as follows: "The general opinion of Winslow Homer ... has been that his art was virile, vigorous, rugged, powerful, and remorselessly truthful as a record of what he saw ... so that he was lacking in charm, in feeling for beauty, in subtlety of sentiment, and above all, lacking in harmony and tonality of color" ("The Watercolors of Winslow Homer, 1836-1910," *Brooklyn Museum Quarterly* 2, 3-4 [October 1915]: 367). And Lewis Hind emoted: "What a master! What force and virility!... Homer prods us wide awake with the shout of Virility. Whistler tantalizes us with the whisper of Beauty" (*Landscape Painting,* pp. 141, 143).

15. Brinton, "Winslow Homer," p. 22.

16. Reuterdahl, "Homer: An Appreciation," pp. 10, 17.

17. The same vocabulary of strength and manliness permeated the critical discourse on Whitman: "[Whitman] is often crude, often grotesque, often unbeautiful. But he is large, consistent, human." Philip Henry Savage, *Harvard Advocate* 1897, quoted in Charles Borromeo Williard, *Whitman's American Fame: The Growth of His Reputation in America after 1892* (Providence, R.I.: Brown University, 1950), p. 101. Homer was compared to Whitman as early as 1895 (Goodrich, *Homer,* p. 138), and also by his contemporaries to Beethoven, Tolstoy, Rembrandt, Mantegna, besides of course his namesake, the Greek poet.

18. G. S. Dickerman, "The Drift of the Cities," 1913, in Roderick Nash, ed., *The Call of the Wild (1900-1910)* (New York: George Braziller, 1970), p. 30.

19. Lears, *No Place of Grace,* p. 36.

20. Brinton, "Winslow Homer," p. 9. Even the American landscape could be manly. Charles Woodbury declared: "One of the characteristics of American landscape is that it has a virility we do not find in Europe. The American people are full of life and their natural expression is force." *Painting and the Personal Equation,* 1916, quoted in Louise Tragard and Patricia E. Hart, *A Century of Color, 1886-1986: Ogunquit, Maine's Art Colony* (Ogunquit, Me.: Barn Gallery Associates, 1987), p. 13.

21. Caffin, "American Painters of the Sea," p. 552. See also Reuterdahl: "[Homer's] physical and mental independence, strong as a rock, became the very foundation of his art. Uncouth as the average

American is in his honesty, so is Homer.... Winslow Homer's art is ... the out-of-door man's. Intense, full of brute strength, the power of the sea which smites the rock is behind his brush.... The great and simple feeling within demanded its outlet, and pushed him on toward the monumental" ("Homer: An Appreciation," pp. 8-9). Willem de Kooning, speaking about Clifford Still and Jackson Pollock in 1959, made essentially the same point: "They stand alone in the wilderness—breast bared. This is an American idea" (quoted in Irving Sandler, "Conversations with de Kooning," *Art Journal* 48, 3 [Fall 1989]: 216).

22. Nicolai Cikovsky, Jr., "Winslow Homer, *School Time:* 'A Picture Thoroughly National,'" in *Essays in Honor of Paul Mellon, Collector and Benefactor,* ed. John Wilmerding (Washington, D.C.: National Gallery of Art, 1986), pp. 47-69.

23. Royal Cortissoz, *An Exhibition of Water Colors by Winslow Homer,* exh. cat. (Pittsburgh: Carnegie Institute, 1923), p. 7. Lewis Hind wrote: "He stands with Walt Whitman, entirely and racially American" (*Landscape Painting,* p. 142).

24. Henry Adams, *The Education of Henry Adams, An Autobiography* (Boston: Houghton Mifflin, 1961; orig. publ. 1906), p. 333.

25. Henry James, *The American Scene* (New York: Horizon Press, 1967; orig. publ. 1905), p. 121. Henry Ward Ranger strikes a distinctly sane note, when asked about American art too closely resembling European art: "[Critics] ask why American art suggests and is reminiscent of European art, instead of being itself; i.e., purely American, and without trace of European influence? This rings with a certain plausibility; but if examined, it appears grotesque. Its basis seems to be a vague idea that our ancestors were American Indians.... We are a European people ... their history is our history.... Our present environment, as regards climate and scenery, is about what we left behind us" (Bell, *Art-Talks with Ranger,* p. 177).

26. Isham, *History of Am. Painting,* p. xvi.

27. Cox, *Old Masters and New,* pp. 1, 146. John Rummell also emphasizes this point: "The most truly national of all our painters ... [Homer's] work never betrays the influence of any school of art or the method of any artist" (*Aims and Ideals,* pp. 106-107). He added: "whatever is idyllic or heroic in the lives of the common people of this great democracy, Homer has closely observed ... always telling the essential truth of his subject in a style at once broad and masterful, sincere and noble" (p. 108).

28. Charles Vezen, "Protests against Psychopathic Art" (letter to the editor), *The Herald,* April 4, 1907, Henri scrapbook, Archives of American Art, microfilm 887, 401.

29. For example, see the table of contents in Holger Cahill and Alfred H. Barr, Jr., *Art in America in Modern Times* (New York: Reynal and Hitchcock, 1934). Hind commented, "Inevitably one contrasts these two remarkable artists" (*Landscape Painting,* p. 140). Kenyon Cox makes the same point (*Homer,* p. 40).

30. Van Dyke, *Am. Painting,* p. 91.

31. Sophia Antoinette Walker, "The Academy Exhibition," *The Independent,* New York City, February 1901, Henri scrapbook, Archives of American Art, microfilm 887, 21. She was discussing Homer's *Signal of Distress.*

32. Sheldon, *Hours with Art and Artists,* p. 139.

33. Hind, *Landscape Painting,* p. 315.

34. Sheldon, *Hours with Art and Artists,* p. 136.

35. Isham, *History of Am. Painting,* pp. 357-58. The last word is the most telling. Homer the poet had been a symbol of unfettered, untaught genius, crude but powerful, standing at the beginning of art not at its polished perfection, since at least Hellenistic times. The same line of thought is revealed in Van Dyke's comments: "He has no comeliness of style, no charm of statement, no grace of presentation. To the last he is a barbarian for all that we may feel beneath his brush the surge and thunder of the 'Odyssey'" (*Am. Painting,* p. 111).

36. Isham, *History of Am. Painting,* p. 355.

37. "Unsuspected Art of Winslow Homer," *Literary Digest* 41, 17 (1910): 700-701. The quotations are from the *New York Evening Post.* Hartmann characterized Homer's work as "a crude and angular art, but classic in its dignity and strength." *History of Am. Art,* vol. 1, p. 194.

38. Brinton, "Winslow Homer," p. 9.

39. Cortissoz, *Am. Artists,* p. 125. *Crisp* and *spontaneous* are terms used by Mather to characterize O'Henry stories and Ashcan painting. See Frank Jewitt Mather, Jr., "Some American Realists," *Arts and Decoration* 7, 1 (November 1916): 13-16.

40. Cortissoz, *Exhibition of Water Colors by Homer,* pp. 7-8.

41. For example, Goodyear wrote: "Winslow Homer is the Millet of the sea" ("Watercolors of Homer," p. 10). For Courbet, see discussion on pages 37 and 50, and Chapter 3, n. 15.

42. John Berryman, "Crane's Art," in *Stephen Crane*, ed. Maurice Bassan (Englewood Cliffs, N.J.: Prentice-Hall, 1967), pp. 36-37.

43. Eric J. Sundquist, ed., *American Realism: New Essays* (Baltimore: The Johns Hopkins University Press, 1982), p. 13.

44. Quoted in ibid., p. 16.

45. Hartmann, *History of American Art,* vol. 1, pp. 193-94.

46. Quoted by Amy Kaplan, "'Absent Things in American Life,'" *The Yale Review* 74, 1 (November 1984): 129.

47. Sheldon, *Am. Painters,* p. 29.

48. Isham, *History of Am. Painting,* p. 352.

49. Mather added: "As a group I think they are the most coherent and American apparition that our painting now affords." The group included Henri, Luks, Glackens, Bellows Shinn, Sloan, Myers, Eugene Higgins. "Some American Realists," quotes from pp. 13, 16.

50. Amy Kaplan, *The Social Construction of American Realism* (Chicago: University of Chicago Press, 1988), p. 2.

51. For example, compare the viewpoints of Amy Kaplan and Eric Sundquist. Alfred Habegger's *Gender, Fantasy and Realism in American Literature* (New York: Columbia University, 1982) fruitfully muddies the waters.

52. Quoted in Richard Wightman Fox and T. J. Jackson Lears, eds., *The Culture of Consumption: Critical Essays in American History, 1880-1980* (New York: Pantheon Books, 1983), p. 49. The authors add: "Written words were valued for their clarity, strength, and above all, their ability to persuade, to impose an idea ... a modified form of 'realistic' discourse that attempted to convey authority, authenticity or expertise."

53. Thus Rensselaer noted: "Never did any dweller in cities more completely ignore on canvas not their existence only, but also the existence of the human types they foster. This would not, of course, be remarkable if he were simply a landscape painter; but while landscape elements are very prominent in his work, humanity is rarely absent, and is usually his chief concern. But it is rustic humanity always." "Am. Artist in England," p. 14.

54. Sheldon, *Am. Painters,* p. 29.

55. Frank Norris, "The Frontier Gone at Last," 1902, reprinted in Nash, ed., *Call of the Wild,* pp. 71-72.

56. Both by Cecelia Beaux and William J. Bixbee, a Boston marine painter, as well as by Harrison Morris, director of the Pennsylvania Academy, who took him "for a successful stock broker." See Goodrich, *Homer,* pp. 150-51.

57. Quoted in ibid., pp. 216, 168.

58. Reuterdahl, "Homer: An Appreciation," p. 9.

59. See Cooper, *Homer Watercolors,* pp. 74 ff., and Eleanor Lewis Jones, "'Deer Drinking' Reflections on a Watercolor by Winslow Homer," *Smithsonian Studies in American Art* 2, 3 (Fall 1988): 55-65.

60. Alan Trachtenberg, *The Incorporation of America: Culture and Society in the Gilded Age* (New York: Hill and Wang, 1982), pp. 208 ff.

61. Henry James, *The American Scene,* p. 345. See also p. 64.

62. Goodrich, *Homer,* pp. 202-203, quote on p. 202. Lloyd Goodrich felt compelled to broach the subject in his first statement on Homer, in "Winslow Homer," *The Arts* 6, 4 (October 1924): 191-92. See also Frank Jewett, Mather, Jr., "The Art of Winslow Homer," *The Nation* 92, 2382 (March 2, 1911): 226.

63. Lears, *No Place of Grace,* p. 305.

Chapter Five: Henri and Homer

1. Lewis C. Hind, "American Paintings in Germany," *The International Studio* 41, 163 (September 1910): 189.

2. For the modernist counter-attack, see Susan Noyes Platt, "Modernism, Formalism, and Politics: The Cubist and Abstract Art Exhibition of 1936," *Art Journal* 47, 4 (Winter 1988): 284-95.

3. Homer, on the other hand, really never knew his fellow artists as a group after he left New York, and sometimes regretted it. Downes, for example, reported: "[Homer] told [Mrs. Joseph E. Baker] that one of the big mistakes of his life had been that he did not affiliate with 'the boys,' meaning the artists." *Life and Works,* p. 241.

4. Also among the artists Henri listed as influences were Renoir, "the Impressionists," and "a few post-Impressionists." He added "Don't, therefore, take the names above as forming a list ... you would find many contemporaries here in America in the list [were I to make one]." Henri to Prof. George Zug, Dartmouth College, August 14, 1919, Henri papers, Beinecke Library.

5. In contrast, Homer's memorial exhibition seems to have excited little interest, perhaps because the paintings selected were not always the best. Henri was disappointed: "Not sufficient show of his work and badly hung." Henri, Diary, March 9, 1911, p. 68, Archives of American Art.

6. See *Index of Twentieth Century Artists,* vols. 1-4, nos. 1-7, for a full list of articles and reproductions.

7. Really any artist whom a critic found frank and direct could suggest a connection to Homer. Lewis C. Hind thought Edward Schofield "as near to the vigorous banner of Winslow Homer as he is far from the tenderly tinctured oriflamme of Twachtman. His art is virile and outstepping, crisp and candid" (*Landscape Painting,* p. 239). Isham even compared the rather refined painters of the Boston school, such as Edward Tarbell, to Homer. He commented more generally: "At present the tendency is rather toward strength both of conception and execution than subtlety" (*History of Am. Painting,* pp. 475, 461). And another critic began a review of the annual exhibition at the National Academy of Design in 1910 by praising Homer and then declared that: "A group, who, for convenience, may be called the naturalists, has at least rediscovered a fresh and vigorous idiom in paint." He named Edward Redfield, Ernest Lawson, George Bellows, and George Gardner Symons. He added, speaking of Cullen Yates' *Rising Fog,* "One could wish this hung by the Winslow Homers" (*The New York Post,* December 18, 1910, Bellows scrapbook, Bellows papers, Amherst College Library, Amherst, Mass.).

8. Henri, *Art Spirit,* p. 279.

9. Henri, "Progress in Our National Art," *The Craftsman* 15, 4 (January 1909): 390; reprinted in Henri, *Art Spirit,* p. 135.

10. Henri to his parents, 1902, quoted in Bruce Chambers, "Robert Henri's Street Scene with Snow (57th Street, N.Y.C.): An Idea of City 'In Snow Effect,'" *Yale University Art Gallery Bulletin* 39, 3 (Winter 1986): 35.

11. In a hopeful note that all was not lost, and that more refined days would soon follow, John Van Dyke placed Homer early in the historical development: "Homer was not the Leonardo but the Mantegna of American art." *Am. Painting,* pp. 111-13.

12. John Cournos, "Three Painters of the New York School," *The International Studio* 56, 224 (October 1915): 239, 240. More recently, John Baur related Homer to the Henri group, especially Kent and Hopper (*Revolution and Tradition in Modern American Art* [Cambridge, Mass.: Harvard University Press, 1951], pp. 86-87, 93). And John Wilmerding has related Bellows to Homer and Sloan to Bellows in their marine paintings *(A History of American Marine Painting* [New York: Harry N. Abrams, 1987], p. 176). Essentially Henri's influence, like Homer's, was virile. Robert Henri declared: "But before art is possible to a land, the men who become the artists must feel within themselves the need of expressing the virile ideas of their country" (Henri, "Progress in National Art," p. 388). John Spargo recognized this aspect of: "Henri's spirited appeal for the recognition and encouragement of the new and virile forces in American art" ("George Luks, An American Painter of Great Originality and Force, Whose Art Relates to All the Experiences and Interests of Life," *The Craftsman* 12, 6 [September 1907]: 600).

Using similar phrases, Charles Wisner Barrell lamented the lack of nationalism in American painting, and the number of younger painters who seem "largely aliens in spirit." Among Henri's students, however, he found a different attitude: "His men lose nothing of their native dignity and masculinity by translation through the Henri paint" ("Robert Henri—'Revolutionary,'" *The Independent* 64, 3108 [June 25, 1908]: 1427 ff., 1431). Lewis Hind found several of Henri's students virile, including Beal: "Gifford Beal is another frank, straightforward painter more akin to the virility of Winslow Homer than the delicacy of Twachtman" (*Landscape Painting,* p. 313).

13. William Innes Homer, *Robert Henri and His Circle,* rev. ed. (New York: Hacker Art Books, 1988), p. 121.

14. Bellows to Dr. S. C. G. Watkins, Montclair, N.J., February 25, 1924, Bellows papers, Amherst College Library. He went on: "And one other American painter or better, two, stand on the same pedestal with him, in my [m]ind, neither of whom you mentioned—Thomas Eakins, and Whisler [*sic*]. Homer Martin follows. [This last sentence is crossed out.]" The letter is quoted in part in Charles H. Morgan, *George Bellows, Painter of America* (New York: Reynal and Company, 1965), p. 272. Frank Kelly movingly suggests that *Shore House* by Bellows be seen as a memorial tribute to Homer. Franklin Kelly, "George Bellows' *Shore House,*" in *Essays in Memory of Daniel Fraad, Jr.,* ed. Nicolai Cikovsky, Jr., and Doreen Bolger (Washington, D.C.: The National Gallery of Art; and New York: The Metropolitan Museum of Art, 1990).

15. Kroll met Homer in 1907. Homer offered a few tips, which Kroll remembered and later found useful. Homer let Kroll and his friends in initially because "one of them had a very nice personality ... [and] was kind of nice-looking." But once he saw Kroll's work he ignored the other two students. Kroll, *A Spoken Memoir,* pp. 12-15.

16. Redfield to Henri, January 20, 1900, Henri papers, Beinecke Library. By "River stuff" Redfield meant his own paintings of the Seine, such as *Evening on the Seine,* ca. 1899 (collection of Mr. and Mrs. J. Elwood Burke).

17. *Herald Tribune,* March 15, 1902(?), Henri scrapbook, Archives of American Art, microfilm 887, 99.

18. Chambers, "Henri's Street Scene," p. 35.

19. For example, Caffin describes Luks' *Dumping Snow* as "the brutal side of life.... The conditions are monstrous, a modern revival of the fight of the earth-folk with the Titans." Caffin, *Story of Am. Painting,* p. 375.

20. For Perrine's biography see Lolita L. W. Flockhart, *A Full Life, The Story of Van Dearing Perrine* (Boston: The Christopher Publishing House, 1939). Perrine's friendship with Henri is mentioned on pp. 138, 144, 211, etc. See also John I. H. Baur, "Rediscovery: Van Dearing Perrine," *Art in America* 57, 1 (January-February 1969): 76-79.

21. Quoted in Flockhart, *Perrine,* p. 202.

22. Quoted in ibid., p. 178.

23. "The Country Sketch Club," *The Art Collector* 9, 15 (June 1, 1899): 230.

24. Another close parallel to Perrine's snow scenes is Henri's *Winter (Central Park Snow),* 1902, sold at Sotheby's, New York, May 28, 1987, lot 257.

25. The biographical information is based on Charles H. Morgan, *George Bellows, Painter of America* (New York: Reynal and Company, 1965).

26. Wanda Corn emphasizes that every artist depicted Manhattan's newness, but that they first used a veil of atmosphere to blur the sharp edges. She mentions the importance of steam clouds, which are so prominent in all of Bellows' paintings of the Pennsylvania Station excavation. Corn, "The New New York," *Art in America* 61 (July 1973): 60-61.

27. "Eight Independent Painters," ca. 1907, Luks papers, Archives of American Art, microfilm NLu 1, 029.

28. George Santayana, "The Genteel Tradition in American Philosophy," in *Winds of Doctrine* (New York: Scribners, 1912), p. 188.

29. Hind, "Am. Paintings in Germany," pp. 189-90. *The Bridge, Blackwell's Island,* 1909, is now in the Toledo Museum of Art.

30. Cournos, "Three Painters," p. 242; Henry McBride in *The Sun,* quoted in *Literary Digest* 84, 5 (January 31, 1925): 26; and idem, "Bellows and His Critics," *The Arts* 8, 5 (November 1925): 294-95.

31. Bellows to Joseph Taylor, January 15, 1914, Bellows papers, Amherst College Library. In a letter to Henri, October 25, 1913, he makes the same equation between winter and the cold ocean that Homer implicitly does in *Maine Coast:* "There has been just one day that amounted to anything. When we had a tremendous sea and clear sunshine. The water looking like a raging snow storm." Henri papers, Beinecke Library.

32. Daniel Catton Rich correctly placed Bellows' snow scenes within the context of Schofield's and Redfield's paintings, and suggested that the purchase of Bellows' *North River* by the Pennsylvania Academy of the Fine Arts was no coincidence, given Redfield's prominence in Philadelphia. "Bellows Revalued," *Magazine of Art* 39, 4 (April 1946): 139.

33. In *The New York Times,* March 16, 1908, the reviewer of the annual exhibition of the National Academy linked the "force and freshness" of Homer's *West Wind* to the "rugged and almost startling reality" of Bellows' *North River* and cited in the same paragraph, as though they shared a basic affinity, Homer's *West Wind,* Jonas Lie's *Heart of the Woods,* Redfield's *December,* and Bellows' *North River,* as well as mentioning Lawson, Kent, and Leon Dabo. Bellows scrapbook, Bellows papers, Amherst College Library; quoted in part in Morgan, *Bellows,* pp. 82-83.

34. Henri, nonetheless, mentioned Homer many times in adulatory tones (see Chapter 4, note 9). He often paired him with Twachtman: "Twachtman saw the seas bathed in mists, the rocks softened with vapor. Winslow Homer looked straight through the vapor at the hard rock; he found in the leaden heaviness a most tremendously forceful idea. It was not the sea or the rock to either of these men, but their own individual attitude toward the beauty or the force of nature. Each man must take the material that he finds at hand, see that in it there are the big truths of life, the fundamentally big forces, and then express in his art whatever is the cause of his pleasure in his art. It is not so much the actual place of the immediate environment; it is personal greatness and personal freedom which any nation demands for a final right art expression" ("Progress in National Art," p. 390, reprinted, *Art Spirit,* pp. 134-35). He added: "Here in America we have a country filled with energetic people.... It is a great encouragement that already fine and strong notes of this voice have come to us. We have had it, as I have already said, in Whitman, in Winslow Homer, and in Twachtman" (ibid., p. 391). See also Hind, *Landscape Painting,* p. 315.

35. Henri to his mother, September 17, 1911, Henri papers, Beinecke Library.

36. In a few instances, Henri later repainted these sketches to simplify the forms and introduce more dynamism. In *Sea and Rocks* (B 111, repainted in 1910), for example, he consolidated the rocks in the foreground into a single wedge, like Homer's *Northeaster.* Other panels reminiscent of Homer are *Surf,* B 135; *Sea and Rocks,* B 147; *Sea and Rocks,* B 159; *Surf near Gull Rock,* B 172; *Rocks and Sea—Fog,* B 180; and *Surf and Rocks,* B 202. Henri Record Book, courtesy of Mrs. Janet LeClair.

37. Henri, *Art Spirit,* p. 115. William Innes Homer credits the specific influence of Homer on Henri in the Maine paintings, as freeing him "from any preordained compositional format" and adds: "His deep involvement with nature as a dynamic force suggests an obvious debt to ... Homer." *Henri and His Circle,* p. 235.

38. Charles deKay, "Six Impressionists," *The New York Times,* January 20, 1904, Henri scrapbook, Archives of American Art, microfilm 887, 196. DeKay mentioned specifically "Cliff and Sea," "Burnt Head, Monhegan," "Island of Manana," and "Monhegan Fishing Houses"; the latter is probably *Storm Tide.*

39. "Art Notes: Robert Henri's Paintings of Monhegan Island at the Macbeth Gallery," *The Craftsman* 21, 4 (January 1912): 454-55.

40. Henri, "Progress in National Art," p. 398.

Chapter Six: Henri's Students

1. For biographical information, see David Traxel, *An American Saga: The Life and Times of Rockwell Kent* (New York: Harper and Row, 1980).

2. *John Sloan's New York Scene,* ed. Bruce St. John (New York: Harper and Row, 1965), p. 121; Bellows to Joseph Taylor, April 21, 1910, Bellows papers, Amherst College Library. Kent temporarily shared Bellows' studio in the spring of 1907 (Morgan, *Bellows,* p. 68).

3. James Gibbons Huneker also compared him to Scandinavian painters. *Americans in the Arts 1890-1920,* ed. Arnold T. Schwab (New York: AMS Press, 1985), p. 503; orig. publ. in *New York Sun,* April 5, 1907, p. 8.

4. Hind, "Am. Paintings in Germany," p. 190. Hind discussed Kent along with Bellows and Homer, and also mentioned "the forceful sea-pieces of Paul Dougherty."

5. Barrell, "Henri—'Revolutionary, '" p. 1432. Barrell discussed Kent's *Winter, Monhegan Island* in conjunction with Whitman and Homer, and also mentioned Kent's *Maine Coast.* Hind described him as: "Rockwell Kent, that art child of Winslow Homer and William Blake" (*Landscape Painting,* p. 311). In 1910 a reviewer for *Art News* found Kent "in a way, a younger Winslow Homer in his somewhat hard and crude color but dramatic intensity" (quoted in *Rockwell Kent: An Anthology of His Works,* ed. Fridolf Johnson [New York: Alfred A. Knopf, 1982], p. 25). In 1915 J. Nilsen Laurvik thought: "Rockwell Kent ... is of the same vigorous, large-minded race as Winslow Homer. He is a worthy successor to the master of Prout's Neck, whose rugged, rock-ribbed coast he has depicted with forthright simplicity and directness that has something of the stark actuality and bitter tang of the sea itself" (quoted in Richard V. West, *"An Enkindled Eye": The Paintings of Rockwell Kent,* exh. cat. [Santa Barbara, Calif.: Santa Barbara Museum of Art, 1985], p. 17). In a summary of reviews of Kent's Newfoundland paintings and drawings, the compiler noted: " 'The paint is laid on by an athlete of the brush,' Mr. Huneker exclaimed in the *Sun....* Everything in these new pictures, for the *Tribune,* is painfully big.... For *American Art News,* ... 'there is still a suggestion in his deep, sometimes crude color of the seas and skies of the Newfoundland coast he so loves, and his virile drawing, of Winslow Homer who has evidently most influenced him'" ("Spiritual Adventures of an American Artist in Newfoundland," *Current Opinion* 62 [April 1917]: 277). Frank Jewett Mather, as late as 1927, declared: "Indeed his closest successor, Rockwell Kent, has infused his even more simplified realism with suggestions

of symbolism.... If one could imagine a Winslow Homer cut free from his realistic moorings, one would have a rough picture of the genius of Rockwell Kent ... perhaps the most powerful among our younger painters" (Mather et al., *Am. Spirit in Art,* pp. 85, 162). Forbes Watson was more dubious of Kent's self-conscious relationship to Homer: "When he was not afraid of Homer he did the best work he has ever done" ("Rockwell Kent, Incorporated," *Arts and Decoration* 12, 5 [March 1920]: 325).

6. "Kent shared with his friend Marsden Hartley an almost mystical reverence for ... the paintings of Winslow Homer." Alan Wallach, "Rockwell Kent," *Arts Magazine* 54, 2 (October 1979): 15.

7. Rockwell Kent, *It's Me O Lord* (New York: Dodd, Mead and Company, 1955), p. 191.

8. Examples of Thayer's winter views of Mount Monadnock are in the National Academy of Design; Freer Gallery of Art; Corcoran Gallery of Art; The Art Museum, Princeton University; and the Metropolitan Museum of Art. A much later repetition of Cleveland's painting by Kent, entitled *Monhegan Headland, Winter,* is now in the Soviet Union. Another painting related to Cleveland's is in the Museum of Fine Arts, Boston: *Maine Coast, Winter,* 1909, 38 x 44-1/2. The original title of Cleveland's painting seems to have been "The Clearing." There is a sketch of the painting with this title in Kent's letter to William Macbeth, February 5, 1908, Archives of American Art, Macbeth papers, microfilm NMc8, 808. Interestingly, the comparison between Thayer and Homer was made in their lifetimes. See Barbara Novak and Annette Blaugrund, *Next to Nature: Landscape Paintings from the National Academy of Design,* exh. cat. (New York: National Academy of Design, 1980), p. 164.

9. Kent, *It's Me O Lord,* p. 186.

10. Richard V. West points to several similar parallels with Homer. *Rockwell Kent: The Early Years* (Brunswick, Me.: Bowdoin College, 1969).

11. Kent from Newfoundland to John and Dolly Sloan, October 20, 1910, Sloan papers, Delaware Art Museum, Wilmington, Delaware.

12. Bellows to Emma, August 9 and August 12, 1911, Bellows papers, Amherst College Library.

13. Bellows to Emma, August 15 and 14, 1911, respectively, Bellows papers, Amherst College Library.

14. Bellows to Henri, September 15, 1913, Henri papers, Beinecke Library.

15. "I painted a sure enough masterpiece today which walks up to the 'Shore House' and says 'Hello, Kid, I'm with you.' It's 'An Island in the Sea.'" Bellows to Emma, quoted in Morgan, *Bellows,* p. 137.

16. Although the quotation is from a critic reviewing in a Chicago paper Homer's *Early Morning after a Storm at Sea,* the applicability to Bellows is obvious (included in a letter from Homer to Knoedler, December 11, 1902, Homer correspondence in Knoedler Archives, Archives of American Art, microfilm NY59-5, 501). As if to underline his connection to Homer, Bellows saved in his scrapbook a review which reproduced together his *Pennsylvania Station Excavation at Night* and Homer's *Northeaster* (*Literary Digest,* September 10, 1910, "Our Lack of an 'American' Art," Bellows papers, Amherst College Library).

17. Bellows to Henri, September 8, 1916, Henri papers, Beinecke Library.

18. Article in *Palette and Brush* quoting J. E. Chamberlain of *New York Evening Mail,* 1913, Bellows scrapbook, Bellows papers, Amherst College Library. *The Dory* is in the New Britain Museum of Art, New Britain, Connecticut, with another version in the Reading Public Museum and Art Gallery, Reading, Pennsylvania.

19. *American Art News* 12, 16 (January 24, 1914): 3. Robert J. Cole declared in 1924: "If he has a kinship, it may be with such an earlier artist as Winslow Homer" (quoted in Morgan, *Bellows,* p. 269). Frank Crowninshield, in his introduction to the *Memorial Exhibition of the Works of George Bellows,* wrote: "We believe that the work of this painter ... will take its place beside the poetry of Whitman and the marines of Homer, and that the three will then be seen to constitute the most inspiring, the most native and the most deeply flavored performances in American art" (exh. cat. [New York: Metropolitan Museum of Art, 1925], p. 21).

20. Bellows was described by the Metropolitan as having "virile talent" ("Recent Acquisitions," *Metropolitan Museum of Art Bulletin* 6, 3 [March 1911]: 67). The next year, in an article entitled "George Bellows, An Artist with 'Red Blood,'" his work was compared to the stories of Rudyard Kipling and Jack London, and was described (quoting Robert G. McIntyer in *Art and Progress*) as: "Bold yet dignified simplicity is the chief characteristic of his painting" (*Current Literature* 53 [September 1912]: 342-45). Ameen Rihani, in a rather silly article, suggested that it was "inevitable" that Luks and Bellows should "adopt the Whitman manner.... They are after the big facts of life." He added: "Neither Luks nor Bellows has a mincing manner in speech or behavior ... [they show] a crude sin-

cerity" ("American Painting, Part III, Luks and Bellows," *The International Studio* 71, 281 [August 1920]: xxi). Equally bombastic, Charles L. Buchanan described Bellows' art as having: "Strength—a great, broad, bulging, muscular strength, a strength with all its imperfections and crudities, its advantages and its disadvantages largely thrown at you in the raw, so to speak, by an apparent sincerity of purpose. There, so I rightly or wrongly take it, you have George Bellows, painter of democracy and a clean hard worker, however much you are at liberty to disagree with his methods and his vision.... The unyielding antagonist of a mere facile prettiness, a colorful confectionery.... Action, force—there you have the sky line of the man's endeavors." He concluded: "He suggests to me the alertness of American journalism turned painter.... He is obsessed by the mere bigness of things" ("George Bellows, Painter of Democracy," *Arts and Decoration* 4, 8 [August 1914]: 370, 371, 373). Bellows himself employed the same kind of language: "The bigness or littleness of art springs from the deepness or shallowness of the workers [*sic*] perception" (Bellows to John W. Beatty, December 13, 1923, Bellows papers, Amherst College Library).

21. Catherine Beach Ely, "The Modern Tendency in Henri, Sloan and Bellows," *Art in America* 10, 111 (April 1922): 138.

22. Frank Crowninshield, "An Appreciation of the Life and Work of George Bellows," *The Art News* 23, 15 (January 17, 1925): 6. Crowninshield puts these words into Bellows' mouth; but Bellows had said pretty much the same thing. Speaking of the independent exhibition in 1910, he wrote to his old professor: "I think the one big impression is that of manliness, frankness and love of the game." Bellows to Joseph Taylor, April 21, 1910, Bellows papers, Amherst College Library.

23. It is a mark of both Bellows' self-proclaimed interest in Old Masters and a change in the degree of sophistication in art criticism that Cortissoz should have felt the need to add defensively: "If he had any artistic forefather it was Manet ... but it does not touch the integrity of that Americanism" (*Scribner's Magazine* 78 [1925]: reprinted in *The Painter's Craft* [New York: Charles Scribners Sons, 1930], pp. 440-41, 44). In an article entitled "The Americanism of George Bellows," the author lamented: "American art of today has lost one its strongest vital forces; ... he is one of our most authentic answers to the call for a native art" (*Literary Digest* 84, 5 [January 31, 1925]: 26). The article also quoted the *New York Tribune:* "He was a racy American; ... his art flowed out of a wholesomely robust nature ... with amazing realism." It is typical of this period that Crowninshield should assert, while discussing Bellows' origins in Ohio, "the painter was not, in a true sense, a product of

that state, his people having derived from the Montauk end of Long Island, where his grandfather had been a whaler of renown" (*Memorial Exhibition of the Works of George Bellows,* p. 12). Crowninshield added: "As time went on Bellows began more and more to embody the geography and democracy of our country. For one thing, he never set foot in Europe" (ibid., p. 13). Crowninshield underlined the point by commenting: "Bellows became the most characteristically 'native' of our painters, not because he avoided Cubism and the movements that come with it, nor because he lived in America, but because his emotions, tastes and personal quality remained so purely and so completely American.... Indeed, the native quality in him was so intense and so immediate that he seemed able ... to imbue his method of painting itself with a character quite unmistakably un-European" (ibid., p. 14).

24. Homer's most memorable advice to Leon Kroll was "you've got too many waves. If you want to do a great sea, use only two waves" (Kroll, *A Spoken Memoir,* p. 5). Bellows understood the admonition instinctively. Kroll's memoirs also reproduce a sketch very close to Homer's *High Cliffs* (ibid., fig. 31). *Breaking Surf, Prout's Neck* was exhibited as *Rocks and Sea,* 1909, in 1970, but the inscription reads: *Kroll 07. Leon Kroll: The Rediscovered Years,* exh. cat. (New York: Bernard Danenberg Galleries, 1970), no. 4.

25. For biographical information, see *George Luks: An American Artist,* exh. cat. (Wilkes-Barre, Pa.: Sordoni Art Gallery, 1987).

26. Spargo, "Luks," p. 601. Rihani felt that "Like Cézanne, [Luks] is pre-eminently a builder. His sense of form and his sense of colour are crude but virile" ("Luks and Bellows," p. xxvi). Guy Pene du Bois noted not Luks' form, but his sense of energy: "There are no static moments in a single one of his successful canvases. They do not flow with the swift urbanity of the lines of Rubens. They have a slower, squarer, less sophisticated rhythm— probably a more homely one—but they have a natural and easy exuberance that is very like his" ("George Luks and Flamboyance," *The Arts* 3, 2 [February 1923]: 110-13).

27. Emma W. Moseley, "George Luks, Noted Artist and Philosopher, Says Maine Leads Them All in Scenery," *Portland Evening Express,* August 22, 1922, Luks papers, Archives of American Art, microfilm NLu 1, 094. Luks painted fifteen canvases (see his letter to Mildred Williams, September 3, 1922, Mildred E. Williams papers, Archives of American Art, microfilm 3482, 223). Some were portraits of "types" but the majority were landscapes.

28. *New York City Tribune,* October 8, 1922, Luks papers, Archives of American Art, microfilm NLu 1, 107; and *Evening Transcript,* Boston, September 5, 1922, ibid., microfilm NLu 1, 106. See also Elizabeth Luther Cary, who particularly noted: "his pigment, however brutally it is thrust upon the canvas" ("George Luks," *American Magazine of Art* 14 [February 1923]: 74). Interestingly, the use of red was noted as it had been for Homer. In a review of Luks' Maine paintings, the restraint of the color is noted, being only "present in the vermilion gleam on the rocks where the waves break over a reef, and in the vivid streak of a sunset sky over black water" (*American Art News* 21, 1 [October 14, 1922]: 2). The spot of red in *Great Waves* seems a very Homeric, accidental touch.

29. *New York Globe,* October 1922, Luks papers, Archives of American Art, microfilm NLu 1, 116. Luks was also compared to Waugh, in an article by Margaret Breuning (ibid., microfilm NLu 1, 109).

30. For biographical information, see Gail Levin, *Edward Hopper: The Art and the Artist* (New York: W. W. Norton and Company, 1980).

31. A. H. Barr, Jr., noted: "Hopper has painted a few pictures in which there are neither men nor houses. The pure landscapes *Cape Ann Granite, Hills, South Truro,* [and] *Camel's Hump* occupy a place apart in his work. They reveal a power which is disconcertingly hard to analyze. Cézanne and Courbet and John Crome convey sometimes a similar depth of feeling towards the earth and nature." *Edward Hopper, Retrospective Exhibition,* exh. cat. (New York: Museum of Modern Art, 1933), p. 14.

32. Helen Appleton Read, "Edward Hopper," *Parnassus* 5 (November 1933): 8, 10.

33. Robert Coates, "The Art Galleries," *The New Yorker,* May 26, 1945, p. 26; see also Levin, *Hopper,* p. 37.

34. Baur, *Revolution and Tradition,* p. 93.

35. Lloyd Goodrich, *Edward Hopper* (Harmondsworth, Middlesex: Penguin Books, 1949), p. 11. Goodrich's terms echo Isham's uncannily (see Isham, *History of Am. Painting,* pp. 352-53).

36. Mary Morsell, "Hopper Exhibition Clarifies a Phase of American Art," *The Art News* 32, 5 (November 4, 1933): 12. Others saw alienation: "Much of his work, particularly his sunlit summer landscapes, is as purely objective as Homer's. But Hoppper has also been acutely sensitive to those hidden tensions which exist below the level of normal human intercourse and to those nameless emotions which loneliness creates in the human spirit.... In a way it is a pessimistic art, its sense of isolation emphasized ... by the paucity of detail and the alienating quality of Hopper's light" (Baur, *Revolution and Tradition,* p. 93). Baur, however, is oblivious to the same tensions underneath the surface of Homer's "objective" landscapes.

37. Charles Burchfield, "Edward Hopper— Classicist," in Barr, *Hopper,* p. 16.

38. Edward Hopper, "Notes on Painting," in ibid., p. 17.

39. Clipping dated February 2, 1908, Luks papers, Archives of American Art, microfilm NLu 1, 045.

40. Giles Edgerton, "The Younger American Painters: Are They Creating a National Art?" *The Craftsman* 13, 5 (February 1908): 512, 521.

41. Arthur Jerome Eddy continued: "Winslow Homer's name has been mentioned and mentioned with the respect due one of the greatest painters this country has produced, but the besetting weakness of picture buyers is undue reverence for the man who has 'arrived,' above all for the master who is dead. Better pictures are being painted in America today than Homer painted, and he would be the first to say so if living. Since he painted his best pictures the art of painting has advanced, painters have improved their technic and broadened their outlook. There are pictures being painted today by young Americans that will be worth far more than Homer's, and that is said with the full realization that no lover of what is big and strong in art could ask for more virile impressions of nature than those of Homer at his best" (*Cubists and Post-Impressionism* [Chicago: A. C. McClurg and Company, 1919], pp. 195-96). In a review of The Eight, Samuel Swift declared: "There is a virility in what they have done, but virility without loss of tenderness; a manly strength that worships beauty, an art that is conceivably a true echo of the significant American life about them" ("Revolutionary Figures in American Art," Luks papers, Archives of American Art, microfilm NLu 1, 034). "The place of so-called ugliness in art" as Caffin put it (*Story of Am. Painting,* p. 370) was also discussed in relation to The Eight. Henri, it was said, "does not fear the ugly" (Huneker, "Henri and Others," p. 494).

42. Edgerton, "Younger Am. Painters," p. 531.

43. See Theodore P. Greene, *America's Heroes: The Changing Models of Success in American Magazines* (New York: Oxford University Press, 1970).

44. It is because of this insistence on character and personal expression, that Henri, ultimately primarily a figure-painter, identified himself with the tradition of figure-painters not landscape painters, omitting Homer in most of his genealogies of artistic ancestors.

45. "George Bellows," *The Nation* 120, 3107 (January 21, 1925): 60. Crowninshield draws at length the comparisons with Whitman, especially "the mysterious and dilating energy of their creations" ("Appreciation of Bellows," p. 16).

46. Ernest Thompson Seton, *Boy Scouts of America* (New York: Doubleday, 1910), quoted in Nash, ed., *Call of the Wild,* p. 21.

47. Ibid.

48. Although Henri later retouched the painting, *Storm Tide* (B122) is listed in Henri's Record Book as being painted in August 1903—in other words, on Monhegan. The houses seem to be those surrounding Fish Beach.

49. Henri Pene du Bois, "Painting out of Doors," October 29, 1905, Henri scrapbook, Archives of American Art, microfilm 887, 410. He concluded: "He has the lyrism [*sic*] of force, the lyrism of power, the lyrism that sings in the philosophy of Nietzsche, in the life of our civilization."

50. The Metropolitan's *Winter, Monhegan Island* was the painting exhibited in Berlin in 1910 as *Evening on the Coast of Maine.* See *Metropolitan Museum of Art Bulletin* 12, 5 (May 1917): 120. (Kent had first given the painting to Henri.)

51. Kent, *It's Me O Lord,* p. 120.

52. Florence Barlow Ruthrauff, *Morning Telegraph,* April 2, 1911, quoted in "Robert Henri, an Apostle of Artistic Individuality," *Current Literature* 52 (April 1912): 344.

53. Robert Henri, "What Is Art?" *Arts and Decoration* 7, 6 (April 1917): 317, 324.

54. Greenberg, *Art and Culture,* p. 186.

Chapter Seven: After the Armory

1. The standard reference is Milton Wolf Brown, *The Story of the Armory Show* (New York: Abbeville Press, 1988).

2. Henry McBride, "Modern Art," *The Dial* 71 (December 1921): 118-20.

3. Thomas Craven, "George Bellows," *The Dial* 80 (February 1926): 136.

4. See, for example, Leslie Katz, "The Modernity of Winslow Homer," *Arts* 33, 5 (February 1959): 24-27.

5. Lewis Mumford, *The Brown Decades* (New York: Dover Publications, 1931), intro.

6. For more information on Hambidge and Maratta, see William Innes Homer, *Henri and His Circle,* pp. 184-94.

7. Bellows to Joseph Taylor, January 15, 1914; quoted by Morgan, *Bellows,* p. 174.

8. Bellows to John Beatty, December 13, 1923; Bellows papers, Amherst College Library.

9. For more information on Sloan, see Van Wyck Brooks, *John Sloan, A Painter's Life* (New York: E. P. Dutton, 1955).

10. Sloan to Henri, September 1, 1911, Henri papers, Beinecke Library. Instead Sloan decided to go to Belmar, New Jersey, with E. W. Davis and Stuart Davis.

11. Henri to Sloan, August 3, 1915, Sloan papers, Delaware Art Museum.

12. Sloan, *Gist of Art,* p. 15.

13. Sloan mentioned seeing Homer's work several times. At one point, while painting an old model who claimed to have worked for Homer, he described Homer as "the most important man in America today." But it is difficult to know if this is Sloan or the model speaking, or if Sloan is being serious or facetious. *Sloan's New York Scene,* ed. St. John, pp. 166, 272, 418, 494.

14. Grant Holcomb, *John Sloan: The Gloucester Years,* exh. cat. (Springfield, Mass.: Springfield Museum of Fine Arts, 1980), pp. 10, 14.

15. *N. C. Wyeth in Maine: A Centenary Exhibition,* exh. cat. (Rockland, Me: William A. Farnsworth Library and Museum, 1982), p. 2.

16. But not always. Willard Huntington Wright, reviewing a show of Homer watercolors in the context of modern painting, wrote: "His reputation is due more to America's ignorance of things artistic, than to his own inherent worth.... The desire to apotheosize Winslow Homer has in it more of patriotism than of pure aesthetic judgement." "Modern American Painters—and Winslow Homer," *Forum,* December 1915, p. 672.

17. Doreen Bolger, "Hamilton Easter Field and His Contribution to American Modernism," *American Art Journal* 20, 2 (1988): 81, 93.

18. Elsa Rogo, quoted in ibid., p. 91.

19. Ibid., p. 93.

20. *The New York Sun,* January 25, 1936, p. 330, reprinted in Henry McBride, *The Flow of Art,* ed. Daniel Catton Rich (New York: Atheneum, 1975), p. 330.

21. Edward Steichen praised "the brilliant virtuoso performance of [Homer's] brushwork—the so-called technique" ("Painting and Photography," *Camera Work* 6, 23 [July 1908]: 5, reference kindly supplied by Geraldine Wojno Kiefer).

22. Eddy, *Cubists and Post-Impressionism,* p. 79. Eddy also owned Homer's *Coast of Maine,* 1893 (Art Institute of Chicago).

23. To show the breadth of his judgment, Eddy added that "Sargent is a Virile-Impressionist." In the index, Henri is cited on the same page with Sargent, but he is not actually mentioned: an error or an interesting Freudian slip? (Ibid., pp. 191-93.) Mather also compared Homer to Cézanne: "Before Cézanne, he loved to see nature as raw planes thrusting and grinding against each other" (*Modern Painting,* p. 178).

24. Gail R. Scott, *Marsden Hartley* (New York: Abbeville Press, 1988), p. 127. Hartley once noted: "I prefer rough textured solid substances than all this flayed and whipped sensuality the French call finesse." Quoted in Barbara Haskell, *Marsden Hartley,* exh. cat. (New York: The Whitney Museum of American Art in association with New York University Press, 1980), p. 79.

25. For biographical and other information, see Sheldon Reich, *John Marin: A Stylistic Analysis and Catalogue Raisonné,* 2 vols. (Tucson: University of Arizona Press, 1970).

26. Marin to Stieglitz, August 7, 1914, *The Selected Writings of John Marin,* ed. Dorothy Norman (New York: Pellegrini and Cudahy, 1949), p. 14.

27. Quoted in Megan Thorn, "John Marin in Maine," exh. cat. (Portland, Me.: Portland Museum of Art, 1985), unpag. [p. 1].

28. For a more detailed analysis and comparison of these watercolors to Homer, see Reich, *Marin: A Catalogue Raisonné,* vol. 1, pp. 106-109.

29. *Rocks and Sea* initiates the series. See ibid., vol. 2, nos. 31.31, 32.38, 32.39, 32.40, 32.41. When Cleveland's acquisition was published, Nancy Coe noted: "His seascapes carry on the great tradition of Winslow Homer" ("Rocks and Sea, Small Point, Maine," *The Bulletin of The Cleveland Museum of Art* 44, 1 [January 1957]: 9). Klaus Kertess also points out the parallels to Homer (*Marin in Oil,* exh. cat. [Southampton, N.Y.: Parrish Art Museum, 1987], p. 48).

30. MacKinley Helm, *John Marin,* exh. cat. (Berkeley and Los Angeles: Art Galleries, University of California, Los Angeles, 1956), unpag. [p. 25].

31. Marin to Stieglitz, July 20, 1931, in Marin, *Selected Writings,* ed. Norman, pp. 139-40. In the same letter, Marin contrasted plein-air painting with studio painting, in terms recalling the general perception of Homer's work: "Out door painting as such is just a *Job*—to get down what's ahead of you—water you paint the way water moves.... If you are more or less successful these paintings will look pretty well indoors for they have a certain rugged strength which will carry them off in a room—though they seemingly bear no relationship to the room. In *indoors* painting—as such—things should bear a close relationship to the room."

32. Marin to Steiglitz, August 28, 1932, in ibid., p. 144. See also his comment "The trouble with most art endeavour it is not sexual" (John Marin, *John Marin,* ed. Cleve Gray [New York: Holt, Rinehart and Winston, 1970], p. 54).

33. MacKinley Helm, *John Marin* (New York: Pellegrini and Cuhday in association with the Institute of Contemporary Art, 1948), p. 67.

34. As Marsden Hartley stated: "Most painters in this medium [watercolor] ... are frequently occupied with the wash as merely liquid substance, and you will find that Winslow Homer and John Marin have found that there is a substance to be achieved in spite of this idea" ("John Marin," in Marsden Hartley, *On Art,* ed. Gail R. Scott [New York: Horizon Press, 1982], p. 78). Paul Rosenfeld also suggests that Marin "seems of a single piece; ... Whistler, Winslow Homer, Cézanne, the Chinese, are forgotten when he works" (*The Port of New York* [Urbana: University of Illinois, 1961; orig. publ. 1924], p. 158). The photographer Paul Strand said of one of Marin's Maine paintings: "This is Maine and nowhere else. We are made to exper-

ience something which is our own, as nothing which has grown up in Europe can be our own" ("American Watercolors at the Brooklyn Museum," *The Arts* 2, 2 [December 1921]: 148-52, quote on p. 152; also quoted in Reich, *Marin: A Catalogue Raisonné,* vol. 1, p. 162).

35. Duncan Phillips, *The Artist Sees Differently,* The Phillips Publications, 6, 1 (Washington, D.C.: Phillips Memorial Gallery, 1931), p. 85. See also Phillips, *A Collection in the Making,* p. 60.

36. Reich, *Marin: A Catalogue Raisonné,* vol. 1, p. 202.

37. For a recent biography of Hartley, see Scott, *Hartley.*

38. "Somehow a Past," unpublished manuscript, Hartley papers, Beinecke Library, p. 11.

39. "American Painting and Poetry," unpublished manuscript, Hartley papers, Beinecke Library, p. 7.

40. Quoted in Scott, *Hartley,* p. 123.

41. "William M. Harnett—Realist Painter," unpublished manuscript, Hartley papers, Beinecke Library, p. 9. Hartley, in the same essay, noted: "His sense of reality is rugged while that of Dalkie and Roy is of a feminine quality" (ibid., p. 4).

42. Rosenfeld, *Port of New York,* p. 99.

43. Hartley, *On Art,* ed. Scott, pp. 112-15.

44. Marsden Hartley, "Winslow Homer," in his *Adventures in the Arts* (New York: Boni and Liveright, 1921), p. 42. Hartley added: "Homer was the frozen one among them. Nature was nature to him, and that alone he realized, and yet it was not precisely slavish imitation that impelled him" (ibid., p. 44).

45. Ibid., pp. 44-45.

46. Ibid., p. 49.

47. Much of the following discussion draws on Vivian Endicott Barnett, "Marsden Hartley's Return to Maine," *Arts Magazine* 54, 2 (October 1979): 172-76.

48. Quoted in ibid., p. 174.

49. "Is There an American Art," unpublished manuscript, Hartley papers, Beinecke Library, p. 7

50. In the poem "What Is Sacrament" Hartley compares the "wild and black and black" sea to bombs which "go spitting out their welltimed [*sic*] murder." Marsden Hartley, *The Collected Poems of Marsden Hartley, 1904-1943,* ed. Gail R. Scott (Santa Rosa, Calif.: Black Sparrow Press, 1987), p. 293.

51. "New England Painting and Painters," unpublished manuscript, Hartley papers, Beinecke Library, p. 3.

52. "Cleophas and His Own," in *Marsden Hartley and Nova Scotia,* ed. Gerald Ferguson (Halifax: Mount Saint Vincent University Art Gallery, 1987), p. 122.

53. Hartley, *Coll. Poems,* ed. Scott, p. 153.

54. "New England Artists," unpublished manuscript, Hartley papers, Beinecke Library, p. 7. Elsewhere he commented, during a too-peaceful summer: "This is a coastal place ... a negligible place. Nature sort of fritters away here into the tidal waters which rise and fall, recede and return—leaving no other trace that it is sea water on whose edges we are living or at least sojourning there are no waves to make a virile music" ("Summer Memory of Maine," unpublished manuscript, Hartley papers, Beinecke Library, pp. 1-2).

55. One of several versions of a composition deriving from *Granite by the Sea,* 1937 (Whitney). Others include: *Rising Wave, Indian Point, Georgetown, Maine,* 1937-38 (Baltimore Museum of Art), and *Crashing Wave,* 1939 (Salander-O'Reilly Galleries, New York City).

56. Other versions include: *The Wave,* 1940-41 (Worcester Art Museum); and *Evening Storm, Schoodic, Maine, no. 2,* 1942 (private collection). The Museum of Modern Art's version is the most monumental; the wave is more clearly reduced to a single form than in *The Wave.* Wilmerding notes, "The water has the brutal force of Homer's late paintings, but not the effervescence. Hartley is in search of permanence, not movement" (*History of Am. Marine Painting,* p. 180). Stein contrasts Marin's gay cubist and Hartley's grim waves, and calls Hartley's *The Wave* "a reinterpretation of the Prout's Neck vision of Homer" (*Seascape,* p. 130).

57. Robert Goldwater noted the similarities in 1947. "Evening Storm, Schoodick [*sic*], Maine," *Kenyon Review* 9, 2 (Spring 1947): n.p., frontispiece. Many artists followed Hartley's lead, or at least, provided other more or less modernist versions of Homeric subjects. See, for example, Lamar Dodd's paintings of Monhegan or Henry Mattson's heavy rocks and seas. Milton Avery's *White Wave,* 1954, in the Milton Avery Trust, is a very close reinterpretation of Hartley's *Evening Storm.*

58. In the poem "Three Loving Men," Hartley imagines building a house with Adelard and Etienne: "each loving each, loving me." But "black went the sky" and nature destroyed both the house and the "two consummate men." Hartley, *Coll. Poems,* ed. Scott, p. 234.

59. Hartley read Eliot's poetry. On the back of the painting *In the Moraine, Dogtown Common, Cape Ann,* 1931 (Georgia Museum of Art, The University of Georgia, Athens), Hartley transcribed several lines from Eliot's *Ash Wednesday:* "Teach us to care and not to care / Teach us to sit still / Even among these rocks." Elizabeth McCausland, *Marsden Hartley* (Minneapolis: University of Minnesota Press, 1952), p. 43.

60. Henry David Thoreau, *The Maine Woods,* ed. Joseph J. Moldenhauer (Princeton: Princeton University Press, 1972; orig. publ. 1848), p. 71.

61. Henri, *Art Spirit,* p. 163. Hopper echoed Henri's words: "It's concerned with saying something that's in the man. Courbet and Homer have physical weight. In Homer those waves after waves come toward you with tremendous weight." Quoted in Brian O'Doherty, *American Masters: The Voice and the Myth in Modern Art* (New York: E. P. Dutton, 1974), p. 40.

Selected Bibliography

Manuscript Sources

Bellows, George. Papers. Amherst College Library, Amherst, Massachusetts.

Hartley, Marsden. Papers. Beinecke Library, Yale University, New Haven, Connecticut.

Henri, Robert. Papers. Beinecke Library, Yale University, New Haven, Connecticut; and Archives of American Art.

Henri, Robert. Record Book. Xerographic copy, courtesy of Mrs. Janet Le Clair.

Homer, Winslow. Papers. Bowdoin College Museum of Art, New Brunswick, Maine; and Archives of American Art.

Kent, Rockwell. Papers. Archives of American Art, Smithsonian Institution, Washington, D.C.

Luks, George. Papers. Archives of American Art, Smithsonian Institution, Washington, D.C.

Sloan, John. Papers. Delaware Art Museum, Wilmington, Delaware.

Published Sources

Adams, Henry. "Mortal Themes: Winslow Homer." *Art in America* 71, 2 (February 1983): 112-26.

Barker, Virgil. *A Critical Introduction to American Painting.* New York: William Edwin Rudge for the Whitney Museum of American Art, 1931.

Barnett, Vivian Endicott. "Mardsden Hartley's Return to Maine." *Arts Magazine* 54, 2 (October 1979): 172-76.

Barr, A. H., Jr. *Edward Hopper, Retrospective Exhibition,* exhibition catalogue. New York: Museum of Modern Art, 1933.

Barrell, Charles Wisner. "Robert Henri— 'Revolutionary.'" *The Independent* 64, 3108 (June 25, 1908).

Baur, John I. H. "Rediscovery: Van Dearing Perrine." *Art in America* 57, 1 (January-February 1969): 76-79.

Baur, John, I. H. *Revolution and Tradition in Modern American Art.* Cambridge, Mass.: Harvard University Press, 1951.

Beam, Philip C. *Winslow Homer at Prout's Neck.* Boston: Little, Brown and Company, 1966.

Bell, Ralcy Husted. *Art-Talks with Ranger.* New York: G. P. Putnam's Sons, 1914.

"Bellows and His Critics." *The Arts* 8, 5 (November, 1925): 291-95.

Bolger, Doreen. "Hamilton Easter Field and His Contribution to American Modernism." *The American Art Journal* 20, 2 (1988): 78-107.

Bolton, Theodore. "The Art of Winslow Homer: An Estimate in 1932." *Fine Arts* 18 (February 1932): 23-28.

Brinton, Christian. "Winslow Homer." *Scribner's Magazine* 49 (January 1911): 9-23.

Brooks, Van Wyck. *John Sloan, A Painter's Life.* London: J. M. Dent and Sons Ltd.; New York: E. P. Dutton, 1955.

Brown, Milton Wolf. *The Story of the Armory Show.* New York: Joseph H. Hirshhorn Foundation, 1963. New York: Abbeville Press, 1988.

Bryant, Lorinda Munson. *American Pictures and Their Painters.* New York: John Lane, 1917.

Caffin, Charles H. "American Painters of the Sea." *The Critic* 43 (December 1903): 548-59.

Caffin, Charles H. *The Story of American Painting.* New York: Frederick A. Stokes Company, 1907.

Cahill, Holger, and Barr, Alfred H., Jr. *Art in America in Modern Times.* New York: Reynal and Hitchcock, 1934.

Carey, Ralph W. "Some Paintings by Gifford Beal." The *International Studio* 44, 174 (August 1911): xxix-xxxi.

Chambers, Bruce. "Robert Henri's Street Scene with Snow (57th Street, N.Y.C.): An Idea of City 'In Snow Effect.'" *Yale University Art Gallery Bulletin* 39, 3 (Winter 1986): 30-39.

Chase, Eastman J. "Some Recollections of Winslow Homer." *Harper's Weekly* 54 (October 22, 1910): 13.

Cikovsky, Jr., Nicolai. "Winslow Homer, *School Time:* 'A Picture Thoroughly National.'" In *Essays in Honor of Paul Mellon, Collector and Benefactor.* Edited by John Wilmerding. Washington, D.C.: National Gallery of Art, 1986.

Coffin, William A. "A Painter of the Sea: Two Pictures by Winslow Homer." *Century Magazine* 58, 5 (September 1899): 650-54.

Cooper, Helen A. *Winslow Homer Watercolors,* exhibition catalogue. Washington, D.C.: National Gallery of Art; and New Haven, Conn.: Yale University Press, 1986.

Corn, Wanda M. *The Color of Mood: American Tonalism 1880-1910,* exhibition catalogue. San Francisco: M. H. De Young Memorial Museum and California Palace of the Legion of Honor, 1972.

Corn, Wanda M. "The New New York." *Art in America* 61 (July-August 1973): 58-65.

Cortissoz, Royal. *American Artists.* New York: Charles Scribner's Sons, 1923.

Cortissoz, Royal. *An Exhibition of Water Colors by Winslow Homer,* exhibition catalogue. Pittsburgh: Department of Fine Arts, Carnegie Institute, 1923.

Cortissoz, Royal. *The Painter's Craft.* New York: Charles Scribner's Sons, 1930.

Cournos, John. "Three Painters of the New York School." *The International Studio* 56, 224 (October 1915): 239-46.

Cox, Kenyon. *Old Masters and New, Essays in Art Criticism.* New York: Fox, Duffield and Company, 1905.

Cox, Kenyon. "Some Phases of Nineteenth-Century Painting, Part I, Naturalism in the Nineteenth Century." *The Art World* 1, 5 (February 1917): 315-20.

Cox, Kenyon. *Winslow Homer.* New York: privately published, 1914.

Crowninshield, Frank. "An Appreciation of the Life and Work of George Bellows." *The Art News* 23, 15 (January 17, 1925): 6.

DeForest, Julia B. *A Short History of Art.* New York: Dodd, Mead and Company, 1924.

Downes, William Howe. "American Painters of the Sea." *The American Magazine of Art* 23, 5 (November 1931): 360-74.

Downes, William Howe. *The Life and Works of Winslow Homer.* Boston: Houghton Mifflin Company, 1911.

Eddy, Arthur Jerome. *Cubists and Post-Impressionism.* Chicago: A. C. McClurg and Company, 1919.

Edgerton, Giles. "The Younger American Painters: Are They Creating A National Art?" *The Craftsman* 13, 5 (February 1908): 512-32.

Ely, Catherine Beach. "The Modern Tendency in Henri, Sloan and Bellows." *Art in America* 10, 111 (April 1922): 132-43.

Faxon, Susan C.; Downey, Alice; and Bermingham, Peter. *A Stern and Lovely Scene: A Visual History of the Isles of Shoals,* exhibition catalogue. Durham, N.H.: University Art Galleries, University of New Hampshire, 1978.

Ferguson, Gerald, editor. *Marsden Hartley and Nova Scotia.* Halifax: Mount Saint Vincent University Art Gallery, 1987.

Flexner, James Thomas. *History of American Painting.* Volume 3: *That Wilder Image.* Boston: Little, Brown, 1962.

Flockhart, Lolita L. W. *A Full Life, The Story of Van Dearing Perrine.* Boston: The Christopher Publishing House, 1939.

"George Bellows." *The Nation* 120, 3107 (January 21, 1925): 60.

"George Luks: An American Artist," exhibition catalogue. Willkes-Barre, Pa.: Sordoni Art Gallery, 1987.

Gerdts, William H. "The Square Format and Proto-Modernism in American Painting." *Arts Magazine* 50, 10 (June 1976): 70-75.

Goodrich, Lloyd. *American Watercolor and Winslow Homer.* Minneapolis: The Walker Art Center, 1945.

Goodrich, Lloyd. *Edward Hopper.* New York: H. N. Abrams, 1989.

Goodrich, Lloyd. *Edward Hopper.* Harmondsworth: Penguin, 1948.

Goodrich, Lloyd. *Winslow Homer.* New York: MacMillian Company, 1944.

Goodrich, Lloyd. "Winslow Homer." *The Arts* 6, 4 (October 1924): 185-209.

Goodyear, William H. "The Watercolors of Winslow Homer, 1836-1910." *Brooklyn Museum Quarterly* 2, 3-4 (October 1915): 367-84.

Greenberg, Clement. *Art and Culture: Critical Essays.* Boston: Beacon Press, 1961.

Hartley, Marsden. *Adventures in the Arts: Informal Chapters on Painters, Vaudeville and Poets.* New York: Boni and Liveright, 1921.

Hartley, Marsden. *The Collected Poems of Marsden Hartley, 1904-1943.* Edited by Gail R. Scott. Santa Rosa, Calif.: Black Sparrow Press, 1987.

Hartley, Marsden. *On Art.* Edited by Gail R. Scott. New York: Horizon Press, 1982.

Hartmann, Sadakichi. *A History of American Art.* Boston: L. C. Page and Company, 1901. Two volumes.

Haskell, Barbara. *Marsden Hartley,* exhibition catalogue. New York: The Whitney Museum of American Art in association with New York University Press, 1980.

Havens, George R. *Frederick Judd Waugh American Marine Painter.* Orono, Me.: University of Maine, 1969.

Hendricks, Gordon. *The Life and Work of Winslow Homer.* New York: Harry N. Abrams, 1979.

Henri, Robert. *The Art Spirit.* Philadelphia: J. B. Lippincott Company, 1923.

Henri, Robert. "Progress in Our National Art Must Spring from the Development of Individuality of Ideas and Freedom of Expression: A Suggestion for a New Art School." *The Craftsman* 15, 4 (January 1909): 387-401.

Hind, Lewis C. "American Paintings in Germany." *The International Studio* 41, 163 (September 1910): 178-89.

Hind, Lewis C. *Landscape Painting from Giotto to the Present Day,* volume 2. London: Chapman and Hall Ltd., 1924.

Hoeber, Arthur. "American Sea Painters." *The Mentor* 1, 21 (July 7, 1913): 1-24.

Hoeber, Arthur. "Winslow Homer, A Painter of the Sea." *The World's Work* 21 (February 1911): 14009-14017.

Holcomb, Grant. *John Sloan: The Gloucester Years,* exhibition catalogue. Springfield, Mass.: Springfield Library and Museums Association for the Springfield Museum of Fine Arts, 1980.

Homer, William Innes. *Robert Henri and His Circle.* Revised edition. New York: Hacker Art Books, 1988.

Huneker, James Gibbons. *Americans in the Arts 1890-1920.* Edited by Arnold T. Schwab. New York: A. M. S. Press, 1985.

The Index of Twentieth Century Artists. Volumes 1-4, numbers 1-7. New York: Research Institute of the College Art Association, October 1933-April 1937.

Isham, Samuel. *The History of American Painting.* New York: MacMillan Company, 1910.

James, Henry. *The American Scene.* New York: Horizon Press, 1967. Originally published 1905.

John Sloan—Portraits and Places, exhibition catalogue. New York: Kraushaar Galleries, 1988.

Kaplan, Amy. *The Social Construction of American Realism.* Chicago: University of Chicago Press, 1988.

Katz, Leslie. "The Modernity of Winslow Homer." *Arts* 33, 5 (February 1959): 24-27.

Kelly, Florence Finch. "Painters of Sea and Shore." *Broadway Magazine* 18, 5 (August 1907): 580-86.

Kelly, Franklin. "George Bellows' *Shore House.*" In *Essays in Memory of Daniel Fraad, Jr.* Edited by Nicolai Cikovsky, Jr., and Doreen Bolger. Washington, D.C.: The National Gallery of Art; and New York: The Metropolitan Museum of Art, 1990.

Kent, Rockwell. *It's Me O Lord.* New York: Dodd, Mead and Company, 1955.

Kent, Rockwell. *Rockwell Kent: An Anthology of His Works.* Edited by Fridolf Johnson. New York: Alfred A. Knopf, 1982.

Kertess, Klaus. *Marin in Oil,* exhibition catalogue. Southampton, N.Y.: Parrish Art Museum, 1987.

Kroll, Leon. *Leon Kroll: A Spoken Memoir.* Edited by Nancy Hale and Fredson Bowers. Charlottesville: University Press of Virginia, 1983.

Kuspit, Donald. "19th-Century Landscape: Poetry and Property." *Art in America* 64, 1 (January-February, 1976): 64-71.

Landscape in Maine 1820-1970: A Sesquicentennial Exhibition, exhibition catalogue. Waterville, Me.: Colby College Art Museum, 1970.

Lears, T. J. Jackson. *No Place of Grace: Anti-Modernism and the Transformation of American Culture 1880-1920.* New York: Pantheon Books, 1981.

Levin, Gail. *Edward Hopper: The Art and the Artist.* New York: W. W. Norton and Company, 1980.

Loria, Joan, and Seamans, Warren A. *Earth, Sea and Sky: Charles H. Woodbury, Artist and Teacher, 1864-1940.* Cambridge, Mass.: The MIT Museum, 1988.

McBride, Henry. *The Flow of Art.* Edited by Daniel Catton Rich. New York: Atheneum, 1975.

McCausland, Elizabeth. *Marsden Hartley.* Minneapolis: University of Minnesota Press, 1952.

Marin, John. *John Marin.* Edited by Cleve Gray. First Edition. New York: Holt, Rinehart and Winston, 1970.

Marin, John. *The Selected Writings of John Marin.* Edited by Dorothy Norman. New York: Pellegrini and Cudahy, 1949.

Mather, Frank Jewett, Jr. "The Art of Winslow Homer." *The Nation* 92, 2382 (March 2, 1911): 225-27.

Mather, Frank Jewett, Jr.; Morey, Charles Rufus; and Henderson, William James. *The American Spirit in Art.* New Haven: Yale University Press, 1927.

Mather, Frank Jewett, Jr. *Modern Painting: A Study of Tendencies.* New York: Henry Holt and Company, 1927.

Mather, Frank Jewett, Jr. "Some American Realists." *Arts and Decoration* 7, 1 (November 1916): 13-16.

May, Henry F. *The End of American Innocence: A Study of the First Years of Our Own Time, 1912-1917.* New York: Alfred A. Knopf, 1969.

Mellon, Gertrud A.; and Wilder, Elizabeth F. *Maine and Its Role in American Art 1740-1963.* New York: Viking, 1963.

Memorial Exhibition of the Works of George Bellows, exhibition catalogue. New York: Metropolitan Museum of Art, 1925. Introduction by Frank Crowninshield.

Morgan, Charles H. *George Bellows, Painter of America.* New York: Reynal and Company, 1965.

Morgan, H. Wayne. *New Muses: Art in American Culture 1865-1920.* Norman: University of Oklahoma Press, 1978.

Mumford, Lewis. *The Brown Decades.* New York: Dover Publications, 1931.

Murphy, Alexandra R. *Winslow Homer in the Clark Collection.* Williamstown, Mass.: Sterling and Francine Clark Art Institute, 1986.

N. C. Wyeth in Maine: A Centenary Exhibition, exhibition catalogue. Rockland, Me.: William A. Farnsworth Library and Museum, 1982

Nash, Roderick, editor. *The Call of the Wild (1900-1910).* New York: George Braziller, 1970.

Nelson, Harold B. *Sounding the Depths: 150 Years of American Seascape,* exhibition catalogue. San Francisco: Chronicle Books, 1989.

Neuhaus, Eugen. *The History and Ideals of American Art.* Stanford: Stanford University Press, 1931.

Pene du Bois, Guy. "George Luks and Flamboyance." *The Arts* 3, 2 (February 1923): 107-18.

Poore, Henry Rankin. "The Many-Sided Waugh." *The International Studio* 74, 297 (December 1921): cxxiv-cxxxv.

Prown, Jules D. "Winslow Homer in His Art." *Smithsonian Studies in American Art* 1, 1 (Spring 1987): 31-45.

Reed, Christopher. "The Artist and the Other: The Work of Winslow Homer." *Yale University Art Gallery Bulletin* 40, 3 (Spring 1989): 68-79.

Reich, Sheldon. *John Marin: A Stylistic Analysis and Catalogue Raisonné.* 2 volumes. Tucson: University of Arizona Press, 1970.

Rensselaer, M. G. Van. "An American Artist in England." *Century Illustrated Magazine* 27, 1 (November 1883): 13-21.

Reuterdahl, Henry. "Winslow Homer, American Painter: An Appreciation from a Sea-Going Viewpoint." *The Craftsman* 20, 1 (April 1911): 8-18.

Rich, Daniel Catton. "Bellows Revalued." *Magazine of Art* 39, 4 (April 1946): 139-42.

Rihani, Ameen. "American Painting, Part III: Luks and Bellows." *The International Studio* 71, 281 (August 1920): xxi-xxvii.

Rosenfeld, Paul. *The Port of New York.* Urbana, Ill.: University of Illinois, 1961. Originally published 1924.

Rummell, John. *Aims and Ideals of Representative American Painters.* Buffalo, N.Y.: E. M. Berlin, 1901.

St. John, Bruce, editor. *John Sloan's New York Scene.* New York: Harper and Row, 1965.

Scott, Gail R. *Marsden Hartley.* New York: Abbeville Press, 1988.

Seaton-Schmidt, Anna. "Some American Marine Painters." *Art and Progress* 2, 1 (November 1910): 3-8.

Sheldon, George Williams. *American Painters.* New York: D. Appleton and Company, 1879.

Sheldon, George Williams. *Hours with Art and Artists.* New York: D. Appleton and Company, 1882.

Simpson, Marc. *Winslow Homer's Paintings of the Civil War,* exhibition catalogue. San Francisco: The Fine Arts Museums of San Francisco, 1988.

Sloan, John. *Gist of Art.* New York: American Artists Group, 1939.

Spargo, John. "George Luks, An American Painter of Great Originality and Force, Whose Art Relates to All the Experiences and Interests of Life." *The Craftsman* 12, 6 (September 1907): 599-607.

Spassky, Natalie. *American Paintings in the Metropolitan Museum of Art.* Volume 2, *A Catalogue of Works by Artists Born between 1816 and 1845.* New York: Metropolitan Museum of Art, 1985.

Stebbins, Theodore E., Jr.; Troyen, Carol; and Fairbrother, Trevor J. *A New World: Masterpieces of American Painting 1760-1910,* exhibition catalogue. Boston: Museum of Fine Arts, 1983.

Stein, Roger B. *Seascape and the American Imagination,* exhibition catalogue. New York: Clarkson N. Potter and the Whitney Museum of American Art, 1975.

Sundquist, Eric J., editor. *American Realism: New Essays.* Baltimore: The Johns Hopkins University Press, 1982.

Thorn, Megan. "John Marin in Maine," exhibition catalogue. Portland, Me.: Portland Museum of Art, 1985.

Trachtenberg, Alan. *The Incorporation of America: Culture and Society in the Gilded Age.* New York: Hill and Wang, 1982.

Tragard, Louise, and Hart, Patricia E. *A Century of Color, 1886-1986: Ogonquit, Maine's Art Colony.* Ogonquit: Barn Gallery Associates, 1987.

Traxel, David. *An American Saga: The Life and Times of Rockwell Kent.* New York: Harper and Row, 1980.

Van Dearing Perrine, exhibition catalogue. New York: Graham Gallery, 1986.

Van Dyke, John C. *American Painting and Its Tradition.* New York: Charles Scribner's Sons, 1920.

Van Dyke, John C. *Art for Art's Sake.* New York: Charles Scribner's Sons, 1893.

Van Dyke, John C. *What Is Art? Studies in the Technique and Criticism of Painting.* New York: Charles Scribner's Sons, 1910.

Wallach, Alan. "Rockwell Kent." *Arts Magazine* 54, 2 (October 1979): 15.

West, Richard V. "An Enkindled Eye": The Paintings of Rockwell Kent,* exhibition catalogue. Santa Barbara, Calif.: Santa Barbara Museum of Art, 1985.

West, Richard V. *Rockwell Kent: The Early Years,* exhibition catalogue. Brunswick, Me.: Bowdoin College, 1969.

Wiebe, Robert H. *The Search for Order 1877-1920.* New York: Hill and Wang, 1967.

Wilmerding, John. *A History of American Marine Painting.* New York: Harry N. Abrams, 1987.

Wilmerding, John. "Winslow Homer's 'Right and Left.'" In *Studies in the History of Art,* volume 9. Washington, D.C.: National Gallery of Art, 1980.

Wilmerding, John. *Winslow Homer.* New York: Praeger Publishers, 1972.

Woodbury, David O. *Charles H. Woodbury, N.A. 1864-1940,* exhibition catalogue. Boston: Vose Galleries of Boston, 1978.

Wright, Willard Huntington. *Modern Painting: Its Tendency and Meaning.* New York: John Lane Company, 1915.

Zurier, Rebecca. *Art for the Masses (1911-1917): A Radical Magazine and Its Graphics,* exhibition catalogue. New Haven, Conn.: Yale University Art Gallery, 1985.

Index of Paintings Illustrated